THE REBEL COUNTESS

The Life and Times of Constance Markievicz

D0300308

MA 1842 **120603** 9335

Leabharlanna Fhine Gall
MALAHIDE LIBRARY
Inv/00 : 00/1092F Price IR£17.03
Title: Rebel Countess
Class:
920 / MARKIEVICZ

In addition to her biographical writing, Anne Marreco wrote, in a literary career which spanned three decades, a number of historical novels under the pseudonym Alice Acland. Based in London and Devon, she also spent much time in Greece. Anne Marreco died in 1982.

Also by Anne Marreco

The Charmer and the Charmed
The Boat Boy

As Alice Acland

Caroline Norton
Templeford Park
A Stormy Spring
A Second Choice
A Person of Discretion
The Corsican Ladies
The Secret Wife
The Ruling Passion

THE REBEL COUNTESS

The Life and Times of Constance Markievicz

Anne Marreco

PHOENIX
PRESS

5 UPPER SAINT MARTIN'S LANE
LONDON
WC2H 9EA

A PHOENIX PRESS PAPERBACK

First published in Great Britain
by Weidenfeld & Nicolson in 1967
This paperback edition published in 2000
by Phoenix Press,
a division of The Orion Publishing Group Ltd,
Orion House, 5 Upper St Martin's Lane,
London WC2H 9EA

Copyright © 1967 by Anne Marreco

The moral right of Anne Marreco to be identified as the author
of this work has been asserted by her in accordance with
the Copyright, Designs and Patents Act 1988.

All rights reserved. No part of this publication may be
reproduced, stored in a retrieval system, or transmitted,
in any form or by any means, electronic, mechanical,
photocopying, recording or otherwise, without the prior
permission of the copyright owner and the above
publisher of this book.

This book is sold subject to the condition that it may not
be resold or otherwise issued except in its original binding.

A CIP catalogue record for this book is available
from the British Library.

Printed in Great Britain by
Butler & Tanner Ltd, Frome and London

ISBN 1 84212 060 3

Ah, my darlings you will have to fight and
suffer; you must endure loneliness, the
coldness of friends, the alienation of love
... laying in dark places the foundations
of that high and holy Eri of prophecy, the
isle of enchantment, burning with druidic
splendours, bright with immortal
presences, with the face of the everlasting
Beauty looking in upon its ways, divine
with terrestrial mingling till God and the
world are one.

Æ (George Russell)

Contents

Illustrations

ACKNOWLEDGEMENTS

I am indebted to Count Stanislas Dunin-Markiewicz for permission to reproduce the illustrations numbered 1, 5, 6, 10, 11, 12, 13, 14, 15, 17, 18, 19, 23, 24, 25, 27 and 28; to Lady Gore-Booth for number 2; to Lady Gore-Booth and the Hon Desmond Guinness for numbers 3 and 4; to Lieutenant-Colonel O'Connell Fitz-Simon MC for numbers 7 and 9; to the National Gallery of Ireland for number 8; to the Reverend Patrick Walsh CC for number 16; to Mr William Griffith for number 20; to Mrs S. O'Sullivan for number 21; to Beatrice Elvery (Lady Glenavy) for number 22 and to the National Library of Ireland for number 26.

Author's Note

In the heart of Dublin lies St Stephen's Green. Walking through the pleasure grounds you come to an open space surrounded by ornamental trees where three statues look onto a placid scene composed of neat flower beds, plaster urns, and two round stone basins where fountains play. The statues are of James Clarence Mangan, poet, patriot and Irish scholar; Thomas Kettle, parliamentarian and poet, who worked for Irish Nationalism but died fighting for England in the First World War; and Constance Markievicz, who was born into a well known Anglo-Irish family yet was condemned to death for fighting against England in the 1916 Rebellion. The three subjects personify the conflicts of Irish politics. Because of the especial relationship of Ireland to England, Irish-born political figures were faced from the beginning with a choice of loyalties. This necessity of choice engendered bitter feuds, misunderstanding, and violence. The subject of this biography is no exception to the rule.

In writing Constance Markievicz's life story I have set out to give a full account of herself and of her times. I have not set out to interpret the political events in which she figured passively or actively because others are far better qualified than I am to do so; for the same reason my account of the Easter Rising is mainly confined to Constance Markievicz's own part in it.

The author of a book in which Irish proper names figure is at once faced with the problem of the English and Gaelic alternative. For instance, should it be Eamon Ceannt or Edward Kent? More confusing still should Pearse be Patrick Pearse, or Padraic Pearse, or Padraig MacPiarais? I have followed what appears to be the official usage.

Another problem concerns what collective name is the most

clear and accurate for the various groups and organizations which represented anti-Unionism. Up to September 1914 I have used the term Nationalist rather than Republican to cover the non-Unionist groups (apart from the Irish Parliamentary Party which I always name as such) because Griffith, the creator of *Sinn Fein*, was not a Republican. After the split in September 1914 between Redmond's and MacNeills's followers when the two groups were named the National Volunteers and the Irish Volunteers, a new problem arises since there is a tendency in Irish writers to use the term Nationalist for Redmondites.

The Easter Rising was called the *Sinn Fein* rebellion by the British, but this was an over-simplification. Of those who fought in Easter Week, the Irish Volunteers (non-Redmondite) consisted of *Sinn Fein* members, IRB members, and some who were neither – not to speak of the Citizen Army (a creation of the Labour movement) who started the Rebellion alone, and Constance Markievicz's militant Boy Scouts *Na Fianna Eireann*.

After the split in 1922 over the terms of the Treaty between Ireland and Great Britain, the main streams of political division became known by the terms Free Staters for the Government; while the Opposition was known as Irregulars, or Republicans, or IRA, or *Sinn Feiners*.

In 1925 the leader of the political Opposition, Mr de Valera, created from some of these elements his new party, *Fianna Fail*, which eventually came into the Dail. This crucial event took place in the same year that Constance Markievicz died.

In writing this biography my thanks are first of all due to Count Stanislas Dunin-Markiewicz,* stepson of my subject. He has put at my disposal his collection of letters from her contemporaries, his scrap-books, his written personal memories of his stepmother's younger days, together with his unfailing courtesy in answering the many questions I have asked him. I am also indebted to him for his permission to make use of material donated by him to the National Museum, Dublin.

I am indebted to Mr Patrick Henchy of the National Library, Dublin, and Mr Oliver Snoddy of the National Museum, Dublin for their kind and patient co-operation, also equally to Miss Nora Niland of the County Library, Sligo. Sir Anthony Weldon most

*Unlike his stepmother, Count Stanislas uses the traditional spelling of his family name.

generously made his collections of press cuttings available to me.

I would like to thank particularly Mrs Moloney (Kathleen Barry) for putting her collection of press cuttings of the 1922 American Tour at my disposal, also for much personal encouragement and assistance. I am grateful to Mr Hilliard, Minister of Defence, for granting me an interview. I would like to thank the following ladies for their generous hospitality, together with their personal recollections of Constance Markievicz: Lady Glenavy, (Beatrice Elvery), Mrs O'Donaghue (Shiela Humphries), Mrs O'Donnell (Eithne Coyle), and Miss Maire Comerford. I would like to thank especially Miss Baby and Miss Doty Bohan and Miss Clayton for their recollections. I am grateful, too, for the courtesy of Professor Liam O'Brien, Mr Padraic Colum, Mr T. P. O'Neill and Mr P. J. Hayes; also to Mr Charles Duff for his illuminating letters. Mr Terence de Vere White has been kind enough to give me invaluable assistance and advice. My thanks are due also to Mr Seymour Leslie for the help he has given me in my task. I am indebted to Sir Paul Gore-Booth KCMG and Messrs Longman Green and Co for permission to quote from the *Prison Letters of Countess Markievicz*. The verses by W. B. Yeats which appear on pages 1, 11, 57, 58, 244, 245, 261 and 262 are reproduced from *Collected Poems of W. B. Yeats* (London, 1958) by courtesy of Mr M. B. Yeats and Messrs. McMillan & Company, Ltd. Miss Elizabeth Coxhead kindly made available to me, with Miss Clayton's permission, the latter's personal recollections. Last, but far from least, I would like to record my gratitude to Lady Gore-Booth, and Miss Gabrielle and Miss Aideen Gore-Booth for entertaining me at Lissadell, and for so kindly allowing me to see everything and everywhere necessary for the setting of the background to my subject.

Port Hall
co Donegal
Easter Monday 1966

CHAPTER I

Lissadell

Five miles out of Sligo on the main road to the seaside resort of
Bundoran the traveller comes to the village where Yeats is
buried. On the opposite side of the road from the windswept
churchyard where his stark grave lies is a signpost marked
Lissadell. This gentle chime of syllables, celebrated through
Yeats' poem in memory of two of Lissadell's inhabitants, spells
the name of a much loved place,

> The light of evening, Lissadell,
> Great windows open to the south,
> Two girls in silk kimonos, both
> Beautiful, one a gazelle . . .

The girls were Constance Gore-Booth and her sister Eva. One
became a revolutionary, the other a poetess.

It is two and a half miles from the turning to the drive gate,
through narrow lanes whose banks and hedges part to show fields
of moon daisies in summer, and beyond them the waters of
Drumcliffe Bay. The house does not show itself to the outside
world but is hidden in thick woods. You would have to be out at
sea, or on the sphinx-like flanks of Ben Bulben to see the pale,
solid mansion built by Sir Robert Gore-Booth, grandfather of the
girls in silk kimonos. Even when you have come into the drive
and follow the roadway by the shore, all that can be seen are trees
and the high brick walls of the walled garden near where an older
house stood. Once arrived, the contrast is revealed between the
heavy sanctuary made by the trees on the north and east, and the
outlook to the south and west of sea and sky and mountains. The
lands round Lissadell are green pastures breaking into dunes by
the shore and open to the wide Irish skies that never stay the same,

contained only by the linked mountains of Sligo, of Mayo, of Leitrim and of Donegal.

There can be few more effective trainings for a female revolutionary than the nineteenth-century childhood of a country tomboy in a troubled land. The child learns to be tough, resourceful and spartan, and because she is fearless and enterprising she gets about and sees things for herself. Her home, if it is large like Lissadell, is full of cold bedrooms, her food plain but wholesome. Stoicism is praised, emotion discouraged. If she is a member of a large family she soon learns the virtue of loyalty in the face of the enemy-authority.

Constance Gore-Booth was a being born to be happy, as a child, in the surroundings which her destiny had allotted her. The haunting Sligo landscape fixed itself in her heart, so that when she was in prison in England years later it was to Lissadell and all around it that her mind returned and where her imagination liked to dwell – fulfilling itself in a series of water-colours of clouds and sea and mountains.

But she was born in London at Buckingham Gate (not in Carlton House Terrace as stated in previous accounts) on 4 February 1868, the eldest child of Henry Gore-Booth, heir of Sir Robert Gore-Booth of Lissadell. That is to say she was born into a family stronghold of the Anglo-Irish world; she was a child by right of the Ascendancy. But this world which claimed her for many years of her life was in the last flowering before dissolution. She is chiefly remembered because when a handful of desperate men in 1916 changed the political face of Ireland for ever, she was in the thick of the fray. Once a woman has proved that she can fight beside men it is as though she divests herself of her femininity in the eyes of the world. Opinion transforms her into a member of some strange, intermediate, sex or category like worker ants. But Constance enjoyed the full scope of a woman's life, given her class and times. When she was young she was a superb horsewoman and an admired beauty (singled out by such different judges of female perfection as Yeats and Edward VII). When she lay dying at the age of fifty-nine the poor of Dublin prayed in the streets for her. 'Whoever misunderstood Madame,' said Mr de Valera after her death, 'the poor did not.'

Constance Gore-Booth developed, changed, and achieved greatness through the turmoil of her country's history, as a stone is shaped by the stress of the sea. If the purpose of human existence is to experience, serve, and shed illusion, she fulfilled her destiny more surely in the arena than on the sidelines where she was born.

In the October of her birth year Mr Gladstone in a speech in Wigan during his electoral campaign compared the Protestant Ascendancy in Ireland to 'some tall tree of noxious growth, lifting its head to Heaven and poisoning the atmosphere of the land so far as its shadow can extend. It is still there, gentlemen, but now at last the day has come when, as we hope, the axe has been laid to the root. It is deeply cut round and round. It nods and quivers from base to base. There lacks, gentlemen, but one stroke more – the stroke of these Elections. It will then, once for all, topple to its fall, and on that day the heart of Ireland will leap for joy ...'[1]

At Lissadell in the 1860s the tall tree of the Protestant Ascendancy still stood firm as ever in the minds of the Gore-Booths. Mr Gladstone was far away and his huffing and puffing seemed unlikely to blow their house down. They were good landlords, respected by their tenants, and they lived the active, self-confident, insulated life of the landed gentry anywhere in the British Isles before the twentieth century brought doubts, world war, political conflict, financial changes, and, in Ireland, finally the toppling forecast by Mr Gladstone. The only, but crucial, difference between families like the Gore-Booths and the landed families of England was that in Ireland their position, although outwardly secure, was held, not freely given. Their forebears had come adventurously and taken possession of conquered lands. 'The Irish landlords continued to be colonists. The very building of their houses, the planting of their trees, the making of the high walls about their estates (raised by the incredibly cheap labour of the natives whom their ancestors had tried to exterminate) declared their intention ... the Irish landlords lived within their demesnes, making a world of their own, with Ireland outside the gates.'[2] There was no village green cricket, no prosperous public house used by ruler as well as the ruled, no local or parochial government shared by all classes, no corporate life, no common aim; there were two worlds which did not meet. George Moore remembered, as though they were foreigners, the tenantry going to church; the married women in special dark blue cloaks, and the girls 'hiding their faces behind their shawls' – the men on the other side of the road. But, all the same, Ireland came seeping in through the high walls of the English ascendancy. Any adventurous child of the big house was made free of the cabins where the turf fire never went out, where the past was never forgotten, and where the walls might be hung (so Maud Gonne records of the cabins she visited in 1882 when a child in Howth) with coloured pictures of Wolfe Tone, Emmet and Michael Dwyer: heroes who had died for an Ireland that was not to be born until 1916.

The first ancestor of Constance to come to Ireland was Captain Paul Gore. He was a seventh son and therefore, presumably, he needed to make his way in the world. He came with Elizabeth's young favourite, Essex, in 1598 and he was made commander of a troop of horse. For his services he was rewarded with grants of land in Ireland by the Queen, and later by James I. In 1621 he was created a Baronet of Ireland. He married a niece of Thomas Wentworth, the great Strafford, and he had thirteen children.

The first Gore to own land in Ireland found a primitive and ignorant peasantry. The native Irish used their ploughs attached to their horses' tails, plucked sheep because they had no shears and burnt corn to divide the grain from the straw. The life of the Irish was nomadic and tribal. They moved their cattle from pasture to pasture. 'This keeping of cows' the poet Spencer wrote, 'is of itself a very idle life, and a fit nursery for a thief.' But the reason for reliance on cattle was that they could be removed from marauders or invaders, while crops could not. The Irish poor of the sixteenth century lived in tents of hide, and no one felt safe, for England had conquered Ireland, but had failed to give her the benefit of English law.

It was the policy of Paul Gore's uncle by marriage, Wentworth (who was Lord Deputy of Ireland from 1633 to 1640) to improve on these agricultural customs and increase prosperity by granting as much land as possible to English settlers. The strong and the enlightened did not then think it a duty to educate the ignorant. In this way began the centuries of division and intermittent strife between the settlers, who brought new methods and ideas, and the native, dispossessed Irish who clung to their myth-haunted past. It was not until Constance's lifetime two hundred and fifty blood-stained years later that paternalism came truly into being with Sir Horace Plunkett's Agricultural Co-operative movement –

of which her brother, Sir Josslyn Gore-Booth became a leading exponent.

Paul Gore built himself a castle at Ardtarman, five miles from the eventual home of his descendants at Lissadell. He built solidly of stone – near the shores where Drumcliffe Bay merges into the larger Sligo Bay – with fortifications, and a staircase in a turret tower looking west; but like his uncle's new wing at Dublin Castle his new home was burnt by accident, and today only the walls still stand enclosing grass while cows peer through the window embrasures at the sightseer.

After the founder of the family line, the next most significant forebear was Constance's great-great-grandmother, Letitia Booth, a Sligo heiress, wife of Nathanial Gore.*

Letitia Gore, née Booth, besides adding her name, her lands, and five children to her husband's family, left a local legend. About seven miles from Lissadell, and within sight of the ruined walls of Ardtarman, there is a semicircular chasm known as the Derk of Knocklane where gulls nest like doves in a dovecot along the grassy ledges that face west, but where opposite them the rocks are grooved by centuries of storms and drop sheer to the sea two hundred feet below. This place can be approached by a level track a few feet above the sea on the opposite side of the miniature peninsular in which the Derk of Knocklane is coiled. One day Letitia Gore conceived the notion of being driven in her coach round the rim of the chasm. This idea with its combination of fearlessness, panache, and wilfulness, had everything in common with the exploits of her great-great-granddaughter, Constance, in youth. The only difference between ancestress and descendant being that anyone who knew Constance would be convinced that she herself would have taken the reins. Letitia's coachman naturally demurred, whereupon she threatened him with her pistol. Under duress he whipped up the horses and accomplished the feat. Letitia was said always to be dressed in white, earning herself the title of Banshee Ban, and her horses were reputed to be shod with gold.

Letitia's grandson was the fourth Baronet and the grandfather of Constance. Sir Robert Gore-Booth still had eight years to live when she was born. He had a long minority, which is perhaps the reason he felt rich enough to pull down the then family home – a

*For a full genealogy of the Gore-Booth family see Appendix 1.

bow-windowed house on the north shore of Drumcliffe Bay – and build another one higher up in the trees.

In 1830 Sir Robert, then a widower since 1828 after only a year of marriage, chose his second bride from a family of beautiful sisters, the Miss Goolds, daughters of Thomas Goold Master of Chancery. Constance's grandmother was the second daughter, Caroline Susan. She was painted by the miniaturist, A. E. Robertson, who shows her to have had the type of looks most admired in her day: symmetrical, static, aristocratic, with large well-shaped eyes, an oval face, a rather long, straight nose, luxuriant ringlets. On her slender wrist can be seen a gold band which widens to hold a miniature portrait in the fashion of the time. She and Sir Robert (he was tall with a red beard) no doubt dominated their large cousinhood.

Sir Robert is remembered by the local Irish for two opposing happenings – a tragedy known as the affair of the Seven Cartrons, and his generosity in the Great Famine. Both happenings typify the total power of the landlord. The Seven Cartrons was a township inhabited by fishermen and small landholders. In 1833, Sir Robert, through a deal over the dinner table, acquired the Seven Cartrons when he bought the town of Ballymote, together with the Fitzmaurice property, from Lord Orkney. Having made the deal, Sir Robert, in the mood of the times, decided to make clearances in his new property. His choice of an agent fell on one, Dodswell, who was notorious in Co Sligo for his ruthless evictions. The hapless tenants were offered plots elsewhere, but tradition states that the alternative land must have been very poor, since virtually everyone took up the alternative offer of passage money to America, plus compensation (£2 passage money and £4 compensation, which was generous by current standards).* Tradition has it that the ship in which these people set forth was unseaworthy and sank when barely outside Sligo Bay with all on board drowned, some of the bodies floating back to the shores of Lissadell itself. This tragedy has become part of local legend, still alive today, still on occasions thrown at the family, but it is hard to disentangle truth from myth.

The incident coming only three years before the Great Famine had every element to intensify and prolong itself in the minds of a people whose imagination inclines to myth-making and who had

*See Appendix 2.

many reasons for making them against Anglo-Irish landlords. In any case, it would appear that the agent was the villain of the piece, not Sir Robert, who was to prove himself later to be an exceptionally benevolent landowner who spent thousands of pounds on food for his people in the Famine. An article on the Lissadell estates in the London *Times* of 1881 states that Sir Robert spent £40,000 on relief in the Famine years. He was also on the spot – as Minute Books of meetings in the near-by hamlet of Carney testify – instead of writing letters from London, like many of his fellow landlords.

Lady Gore-Booth, the pretty Caroline, was constantly out on her pony with panniers filled with food. The parish priest of Drumcliffe wrote an address of thanks for the help his people had received, 'It will be consoling to her Ladyship to learn that the humble prayers of God's humble creatures were offered every night in every home for the spiritual and temporal welfare of every member of her Ladyship's family.' Archdeacon O'Rorke, the historian of Sligo, wrote of Sir Robert as a landlord, 'Sir Robert must be classed with the best for he let his lands at their value and never pressed for rent . . . always allowing his tenants plenty of time to wait and sell in the best market.'

It is also said in the neighbourhood that when Sir Robert died in midwinter his tenants carried his coffin in relays the whole three miles from the house to Drumcliffe churchyard on its way to Sligo Cathedral. After his death a clock was erected in the tower of Lissadell Church with a tablet inscribed to 'the memory of Sir Robert Gore-Booth Bart MP by a Grateful Tenantry not Unmindful of the Unvaried Kindness and Liberality of their late landlord.' The spontaneity of the first tribute is possibly more certain than the second, when it seems possible that a non-subscribing tenant might have suffered for his lack of gratitude.

Between 1834 and 1836 Sir Robert was engaged in building himself a new home. He chose Francis Goodwin as his architect and built his house of Ballysadare limestone in a self-contained, ample, two-storeyed block with a huge porte cochère on the north, and broken on the south by a bay the height of the house containing three windows on each floor. From these and the six flanking windows the inmates could look over the water to the mountain of Knocknarea beyond Ballysadare Bay, with its cairn which is the monument to Maeve, Queen of Connacht in the first century

AD; legendary as a burial place too, of a warrior king whose dying command was that he should be buried standing upright with his red javelin in his hand and his face to the north, 'on the side of the hill by which the northerns pass when flying before the army of Connacht.'

Sir Robert obtained black marble from Kilkenny to floor his hall and make his staircase and columns, the same kind of black marble Wentworth had chosen in the 1630s for his vast pile, Jigginstown, never completed. He made a picture gallery lined with fat white columns, a hundred feet long and the height of the house, with a chimney piece of yellow Italian marble. Here he hung his pictures of the Italian school – bought when he was making the Grand Tour – and put in an organ. He settled down to a life well divided between duty, sport and the arts. He was musical and played the cello, giving private recitals in his London house in Buckingham Gate; he was a Member of Parliament from 1850 until his death; and he kept up the Lissadell Harriers, of which he was master, at his own expense.

In 1865, the other Ireland which would never admit itself to be finally conquered was once more astir. The Irish Republican Brotherhood (founded in 1858 with the aim of making Ireland free of England, if necessary by force) was finding many new recruits in the villages and in Dublin, where Irish-American officers disbanded after the Civil War had nothing to come back to but poverty and disaffection. There were rumours of an impending rising. The British Government took alarm and began to arrest the leaders. The notorious Fenian trials followed with packed juries in the courts of Judge Keogh, detested for his lack of impartiality. Two years later, in 1867, the execution took place in England of the three Cork men who came to be known as the Manchester Martyrs (the vast demonstration in Dublin on their account had a lasting effect on Parnell as a young man). The men were executed because they had accidentally shot a police officer when trying to rescue two of their organization. In the same year police protection was offered to the Gore-Booths at Lissadell, but they refused it in view of their good relationship with their tenants. In this year, too, Sir Robert's eldest son, the father of Constance, got married.

Henry Gore-Booth was brought up as a younger son, his elder

brother being twelve years older than himself. When Henry was eighteen his brother died, a married man, but childless. In 1867, when Henry married, he was twenty-four. In the family tradition of suitable brides he won the hand of Georgina Hill, whose home was Tickhill Castle in Yorkshire, and whose mother was the daughter of Lord Scarborough. A portrait of her at this period shows a young woman as fair as Hebe, but when the Irish portraitist, Sarah Purser, painted her about fifteen years later, she depicted a tight-lipped matriarch.

The young couple had two babies in rapid succession: Constance in 1868, and a year later, a son, Josslyn. They lived at Lissadell with Sir Robert (whose wife had died in 1855) and paid long visits to their friends and relations for shooting. It seems a pattern of perfect orthodoxy, and yet this couple were to produce out of their five children, a revolutionary, a poetess, and the landlord, who out of principle, was the first to sell a large part of his estate to his tenants under the Land Act of 1903. But it is one of the paradoxes of Irish history that many of the adventurous British families who obtained property in Ireland through a conqueror's prerogative bred adventurous sons whose lifes' work was to annul the reality of this conquest of the land of their own birth.

Constance's grandfather died in 1876 when she was eight. Meanwhile, three more children had been born to fill the nursery: Eva in 1870, Mabel in 1874, and another son, Mordaunt, in 1876, the year his grandfather died. Constance, therefore, had four younger brothers and sisters to lead, dominate or protect in her nursery days, and everything that her subsequent life and actions tells us about her character makes one suppose that she did so.

The new Baronet, Sir Henry, the fifth of his line, became known as a good landlord, in the sense that he took a personal interest in his tenants and reduced their rents when they were in distress. In fact, by 1879, three years after he had come into the property, he had brought most of his rents down to the Griffith Valuation, for which the Land Leaguers had begun to fight all over Ireland. There are many first hand stories of Sir Henry's benevolence to tenants in distress – remitting rents, giving free Quicks* and giving rights of Turbary.† He was also, in a time of intense religious bigotry, remarkably unprejudiced towards Catholics. Sir Henry

*Thorn for fencing.
†Turf cutting.

was peace-loving in domestic life, he loved shooting and fishing, and he especially loved the sea. Ever since his Eton days he had owned a boat; before he married he spent three summers running yachting and salmon-fishing in Norway. It was the North which drew him, not the South, the traditional love-affair of the natives of the British Isles. In 1873 he penetrated even further into the North, so far as the Polar regions, when he made a trip in a friend's yacht to Spitzbergen bringing back his spoils in the shape of a collection of Arctic birds, the skull of a bottle-nosed whale, walrus tusks and two huge salmon. Five years later he returned again there, leaving for the time his five children ranging from ten to two years, his devoted wife, his 25,000 acres, and the cares of a conscientious landlord.

CHAPTER 2

Under Ben Bulben to the meet

Constance was born with three assets which early endeared her to her father: she was fearless, handsome, and she loved horses. Stories of her childhood prove her to have been of the breed of cheerful, gallant, and slightly zany Anglo-Irish girls whose impetuosity shocks their more restrained English cousins. But her nature held deeper reserves than mere dash, or else her story would not be worth telling.

Her father taught her to ride and shoot when she was very young. From the first she was a familiar of her mysterious, unforgettable countryside, where the low-lying land seems to float in tranquillity between the fierce Atlantic to the west and the line of the mountains to the east which crouch like archaic, stone lions – flat-topped, spare, yet formidable.

Yeats remembered Constance in her youth,

> When long ago I saw her ride
> Under Ben Bulben to the meet,
> The beauty of her countryside
> With all youth's lonely wildness stirred,
> She seemed to have grown clean and sweet
> Like any rock-bred, sea-borne bird.

Constance's childhood years were peppered with rash escapades, which her mother tolerated less readily than did her father. She must have been the sort of child dreaded as a cousin by a quiet visiting muff, but adored by grooms, cottagers and brothers. She administered a rough-and-ready justice, as when she found her sweets were being pilfered by a maid. She put an emetic into them, making the maid badly sick. For this she was locked up and her clothes taken away.

There is a photograph of her at the age of six on her shetland pony, dressed formally in a miniature light-coloured riding habit, gloved, straw-hatted, and seated side-saddle. At this period she was not allowed to ride alone, but was led on a leading-rein either by her governess or a groom, much to her disgust. She waited for her opportunity. One day when her attendant was panting along beside her while she trotted, she kicked her pony into a gallop, shook off the groom and had her first taste of freedom won. After this she was allowed to go out with a mounted groom; and it was not long before she persuaded her mother and father to let her dispense with an escort of any kind. She showed even then a tendency to self-dramatization – which was part of her public courage and probably a necessary part – in that she spared her family no detail of her exploits and narrow escapes when she got home. Much later in life she showed she also possessed the harder private fortitude which gives her character its depth and interest to posterity.

In these years of childhood the expression of an ardent nature was always through her riding life. She liked to ride her chestnut pony, Storeen, up the forty steep embankment steps which led by a short cut to the stables; her pleasure was to give the schoolroom a miss and gallop over the country (where she early became a well-known figure) missing meals and lessons, and undaunted by the subsequent classic punishment of being sent to bed supperless. She was a frequent visitor to the houses of the poor, 'slipping in and out like a little fox'. In the words of the family butler, 'She was everything that was nice and good, always full of life and energy, and as innocent as the wild birds of the air; there was no guile in her, ever sympathetic, ever fond of an innocent joke . . . she was beloved by all.'

The Ireland which was to claim her and change her life utterly lay all around her in travail, but it was only the background, then, and for many years to come, to the absorbed, extrovert life into which she fitted like her stirrup leather into its saddle.

A contemporary of Constance's who was brought up two counties away in Galway on the edge of Connemara, wrote of her country upbringing, 'In my childhood the people were terribly poor, and bore their poverty with apparently complete resignation. They were deeply religious, and accepted literally the teaching that this world was only a road to the next. What did it matter, then, if it was hard to walk, when it led to such unimaginable bliss '[1]

The Ireland of Constance's childhood and youth was dominated by the Land question and the Home Rule controversy. In 1879, when Constance was eleven, over 6,000 tenants were evicted from their homes, the next year it was 10,457. In four years more than 23,000 people were evicted and sank into abject poverty and despair. In the year 1880 a farmer called McGrath had his rent raised from £60 to £105. He could not pay so he was evicted. He had to take refuge with his family under an upturned boat where he died of exposure (receiving the Last Rites in the pouring rain under the priest's umbrella). His wife, then his sister, then his children successively tried to retake possession of their home, and were put into prison. For protesting against this, Tim Healy, a young Land Leaguer, destined one day to be Governor-General of a free Ireland, was arrested.

The painful history of large-scale evictions dated from the Famine years. The land question itself was rooted in the whole treatment of Ireland by England as a conquered country. It was a problem which could never have been far from the thoughts of a conscientious landlord such as Sir Henry. The affair of his father and the Seven Cartrons was always alive in the minds of the people, and ten miles away on the estate of his father's neighbour, Lord Palmerston, at Classiebawn, some of the worst of the evictions had taken place (undertaken by agents in Lord Palmerston's absence) many of his tenants (2,000 in number) arriving in Canada half naked and totally destitute.

The power of the landlord was absolute. It was expressed in round terms by Lord Brougham in 1846 commenting on the public outcry against a Mrs Gerrard of Ballinglass who had evicted three hundred paying tenants with a view to turning the holdings into pastures. 'Undoubtedly,' said Lord Brougham in the House of Lords, 'it was the landlord's right to do as he pleased, and if he abstained he conferred a favour and was doing an act of kindness ... property would be valueless and capital would no longer be invested in cultivation of land if it were not acknowledged that it was the landlord's undoubted, indefeasible and most sacred right to deal with his property as he list.'[2]

Landlords as a class were completely identified in the mind of the native, Catholic Irish with their English conquerors. Land hunger was the ulcer of the Irish nation. Under the Penal Laws passed in the period 1695 to 1727 no Roman Catholic could buy land or take a lease of over thirty-one years. The estate of a Catholic landowner on his death had to be divided amongst his sons unless the eldest conformed to the established church within a year. The meagre concession of the 'Bogland Act' in 1771 enabled Catholics to take leases for sixty-one years of unprofitable land. But there was no security for a tenant. If he had a lease and got into arrears with his rent he was liable to eviction, if he was a tenant-at-will (and as late as 1870 out of 680,000 farms in Ireland over 525,000 were occupied by such tenants) he was expected to provide his own fencing and buildings and he could get turned out at his landlord's whim, obtaining no redress for any improvements which he had made out of his own pocket.

There was a built-in penalty for good husbandry. The poet, Padraic Colum, wrote of how men looking back to the eighties recalled that if a landlord or a landlord's hanger-on saw a well-clothed family, a comfortably spread table, it was the signal for the rent to be raised. 'The higher you load the horse, the tighter he draws.' When a landlord turned out a tenant he could always get two others to bargain for the holding.[3]

Before the Ballot Act of 1872 a landlord would lead his people to the poll to vote as he told them. Elizabeth Countess of Fingall relates how in her childhood a neighbour watched his tenants go to the poll in 1874 to vote secretly and freely for the first time, and to vote against him. He left the district shocked and broken-hearted. Among these Irish people whose real lives flowed like an underground river beneath the heels of their conquerors tradition never died. Parental authority was Roman. Everything was for the family – 'one child should rear another' – when the Irish emigrated they stayed in the cities and made a clan, emigrants from a particular district in Ireland always going to the same city. In the homeland, which so many had to leave, there was in the eighties a precarious self-sufficiency and a simplicity in domestic life which Wilfred Scawen Blunt, writing of Donegal, says reminded him of a Bedouin camp. The Irish who were not evicted kept healthy on buttermilk, meal and potatoes. They had their perpetual turf fires. They looked after the old and the infants in arms. They clung to their religion.

The dark picture of landlordism in Ireland is lightened by

an account such as Lady Fingall's of her father 'Blind Burke' who looked after his people like a patriarch. There were good landlords, but they were the exception, not the rule.

A Special Correspondent writing in the London *Times* of 7 March 1881 deals at length with the conditions on the Gore-Booth estates, which were considered to be administered by a tradition of good landlordism. A typical house would be built of mud and rough stone with no lath or plaster. There would be one room shared by the family and the donkey and the cow. The furniture would consist of one or two beds, a rough table and a few benches. The children were bare-footed; the older people could seldom speak English, and the diet consisted of milk, oatmeal and imported Indian meal.*

Families like these were the survivors of the terrible Famine years when near-by Sligo had seen the 'coffin ships' leave with their human cargoes of destitute, diseased, ignorant victims. The Great Famine, that watershed in the many tragedies of Ireland's history, brought a new spiral of disasters into an already precarious agricultural situation. Through the failure of the potato crop the landlords lost their rents and found they could not pay their rates (calculated on holdings rated at £4 and under). Many of them declared they were forced to evict tenants in order to survive themselves. Lord Clanricarde wrote to the Viceroy explaining that the landlords were '*prevented* from aiding or tolerating poor tenants. They are compelled to hunt out all such, to save their property from the £4 clause'.⁴ It was of this same landowner that Maud Gonne – who one day was to be a fellow-prisoner of Constance's – wrote bitterly that he was a murderer of evicted tenants, living in London clubland.

One of the most ignoble stipulations regarding famine relief made by the British Government was the quarter acre clause, by which it was laid down that tenants who owned more than a quarter of an acre should not be eligible for outdoor relief. This was relaxed in 1849, in favour of the destitute wife and children, but not before thousands of peasants had been faced with the choice of holding on to their then useless land or starving. As a

*At a later date John Redmond in the House of Commons, quoting a Report of the Congested Districts Board, said that the total income of an average Irish family was £23 8s 7d and they could not afford bread but lived on 'the kind of meal you feed your dogs in this country'.

result, smallholdings diminished and larger ones increased. But the landlords were ruined by the disappearance of their rents so the Government put through the Encumbered Estates Act, a measure which was designed to ease the transfer of land to new owners and create a new plantation of efficient English or Scottish farmers. But, on the whole, this type of buyer did not hurry to fill the gap, looking, as people did, on Ireland as a lost land of disaster. The new act tended to help the 'gombeen men' to buy land – (i.e. money-lending shopkeepers or small merchants), who often proved more merciless as landlords than their predecessors.

In 1870 a Land Act was passed which had been designed by Gladstone to protect tenants from rack renting and the fear of eviction; but compensation was only to be given if it were proved that the evicted tenant had not been at fault, and since arrears of rent were held to be the tenant's fault, the Act did little to help small farmers and peasants.

1877 and 1878 brought bad harvests and the impact of foreign competition, especially from America, which affected Irish agricultural prices. The British farmers were also hit, which meant that Irish seasonal labourers, whose wages were counted on to help the family at home, did not find their usual employment. Small farmers (the average Irish farm was from fifteen to twenty acres) were also deep in debt to the banks and the gombeen men, following the original optimism engendered by the Land Act of 1870.

In 1879 Michael Davitt (a Fenian, a selfless patriot, a native of Mayo who had spent seven years in Dartmoor and was now released on ticket of leave) told Parnell, whose obstructionist tactics at Westminster had won the admiration of the extremists, that there must be 'a war against landlordism for a root settlement of the land question'. In the spring of 1879 Davitt launched the Land League, whose activities were to become a thorn in the flesh of the landlords and of the authorities. On October of the same year the first conference of the Land League was held in Dublin, when Parnell was elected President. The purpose of the new organization was to give the tenant farmers protection for the first time against the rack renters; it was an organization which looked ahead to making the occupiers the eventual owners of the soil. More immediately it set out to protect the evicted tenants by uniting the dispossessed with those tempted to take their place, in a common cause against the enemy.

1879 was the year of another potato failure – not so serious as the Great Famine, and promptly dealt with by public and private relief – but a thrill of apprehension went through the country; the horrors of the famine of 1846–7 were still remembered; 'clearances' had been carried out, and further 'clearances' were threatened by owners of property. When those who remembered '46 and '47 looked upon the wasted fields again, they thought it plain that the will of God was against the people of Ireland.[5]

At Lissadell the Gore-Booth family threw themselves into relief work. They made a provision store in the house and dealt out 'with their own hands from morning till night, food to the needy . . . an event unique of its kind, at the time, in Ireland,' in the words of 'a gentleman who was a contemporary'. Sir Henry made personal inquiries over all the estate, returning on one occasion to exclaim, with a feeling his hearer never forgot, 'Oh, the poor people have no potatoes! They will have no food, God help them.' He reduced rents by 40 to 18 per cent and this made such an impression, together with his charity, that when he was spending a night with his neighbour, Captain Gethin, at Earlsfield, 'hundreds from the surrounding countryside flocked into the town. There a torchlight procession was formed, and headed by the local Temperance Band it proceeded to Earlsfield and in an orderly manner marched past the big house, while cheer after cheer went up for Sir Henry Gore-Booth.'[6]

Not long after this Lady Gore-Booth was driving through Maugherow when she saw a Land League meeting taking place. She stopped to listen and was surprised to hear the speaker (Tom Sexton) attacking the Gore-Booths. She sent him an invitation to Lissadell, but he refused, 'inferring that he had come down to defend the rights of the people, and not kowtow to their oppressors'.[7] An early, if unsuccessful, example of the skill the English upper classes are supposed to display in domesticating their enemies.

While Constance at this period was still a child absorbed in her active outdoor life, going out stalking the special breed of deer introduced by her father to Lissadell (which produced herds of record size), going out with the Co Sligo Harriers on her pony with her auburn hair flowing on her shoulders, a forerunner in the shape of a militant political woman, Anna Parnell – one of the first of the Irish furies – had formed a Ladies' Land League. She was travelling the length and breadth of the country inciting women to resolutions, a course of action which was looked on by her brother with qualified approval.

In 1880 Gladstone forced a Bill through the House of Commons as a stop-gap measure to aid Irish tenants. For the first time this compelled landlords to compensate tenants in certain circumstances when they evicted them. Lord Lansdowne, a great Anglo-Irish landowner, and Under-Secretary of State for India, resigned in protest and in the House of Commons twenty Liberal members voted against the measure. Evictions rose that year to more than ten thousand. Gladstone went on to draft a new Land Bill which was said to be so complicated that no one understood it except himself and the Treasury Counsel, Sir Henry Thring. Gladstone only got his Bill through by also passing a Coercian Act which was said virtually to give the Viceroy power to lock up anyone he chose for as long as he wished. The Land Bill was passed in April 1881 (the Duke of Argyll resigning from the Cabinet in protest). This Act conceded the tenants what were known as the three F's: fair rents, fixity (i.e. security of tenure) and free right to sell a holding. It was the beginning of the slow painful road to a reborn nation; but at the time no one was satisfied. The landlords felt they had been betrayed by their Government, and the tenants had no capital to improve their land. Even though the Act enabled a peasant to borrow three-quarters of the price if he wished to buy his land, there was little enthusiasm. The people found it hard to understand and believe that they were at last protected from rack-renting. They were like passengers escaped from a tempest at sea who still feel the ship tossing when they are on dry land.

Parnell and the Land Leaguers opposed the Bill, asserting that the peasant should own his land and not pay rent to an alien landlord. In October 1881 the Government had Parnell arrested under the Coercion Act and put into Kilmainham Jail – where Constance was to find herself more than thirty years later, for Ireland's sake. The Land League declared a rent strike. Parnell's imprisonment had the opposite effect of that intended by the Government. During the seven months he was in Kilmainham agrarian crimes and agitation increased alarmingly (the prisoner's sister, Anna, playing more than her part in fanning the flames). Parnell, therefore decided to veto any further payments to the Ladies' Land League.

The political pattern became all too familiar in the next forty years: a vicious circle of outrage and counter-outrage. Such magistrates as Clifford Lloyd, installed by the Chief Secretary for Ireland, Forster, were reputed to put respectable women in prison in virtually solitary confinement for months at a time. Beatings-up by the police were frequent in some districts. A boy could be arrested for whistling – an edgy sub-constable bayoneted a girl for singing *Harvey Duff*.*

In her autobiography, Maud Gonne records a conversation at dinner which reveals the attitude of the die-hard landlord – and these were the rule, not the exception.

That damned Land League is ruining the country . . . We will see who will hold out the longest. They would stop us hunting, would they, the . . . so and so's. As I was coming home this evening I saw Paddy Ward and his family lying out in the ditch. His wife doesn't look as though she will live till the morning. I stopped and told him he would be respon-sible for her death. I had warned him as to what would happen if he joined the Land League. Now he has no roof to shelter his family and the woman will be dead before tomorrow.

Maud Gonne exclaimed in dismay, 'And you did nothing about it?' Her host replied, 'Let her die. These people must be taught a lesson.'[8]

In March 1882 Sir Henry Gore-Booth received an unstamped letter, surcharged 2d, the double fee, which read,

My dear lucifer – I must inform you that you have the poorest tenants in Ireland and all owing to your bad treatment but do you see bad [*sic*] the time has come that by God we dont care for man or the divil is that you are stuck in Lissadell like the divil in hell but I'll meet you like parson Bell.[9]

On the reverse side of the sheet of paper was a sketch of a coffin, marked 'Died 1882' and the words 'Captain Moonlight' printed in large letters.

Sir Henry had in his possession an earlier threatening letter sent to his father's agent, which indicates that even landlords like the Gore-Booths who were just and fair according to their lights,

---

*Unlike policemen in England, The Royal Irish Constabulary (RIC) were armed and they lived like a military force in barracks. It was the policy to post RIC men out of their home counties.

and exceptionally generous in the Famine, were not immune from the general and ever-mounting dissatisfaction. The earlier letter was written to Michael Boyle, a bailiff in charge of the oyster beds.

Michel Boyle – when you are takin beyond Carny or in Sligo you may have your coffin allong with you – we will let you now that you will say that it was better for you to be at home in the corner than to be proper-tiction Sir Roberts oyster the will be the dear oyster to you any day for five years you will be taking yo will be treated like a mad dog that is quartered and Berried under ground and that is the death yo must get – the crew that was with you if the can be nowing the will get bad treatment but not half as bad as you will get we are the lads that dis not feare to do you. Be sure of the words i have said . . .[10]

The lads 'that dis not feare to do you' were to become an increasing and ominous feature of rural and urban life through the troubled years.

By May 1882 the Government were forced to admit themselves beaten, so Parnell was released from Kilmainham on the condition that he would support the Land Act. The Viceroy and the Chief Secretary for Ireland resigned (the Viceroy on account of ill health) the Chief Secretary saying, 'If England cannot govern the honourable member for Cork, then let us acknowledge that he is the greatest power in all Ireland today.'

With the release of Parnell from Kilmainham, and also of Michael Davitt from his long ordeal in Portland Prison, with a new Viceroy (Lord Spencer) and a new Chief Secretary who was young and idealistic (Lord Frederick Cavendish) it looked as though better times might at last be on the way. But with the malign fatality which seemed to dog the destiny of Ireland a new tragedy was already preparing itself. In the teeming slums of Dublin, some of the worst in Europe, a murder group had formed whose members called themselves the Invincibles. They had already made nineteen attempts to murder the newly retired Chief Secretary, Mr Forster, who, certainly, the Irish had no reason to love, and they were now out to get Mr Burke, the Permanent Under-Secretary. The new Viceroy made his state entry on 6 May, the day after a torchlight procession in Dublin in honour of the newly freed Leader and the Fenian. The Invincibles, having missed Mr Burke twice, now set out on their third attempt. They split into two groups, one in a cab, and the other in a jaunting car. At twenty past seven on that May evening Mr Burke and Lord

Frederick and the gang came face to face in Phoenix Park. Mr Burke was stabbed, then Lord Frederick. After this Mr Burke's throat was cut. Lord Frederick was unknown to the terrorists; he was killed because he tried to protect his companion.

When the news was broken to Lady Frederick in London by the Gladstones, Mr Gladstone said to her 'Be assured it will not be in vain' and, her Journal entry continues, 'across all my agony there fell a bright ray of hope, and I saw in a vision Ireland at peace, and my darling's life blood accepted as a sacrifice for Christ's sake, to help bring this to pass.' In her semi-mystical reaction Lady Frederick anticipated by thirty-four years the words of Padraic Pearse, the leader of the Easter Rising. In the peroration of his speech to his pupils before they broke up for the Easter holidays in 1916, he said, 'It took the blood of the Son of God to redeem the world. It will take the blood of the sons of Ireland to redeem Ireland.'

If anything more was needed to convince the English people and their Government that the Irish were a treacherous, ungrateful and degraded race it was the Phoenix Park murders. Gladstone was compelled to bring in an even more drastic Coercion Bill. Three days later he introduced an Arrears Bill which enabled tenants of land worth less than £30 a year to cancel their arrears of rent. There was much opposition, but the Bill became law in August. By 1883 the incidence of reported agrarian crimes had dropped to 870 as against 4,439 in 1881.

In the same turbulent year of 1882 Sir Henry Gore-Booth bought a fifty-ton yawl – the *Kara* – and set out to rescue a friend marooned in Franz Josef Land. It was evidently an irresistible quest, for Sir Henry had been within eighty miles of Franz Josef Land (at Cape Mauritius) in 1879, and the explorer who had set out, Mr Leigh Smith, was a friend whom he had promised to go in search of if he did not return from his expedition. Sir Henry, undaunted by not having obtained his Master's certificate (which he did not gain until 1886) acted as his own sailing master, and found his friend, who had reached Matoshkin Mar in his lifeboats. The *Kara* sailed north along the coast of Novaya Zenia, got icebound, suffered a severe gale, survived it, and sailed for home. North of Shetland the *Kara* encountered another gale, but after five days hove-to was able to proceed. It is impossible to imagine that such adventures recounted in the home circle by the father of the family would not fire the heart of an adventurous daughter – although Constance's spirit was to express itself in more unorthodox ways.

As she grew into her teens, Constance's life was full both indoors and out. Like most people she applied herself only to the subjects which interested her – in her case literature and art. She was clever with her hands and throughout her life through all its vicissitudes she drew and painted, did wood-carving, fretwork and poker work. She took trouble to learn French and German and, later, Italian, so as to read the literature of those countries in the original. Schiller, Heine and Goethe were her favourite German poets. She loved all poetry and had the gift of memorizing long passages. In late middle age, sitting with her stepson, she would take off her spectacles to rest her eyes from her embroidery and recite the favourite lines of her youth.

Of her brothers and sisters – quiet reserved Josslyn, fragile Eva, energetic Mabel and red-headed Mordaunt – it was Eva who was able to give her the closest loyalty of siblings: love, moral support, understanding; firm even through the later events of Constance's life which bewildered and estranged the rest of her family.

Eva was two years younger than Constance and they shared their life on all levels as children. Eva's character and disposition provided the perfect counterfoil to her sister's. Constance expressed herself through action: she was generous-hearted, restless and outgiving. Eva was gentle, more thoughtful, more subtle, a dreamer and a scholar. She read Greek and Roman history and knew Latin. She taught herself Greek in later life. She became an admired poet, and a social worker. Her life-long friend and colleague, Esther Roper, records it as her opinion that Eva was not altogether happy as a child. 'Her enjoyment of the beauty of life was tempered by a passionate sympathy for suffering and injustice and a strange feeling of responsibility for life's inequalities.' It would have been hard for Eva, born as she was a sensitive, introspective humanitarian not to have brooded on the lot of the poor who surrounded her. Everywhere the girls went in Co Sligo, whether on horseback, on foot, or in the family carriages they would have seen the tumbledown cabins and the barefoot children. Constance wrote in later life that politics were not discussed in the family circle and that Irish history was dismissed as brooding on past grievances, but politics, history and grievances were part of the Irish air they breathed and it must have been impossible as the girls grew older not to have taken up some mental attitude. Either you agreed with your parents that the Land Leaguers were misguided (and wicked) or you were in sympathy with their aims; you either thought Parnell a disaster, or a hero; Home Rule the scheme of a madman, or the one hope for Ireland.

When Constance was twelve her mother invited the then unknown Irish artist, Sarah Purser, to paint the two girls. In the double portrait the children are shown in the woods of Lissadell – Constance standing upright as a larch post with her hands full of blossom and wild flowers, Eva, in a pinafore printed with leaves, crouched like a faun beside her, picking a primrose. In a short piece *The Inner Life of a Child* found after her death and known to refer to her own childhood, Eva writes, 'In one's childhood there are sunsets one will never forget, blue skies that never fade, Atlantic breakers that are immortal in their opal arches of green water, flashing with unknown light. There are twilights in spring, and primroses, and cloud shadows that flit across blue mountains and green meadows . . .' An extract from a two hundred line early poem of Eva's dedicated to 'Con' holds the retrospect of a youth filled with innocent poetic fancy.

Who shall venture to intrude
In the dim secluded wood
Where the birds have hushed their song,
Fearing to do silence wrong,
And the wind's breath scarcely stirs
In the midst of shadowy firs:

Hush, the silence grows intense,
Soon a shade shall issue hence;
Some fair Goddess white and tall,
Shadowy-limbed, majestical;
Leaning on her bow and spear,
Cynthia's self might venture here; . . .

Down to where the great waves are
Breaking on the sandy bar,
Surely we shall find the vision,
Of the sunset land Elysian,

Where the clouds and mountains go
In the dreamy afterglow –
Hush – the silence grows immense
Till a Presence issues thence;

High she sits, alone, serene,
Holy Universal Queen,
Snowy limbed and white and nude
Ocean Maiden Solitude.

Miss Purser found Constance a difficult sitter and liked Eva the best of the two sisters. She noticed, however, that all Lady Gore-Booth's hopes seemed to be centred on Constance (a state of affairs which turned out sadly when Constance reached her twenties and was irritated and irked by her mother).

The children had a governess who had been rash enough to confide in them about her affairs of the heart. The visiting painter recalls that Constance delighted in embarrassing her parents and the other older people by recounting these confidences in the dining-room. One can imagine her, having spent a trying morning posing, fidgeting in her seat in the long, high, dining-room with its view of Ben Bulben, taking it out on authority with her clear-voiced disclosures.

In its conception Sarah Purser's double portrait embodies the idyllic side of the sister's childhood: the long summer days crowned by the endless Irish twilight when the children hardly left the beach, paddling, bathing and shrimping, eating picnic teas of cockles and shrimps, sailing in the bay; the picnics at Knocklane when every conveyance was called into use, brakes, carriages and the outside cars that Lady Fingall describes as being so typical of the Irish character, 'Two people can drive on one through the same country and yet each see quite a different view. One looks one side, one the other. The only person who can see the whole truth of the landscape, is the jarvey who sits in the middle.

Knocklane is some six miles from Lissadell through lanes from which you see how the long flanks of Ben Bulben and King's Mountain dominate the sky to the south-east. The chasm – the Derk of Knocklane – is celebrated, as has been seen, by Constance's great-great-grandmother Letitia through her circus feat. Below the hill and Knocklane there is a great curving sandy beach and dune-land, and the view across Sligo Bay to Ocris Head.

Many years later Constance's husband wrote a passage based on his memory of such a day. 'The boundless ocean – the Atlantic on a languid summer's day – basking in the July sunshine – its waters reflecting the rays of the sun like a silver mirror sparkling with gold, rainbow opals and violet of amethysts and translucent with the green of emeralds. One is almost blinded by the strong white light, like an eagle by the glare of the sun . . .'

In the winter there was pheasant, snipe and woodcock shooting, in the Mountain Plantation on the slope of Ben Bulben, or in the bogland up to your waist in water. Duck came into the reeds and marshes round the lake in the Upper Glen, fed by a stream which rushes down the side of Ben Bulben. In March and April flocks of barnacle geese from the Arctic came into feed on the sandbanks and dunes of Lissadell and provided more sport.

The self-contained life in the Lissadell demesne, rooted in family, in horses, in sports which entailed physical exertion and discomfort, the untamed country with the ignorant, deeply religious poor who inhabited it, is reminiscent of life on estates in Russia before the Revolution. The less sensitive inhabitants of a large house set in an estate such as Lissadell must have found it hard to feel the reality of the political problems which surrounded them. Between the Protestant Anglo-Irish absorbed in the time-consuming, full and yet leisurely life of their class, and the Catholic dispossessed scratching a wretched living, resigned or unsuccessfully rebellious, there was the gulf of centuries of strife.

Even though Constance was outstanding from the first in the immediate, practical help she gave to anyone in trouble, help involving more than putting her hand into her purse, she does not appear in her youth to have questioned seriously the state of affairs which led to the various urgent needs. She always tended to live and act rather than reflect – it would, no doubt, have been Eva who pondered on the larger implications. Although Constance would do all the housework and cooking and buy the food out of her own pocket for a mother of six, ill after childbirth, or give her shoes to a girl in the road, in these early days she would come back home and plunge straight back into her own active life. There is always a first moment of illumination for heroes and heroines, from St Paul to Dick Whittington: hers did not come for many years.

A year or two after Miss Purser's first visit – in 1882 – there was a particularly violent thunderstorm which wrecked the roof of the church at Maugherow during Mass, killing one member of the congregation and injuring several others. 'Lady Gore-Booth and Sir Henry flew on the moment to the scene of the calamity, and then and for months afterwards seemed to have nothing on hand, or at heart, but to help and console the afflicted, and to repair the damage done to the place of worship.'[11] This aid was given at a time when religious intolerance was extreme.

Constance's childhood, therefore, was spent in a kindly, unpretentious family circle in which she shone from the first as the most vivid character. Whether she was risking her life sailing alone in her centreboard skiff in the treacherous waters of Donegal Bay, or getting herself injured through a bad fall because she put her horse at a cow and the cow got up, or planning and carrying out practical jokes, she must always have been a life-enchancer, a centre of activity and enterprise. But all this activity and enterprise went with the stream, not against it, she was simply braver, kinder, more lively than others of her background, not different, then, in action or outlook.

CHAPTER 3

Salad Days

In 1886 in Constance's troubled country the hero of the hour was the Parnellite William O'Brien, the brilliant, charming, editor of *United Ireland*, whose name is connected forever with Tullamore Jail. Here, in protest against being forced to wear convict clothes when he was a political prisoner, he lay in bed naked for weeks – becoming the subject of many a popular ballad (as Parnell had before him in 1882 when imprisoned in Kilmainham over the Land Act). O'Brien was finally delivered from his ordeal when a sympathetic warder smuggled in a suit of Irish tweed.

In the three years 1886 to 1889 when Constance was making her début in Dublin and London, liked and admired by everyone she met, other figures destined to be more significant in her life than her hostesses and dancing partners were beginning to take their places on the chess board.

The woman whose life formed the counterpoint to that of Constance (like two voices in a fugue) was Maud Gonne. She was the elder by two years, being born in 1866. Her father was a regular soldier, and became in 1882 Assistant Adjutant-General in Dublin. Mrs Gonne had died when Maud was four years old, and she and her younger sister, Kathleen, spent most of their childhood in France. Maud Gonne and Constance, who became allies and close friends, were unacquainted then, although at different periods their social life centred round Dublin Castle. But they shared more than the experience of a particular kind of colonial social life grafted like a bright parasite on the body of Ireland, the ailing Cathleen ni Houlihan of Yeats' play; the two young women had many traits and tastes in common. They were both admired as beauties (Yeats called Maud Gonne the most beautiful woman of her time. 'Tall and noble,' he described her beauty as 'like a tightened bow that is not natural in an age like this'); both Constance and Maud were horsewomen, and animal lovers from monkeys and snakes to Great Danes. They both took up acting, both studied art; and more than all else both are remembered for their militant role in Irish politics. Perhaps, even so, they would not be remembered in quite the same way if Yeats had not celebrated their personalities through his genius. He liked Constance, but he loved Maud Gonne.

In 1886 Maud Gonne had not yet met the poet. She was already far more politically aware than Constance. In 1886 she was in France recuperating from an illness, and falling in love with the man whose influence on her life was decisive. He was Lucien Millevoye, a politician and journalist, a militant like herself, an anti-monarchist and one of the leaders of the anti-British and pro-Russian group in France. He fired Maud Gonne with the ambition to work actively to free Ireland 'as Joan of Arc freed France'. The next year she went to Russia on a secret mission for Millevoye and the Boulangist Party, and there met the distinguished journalist, Wickham Steed, who talked to her about the Fenian prisoners rotting in English jails. She came back to Ireland determined to begin an active political life – fighting the British Empire. She installed herself in rooms in Nassau Street 'with peaceful faded carpets and not too comfortable armchairs' with her Great Dane, Dagda, as sole chaperone. She was fiery and determined – a Valkyrie straight from Wotan. She quickly made friends, with Yeats, and with such Gaelic Leaguers or Nationalists as Arthur Griffith, Willie Rooney, Douglas Hyde, and eventually James Connolly, the future Trades Union leader and Labour politician.

The last-named patriot became as decisive an influence on Constance as Millevoye was on Maud Gonne. Born the same year as Constance, James Connolly opened his eyes on very different circumstances: his father was an Irishman working as a lamplighter in Edinburgh. He was brought up in poverty and, after working at various jobs from the early age of eleven, at fourteen years of age he joined the King's Liverpool Regiment. In 1886 he was serving in Ireland and learning about Irish Nationalism through *Penny Readings*.

In 1886 another significant personality and future friend was emerging as an Irish patriot. This third future influence was the poet, painter, theosophist and agriculturist George Russell – self-named Æ – then aged nineteen. Born into a middle class family in Lurgan, County Armagh, Æ early displayed a marked determination to follow his own course. While walking alone in the country he experienced a mystical intuition of the soul. It was 'no angelic thing, pure and new from a foundry of souls, which sought embodiment, but a being stained with the dust and conflict of a long travel through time, carrying with it unsated desires, base and august ... myriads of memories and a secret wisdom.'¹ For Æ the inauguration of the Theosophic Movement in 1886 was both a confirmation of his intuitions and the inspiration for the future. These beliefs remained the centre of his life.

The genesis of the Theosophic Movement took place in 1885 under the roof of Professor Dowden, who was not, as it happened, a supporter of the Irish Literary Renaissance, saying an Irish book could be known from its smell of rotten glue. Someone present spoke of a recently published book called *Esoteric Buddhism* by A.P. Sinnett. Yeats read it and gave it to an old schoolfellow, Charles Johnston, the son of the Orange Member of Parliament for Ballykillbeg. The result was a striking example of the power of the written word. Charles Johnston, who was planning to be a Christian missionary, was converted to esoteric Buddhism. He immediately founded the 'Hermetic Society' which met in a room in York Street. In 1886 he went to London to meet Madame Blavatsky (whose niece he eventually married) and came back to found the Dublin Branch of the Theosophical Society. For many years the Society met in a house in Ely Place. Here, where there was an orchard to walk in and the back windows overlooked a convent garden, Æ quickly took the lead, until he withdrew in 1898 and revived the original Hermetic Society. 'The Dublin Lodge of the Theosophical Society,' wrote Ernest Boyd, in his *Ireland's Literary Renaissance* 'was as vital a factor in the evolution of Anglo-Irish literature as the publication of Standish O'Grady's *History of Ireland* ... The Theosophical Movement provided a literary, artistic and intellectual centre from which radiated influences whose effect was felt even by those who did not belong to it.'

Already the diverse strands of the Irish national resurgence were becoming clear. The imprisoned *Cathleen ni Houlihan* had many and various champions who sometimes, like Tweedledum and Tweedledee, tended to charge in different directions. There were those who resisted the call. 'And I began to tremble lest the terrible Cathleen ni Houlihan might overtake me,' wrote George Moore, 'She had come out of that arid plain, out of the mist, to tempt me, to soothe me into forgetfulness that it is the plain duty of every Irishman to disassociate himself from all memories of Ireland – Ireland being a fatal disease . . .' But of those who flung themselves gladly, even triumphantly, into the arena, Maud Gonne, James Connolly and Æ were representative of three important ideals in a complexity of aims and ambitions. The first was a spirit of pure nationalism with the aim of complete independence from England, by whatever means. The second kind of patriot looked first upon the urban poor festering in their rookeries of slum tenements – for James Connolly and his supporers it was workers' rights which were paramount, and Cathleen ni Houlihan's release as an accessory to a workers' republic. 'You cannot teach starving men Gaelic,' he stated in 1898. Thirdly, Æ, mystic and poet from his youth, practical agriculturalist by adoption, looked for inspiration far back into the centuries, and forward to a future transformed through myth – 'a flame of consciousness lit from a divine origin in the Celtic past'. He glorified the ancient gods of Ireland. Together with the other writers of the Irish Literary Renaissance, with the Gaelic Leaguers, the collectors of folklore, the playwrights and poets and story-tellers, his gift to Ireland was the renewal of her national identity.

In 1886 the delineation and eventual fusion of these shifting new elements was many years away. The Gaelic League was founded in 1893, Arthur Griffith founded his influential paper the *United Irishman* in 1899, Maud Gonne founded her woman's league *Inghinidhe na hEireann* (Daughters of Erin) in 1900. On the political front it was not until 1914 that Labour and Nationalists sank their differences in the common cause of Ireland's freedom.

Meanwhile in 1886, Constance herself, unknown by her future comrades and unknowing of her future divergence from her own class, in the tradition of young ladies of her class, spent six months in Florence, chaperoned by the governess who was her favourite of all her governesses – Miss Noel, known lovingly as Squidge. When Constance was not occupied in private drawing lessons or copying old masters in the Uffizi, or having Italian lessons, she harassed the devoted Squidge through her indulgence in the jokes and pranks which spark through her life story like fire-crackers.

About this time she was secretly engaged to a young man called Phil Percival. He had his way to make in the world and went to Australia. In his absence, without the stimulus of a secret romance upheld through meetings and the memory and prospect of meetings, she changed her mind and the engagement was broken off. It is evident later from the Journal covering the years 1892 and 1893 (when she was still living at home unmarried), that she looked for something further and outside her allotted scope – through love or achievement. It was never likely that she would settle for quiet domesticity with a country neighbour.

When she came back from Italy in 1886 she had plenty to divert her. Her passion for hunting was undiminished; during the next few years she established herself as one of the best and bravest riders in the County Sligo Hunt. The horse most connected with her name, the only real hunter she ever owned, was given to her by her Aunt Augusta Gore-Booth (known in the family as 'Wee Ga') and he was called Max after a hero in German literature whom she admired. Before she owned Max she got what mounts she could; cobs from the Lissadell stables, or mounts for the day offered by friends. In the words of Mr Edward Rowlette, farming neighbour, ally, Master of the Sligo Hunt Club:

Miss Gore [*sic*] and Max came to be regarded by the regular followers of the Hunt as being so much in a class of their own as to be altogether outside the ordinary realm of competition, and this supremacy was accepted by everyone as a matter of course. How often have I heard some exceptional 'run' or some wonderful jump described, and the story invariably ended with something like this: 'There wasn't one at the finish, except myself and . . . Miss Gore' . . . I have known a number of hunting people whom I regarded as very courageous riders, who would ride anything anywhere, but they sensed where real danger lay, and would always have to force themselves to risk a bad fall if the occasion warranted. But Miss Gore-Booth never had to force herself – for she enjoyed the risk . . . in all the years I knew her I never saw her take a bad toss. She was not only fearless, but attracted by danger.

With all this she had such a light hand that no one else would ride Max as she did. Mr Rowlette remembers seeing the horse in his comfortable old age at Lissadell without a blemish on his legs, so carefully and expertly had he been ridden, for all the dash of his owner. Many women of Constance's period, upbringing, and background would have been content to fulfil themselves, outside marriage or useful spinsterhood, through an indefinite continuation of this highly approved outlet for vitality; but another element came into her courage and bravado: a concern for humanity as represented by the sufferings of the Irish poor which transcended any present project or achievement. Hunting field walls turned into barricades, the sporting guns of Lissadell into the revolvers of civil war.

Together with her marked Amazonian side Constance combined a charming and natural wish to play the Fairy Godmother. This reached its ultimate conclusion when in late middle age she carried sacks of peat on her back up the tenement stairs of the Dublin poor. In her young womanhood this instinct found expression in a less practical manner. Constance and Eva were interested in the occult (although it is not known if they were aware then of the Dublin Branch of the Theosophical Society) and, as Irish girls, they had been brought up on stories of the Good People. It is the tradition that on May Eve the Good People concern themselves especially with humans. Constance decided to stage an elaborate charade for a local family. Mr Rowlette (who appears to have regularly brightened his life through being a member of Constance's inner circle of cronies) was asked to find a large family living in a lonely place some distance from Lissadell, preferably near a high hill, and with at least half a dozen children under teenage. He found such a family, and on May Eve the actors set out. The party consisted of Constance, her younger sister Mabel, and Mr Rowlette to carry the dressing-up trunk. They went into a wood near the chosen cabin, where Mr Rowlette left them to change their clothes. Mabel was the Prince, in a long green jerkin and a yellow scarf fastened under her chin with a large jewelled brooch, Constance, as the Princess, wore flowing robes and a hawthorn wreath in her hair, which streamed to her waist. 'It was illumined from its hidden depths by myriads of fairy lights struck by the rising moon from countless facets of multicoloured glass.' Mr Rowlette continued, 'I was too dazzled to be coherent. I can only say that she radiated all the beauty of a rare kaleidoscope.' Constance had also managed to incorporate some unnamed musical instrument or instruments which are described as numerous gadgets dangling. Mabel knocked five times on the door - the mystic number – while Mr Rowlette hid behind a turf stack. The visitors were left in and they proceeded to dance to the faint tinkling of Constance's music. Mr Rowlette crept up to the window and saw seven girls and three boys watching, while the younger children hid behind their mother, and the father leant against the dresser, his clay pipe in his mouth.

Later as they harnessed the pony with Mr Rowlette, Constance remarked that the man of the house had said that she was a 'real nate, tight woman'. Mr Rowlette adds that of all his memories of Constance this was the most vivid, and that so far as he knew the family never came to connect the visitation with 'the Lissadell young ladies'.

Constance did not often dress up as a princess. She preferred the role of beggar girl. She once went so disguised to the back door of Lissadell, and was sent away by the servants, unrecognized. On another occasion she took a bet with two young men staying in the house that she would beg from them on the high road without being recognized. Her Journal of 1893 records, 'My grand joke comes off. Armed with an old ass, a child (Mickey Mashy) and much broken crockery we arrange the tableau on the high road,' i.e. the donkey was saddled with panniers whose bottoms opened with the touch of a lever. Constance released the crockery, the child and she wept, and the young men, coming upon her, gave her money to buy more china. A third begging story is that she decided to teach a lesson to a man friend whom she considered was unkind and rude to poor people. In her role as beggar girl she arranged to come across him on the road. She solicited him for alms. As she expected, he let fly at her, so after a suitable interval she gleefully discussed her identity.

Young men who stayed at Lissadell found hazards other than Constance dressing up as a beggar maid. She had a tandem of her own invention in which she liked to drive the ponies Kelpie and Storeen. The individual feature of the tandem was that the seat was not fixed but lay across like a board. Constance would invite a selected guest for a drive and take him along the sandbanks which were honeycombed with rabbit holes. When the wheels struck a hole she waited for him to pitch forward on his head. An older guest of a status above drives with Kelpie and Storeen annoyed her by his attentions at this period of her life. One evening, during a large, formal dinner party, she suddenly felt his hand on her dress. She picked it from her knees like a dropped pear, held it up to attract everybody's attention and said 'Just look what I have

found in my lap!' Another middle-aged guest had the feminine
habit of slipping off his shoes at dinner to relieve his feet, so
Constance, sitting next to him, put the pumps over her own shoes
and left the dining-room in them. At this time she had a pet
monkey, and a tame snake she liked to wear round her neck. One
feels that her warmest admirer could not have found her a restful
companion.

In spite, however, of the hazards of monkeys, snakes and
drives on the dunes; in spite also of an experience like that of
young Mr Godley of the Royal Dublin Fusiliers (in love, he says,
with Constance like all Ireland to a man), who had to throw his
cap in the air so that she could shoot at it with her revolver,[2]
Lissadell must have provided space, leisure and delight for the
guest. On arriving he would find himself in a large hall pillared and
floored in black Kilkenny marble, while his luggage was presided
over by the benign presence of the butler, Mr Kilgallon, who had
been taught to read and write by the Gore-Booths. To the left, a
double staircase, with the charming feature of a fireplace on the
half landing, leads up to a large main landing also pillared and
floored in black marble. Downstairs, ahead of the guest, lies the
long gallery which runs the length and height of the house and
leads into the Bow Room with its shallow bay looking south to
Knocknarea Mountain, and nearer, in Constance's day, on to a
gentle green slope and the cricket pitch below. A white-painted
wooden flight of steps spans the gap between the basement and the
centre window of the bay. Next door is the drawing-room with its
four long windows looking south to Knocknarea and east to
Ben Bulben; with its elaborate white marble chimneypiece holding a clock set in a laurel wreath; with the water-colour by Sir
Frederick Burton of pretty Caroline, wife of Sir Robert, sitting on
a yellow sofa (with a view of Knocknarea painted in later) reading
to her two older daughters Emily and Augusta; and with the
drawing of the old house by the shore. Next to the drawing-room
on the east side is the room known in Constance's day as the Glory
Hole. The fact that this room, where she cut her name into the
pane, where she painted and read and gossiped and sometimes
dined with friends, was between the main formal rooms of the
house – the drawing-room and dining-room – speaks much for
the easygoing family atmosphere of Lissadell.

Constance's own bedroom was a small room which leads out of

the nursery. The window looks south over Drumcliffe Bay to the distant Knocknarea. If Constance wanted to see Eva in her room, which was on the ground-floor next door to the Bow Room, she could run down the near-by back stairs, a winding corkscrew with stone steps, and meet none of the older guests on her way. The house was then flanked on the west by a magnificent line of beeches. The tall woods still crowd round the north side of the house today, where the porch with its great wooden doors gives a misleading sombre effect. Lissadell was a place filled with laughing voices and many comings and goings, with riding for pleasure and polo on the sands, with long expeditions into the hills, with Constance always oversetting the more conventional 'English' ways of her mother, and Sir Henry appealed to as being the 'Irish' parent who would understand and condone the escapades of his eldest child. The centre was invariably Constance; threading oranges for the Christmas tree which she always decorated; getting elected as Beauty Queen of the West in a charity competition; galloping across Moffat's Flat to neighbouring Classiebawn dressed in a brown corduroy frock and hatless in the sunset; lying on the drawing-room hearthrug laughing 'like a foolatic' instead of sitting sensibly in a chair; reciting Christina Rossetti as she climbed Knocknarea – 'Does the road wind uphill all the way?'; risking her life in her little sailing-boat. Hers was a personality which effortlessly dominated those with less of a flame for life.

Constance was presented at one of Queen Victoria's Courts in 1889. She quickly made her mark as 'the new Irish beauty'. She was noticed at Ascot in a 'pale blue gown draped with old lace', and on another occasion, in an outfit which one feels was nearer to her heart, of a red dress slashed with black satin stripes, crowned by a black hat with three ostrich feathers. She had the entrée into the close society of Victorian England through her large cousinhood which threaded its way through the families of Scarborough, Dunraven, Zetland, Bradford, Bolton, Westminster and Carlisle. Lady Fingall describes the London Seasons of the eighties:

All the houses had bright newly watered window-boxes. There were flowers everywhere and sunshine and jingling hansoms. It was great fun to be alive and to be young. There were Sunday Parades in the Park, where people walked up and down after church, met their friends and talked to them. The women were beautifully dressed. It was the time of big hats and full rustling silk dresses.[3]

A studio photograph of this period shows Constance in a snowy dress garlanded with white flowers, a fan in her gloved hands, pearls round her throat and her hair neatly piled on top of her head. But in spite of this regalia of late Victorian maidenhood she has the look of a priestess of Diana strayed into the wrong century.

The Dublin Season possessed an intimate charm which the London one lacked. Dublin social life was dominated by the Castle – its levees, drawing-rooms, state balls and the sought after small dances in the throne-room, with its fluted columns and plaster wreaths. The official Castle season was short, from February to the St Patrick's Ball on St Patrick's night in March. The opening of the Castle Season came with the Lord Lieutenant's Levee. This was followed the next day by the Ladies Drawing-room, when the young girls in their white plumes waiting to enter the stronghold and receive their seal of entry into Vanity Fair – the Viceroy's kiss – sat in their carriages which lined Dame Street. When they eventually reached St Patrick's Hall to make their curtsey, they saw their Excellencies enthroned, surrounded by the members of the household, and attended by two young pages dressed in St Patrick's blue poplin, with puffed breeches, capes, gold-frogged and tasselled tunics, and plumed tricorne hats.

The Viceroy brought over his own pictures, plate and glass – and often furniture as well. It was said that Lord Dudley spent £80,000 out of his own pocket in his first Season in 1902. In his day thirty-two black horses were hired from London, only four of which were used regularly. The rest were fed and exercised (and paid for by Lord Dudley) to add their glossy splendour to the Viceregal state entry at Punchestown and the Horse Show.

The Castle was administered socially and domestically by a hierarchy of officials: Chamberlain, Vice-Chamberlain, Comptroller, State Steward, Master of the Horse, Gentleman Usher, acting Comptrollers, Private Secretaries and assistant Secretaries, Gentlemen-in-Waiting, several Aides-de-Camp, and two Gentlemen at Large.

'It was a friendly world,' writes Lady Fingall, 'Irish society was too small to have the circles and cliques of London. Everyone knew everyone else. The girls had a wonderful time. There were plenty of men, and they, being numerically superior, used to 'cut in' on our dances. A colonel did not disdain to share a dance with his subaltern . . . It was a romantic time. Many an English heart was lost to Ireland for ever and ever during those Dublin Seasons.'

It was a friendly world, but one almost totally isolated from the real Ireland which suffered and endured as though behind a mountain of ignorance and indifference.

The personalities of the successive Viceroys and Vicereines were as important to the small Anglo-Irish world as a new colonel and his wife to a regiment. When Constance first started going to large functions the Londonderrys ruled at the Castle. The Londonderrys came in on memories of Lord Spencer's tenure which had been formal and magnificent, but the new Viceroy and Vicereine were well equipped to make their own mark on Dublin society. Lady Londonderry, who, Lady Fingall writes, had the proudest face she had ever seen, was a power socially and politically. It was a time when an able and determined woman married to the head of a great family could make herself felt through every nerve of the interlocked social and political world. Her position (so long as she avoided scandal) was impregnable. Like the Pope she was enthroned for life. Politically, the Viceroy had little power, which was vested in the English Parliament and wielded through the Chief Secretary. The Viceroy was supposed to be above politics, yet he was a member of the Government. Justin McCarthy says in his *Recollections* that the Viceregal Court was not considered by the Young Irelanders to be in the 'true sense a political institution or even, in its own capacity, a political despotism, but only a school of fashion, and an institution for the maintenance and the creation of new gentility'. He also records that many Irishmen (particularly young ones) then thought there would be a much better chance for Ireland (i.e. Home Rule) if she were placed under the control of a Viceroy given 'absolutely despotic power' like Lord Durham who, when he was sent to Canada invested with almost dictatorial powers for the suppression of a rebellion, ended by successfully giving Canada self-rule.

Lord Londonderry is remembered in Ireland for his bitter hostility to Parnell, and for reducing the period for eating the Viceregal dinners to half an hour, for he hated food. He was succeeded in 1889 by Lord Zetland. Lady Zetland (kind, short-sighted and vague) was a cousin of Lady Gore-Booth's. She is remembered for starting the fashion for Balls with a theme, with a White Ball. Lady Cadogan followed suit during her reign with Flower Balls, and it was left to the serious-minded Lady Aberdeen in her second period as Vicereine to combine a theme with a good deed when she had a Lace Ball in aid of charities.

At this time Lady Gore-Booth used to borrow a house for the season in Harcourt Terrace – belonging to some cousins, the Coffeys. Harcourt Terrace, known then as Joly's Buildings, consists of a stately centre house with a large corinthian portico flanked by two pairs of houses each side, linked by low colonnades. At the end of the street lies the tranquil canal. The creator, Dr Joly, was a Huguenot refugee. His own house, which was the one in which the Gore-Booths stayed, has an historical connection with Lord Edward Fitzgerald who, when on the run, hid in a dried-up well in the garden before jumping on to a passing barge on the canal.

Lady Gore-Booth was often unwell at this time, so Lady Fingall chaperoned Constance when her mother was absent. Lady Fingall was only three years older than her charge. She had married at the age of seventeen the twenty-four-year-old Lord Fingall, the State Steward, known later to the Londonderrys as the somnolent Earl due to his habit of falling asleep at dinner. His fascinating wife was anything but somnolent, and one cannot imagine a more amusing and delightful chaperone. Of her charge, she wrote, 'Con was then a wild beautiful girl and all the young men wanted to dance with her. She was lovely and gay in her youth at Lissadell and she was the life and soul of any party. She was much loved as well as admired.'⁴

One night Lady Fingall and Constance returned in the Vice-regal carriage from a Castle ball and found a drunken soldier in uniform clinging to one of the gate posts. Constance told him not to make so much noise as it would wake her mother, adding to Lady Fingall that she could always manage drunkards. Lady Fingall writes,

She took him by the arm and led him out to the gate, put him outside and shut it. She had sympathy with him even then, for he must be out without leave and would get into trouble. We closed the door behind us and tiptoed upstairs. We had just got into our dressing-gowns when the peace of the quiet terrace was rudely disturbed by drunken singing. Our friend had returned. Constance never hesitated, and I could do nothing but follow her. We just stopped to throw our coats hastily over our dressing-gowns – otherwise we must have died of cold – then went downstairs and out again. 'Now we'll have to take him to the canal,' said Constance. She took the man by one arm and I by the other and we walked him along to the canal bank and set him on his way to the barracks.[5]

When the two young women got upstairs again, Lady Fingall saw herself in the mirror still wearing her tiara with her coat, dressing-gown and bedroom slippers. She was not allowed to go to bed until Constance had made a sketch of her dressed like this.

Two more incidents, which took place in England, again show aspects of Constance's nature rare in so young and fortunate a woman: her impulsive, unconventional generosity, and her fearlessness in coming to grips with disconcerting events. The first anecdote concerns her return one night from a party where she had won a little money at bridge and seeing the tramps sleeping on the Bayswater Road benches, she stopped her carriage and ran from vagrant to vagrant putting her money into their hands until it had all gone. In the second anecdote she was driving to the theatre in a friend's carriage when she saw two drunken men fighting. She leapt out of the carriage, flung herself between them and shamed the onlookers into helping her stop the fight. Anyone who has seen a road accident and longed cravenly to pass on, or heard screams from a house and failed to try to investigate must admire and envy Constance's effortless courage.

In 1890, when Constance, for all her occasional unorthodoxy, was still leading the conventional life of an Anglo-Irish young lady, her contemporary and future co-revolutionary, Maud Gonne, far now from the Dublin Season in place and spirit, had made herself a legend in Donegal, where she had been helping evicted tenants. She saw heart-breaking scenes – a woman with a day-old baby, an old blind woman on a mattress who had not been out of the cabin for years, with her daughter, whose husband was looking for work in Scotland, an old couple who had built their house fifty years before when they first married – all these people and many more saw their houses smashed by the battering ram and knew that anyone who sheltered them would be evicted as well. Maud Gonne tirelessly organized the building of what were known as Land League Huts. 'For a moment, at least,' she wrote, 'they made the evicted tenants forget their misery, but the misery was there because Ireland was not free, because we had no land and the people no means of living and the keen soon replaced the songs, as the emigrant trains, like poison snakes, wound their way continually through the green deserts of derelict farms down to the coasts, where big ships carried away the boys and girls, leaving the old people wearily watching their evicted farms, till the evicted tenants became a nightmare which every politician tried to forget.'[6]

On the larger stage, Parnell was approaching his fall and death, which set the clock back for Ireland for many years. The newspapers of 17 November 1890 carried the first instalment of the divorce proceedings. Michael Davitt attacked him in the *Labour World* saying he should retire from public life and return on marriage 'having paid the penalty which the public sentiment rightly inflicts for such transgressions as this'. About this time a Methodist minister publicly denounced Parnell as the most infamous adulterer of the century. With the inevitability of a Greek tragedy, fate, character and conflict of moral views led to disaster. In December the Irish Parliamentary Party split into Parnellites and Seceders. By 8 December the final insults had been exchanged. Tim Healy had used the unforgivable phrase, 'Who is to be the mistress of the party?' and Parnell had retorted by calling him: 'A cowardly little scoundrel who dares in an assembly of Irishmen to insult a woman.' Parnell returned to Ireland. From then onwards the events mirrored the tragic spectacle of Irish patriots verbally savaging one another. Some went further: a priest in a country district said to his congregation at Mass, 'There are several Parnellites here this morning. You know what to do with them when you get outside'; another priest heard a boy cheering for Parnell and knocked him senseless.

In the spring of 1891 the storm approached peaceful Lissadell when there was an election in North Sligo, and Parnell's candidate V. B. Dillon, a cousin of John Dillon, was opposed by a Sligo alderman called Bernard Collery. Parnell, amongst other places, spoke in the small village of Grange, near Lissadell. Constance used to relate to her friends that she and Eva caught up two horses and rode secretly to the meeting. There is no record of what they thought of the melancholy spectacle of the great man at bay in what was to be the last year of his life – but his candidate lost the election. Six months later Parnell died in England, and an era ended.

CHAPTER 4

The Diarist

There are two periods in Constance's life when she speaks to us in her own voice. One is through her *Prison Letters* published in 1934, seven years after her death, and the other is through the unpublished Journals of 1892 and 1893. In 1892 she was twenty-four, and still living at home.

'May the whole year be as happy as today,' reads the entry for 1 January 1892. There was a shooting party at Lissadell including the Gore-Booths' cousin Lord Dunraven, and a neighbour – W* – a year older than herself, between whom and Constance a close friendship was growing. (On Sunday 3rd he left) 'Such a dull lonely feeling waking up and knowing the friend is gone,' she writes, 'What is it that makes me so fond of him, something deep down somewhere in both of us that meets and meets . . . "The Laws of Friendship are austere and eternal, and of one web with the laws of nature and morals."' She adds that the parson preached a very good sermon against selfishness on a long text from Isaiah which escaped her memory.

On the nights of 4th and 5th she showed her great devotion to Eva by sitting up with her because she had bad toothache, stroking her face for 'many hours' and trying to get her to drink spirits to kill the pain.

Between 9 and 14 January the house-party was absorbed in preparing for an amateur theatrical performace for a play called *Pilot Rosalie* for which W had evidently returned. After it, she says, it was a whirl of excitement, but 'nobody real, nobody themselves, nothing but shams, acting and falseness'. She is 'in the blues most thoroughly having mortally offended W . . . He threw me over for a dance. I was very X and he went off to the billiard-room

*Wilfred Ashley, later Lord Templemore.

with Joss.'* The next day she records, 'we avoid each other with determination and make a boast of it'. However, out shooting he offered her a piece of chocolate and they made up their quarrel.

Tuesday 19th [*January*] '*Every man's life lies within the present which is but a point of time; for the past is spent and the future uncertain.*'

Thursday 28th [*January*] '*Let people talk and act as they please. I must be an emerald and I must keep my colour.*'

She spent her birthday, 4 February, with the great friend 'fishing on the lake for trout in the collapsible boat with scores of cushions and rugs. We rowed into the mud to steady ourselves and fixed our little ship steady by sticking an oar into the mud and ate our frugal meal *tête-à-tête*. It was an idyll.'

On 6 February the friend left (he had been laid up with a sprained ankle which the doctor came to set in starch and which she found 'very interesting'). She writes that she is sad not to have him to fuss over, 'Nothing to tie one down – in fact – no responsibilities. Its so good for one to have someone to look after, shut doors and windows, and seek out stray draughts for and run messages for, its rather nice to be indispensable to someone.' It appears that Constance, like many daughters, found it easier to devote herself in these small ways to an interesting man, than to her mother who ailed, but who irked her a dozen times a day.

An entry of a week later records how she loves to lie late in bed 'half awake half asleep and dream. The sky is blue and the sun shines into my little room and I feel so happy and at rest. I hear Eva's canary in the far distance, its voice quite modified and sweet "Distance lends enchantment" even to that discordant fowl. There is nothing like those late morning hours, one is so pleasant and Contented with oneself. Mama is raging in the Doorway so I cannot go on writing.' (Constance has hardly been down to breakfast for the last couple of months so one can sympathize with Lady Gore-Booth.) Constance goes on to complain that her mother does not leave her alone enough and tries to force her confidence.

On 18 February she is in London staying with her cousin Josslyn (Lord Muncaster) in Carlton Gardens. He takes her out

*Her brother Josslyn.

shopping and gives her 'many pretty things'. In the evening they go to see *Fourteen Days*. 'Wyndham is capital,' she comments, 'the rest bad.'

19 February. What vulgar people the Royalties must be. This is the conclusion I have come to after being to the Victorian Exhibition. No taste in anything and every family event, birth and marriage being celebrated by an awful daub by an incompetent painter . . .

After this experience she went in the evening to dance at 'the Club' with 'Rhoda';* they were insulted by a 'vulgar American' and a Miss Smalled tried to snub them.

On 21 February she gives a long account of a 'first-rate sermon from Mr Eyton' at St Paul's on the subject of duty to God and duty to your neighbour: the danger of morality without religion. 'Because scientific men could not find heaven among the stars with a telescope it did not exist. (This to me is Bathos) . . .'

She went to stay at a house called Burton Hill and records on 1 March that she went to a Fancy Dress Ball at the Bell Hotel, Malmesbury, where she met an old friend and danced a great deal with him.

Sat 5th [March] [at Burton Hill] 'I have read Ariadne *and loved it, unnatural and overstrained it may be, but there is a spark somewhere, the indescribable touch that carries one away and makes one believe in Love – real true love – God is love – and I do not know Him. How I hate the English language where I want to think in it, it seems poor and I feel a fool. Molly† has her God whom she worships and why mayn't I have mine. To my eyes he‡ is . . . goodhearted, thoroughly English and loves her as well as men do love and for that he is her God. She keeps nothing from him and every idea and word she speaks radiates to him, her very face in repose is nothing but a thought of him and for him . . . Its indecent to parade happiness, it makes one feel that there is something in it all – not something, this won't do – Everything – and I don't want it to be so – what do I want? I don't know. Every thought has a contradiction tonight and I don't understand why. I wish Eva were here – she might.* Anna Karenina *loved and saw nothing wrong in her folly . . .'*

It seems certain that the book Constance mentions must have

*Miss Rhoda L'Estrange, later Lady Morpeth.
†Constance's sister Mabel.
‡Mabel's fiancé and later husband, Percival Foster.

been *Ariadne* by Ouida, published in 1877. This story, set in Rome, of Gioja who loved Hilarion – a millionaire poet, beautiful as a god, who mocked at everything – evidently produced a strong effect on the innocent, romantic young women of the period. Marie Bashkirtseff (who like Constance, later, worked at Julian's famous art school in Paris) writes in her Journal entry of 10 August 1877 that she has just finished *Ariadne* and that she almost envies the fate of the heroine 'she loved with her whole soul. And if she was abandoned, it was by *him*; if she suffered it was through him. I do not see how one can be made wretched by anything that comes from him one loves.'[1]

On 20 March a middle-aged self-centred guest came to stay who was 'on hand all day, wandering about and buttonholing people. How sick I am of *his* delicate boyhood, *his* fainting fits – all rubbish I'm sure – *his* shooting, *his* fishing, *his* deerstalking, *his* yachting, *his* powers of managing people. Duck* and I do goose-berry for Molly and her lover.' She goes on to say that she wishes she too had someone to love.

'I feel the want. Women are made to adore and sacrifice themselves, and I as a woman demand as a right that Nature should provide me with some-thing to live for, something to die for. Why should I alone never experience the best and at the same time the worst of Life's Gifts? The happiest and the Saddest. E – W has her lover and the world says she is wicked . . . She affects and alters 3 lives – His, Hers, His wife's. She is abused and called hard names by friends and enemies . . . and the thing they call love is worth it all, worth all Peace, all religion, respectability, good name, friends, all Hope of Heaven . . . Poor girl, poor man – and they probably consider themselves above pity; and look down on the World from a lofty pedestal of Happiness.

On 28 March Constance left England for Ireland on the night mail. On 2 April she 'took part in fine style in the final run of the Sligo Harriers'(riding Max).

7 April 'Eva and I took of lunch to Knocklane – us two and the little tandem. We took no account of time having left our watches behind.'

8 April 'Planted the Beautiful Bed of White Arabis with coloured Hyacinths. All day I worked barring lunch and tea. In the Evening the canoe was launched and I paddled out and sailed back before the wind.'

*Constance's sister Eva.

44

10 *Sunday 'Walked from Church with Lily through the Paddock. Tea on the shore. A most Amusing Scene. Lily insisted on going in the Canoe. Colonel G. and Mama doing their best to prevent her. Mama primly relating a wonderful anecdote over and over again of how Papa's Brother was nearly drowned . . . "close where I was."'**

On 16 April she indulged in her unfailing propensity for practical jokes by stealing 'The Dillon's cow and calf' and hiding them in Johnsport. The Dillon family were heard calling 'Sucky Sucky' on the Sligo road until midnight.

On 25 April she went to stay with her cousins, the Viceregal family at Viceregal Lodge for Punchestown Races, and found Mr and Mrs Willie Jameson (Mrs Jameson was known as 'Soft Eyes' and was charming and clever; Mr Jameson was a well known yachtsman, owner of the *Magdalena*), Sir William Eden (of whom George Moore said a valet was as necessary to him as a boon companion to himself, George Moore) and Lady Eden, Lord and Lady Langford and Miss Sutton, Lord Carlton and Lord Romilly and Captain Matthews. The next day was remarkable for Lady Eden being so late that they nearly missed the train, and when they had removed to the carriages a postilion being so drunk that he fell on to the other horse four times. With the characteristic humanity which was the other face of her occasional tomboyish insensitivity Constance adds it was unsafe for him as well as them since they were in 'the wheeler'. Lord Langford came to the rescue by riding the postilion's horse himself, 'tall hat – smart trousers' complete, leaving the man 'rolling about and swearing in the road'.

On 1 May Constance left the Viceregal party in the morning to visit her Aunt May Wynne,† and her cousin and admirer Captain Graham Wynne who had just come back from India. Coming back, she writes, 'I drove through 3 "Demonstration Processions". In the afternoon we walked out and looked at the meeting in the Phoenix. Early Dinner, during which Hilda‡ and I ran out and dug up Jack's biscuits as fast as he buried them – the poor

---

*There was a local tradition that because of the Seven Cartrons incident there was a curse on the Gore-Booth family– expatiated through the death by drowning of Sir Henry's elder brother. In fact it was Lady Gore-Booth's brother who was drowned at Lissadell.

†Constance's Aunt Emily – wife of Captain Charles Bradstreet Wynne.

‡Lady Hilda Dundas, daughter of Lord Zetland, who married Lord Southampton in the summer of that year.

animal was most bewildered. His Ex. left ½ hour before I did.'

(The Demonstration Processions mentioned by Constance were probably for the Amnesty Movement. One must infer from her lack of comment – compared to the interest she took in sermons – that she was still blindfold as regards Irish politics.)

On Monday, 2 May, on her way home she found a lost yearling which, one need hardly add, she drove home and 'hid in the riding-school'. A 'dear little boy' called Strut had arrived at Lissadell, and she writes, 'We pulled Strut's leg awfully. The family had told him that I was very stiff and cross, so I took it up and flew at the boys for everything they did. He was entirely taken in. After lunch we told him and ragged him awfully.'

On 7 May her father's yacht arrived home from Greenland where he had been game-fishing after whales. The summer was bad and the quest for whales was abandoned in favour of seals, but without much more success. She writes, '*Kara* arrived. We started to meet her in the *Mabel* (i.e. the centreboard skiff she called the canoe) *Brig* and *Flora* crew met us in their whaling-boat and were much astonished at our "courage". Certainly we were nearly swamped. We came on the ship and stayed on board until dinner-time.'

Sunday 8th. '*Spent the afternoon on* Kara. *All the countryside came on board.*'

11 May. '*Mordaunt left. His Mama saw him off so I did not. We dined on the ship and had an excellent dinner. After Dinner the crew entertained us with songs and Dances and we were much amused notwithstanding Mama and W.G. came on board to sit in judgement which stiffened our marrow and wet our thirst.*'

The menu of the dinner runs:

> Tortue Franz Josef Land
> Poulet Sauté au Maharajah
> Boueff rote [*sic*]
> Pomme de Terre au Novaya Zemblia
> Choux Tomates au Jus
> Anglia Gooseberry Tart à la Creme
> Riz a la Kara
> Abricots Greenlandoris
> Rare Bit au Whales
> Songs Step Dances Etc Etc from Sir Henry's brave crew of his Gallant little Ship *Kara*.

Five days later two of the houseparty left and she writes that she dreads 'a narrowed bosom which it will be with a Vengeance'. The next morning, perhaps to cheer themselves up, she and Eva got up at four to see the sunrise and hear the birds sing; but the sun rose behind 'thick barriers of grey woolly cloud – quite as secret and respectable as the Aunt in her Bath' and although the birds sang the expedition was not counted a success. Back in the house Constance found and ate a large amount of cheese, and slept late thereby once more missing family breakfast.

On 24 May the *Kara* sailed, and those left behind (including Constance) got up at three in the morning to see the last glimpse; she writes 'it was so dreary and sad watching the ship getting smaller and smaller, sitting on a bank . . . and passing a telescope round'.

Soon after this the family removed itself to London for the Season. It was the custom, the proper thing to do; very expensive, but presumably essential to family pride. It is symptomatic of the rigidity of nineteenth-century convention that of the three Miss Gore-Booths for whose benefit this move was undertaken, Mabel (aged eighteen) was in love with, if not actually engaged, to her future husband; Eva (aged twenty) could never possibly, given her tastes, health and ideals, have liked the London Season, and Constance by this time was in complete rebellion against it. When it is over she writes,

'Hilda married, Evey marrying, a whole London Season older and not engaged or even wishing to be. If I could only cut the family tie and have a life and interest of my own I should want no other heaven – and I see an opening – Daylight and Freedom – if I can only persevere and drudge and get my . . . family to pay. All this season I have worked 4 hours daily with Miss Nordgren* . . . and I have got on beyond my wildest dreams and am encouraged to see success at the end if only, if, if, . . . 3 years hard work and no money to do it on and no hopes of getting it. Nothing but the burden of Dreams and Ideas . . . If I was sure of myself and I knew I could succeed for sure and make a name or money I would bolt and live on a crust. But to do all that with the chance of having no return and throw oneself on the charity of ones family a miserable failure is more than I can screw up courage to face. So many people begin with great promise and greater hope, and end in nothing but failure'.

On 28 July of the same year, 1892, Lady Gore-Booth set out

*Anna Nordgren, Swedish portrait and genre painter.

with Constance and Eva and Rachell Mansfield for Bayreuth. It was a leisurely trip and one undertaken by many worldly and unworldly music-lovers. The Gore-Booth's party's itinerary was repeated in many respects by two distinguished literary compatriots a few years later and recorded by one of them George Moore, who travelled with Edward Martyn, and wrote of his experiences in his memoirs *Ave, Atque, Vale*.

Constance writes, 'We start and have three-quarters of an angry hour to wait for our train' (presumably at Victoria). Once on the boat things looked up, 'A bright sun and a fresh breeze blowing the spray about in light sparkling showers. We trod the deck with all the airs of born sailors. Eva and Rachel went to read by a paddle-box while I took exercise. The breeze got brisker . . . We were all sick. Mama nearly died. She will never recover I'm afraid. We put her to rest and went out. We ranged the town [Boulogne] and saw the *Dome*.'

The next day Constance and Rachel Mansfield got up at six and went to sketch in the market. Another artist was already there 'drawing a lovely water-colour, a big broaded-minded picture full of light and air'. Lunch was in an 'awful place found by Mama' and in the afternoon after lunch there follows an incident typical of Constance's hardihood in the face of unpleasantness. The afternoon began peacefully enough with she and Rachel Mansfield finding 'an angel called François' to carry their bags.

'We selected a meadow from which there was a lovely view and began to sketch, but Alas, Alas we did not notice a school in the background, suddenly I and François were surrounded by imps, boys and girls hemming us all round gabbling fighting snatching our things and pulling our clothes. We tried civility & remonstrated with them, also brute force which was more efficient as they all scampered when threatened & retired but returned as soon as we had seated ourselves again. At last I went to the school & got a mild, helpless Sister of St Vincent de Paul, at whose sight they all vanished & we had a short respite – but when they came back they were worse than Ever, François had a hand to hand fight with a thing quite twice his size. I rescued him & nearly killed his opponent, boxing several ears and raging. At last I saw St Michael in the form of a policeman to whom I poured out my rage. He was very comforting and I had quite an hour's peace. Mama returned having mended her cane.'

The next day the party left Boulogne by train for Aachen.

Constance writes, 'I lied freely about Mama being ill but inexorable guards rammed 3 fat French in on us. We had a dusty mile to walk before we got to the Grand Monarch.' Here the rooms were bad but the food good. The next day they moved on to Cologne and dined in a 'low pot house, well and cheaply'. The day after (31 August) Constance enjoyed High Mass at nine o'clock in the Cathedral, finding the Cathedral 'sublime' and the treasure 'wonderful'. (George Moore and Edward Martyn, on the other hand, considered the cathedral an ugly building because 'it was begun in the Middle Ages and finished somewhere in the middle of the nineteenth century'.) The Gore-Booth party visited the shrine of St Ursula which Constance found 'quite comic, built up everywhere with skulls and bones. Mama kept saying in a loud voice "Professor (illegible) says all the Bones are Those of Inferior animals." ' Constance adds, 'I think Faith is a very pretty Quality & am greatly interested to know if it can be combined with Knowledge and common sense'.

Rachel Mansfield and Constance then set off by tram round the town and had another unpleasant adventure while waiting for a return one. It was raining and they tried to shelter in a hut, 'A drunken man first tried to kiss & then rudely turned Rachel out and raged at us, we laughed and used our only weapon to annihilate him, i.e. we snapped him with the Camera.'

Coblenz was the next stop and the party had a day on the Rhine, meeting one of Constance's suitors, Mr William Max-Muller. Constance rowed Rachel Mansfield across the Rhine and comments, 'such boats such oars my fingers are blistered'.

On Wednesday 3rd Constance's entry reads, 'All the German Army were having breakfast when we came down. R. and I sketched them, at once suddenly a very tall solemn and beautiful one got up with much dignity & walked over to us clanked his heels together & spoke, "It is very disagreeable" ... (Bang bang went our sketch-books, Ma blushed & flustered) he finished ... "to you if we smoke" ... Mama was nearly killed by a window falling in on her.'

The party moved on to Nuremberg, and met Mr H. Graham – who had lost all his luggage at Mainz Bahnhof – Miss Graham, Rhoda L'Estrange and Mildred Grenfell.

On the 5th they visited the old citadel and photographed a sentry. As they were leaving they were told they had missed the best sight – the tortures. These were quite up to expectations and 'the Iron Maiden gives me the creeps'. Constance admired 'the little old-fashioned chappelle & the peculiar roofs painted with black eagles & other crests'.

On the 6th they arrived in Bayreuth and were 'much cheated by porters' – but their lodgings were clean. George Moore speaks of the 'fly-haunted privies' of the Bayreuth of the late nineteenth century, and non-existence of bathrooms, so perhaps Lady Gore-Booth, unlike with the opera tickets, had booked in advance.

On the 7th they heard *Tannhauser* – 'one of the greatest sermons ever written' – Constance writes, and adds that Eva and she were in the gallery and 'R. and Mama in the stalls. What comes of getting your tickets after you arrive.'

Monday 8th 'Parsifal. *Our seats were good and next me sat a man with a very interesting & nice face. I had a great many possessions — dropped them all. He retrieved them & offered to take care of them for me. That man must have a sense of humour.*'

Tuesday 9th. 'Off Day so saw the town. *I sketched Listz's grave for Squidge* & made great friends with a small boy who sketched it too I supplying him with Paper etc.*'

On Friday 10th, there was another performance of *Parsifal* but, Constance writes, 'alas, alas, my charmer was replaced by a decrepid bore'.

The next day was an off day (i.e. when there are no performances) and the party went on an expedition and gathered flowers and bilberries.

Friday 12th. 'Tannhauser. *We saw Wagner's grave and photographed his House*'.

After this there was a tiff with Miss L'Estrange at lunch at the Opera House who 'bolted from lunch with a book we wanted'.

Miss Grenfell followed her to calm her, and they failed to hear the horn which announces the start of the opera, so missed the first Act. Miss L'Estrange seems to have been the least happy of the party, changing her lodgings with bad grace in Nuremberg,

*The ex-governess.

and also suddenly quitting a day's sightseeing because she remembered she had promised to have tea with Miss Graham – a diversion she could have any day in London, as Constance pointed out. It is sad to think that she did not enjoy her lunch in the place George Moore described as 'the little green-painted restaurant higher up the hill in the orchard close . . . under the trees', where you could drink Rhenish wine mixed with water from stone jars. Perhaps the 'plod through the glare up the long street past the railway station into the avenue of chestnut trees' (a plod Constance undertook that day with Miss Grenfell and not with Miss L'Estrange) upset the latter.

Saturday the 13th was an off day, and on Sunday they saw their last opera – *Meistersinger*. There was another incident with Miss L'Estrange because Constance settled to spend the long interval with Miss Grenfell. Constance writes the sunset was 'lovely' but the heat 'too appalling'.

Monday 15th was 'such a sad day' for Constance, packing to leave. She met Mr Stuart-Wortley in the street who told her that her cousin, Lady Sibell Grosvenor, was in the town, so Constance dashed off to see her and found her dressing. Lady Sibell was the wife of George Wyndham, future Chief Secretary of Ireland and a great grandson of Lord Edward Fitzgerald.* Lady Sibell (who was rich, lovely, kind and devout) must have appeared like the visiting Englishwomen described by George Moore at the station when he says how full of smart ladies Bayreuth has become, 'Ladies in long fashionable dust-cloaks . . . beset by maids with jewel cases in their hands.' The same day the Gore-Booth party travelled to Wurzburg in baking hot carriages and stopped for the night in a 'pleasant pot house with a pretty Babette to wait . . . no baths and dirty rooms.' Then another hot journey and an hour to get cool in Mainz, which George Moore describes as a 'pompous town – imitation French, white streets with tall blue roofs, and some formal gardens along the river.' In Cologne Lady Gore-Booth became very agitated 'tearing furiously up and down after dim officials', but Constance does not give the reason. The trip was nearly over; on the 17th they were in London . . . Constance writes that she 'went to the studios. Miss Mackay

*Lady Sibell was a daughter of Lord Scarborough. She first married Earl Grosvenor, who died. On re-marriage she retained the surname of her first marriage coupled with her courtesy title as an Earl's daughter.

gave me a kiss and tea, Miss Pfeiffer much good advice & I was happy. How nice these people are. So natural & simple, openly critical & straightforward.' She adds, 'Mama awfully X and Squidge came to tea.'

On the journey back to Ireland Constance slept the whole way from Euston to Holyhead and arrived home 'as fresh as a new pin, bathed & revelled in a cool green country, a blue sky and a bluer sea. Tea on the shore & laziness & a sail in a boat. Oh the joy of seeing the People, houses trees and mountains of home again.'

One hopes that Lady Gore-Booth was also able to revel in her return. The reader must feel a pang of pity for her in her role as cicerone without the support of her husband – sea-sick, hit by the falling window, breaking her cane, exhausted by the hot train journeys, finding the wrong sort of eating place, failing to get good seats at the opera; and all under the critical, although affectionate, eye of her eldest daughter. In fact, although Lady Gore-Booth's health was not good at this time she survived to know the days when the newspapers blazoned the arrests and imprisonments of this loved daughter. 'Oh dear, Oh dear, this will be the death of me some day,' she is remembered as saying to the friends whom she met when she was driving round Sligo in her pony-trap; but she lived on until the year Constance herself died.

Constance was hardly home before she left again for the Dublin Horse Show. She writes on 23 August that she went 'for Economy by Slow train. Damn economy, say I.' She met many friends, but 'missed W.', and one day got in free as a groom. She went to the ball given by Lord and Lady Wolseley (who was Commander-in-Chief from 1890 to 1895) in the beautiful Royal Hospital, Kilmainham, and 'Danced most of the time with little Captain B. a silly little flirt quite in his element at a Ball.' She got home on Sunday the 28th and felt 'at peace with the world' spending the day on the shore. She was off again the next day, however, to stay with Lord and Lady Erne at Crom where she sailed, played cards, canoed until the moon was up, and went to Enniskillen Fair where she saw 'the O'Haras and Mauds in troops'.

Back home again she spent nearly three weeks working at her drawing, visiting the cottages for her models. On 24 August she rode Max over to Classiebawn (the neo-Gothic home of Mr Evelyn Ashley) 'and didn't I just gallop across Moffat's flat . . . Max was fresh, the day cool and my spirits Spring like.' Of the guests at

Classiebawn she comments that 'Mr B. is a sleek and youthfully bald nonentity', and that Lord Shaftesbury (first cousin of her host) 'has a nice face, beautiful eyes, a kind affectionate weak face & a good strong very young & plump figure'. Also staying at Classiebawn was Mary Leslie* daughter of another great Anglo-Irish house, the Leslies of Castle Leslie, Glaslough. The two girls made friends. (Constance thought Mary Leslie so charitable in her judgement of people that her critical faculties were 'often blinded by the milk of human kindness'.) The new friend wrote in later life of this first meeting. 'I thought I had never seen anyone so lovely. In the evening she started off at a hand gallop over the shore as if she feared the tide would come up and stop her. Hatless, dressed in a brown corduroy frock, not a habit, she was startlingly beautiful as the sun caught her fair hair.'

At the end of November Constance went to stay with the Leslies at Castle Leslie, and found a houseparty of Monaghan neighbours. She made great friends with Mr John Leslie and his wife, particularly the former, who walked with her in the moonlight, gave her grapes in the greenhouse ('forbidden fruit'), took her out in a velocipede to look at wild duck on the lake which mirrors the great grey house and the hanging woods on the far shore, and lost to her at picquet, taking a beating 'as lightly as most things'.

Constance was urged to prolong her visit, and several days later we find her 'doing a round of Poor visits' with Mrs Leslie when they 'finish up in a tiny cottage where a handsome young man plays the fiddle and O. and his pretty sister dance jigs'. Finally she left, having stayed from 29 November to 8 December. Before she left Mary Leslie gave her a vellum-bound album of *Great Thoughts* collected by herself through the long leisurely days of an Anglo-Irish lady, from sages such as Plato, Thoreau, Emerson and Oscar Wilde. She went on to pay another visit and on the 12th received letters from Mr John Leslie, and her sister Mabel. 'Jam, Jelly and Bread,' she comments. On her way home again Mr Leslie got up early to bring her grapes to the train when it stopped at his local station.

On Christmas Day she writes, 'A very long and depressing Sunday. Three services. After the third I meditated on Heaven

*Later Mrs Murray Guthrie.

and thought Perpetual Hymns and Carols might get monotonous. Why are old People so consecrated? and shall I when over 50 suddenly take to singing solos in church? having failed all my life to get People to go voluntarily to listen to me?'

Constance spent the early part of 1893 hunting at Lissadell, and whatever she may have felt about the frustrations of her artistic life she does not record her thoughts. The entries become more scanty. On her twenty-fifth birthday, 4 February, she comments that there is no birthday cake and only one present (which seems strange in such a large and affectionate family circle) and, later, several entries laconically record her going to carving classes and polishing some furniture she has bought.

The Journals end with her Easter visit to Mr George Wyndham and his wife Lady Sibell Grosvenor at Saighton Grange, Chester, described by Lady Fingall in the same period.

Saighton was an old house with battlemented walls, which made a lovely background for Sibell's tall flower borders, and there was a monastic feeling in George's turret room. It was lined with beautiful books and had deep seats in the windows which looked over the Cheshire country to the spires of Chester Cathedral.* George used to recite poetry in that room and read Shakespeare aloud in his beautiful voice.

No doubt Lady Gore-Booth encouraged and fostered all such visits to large country houses belonging to the privileged and the right thinking, hoping that a suitable husband for her unpredictable eldest daughter would finally emerge. A good match was the panacea – the final solution of the problem of difficult daughters. Through a husband, longings for freedom to pursue Art would be buried, and any glimmering of awkward political ideas quenched. But Constance was born to disappoint her mother in spite of her effortless success in the social scene. Typically, the last glimpse of her through the Journals is at Saighton escaping from the other guests to read her book 'in the Sun under a beech tree on a bank of leaves'.

*Lady Fingall's memory seems to play her false here, since the turret-room at Saighton looks in the opposite direction from the cathedral.

CHAPTER 5

Pictures of the mind

In the year 1893 Constance's name was entered on the roll of the Slade. This was a significant event for it meant that at long last she had persuaded (or badgered) her family into taking her seriously. It was the first breakaway and it set her on the path of her destiny. There was a world of difference between having private drawing lessons in the intervals of the conventional social round supervised by Lady Gore-Booth, and living the independent life of an acknowledged art student. The fact that Constance was no more than a gifted amateur had nothing to do with the deeper implication of her longing to identify herself with something true and important for her. Her art studies were not a false trail, because they led eventually to the militant political life which was her destiny. It was not a question of an interlude outside the fold and then back to marriage with clever, promising Mr William Max-Muller (later British Minister in Poland) or Mr Christopher Howard, son of Lord Carlisle – she stayed outside the inner-ring fence.

Now in 1893 she was about to exchange the London Season with its balls and visiting and dressing up – and the strain of trying to work as well – for the life of a serious art student. The opening to 'Daylight and Freedom' she saw in the Journal entry of July of the previous year, the opening she feared never to have, was shining ahead.

At the Slade she worked under Alphonse Legros, then an elderly man, who had been a pupil of Ingres. She also continued to work with her great friend, the Swedish artist, Anna Nordgren, in her studio at 16 Bolton Studios in Redcliffe Road. There is a letter of Miss Nordgren's to Constance dated April of this year asking her to submit one or two sketches for the election of new members to the 91 Club, and promising to do her best to get her

in. Presumably she succeeded, for in December Mr Solomon –
Joseph Solomon* – wrote saying he was sorry he could not come
to a party Constance was giving at the club.

A contemporary has left her impression of Constance at this
time,

> It was in one of a long row of London studios – The Boltons – off the
> Fulham Road, that I first saw Constance Gore-Booth. She was in her
> first freshness of youth and beauty. It was still the time of the aesthetic
> movement and the studios were full of artists in more or less shabby
> blouses, gay, hopeful, chattering. One day into their midst sailed Con-
> stance Gore-Booth in some long frock of the period which I can only
> remember as part of an enchanting picture. It was not as a pastime that
> she took up art. She worked hard and seriously for some hours each day
> drawing from life. And later on when Miss Nordgren came to stay at
> Lissadell and they painted out of doors together her work gained
> constantly in technique and light and colour.[1]

One of Constance's lodgings was the Alexandra House Hostel
for Girl Art Students, where she was the centre of an incident
typical of her time and of her character. The hostel rules were
strict, and Constance, having been out to Twickenham one evening 'with a cousin' (presumably Captain Graham Wynne) got
back an hour after the official time, which was ten o'clock. She
was locked out and refused admittance; so she found herself in the
invidious position in Victorian London of having to find a hotel
to give her a room late at night without the passport to respectability: luggage. Infuriated by this event, she wrote to her father,
who was so fired by her letter that he had an interview in London
with Sir Francis Cook who had built the hostel and dedicated it to
Alexandra, Princess of Wales.

Sir Francis provides an interesting link with Ireland, for he was
the great-uncle of Maud Gonne. In fact, it was her contention that
Sir Francis's magnificent inherited collection of pictures (which
had been made by her grandfather) should have come to her
mother. It is not certain if it was pure coincidence that Constance
should have been lodging at this particular hostel, which Maud
Gonne must have known of, since there is no precise record of
their first meeting. At this time Maud Gonne was absorbed in her
work for evicted tenants and the Treason Felony prisoners. Meanwhile, Sir Francis was subjected to such a fatherly fuss by Sir

*Painter of portraits and classical and biblical scenes. Made R A 1906.

Henry that the hostel authorities were forced to apologize and to offer to reinstate Constance. She refused to go back, so Sir Henry found himself installing her in a studio of her own at Stanley Chambers. As a result of the incident the hostel rules were relaxed so far as to allow students to stay out until 10.30 pm instead of ten o'clock.

One Christmas time after Constance was settled in her own studio she noticed a strikingly lovely young woman with a baby in the street. She jumped off her bicycle and exclaimed impulsively, 'Oh, how beautiful you are!' The girl, who was not more than seventeen, told Constance that she had just been turned out of hospital to make room for others, and had nowhere to go. Constance took her back to the studio where a Christmas hamper from Lissadell had arrived (lovingly packed, no doubt, by the housekeeper, Mrs Bailey, who adored Constance) and she fed the forlorn mother on turkey and plum pudding. She gave her clothes and later found work for her as a model.

The winter of 1894–5 was memorable at Lissadell for the two visits of Yeats, commemorated by his poem, written thirty years later after the death of both Eva and Constance.

> The light of evening, Lissadell,
> Great windows open to the south,
> Two girls in silk kimonos, both
> Beautiful, one a gazelle.
> But a raving autumn shears
> Blossom from the summer's wreath;
> The older is condemned to death,
> Pardoned, drags out lonely years
> Conspiring among the ignorant.
> I know not what the younger dreams –
> Some vague Utopia – and she seems,
> When withered old and skeleton-gaunt,
> An image of such politics.
> Many a time I think to seek
> One or the other out and speak
> Of that old Georgian mansion, mix
> Pictures of the mind, recall
> That table and the talk of youth,
> Two girls in silk kimonos, both
> Beautiful, one a gazelle.

> Dear shadows, now you know it all,
> All the folly of a fight
> With a common wrong or right.
> The innocent and the beautiful
> Have no enemy but time;
> Arise and bid me strike a match
> And strike another till time catch;
> Should the conflagration climb,
> Run till all the sages know.
> We the great gazebo built,
> They convicted us of guilt;
> Bid me strike a match and blow.

Compelling though the images of genius are, the poet's view seems unnecessarily sombre in the face of two such absorbed and useful lives (to put it at its barest) as those of Constance and Eva Gore-Booth. He was certainly consistent in his attitude to women in politics. Two years earlier than the Lissadell visit, when Maud Gonne was recovering in France from an illness incurred through her efforts to help the evicted tenants of Donegal she received a poem in the post entitled *An Epitaph* which began,

> I dreamed that one had died in a strange place
> Near no accustomed hand;
> And they nailed boards above her face,
> The peasants of that land . . .

By 1894 Maud Gonne was in good health again, and at Lissadell the two girls – 'two beautiful figures among the great trees of Lissadell', part of the 'dear memories' of the poet's youth, gave no disturbing signs of political militancy. 'A very pleasant, kindly, inflammable family' he wrote of them after his first visit, 'ever ready to take up new ideas and new things. The eldest son is "theoretically" a home-ruler and practically some kind of humanitarian, much troubled by the responsibility of his wealth and almost painfully conscientious.'[2]

Yeats was spending the winter with his bachelor uncle, George Pollexfen, at his house, Thornhill, outside Sligo. At this time Yeats was rewriting *The Countess Cathleen* which he had written for Maud Gonne (the first version having been published in the summer of 1892). His other play *The Land of the Heart's Desire* had been produced in March 1894 in London, where George Moore saw him for the first time striding to and fro at the back of the dress circle – 'a long black cloak drooping from his shoulders, a soft sombrero on his head, a voluminous black silk tie flowing from his collar, loose black trousers dragging untidily over his long, heavy feet.'³ In spite of the fact that the play was not a success, Yeats was beginning to be known and talked about in London. He was twenty-nine, three years older than Constance. He had achieved his labour of love in the editing, together with the poet and painter, Edwin Ellis, of the works of Blake for Quaritch. He had published *The Wanderings of Oisin* and the poem *The Lake Isle of Innisfree*. He was much involved in the Gaelic literary revival and in Irish nationalism. He was also an initiate of a Christian Cabalistic Order called the Golden Dawn, the founder being a museum curator called Mathers. (Mathers married the sister of the then unknown Henri Bergson.) Yeats had come to the Society of the Golden Dawn via the London Theosophists, whose company he had sought out on arrival. He resolutely defended his beliefs to the eminent old Fenian, John O'Leary, who disapproved of Yeats and Maud Gonne becoming members of the Society of the Golden Dawn. 'If I had not made magic my constant study,' Yeats wrote to O'Leary, 'I could not have written a single word of my Blue books, nor would *The Countess Cathleen* have ever come to exist. The mystical life is the centre of all that I do and all that I think and all that I write. It holds to my work the same relation that the philosophy of Godwin holds to the work of Shelley . . . the revolt of the soul against the intellect.'⁴

At Lissadell Yeats was asked to lecture on Irish folklore in the school house by the Reverend Fletcher Le Fanu – a fine-built man with a hare-lip, a nephew of the novelist. Yeats found a physical resemblance between Constance and Maud Gonne, but it was Eva he made his real confidant during these visits. He told her of his unhappy love for Maud Gonne and encouraged her to study the old Irish legends. He found her poetry interesting, but formless. It would be strange if Yeats' accounts of his beloved did not fire the imagination of the two Gore-Booth girls. Both sisters felt at odds with the society which had nurtured them, but their reasons differed until events brought Constance nearer to Eva's role as a Good Samaritan. Maude Gonne was a young woman from an Anglo-Irish background, who, like them had done the Dublin Castle social round, who was beautiful and elegant, who shared many of their tastes, but who had broken away completely from what still partially held them. No one acts in a vacuum. There is always an example, a challenge or a conflict. From now on, even though they did not meet yet, Constance must have been aware of this contemporary who was always a step ahead; whether having a social success in Dublin, or studying at Julian's in Paris, or acting, or taking up the cause of Irish nationalism. Women are invariably curious about the women their men friends love, and here was an exceptional human being, endowed with all the characteristics Constance would have most admired.

Constance went on seeing Yeats in London after his visits to Lissadell. She took him to a séance. She tried to involve him in a fight. Sarah Purser recalls that she and Anna Nordgren considered a man called Brown had insulted them and tried to induce 'Willie Yeats' to challenge him to a duel on their behalf. They were not successful in this. It was probably Yeats who introduced Constance to Oscar Wilde. Constance told an Irish man of letters that when she visited the Wildes they had just become reconciled after he had been pursuing Mrs Lily Langtry.

Constance was still at home often enough to continue her feats on Max. She took part in a drag-hunt of the Sligo Harriers on 27 March 1894, when she only failed to finish first because she was 'led astray by the crowd which had collected at the last fence'.[5] In the following year she became the only woman in Ireland to ride in a Point-to-Point Race. The Sligo Harriers challenged the followers of Major O'Hara's Harriers, and Constance rode for her home pack. There is a description of her in a local newspaper at the Point-to-Point Races of November 1897:

When Miss Gore-Booth arrived well mounted and in good hunting form, she shed a bright ray of warm sunshine all around, and as her grandfather did in 1867, she entered into the spirit of the day's doings with a heartiness which made us all feel comfortable. The young lady would blush if she heard a twentieth part of the expressions of admiration of those who watched her as she rode up seated on her palfrey with an ease that would do credit to Diana herself.[5]

Constance's stepson remembers that the house was filled with her cups and trophies, which she still kept out even after marriage.

There is a story of her at this period driving a four-in-hand round and round the front of Hazelwood, her aunt's house, to amuse the elderly temporary tenant, Mrs Horsbrugh-Porter.

During these years when she was at home from her Slade studies, Constance's practical jokes became more elaborate and daring. One was a plan to blow up a munition magazine belonging to the Sligo Militia at their training ground at Rosses Point (which is a headland the other side of Drumcliffe Bay from Lissadell). Fortunately, Mr Rowlette records, the weather was so bad the Militia went back to barracks a week early and the scheme had to be given up.

On another occasion Constance turned her attention to the religious life of Lissadell village. This was dominated by the Church of Ireland. The school house was as much under the control of the Vicar (together with the Gore-Booth family) as the church. There was also a considerable Methodist following in the district, and they were allowed to use the school building for 'special services'. The Vicar began to have the idea that the Methodists were being favoured too much – presumably because he feared defections from his own congregation. His objections reached a climax when the Methodists decided to have a series of special services in the school house. It was Constance's view that the Methodists had as much right as the Protestants to hold services and to have due publicity of the time and place. Since she and Mr Rowlette thought it unlikely that the Vicar 'in his then frame of mind' would agree to announcing the Methodists' special services from his own pulpit, Constance and her group (i.e. Mr Rowlette, Mabel, and Eva when she was well enough to take part) decided to attach a drawing-board to the steeple of the church bearing the announcements in large print for all to see. As usual, the most arduous part was left to Mr Rowlette. With a 'specially constructed collapsible ladder in sections, a hammer, hold-fasts and a supply of rope' he managed to fix the board too high (he thought) to be easily removed. Unfortunately when Sunday morning came it was found that the board had been taken away. A few days later Constance sent Mr Rowlette an anonymous blackmail note regarding his actions on the Saturday night, demanding money unless he wished to be exposed, and making a rendezvous between midnight and 2 am on the road from the church to Carney. He set out blithely, met two figures dressed in great-coats with rifles, who he took to be Constance and Mabel very well disguised, pushed them over, and discovered they were real members of the Royal Irish Constabulary.

From these examples of Constance's exploits it appears that each time fate intervened and stopped the fulfilment of her plans. But since 99 per cent of the amusement of practical jokes is in the planning and the anticipation one supposes she was happy in that. Mr Rowlette must have found life less arduous but more ordinary when she was away.

The last recorded event in Constance's life before she went to Paris to continue her painting, is her local activities in the cause of women's suffrage (a cause to which Eva was to devote most of her life). Mr Rowlette writes that the three sisters became so occupied with the problem that little else was discussed even between runs on a day's hunting. But Constance and Eva did not think that talking was enough; they decided to form a committee which would be representative of the whole county of Sligo. Sir Henry and Lady Gore-Booth were not best pleased by this new development, in view of their attitude the more ambitious project was given up and it was decided to start step by step with a Parish Committee to 'gain the active support of Nationalist MPs'. The first meeting was held in December 1896 in Ballinful school house. Eva was in the chair, and the occasion (which passed off as blandly as a church bazaar) is to be noted for its being the first time that Constance made a public speech. This first time, unlike in her militant future, her mother and father were prominently in evidence 'in the body of the hall'. The whole audience was 'sympathetic and enthusiastic' and every resolution was passed unanimously.

Another, larger meeting – fully reported in the local press – was held in Drumcliffe in the same month of December. Constance, in the chair, as President of the Association, said in her opening speech, 'Ladies and Gentlemen, you have, no doubt heard . . . a good deal about Woman's Suffrage . . . I have been told, amongst other things, that it will cause women to ape the other sex, to adopt their clothes, copy their manners and peculiarities; that it will cause women to neglect their homes and duties, and worst of all, prevent the majority marrying (cries of "Oh").' She went on to say that in order to achieve any political reform

you all know that the first step is to form societies to agitate and force the government to realize that a very large class have a grievance, and will never stop making themselves disagreeable till it is righted. . . John

Stuart Mill said thirty years ago that the only forcible argument against giving women the suffrage was, 'that they did not demand it with sufficient force and noise' . . . Now, one of the many sneers I have been accustomed to hear against women is that they make too much noise; and yet we are told the principal argument against our having votes is that we don't make noise enough [laughter and cheers]. Of course, it is an excellent thing to be able to make a good deal of noise, but not having done so, seems hardly a good enough reason for refusing us the franchise. [Loud cheers and laughter.]

Constance went on to recount the various exclusions of women from the franchise since 1832 (one imagines Eva did the research) and mentioned to cries of 'oh' that the number of women signing a petition to Parliament had increased from that of 1873 when 11,000 women signed, to 257,000 in 1893.

Constance was followed by other speakers, who included Mabel, Eva, and the faithful Mr Rowlette. Despite some opposition and barracking (including a brisk interchange between the Chairwoman and a voice in the crowd, 'If my wife went to vote she might never come back' . . . 'She must think very little of you then'), a resolution advocating the extension of the franchise to women was carried amidst frenzied cheers.

Throughout the meeting there had been an undercurrent of amusement hardly justified by the speeches, and it was notable how long and uproarious was the applause which greeted Constance as President when the platform party arrived – by arrangement a few minutes after the hour fixed, when the audience was settled. After all was over that evening, Constance and her platform supporters realized that someone had hung a large bunch of mistletoe 'almost as large as a sheaf of oats' on the rafters above her head. It was too late to remedy the sabotage. But who had done it? Mr Rowlette had his suspicions of an unnamed helper who had entered into the plans for the Woman's Suffrage Meeting with 'unexpected wholeheartedness', but he did not want to give him away for fear of 'creating a civil war in the Lissadell dovecot'. He was therefore much relieved when Constance with characteristic determination found out for herself and told him that she would deal with the matter herself, 'and efficiently, believe me'.

One further meeting is recorded in the school house at Drum where Constance is said to have made a good speech in reply to Mr Clark who 'endeavoured to draw up an unfavourable comparison between Mr Lyons, the big draper in Sligo, and the numerous girls he employed, in the event of general suffrage being introduced'.

After these happenings politics appear to have faded from Constance's life for several years. A new phase was about to start, leading to further independence and to marriage.

CHAPTER 6

Art, Love and Marriage

From 1898 to 1900 Constance's life was centred in Paris. She
worked in the well-known art school belonging to Monsieur
Rodolphe Julian in the Rue Vivienne – known to this day as
Julian's studio. Although her allowance from home was small, she
did not live in an attic, but chose first of all the Parc Monceau
district, and, later, an English Pension in the Rue de Rivoli, where
Daisy Forbes-Robertson was a co-boarder. Her friends described
meeting in the Crémerie Léopold Robert: Constance 'a tall thin
slip of a girl, with tawny red-gold hair which she wore *à la Mérode*
over her ears under her sailor hat' and wearing 'a pink cotton
blouse, much open at the collar from which a long throat rose
very triumphantly'.

Constance was now thirty, and evidently her mother and
father had been unable to hold out any longer against her wish
to have a completely independent life. Eva had taken wing already.
In 1896 she met Esther Roper in Bordighera, through George
MacDonald.* The two women made friends, and subsequently
Womens' Suffrage and pacifism became their life work.

In 1898 Eva published her first volume of poems. Her path was
now clearly set. She continued to be a poet, often giving her poems
to 'obscure little journals standing for causes in which she believed'
and she spent the rest of her life working with Esther Roper for
women's rights and pacifism. When Constance was in Paris, Eva
and her friend had made Manchester the centre of their activities.
The sisters were worlds apart, then, but emotionally they always
remained close, however divergent their paths.

Julian's art school, where Constance worked under Jean-Paul
Laurens in the women's studio for eighteen months, is vividly

*Author of *Back of the North Wind*.

65

recalled in the *Journals of Marie Bashkirtseff*. This gifted, febrile, extraordinary girl worked under Julian from 1877 until her death, at the age of twenty-five, in 1884. In her Journal we have a picture of an atmosphere and a creative life which cannot have changed greatly in the fourteen years between her untimely death, and Constance's arrival on the scene where Marie Bashkirtseff was a star pupil. We see Julian, with his great size and the Marseillais accent he never lost; the jockeying for the best place in the studio; the jealousies; the visits of the distinguished outside artist teachers; the tension over whether a picture would be considered worthy to be 'shown downstairs' to the men, and, more crucial still, worthy of entry for the Salon. Having achieved this distinction and been accepted there remained the hurdle of the 'number' you would be granted by the committee, whether you would get a medal and what class, and where you would be hung – the worst fate being the outer gallery, 'the morgue', where beginners tended to get placed.

It seems probable that Constance's friend, Anna Nordgren, had some part in getting her into Julian's studio, for she was working there herself in Marie Bashkirtseff's day. Julian's studio was 'the only good one for women,' Marie Bashkirtseff writes. Here, she says, 'all distinctions disappear; you have neither name nor family; you are no longer the daughter of your mother; you are yourself. You are an individual with art before you – art and nothing else ...' In this tiny, international democracy Constance made her mark. She was nicknamed 'Vélo' because she arrived every morning on her bicycle. She wore a ring and declared herself married to art. She frequented the Crémerie Léopold Robert with the other students (perhaps the same crémerie where Marie Bashkirtseff had breakfast for three sous before seven o'clock one morning in May, and saw 'the workmen, the gamins in their blouses, come to drink their poor cup of chocolate'). In the women's studio upstairs at Julian's Constance was not immune from the petty jealousies which Marie Bashkirtseff complained of. She was much teased, and her English speaking mimicked. Her revenge on her chief tormentor came straight from her tomboy past. She seized the girl, marched her to a tap, and held her head under it, in the way she would have treated her brothers to teach them a lesson.

In Paris, Maud Gonne, if not Constance, knew the twilit

world of the Irish-French expatriates – descendants of the 'Wild Geese' who had fled Ireland through the centuries to serve in the Irish Brigades of the continental powers. Maud Gonne describes a banquet given by L'*Association du Saint Patrice* where they ate Potage Shamrock, Poularde Irelandais and Glace Killarney; and where she sat beside the Comte O'Neill de Tyrone, and opposite Comte Bonaparte Wyse, and met, too, the Comte O'Kelly de Galway. These elderly, distinguished gentlemen were more interested in proving their descent from Irish kings than in Maud Gonne's aspirations to free the land of their origin. They and their families lived like *revenants* in a pattern of formality far removed from the sombre truths of contemporary Ireland.

In 1897 in the real Ireland which became Constance's fate, a friendship began between Maud Gonne and Constance's future mentor, James Connolly. The occasion was the series of demonstrations arranged by Maud Gonne and the Nationalists against Queen Victoria's Jubilee celebrations. It was felt that something must be done, in the face of the Unionist displays, to show that all did not love the British Crown. James Connolly, for his contribution, headed a procession escorting a large black coffin symbolic of the fate of the British Empire. When opposed by the police he ordered the coffin to be thrown into the Liffey. He was arrested. Maud Gonne paid his fine and obtained his release. She promised to speak at one of his meetings, but when he came to see her a few days later she told him she was not a Socialist since she could not attend. He protested that she would discredit him, for no one would believe that she had agreed to come, and went sadly away. Yeats, who was also involved in the anti-Jubilee arrangements, suggested that she should follow him to his home. She did so and was so struck by the state of the tenement where Connolly and his family lived that she changed her mind and spoke for him next day.*

Two years later the Boer War broke out. All Irish Nationalists were pro-Boer. Constance herself proclaimed in Paris, 'Je suis Irelandaise', thus disassociating herself from England. Maud Gonne was dangerously involved in a plot against the British

---

W.B. Yeats Joseph Hone p 149. It must be noted that a contradiction, in time, of this account of the effect of Connolly's tenement home on Maud Gonne is implied when she writes in *Servant of the Queen* on p 276 that she went to see Mrs Connolly the day after Connolly was arrested, at his request, to tell his wife what had happened to him.

Government. Yeats visited Paris and begged her to give up politics and to marry him, but it was in vain.

It was in Paris, too, in January of this year, 1899, that Constance met Count Casimir Dunin-Markievicz at a students' ball. The man who introduced them, the Polish writer, Stefan Krzywoszewski, has left an account in his autobiography *A Long Life* of how Constance first set eyes on her future husband. Krzywoszewski had been invited to dine by Casimir Markievicz before the ball. The two young men ate a two-franc dinner of Chateaubriand steaks and fried potatoes in a small restaurant. At the sight of the steaks Casimir startled his fellow-diners by loudly neighing in token of his recognition of the real origin of the meat. Thus fortified, the friends went on to the ball where Casimir had promised Krzywoszewski they would meet many 'swell foreign women students'.

At about ten pm we found ourselves at the ball. It was a bizarre gathering, every class and nationality was represented, and the clothes echoed the diversity . . .

Near me stopped two Englishwomen. The older was of the type that you could meet ten or twenty times and yet not be able to recognize her five minutes later. The other one [i.e. Constance], who appeared to be about twenty years of age, was conspicuous for her proud bearing. She was a living Rosetti or Burne-Jones. Her profile was delicately drawn, her eyes grey-blue. Her ball dress, an over-stylish one and not too fresh, barely covered the skinny shoulder-blades and the smooth planes where men gladly look for convexities.

Since she was looking at me in a friendly manner I asked her in French: 'Madame, don't you dance?'

'I have no one to dance with, I do not like to dance alone.'

I bowed, she stooped down a little towards my arm. We squeezed into the dense crowd of waltzers. A brief conversation enabled me to orientate myself to this new acquaintance. In spite of her easy, woman-of-the-world manners, typical of the Parisian art student world, this was an intelligent Miss with a background of good society. No sooner had the music started again than the Englishwoman wanted to dance once more. Markievicz was passing at this moment. I stopped him: 'Do dance with this lady. You will be well matched in height and bearing.'

Markievicz immediately seized her and started to talk animatedly in his broken English. They looked well together – outstanding in the lively, dancing crowd . . .[1]

A week or two later Krzywoszewski was sitting on the terrace of the Café Flore, when Casimir and Constance suddenly appeared with their bicycles, obviously on the best of terms, using the second person singular, teasing one another, quarrelling like intimates of long standing and absorbed only in their new relationship. They stayed for a little and swept off on their bicycles as suddenly as they had arrived.

Casimir Dunin-Markievicz was an immensely tall, dramatically handsome man, a painter, an original, a light-hearted womanizer with a serious streak: a man, in fact, for Constance to love and to admire. Constance was now thirty-one; her nature was not celibate, but she still had not found the one true object for which her heart craved. She believed in romantic love, but so far it had eluded her. Here was the kind of man who could evoke the suppressed feelings which lay behind her extrovert, energetic, public personality. She may have been tomboyish, brave, independent, but she was also a woman, and a woman in an age when every social and emotional pressure was directed towards the idea of fulfilment through marriage. For Constance marriage without love would have been unthinkable. At times she may have felt that her painting was her whole life, but in spite of wearing of rings and declarations of being wedded to art it is impossible to believe that she did not still hope for more.

Although Casimir was six years younger than Constance, he was more experienced in life. He was already the father of two sons, and his estranged wife was mortally ill far away in the Ukraine. In that spring she died, and soon after the second son died too, leaving Stanislas (the elder) to be cared for by his paternal grandmother.

Count Casimir Dunin-Markievicz came of a long line of Polish landowners who were settled first of all in the Minsk district, and later in the Government of Kieff in the Ukraine, which had become Russian territory. The family traced its descent, even farther back than the Gore-Booths, to Peter Dunin ('the Dane') who settled in Poland in the twelfth century, and gave his name as prefix and a swan for coat-of-arms to all his descendants. Casimir had a country upbringing on the estate of Zywotowka, bought by his grandfather in the Ukraine. He went to school at the State Gymnasium in Kherson, passing out with a silver medal, and went to study law in Kieff. He stayed for two years, then rebelled against his family. The trouble was that, like Constance, he had set his heart on the career of an artist. Like her, he finally persuaded his parents to let him go to Paris on an allowance. What they had not bargained for was that he would be followed to Western Europe by his boyhood love, Jadwiga Splawa Neyman, who had persuaded *her* parents to let her go to study music. Inevitably they married, and lived on love and hope on the fourth floor of 24 Rue Bonaparte in the Quartier Latin. But love died and hope faded; the young wife fell ill, and by the time Constance met Casimir this phase of his life was nearly over. His future lay with her, and in Ireland.

Casimir was not a pupil at Julian's studio. When he came to Paris, which was five[2] years before he met Constance, he enrolled at the State School of Art. He was successful enough as a painter to justify his deviation from the path mapped out for him by his family. For him, as for many of his fellow-inhabitants of the vast, mysterious, semi-barbaric land of his birth, the pull of Europe was strong. In fact, he was made for the life he was now leading. He had congenial work, and a social life whose informality made up for any lack of luxury. By nature Casimir was warm-hearted, hedonistic and unconventional. He had a strong strain of egalitarianism which showed itself in hobnobbing with those he found amusing and agreeable whether they were stage carpenters or barmen, and in making irreverent jokes against the proud and pompous (such as when later in his life he was asked by a shipping line magnate what costume he had chosen for a fancy-dress ball, he replied 'I will paint my bottom red and come as a liner.') At the same time he was no political rebel, his reactions were purely personal and instinctive. He had the especial tolerance (which can border on indifference) of a large handsome man who has never in his life had to compete for attention. Now he had met a woman, who, although she was also high-spirited, unconventional, and from a background curiously similar to his own – although so far removed geographically – had the capacity to evolve more deeply, more dangerously and farther than he could. Temperamentally they were as unalike as they could be. But there was enough of shared tastes and aims to draw them together. Constance wrote of him to Eva, 'He fills me with the desire to do things. I feel with the combination I may get something done, too.'

What they shared immediately was their ambition as painters. When they were not working they plunged into the *vie de bohème* that they found in their own circle in the Paris of the turn of the century. For them it was still the Paris of Tissot, of de Musset and Offenbach. They sat in cafés, the Flore, the Procope; went to student's balls; drank champagne; bicycled in the Bois de Boulogne; and regularly overspent their allowances. When really pushed for the next franc Casimir would go and wash trams in the depots at night. It seems probable that Constance was the first to fall deeply in love. Everything in Casimir's temperament and circumstances would have caused him to drift contentedly without thought for the future. But, all the same, he was irresistibly drawn to the vivid, restless creature who had come into his life, and as the weeks went by, weeks which brought the death of his pathetic, young wife, and of his second son, he became more and more bound to the new relationship. But the love each felt for the other must have been from the first of a different kind, since Casimir was a sensual realist, and she an unsexual idealist. She had the need of such natures for the loved one to represent some cherished interior image. He must be more than just himself. And this need was fulfilled for her, then, by Casimir through his chosen career, his background of a remote, strange land, his almost gladiatoral good looks. What she could not know – and the fact of his speaking no English, so their confidences were exchanged in French, may have interposed a veil between words and inner meaning – was that all the outer factors concealed a total difference in needs and impulses. What they had in common as human beings was a quality of individuality. Neither could be type-cast into any of the available categories. She was no ordinary wild Irish colleen, neither was he simply an *artiste-boulevardier* with a kind heart beneath a velvet coat.

By September 1899 they were engaged to be married. There is no record of Lady Gore-Booth's reactions to the news of her eldest daughter's affianced being a recently bereaved widower, a Roman Catholic, an artist without an income, a foreigner from a far land, and six years younger into the bargain. Loyally and devotedly the family came over to meet him. It was, perhaps, for one of these occasions that Constance bought the green dress with a high ruff at the back which caused her to exclaim, '*Mon Dieu!* I look like a rabbit sitting in the heart of a cabbage.'

In the year 1899 Casimir celebrated their love by painting a large oil of Constance *Constance in White*, which was exhibited in the Grand Palais during the Great Exhibition of 1900. In this year, too, he completed a life-size allegorical oil of two nude lovers *Amour*, based on the Slav legend of St John's Eve.* This picture had a great success, was exhibited with *Constance in White* in Paris, and also in St Petersburg and Warsaw, and ended by being presented by an American lady, Mrs Longworth, to the Polish Embassy in London. Because of it, the Grand Duke Vladimir Alexandrovitch of Russia, who was president of the Imperial Academy in St Petersburg, came especially to Casimir's studio to see his work. He asked why the Count was not studying and exhibiting in St Petersburg. Casimir, as a Pole whose home was in what the Poles considered to be annexed territory replied, 'The climate there does not suit my health, Your Highness.'

A striking portrait of Casimir exists of this period in which he is dressed as a Napoleonic officer of the *Hussars de la Mort*. Like Constance, he enjoyed dressing up, and he originally wore the uniform at a fancy-dress ball. A fellow-painter, Bolesles Szankowski (later Court painter to the Kings of Saxony and Rumania) was so struck by his appearance that he persuaded him to sit for his portrait. In it the Count looks like an Ouida hero facing a legion of phantom enemies, with a stage battlefield behind him. Szankowski also painted Constance in 1901, dressed in black. This boldly conceived study in the manner of Sargent shows her as a typical Edwardian beauty – proud face, long neck, dramatic hat – and is now housed in the Municipal Gallery of Modern Art in Dublin.† Both portraits bring out the theatrical side of the sitters; but in Casimir this trait was satisfied by actual performances on the stage, while in Constance it was symptomatic of her need to find a wider outlet for her creative energy and her dynamism.

It must be said that in his Paris days it came naturally to Casimir to behave in the tradition of a romantic hero as well as to look like one. Before he had met Constance he had fought a duel over a model whom he thought was ill-treated by a fellow-artist; after he was engaged to be married he fought a duel over Constance, whom he considered had been insulted at a masked ball. She was in an Empire dress, and wore an eyeglass on a wide black ribbon.

*On St John's Eve a rare fern flowers at midnight in the enchanted forest. Those who brave the dangers and pick the fern have any wish granted, provided they show no emotion or fear, otherwise they are struck dead. In Count Casimir's picture the man has wished for love, but when love embodied as a nymph appears he cannot conceal his delight, and therefore dies.

†By gift of Count Stanislas Dunin-Markiewicz, surviving son of Count Casimir.

A Frenchman came up to her and flicked the eyeglass away, saying 'Why veil that glance with this cold glass, *ma petite*?' Casimir (dressed as Maréchal Ney) took offence and knocked the man down. A challenge ensued, and in the resulting duel, Casimir, who was far from a paper romantic hero, being a champion fencer, wounded his opponent deeply in the thigh.

The period of courtship was not unclouded for Constance either. She had a beautiful friend called Alice by whom Casimir became much attracted. He resisted the temptation because she was Constance's friend. This young woman later married well, but tragically died in childbirth. She left Casimir a ring, and it is said that his child by Constance was given her second name, Alys, after the beautiful, dead girl.

A charming remembrance of the Paris days exists in a photograph of Constance and Casimir in bicycling dress. They had just returned from a 180 kilometres overnight excursion to Dieppe (an example of Constance's endurance) and went immediately just as they were to record the feat. Casimir had a machine especially built for him, and competed in the great Paris–St Malo race. He was near winning, but his chain broke at the last moment, watched by Constance who had gone to stay with her cousin Mrs Bryce at St Lunière, near St Malo.*

In January 1900 the halcyon days were clouded by the death of Sir Henry. He had been in ill health for some time, due to the rigours of his arctic voyages, and he finally succumbed to pneumonia. Although Lady Gore-Booth continued to rule firmly at Lissadell, as she was accustomed to do in her husband's long absences, for Constance it was the loss not only of her father, but of one of the men she most admired in life. It was an admiration she cherished through the years.

In May 1900 Casimir came to stay at Lissadell to meet the aunts and the cousins and the friends who, one imagines, were burning with curiosity to see with their own eyes the man who had at last won the hand of the interesting, unpredictable Constance. He went back to the Ukraine in July to visit his mother and his young son, returning in September for the wedding. There is a charming story told by Constance to her stepson of how, as Casimir spoke hardly any English, she used to rehearse him

*Wife of Annon Bryce, Liberal MP for Aberdeen.

in his marriage service responses while travelling in a bus (characteristically on the top), undaunted by the lively interest aroused in their fellow-passengers by: 'Will you take this woman for your wife.'

She was married three times over – in a registry office, in the Russian Legation, and in St Mary's, Marylebone,* on 29 September 1900. Constance reverted to the traditions of her family background. A large trousseau was bought. She chose a wedding dress of white satin with a bodice of lace and chiffon and a full court train of silver brocade. Her jewels for the great day were gifts from her mother: a pearl necklace, a diamond pendant, and a diamond crescent. She dressed for the ceremony in her cousins', Lord and Lady Muncaster's, house. She was supported by four bridesmaids – her two sisters dressed in violet satin, and her friends, Miss Rachel Mansfield and Miss Mildred Grenfell, in green trimmed with lace in compliment to Ireland. The bridegroom wore a nobleman's court uniform consisting of a black tunic trimmed with gold braid, and white trousers. The ceremony was performed by the bride's old friend and vicar the Reverend Fletcher Le Fanu, now rector of Sandymount, Dublin. The reception was given in the home of her third intimate woman friend, Miss Rhoda L'Estrange, now Lady Morpeth. But even in this scene of solidarity and conventionality, she managed to introduce an individual note. She omitted the word 'obey' from her responses, and in addition to the usual wedding ring there were two extra rings – replicas of an heirloom of the Markievicz family made of steel lined with gold, engraved with a skull and cross-bones surrounded by a thistle, and bearing the inscription *'jusqu' à la mort'*. (These were thought, erroneously, by her more dramatically minded friends to have been made out of iron fetters worn by an ancestor of the Count's when imprisoned by the Russians.)

The bride left for her honeymoon dressed in pale blue cloth trimmed with lace and fur, and a hat to match. There was an official send-off at Victoria when the couple caught the boat train, but in fact, so Constance recounted to a friend many years later, they returned secretly to London to have their own unofficial reception for favoured cronies. The honeymoon, also, was less in

*It seems an indication that Constance was always the dominant partner of the two, that, although the Count was a Catholic, he got married in a Protestant church.

74

the prescribed pattern than the wedding. They spent it bicycling in Normandy, eating large quantities of oysters and lobsters, and staying where the mood took them. They were only away three weeks because they wanted to get back to their work in Paris. They settled into a studio and four rooms at 17 Rue Compagne Première, off the Boulevard Montparnasse. These they rented from their friend the painter Szankowski. They had one maid, Josephine, who followed their fortunes for several years. A photograph of Casimir of that period in that flat shows a crowded interior that must have possessed both personality and charm; with his portrait hanging above a narrow Empire cabinet full of silver (presumably polished by Josephine) with two painted Empire stools, and with the walls and divan covered in strikingly patterned materials. Soon after his marriage Casimir had several important portrait commissions, including Baron von Stransenberg, and Lady Westmacott. Constance painted her sister Mabel (who married Percival Foster in December) and a charming fifteen-year-old blonde who later became Lady Townshend. Christmas was spent at Nice, and they resumed their Paris life until the summer of 1901. By this time Constance was with child, and they planned for the newcomer to be born at Lissadell, arriving there in July.

Constance's only child, Maeve Alys, was born on 13 November 1901. It was a difficult birth, and Constance nearly died. The child was christened Maeve, in memory of the warrior queen whose legendary grave is on Knocknarea – the mountain to be seen from nearly every window in Lissadell. This child became the favourite of her grandmother, Lady Gore-Booth, who virtually brought her up. Almost at once the pattern was set. When the Markieviczs went back to Paris in 1902 they left the baby at Lissadell – presumably having been persuaded that a four-room studio flat in Montparnasse with only Josephine as help was not a suitable environment for a baby.

Constance and Casimir had now been married for more than a year and she still had not seen his home and his people and country. In May they set out on the long journey to the Ukraine – travelling, no doubt, in the Russian trains which Marie Bashkirtseff (who also came from the Ukraine) found so delightful because only wood was used for fuel and there were no smuts. Casimir arrived with his right arm in a black sling from a bicycle accident at Lissadell, so he could only lift up his son with his left arm – a fact always remembered by his son, together with his father's wide and bizarre coloured ties. Constance he remembers as 'tall, slim, exquisite in neat artist's overalls', with soft golden brown hair and her own especial smell compounded of delicate scent, paint and cigarettes.

Family life on the estate at Zywotowka came easily to an inhabitant of Lissadell. Constance found a two-storeyed, white manor house set in a large park, surrounded by the famous black, fertile land of the Ukraine which produced huge crops of wheat and sugar-beet. Her mother-in-law, the recently widowed Countess Maria, was an active, Eton-cropped, matriarchal figure who ruled her household benevolently and well. The actual estate was managed by Casimir's elder brother, Jan (whose appearance in a family photograph, with pale, keen eyes and brisk moustache tells much of the difference between him and the strikingly yet indolently handsome Casimir). Count Jan had a house of his own on the property, called Rozyn – the place of the roses. Here, his wife, Lena, caused the house to deserve its name, for she was an ardent gardener. Here, too, Count Jan kept the English thoroughbreds, whose names always began with 'M', that were his pride. There were two more surviving brothers, Stanislas, and sixteen-year-old, Peter, and four surviving sisters: Wanda, Bronia, Adele and Sophie. The dead sister, Maria, had died tragically after taking an overdose of sleeping pills following examination strain.

There was much to remind Constance of home – yet the daily life of a remote country house, and estate, familiar to her since early childhood, took on new shapes and colours here. There was parkland, but it contained an especial tower for the storks. There was hunting, but only of hares, with great Borzoi hounds. There were flowers but they were enormous scarlet poppies, and sunflowers twelve foot tall. There were servants, but they slept like dogs before their masters' doors. There was harvest-time, but here the harvest fields rolled like sea to the horizon, and when the corn was stacked in ricks the rows were as unending as the encampment of a vast army. Winter came suddenly. The storks went, and the swallows, the rains began; then one morning the inhabitants would wake to find the snow world which would be theirs for many months to come.

Constance was popular with her Polish in-laws. They admired her dashing and skilful horsemanship, a supreme feminine accomplishment in their eyes, and they found her gregarious, vital and uncomplicated. It went to their hearts when she adopted a stork with a broken leg – which was fed nightly with frogs from the garden and learnt to answer to the name of 'Ptak' (Polish for bird). They were pleased when she bought herself a peasant's feast-day dress – embroidered blouse of fine white linen, full skirt, beribboned head-dress, high red boots. They were impressed when she lassoed a fruit-stealer in the orchard and dragged him along behind her horse. (He turned out to be one of the under-gardeners, and with as much spirit as Constance had shown in catching him red-handed, sued her for assault.) One sometimes gets the impression of the early Constance that she belonged, then, to the especial section of humanity which feels the plight of animals more poignantly than that of human beings. Or, possibly it was that she responded to immediate human need, but she failed, until later in life, to connect cause and effect.

The young couple did not give up their work. They improvised a studio in a small annexe in the park, but they painted out of doors from nature and life. No breath of Impressionism disturbed the manner of the Count's work. He was a gifted painter, but in the most conservative tradition of his time. In the Ukraine he painted the picture which became the favourite of all for Constance, and which she had until her death. It is a triptych called *Bread* and shows in one panel a peasant sowing seed, in another a peasant woman with her sickle standing beside some stooks of corn, and in the centre a peasant interior, where the sun blazes symbolically through the small window on to the finished loaf lying on a white, embroidered cloth.

The Ukraine visit lasted from May until October 1902. When Constance and Casimir returned to Paris they gave a ball for 150 people, who arrived mostly in fancy-dress, including 'an English girl who was rather plain, and who came dressed as a curé'. The Count made a cup from fourteen different drinks and a merry time was had by all. Christmas was spent at Lissadell, where the other grandmother watched over the baby, Maeve, with as much solicitude as was lavished on Stanislas in the Ukraine.

In 1903 the May to October visit to Zywotowka was repeated. This time Constance and Casimir pleaded for the seven-year-old Stanislas to go back to Western Europe with them. Their life was about to change. Some time in the preceding months the decision had been taken to settle in Dublin. Presumably it was Lady Gore-Booth who made this possible, since she bought and furnished the house in Frankfort Avenue which became their home. The Polish grandmother was at first shocked and disturbed at the idea of losing her favourite grandchild, but in the end she was persuaded and gave her reluctant consent. She wanted assurances that he would not be allowed to forget his Polish language and origin, or the Roman Catholic religion in which he had been brought up. Historically, the situation of the Markievicz family was the opposite of that of the Gore-Booths. Whereas the Gore-Booths lived as Anglo-Irish landowners on Irish property granted to their ancestors by a conquering power, the Markieviczs and their fellow-Polish landowners held on to their own estates, in what had been Polish territory until the partition of the eighteenth century gave it to Russia. In spite of Russian persecution, reminiscent of English treatment of the native Irish, these Poles of the Ukraine were tenacious in matters of their language, religion and customs. Therefore, when Constance heard stories, as she must have, of wrongs and difficulties, it was as though she were living with a family of the Old Irish who had been dispossessed by families such as her own. There is no record of whether this struck her as it strikes us sixty years later; but she wrote home that although she liked the Ukraine so much that she almost wished she and Casimir were not going to live in Ireland, yet 'there are tiresome things about it as well. The peasants are miserable. Yesterday we went for a long drive and passed a man lying drunk in a ditch by the roadside. I wanted to get out and help him, but the horses galloped past and Casimir said he would be all right. So there was nothing to be done.'² (Marie Bashkirtseff when on a visit to her family, also in the Ukraine, records how shocked she was when she saw a young nobleman kicking and digging his spurs into a drunken coachman.) One wonders what Josephine, who was also present at these visits, thought of it all.

In spite of occasional jars to her humanitarian conscience the weeks passed happily for Constance in painting, and sport, and parties held in her honour by the gay, hospitable neighbours. In the late autumn came the day of departure with the young Stanislas. He was so excited at the idea of his new life, and the journey to it, he failed to make the gestures of grief at parting which would have assuaged his grandmother's distress. The train thundered into the small station of Oratowo, looking all the larger for the station having no platform, the four travellers finally climbed aboard and the long journey via Warsaw, Berlin and Paris began. Constance never saw the Ukraine again, and Stanislas not for twelve years.

CHAPTER 7

Constance and the Castle

The next stage in Constance's life was heralded by her future friend, Æ, in a letter to Sarah Purser of March 1902. After mentioning that he has about thirty pictures ready for an exhibition which will take place when he has courage enough, he goes on to relate that the 'Gore-Booth girl who married the Polish count with the unspellable name is going to settle near Dublin about summertime'. He adds 'as they are both clever it will help create an art atmosphere. We might get the materials for a revolt, a new Irish Art Club.' In this same letter Æ tells Miss Purser that he had discovered a 'new Irish genius . . . only just twenty, born an agricultural labourer's son'. This was the poet and playwright, Padraic Colum, who fulfilled all Æ's hopes for him. It will be seen that it was Padraic Colum who indirectly caused Constance's conversion to nationalism. Thus the elements of her Irish future were already assembled while she was still packing up in Paris.

The Markievicz ménage finally arrived in the early autumn of 1903, together with sixty-four cases of furniture and effects, young Stanislas, Josephine, and Janko, a Polish Jew who Constance had rescued from the prospect of military service with the Russian Army. Janko's father was the tenant of a big water-mill belonging to the Markievicz family and he had pleaded with the young couple to take his son into their employment, promising to get him across the Russo-German frontier. Constance and Casimir found Janko duly waiting for them in Berlin; they brought him to Dublin where he was fitted out with a livery and called a footman. This metamorphosis did not last for long and Janko was sent off with ten pounds to find more congenial employment. But he never forgot Constance, and when in 1913 she was trying to collect money for the starving wives of the strikers he rang the doorbell of

Surrey House, Rathmines, where she was then living, and told her he had come to give her money in token of her past kindness. In fact, it is certain that he ended up far better off financially than she did.

The new home, St Mary's Frankfort Avenue, Rathgar, stands in a quiet leafy suburb, west of St Stephen's Green, where some of the houses have the charming feature (characteristic of Dublin houses built at the beginning of the century) of a graceful flight of steps arching over the basement and leading to twin front doors flanked by recessed columns. St Mary's itself (now a presbytery) is a one-storeyed early Victorian house with a sub-basement. The house has a prominent feature in three long arched windows each side of the classical porch, which is surmounted by an imposing architrave and pediment. There is room to park a car in the drive-way. In Constance's day the front windows looked on to a tangle of holly and veronica; today there is a cedar which must have been only a small tree during her tenure, but in her time there was a large Irish yew to lend its shade and sombre dignity. At the back there was a good lawn, a rockery, and a greenhouse with a vine in it; there were fruit trees and borders. There were even stables, but no horses in them. To console herself Constance gardened assiduously. All through her life she never lost her love of gardening.

In the first years the household ran on conventional lines. Guests were waited on, silver and flowers abounded. Josephine was succeeded in 1904 by Ellen Banks, who reigned as cook-house-keeper assisted by two dailies. Ellen Banks, whose small, neat, pale person concealed a strong will and strong opinions, had a hidden story. Unknown to her employers she had a husband in the Scots Guards whom she had left, returning to him after ten years' separation in 1910, and living happily with him afterwards.

Constance had plenty of time to spare from domestic chores. Maeve still mainly lived with her grandmother; Josephine helped to look after Stanislas. Constance was now thirty-five. She had passed two great watersheds in a woman's life; marriage and maternity; but neither of the roles of wife nor mother came first for her in the secret priorities of the psyche, priorities which, what-ever the received ideas of the subject, project themselves in the end as surely as light through dark. As a wife she early defined her limits; it is recorded that she told a close friend that she had no need of Casimir as a lover after Maeve was born. He consoled himself, where he could. As a mother she was loving but slapdash. The small tediums of the nursery and the schoolroom were alien to her nature, and, indeed, her conditioning. She came of a breeding, class, and generation which did not think it necessary for the mother personally to go through the day-to-day routine of her children's life. So it came about that she had arrived at this juncture in her life's journey with all her splendid energy and verve intact. Casimir was not the man to replace a sensual relationship with a strongly spiritual or intellectual one; perhaps even so early as their arrival in Dublin they both knew that *camaraderie* would have to be the basis of their marriage. But no lasting quarrels or overt disharmony clouded their days, then or later; they never indulged in the icy feuds and hidden tensions of a conventionally difficult marriage. They were saved by their projects and by interests existing outside their personal relationship, and by the attributes both possessed of a 'good sport'.

Whatever the hidden strains may have been, the Markieviczs' first appeared in Dublin as a devoted couple – a talented and high-spirited pair. Friends would see them walking up and down their drawing-room at St Mary's, hand in hand – like lovers still. They were handsome and gay; ready to entertain and be entertained. Judging from the recorded opinions of some contemporaries they were each possessed of endearing imperfections. When Constance got married R. D. Blumenfeld of the *Daily Express* commented that she was a clever but rather erratic girl who 'prefers to talk Irish politics'. M. J. Bonn describes in his autobiography *Wandering Scholar* Constance's difficulties as a painter owing to her bad eyesight, and how, when the portrait she undertook of him failed to please her, she threw the brush in his face. (He also describes her as one of the reigning Irish beauties of her day.) Stefan Krzywoszewski (who it will be remembered first introduced Casimir to Constance) criticizes her in his autobiography *A Long Life* for overdressing and untidiness – but he had no cause to love her, for in a series of articles called *Letters from Ireland* that Casimir wrote in 1924 he mentioned that already at that first meeting Krzywoszewski was bald and Constance was much amused by this.

An impression of Casimir is given by a Polish writer, Kornel Makuszynski, in an article written in 1935.

I remember you, my very dearest old friend. I remember you, wonderful old boy, friend of everyone – of monumental stature – Casimir D-M. . . a giant of about two metres high . . . Such was the body in which lived a kind, soft and friendly heart. In that great vessel there was no black tar, nor guile nor jealousy. He was a kind and friendly giant, always happy, a good pal, refined in his friendship and sensitive as an artist. For a friend he would pull the shirt off his back, except for the fact that this shirt could be used as a tent for boy scouts, or as a sail for a boat, and would trail behind the beneficiary like a lady's evening gown . . . He would have made a fortune writing his life story, so much more so, as the Good Lord bestowed him with a vivid imagination . . . Always smiling, from dawn, to sunset noble artist, painter and novelist – the good giant, the royal tramp . . .[1]

To imagine Dublin in the early years of this century an English reader must think of Bath or Bristol without their hilly streets. The unity of architecture was the same, the same space and cohesion of a planned city, the presence of water, the soft climate of the west. Dublin was made for man and not man for it. Padraic Colum wrote of pre-1914 Dublin, 'It is a city that is commercial and bureaucratic and not industrial; little business of an absorbing nature is transacted there, and the citizens are leisurely in their ways and disengaged in their minds.' Dubliners could be out of their city within the hour, riding or walking on the long beaches at Sandymount or on the eight miles of sand at Portmarnock. They could make the twenty minutes drive out to Lamb Doyle's public house and sit on the bench outside and look at the silver sweep of Dublin Bay and the rocky peninsular of Howth. And at Howth itself, as Oliver St John Gogarty describes in a letter to a friend you could lie in 'one of the beautiful brakes whose rhododendrons flush the air and the ground is soft with moss or bracken . . . Hazels, oaks ashes and banks of broom on one side, rhododendron-covered rocks on the other – and rushes which had tufted heads'.[2] Near Constance's suburb, Rathgar, 'the Dartry woods were as picturesque as any', George Moore wrote, 'and even at Lansdowne Road there is a road and a turnstile, and at the end of the wood a pleasant green bank overhung with hawthorn boughs'.

In the city, wherever you were, you felt the presence of the countryside and of water; whether you looked down a street or over the roof-tops to the shifting lights and shadows on the Wicklow mountains, or whether you heard the gulls crying on the

Liffey. Phoenix Park was, and still is, a rural enclave bowered in oaks, limes, chestnuts; an idyllic approach to the bridges, steeples and grey buildings flanking the Liffey, whose quays lead to the heart of the city. In Dublin, even today, you can visit the *Dail*, the National Gallery, the National Museum and Library, Trinity College and the Botanical Gardens within the hour. In London to visit the Houses of Parliament, the National Gallery, the British Museum, London University, and Kew Gardens would take all day. The factor of size is more than geographical. It conditions the life of the mind – the life of a family, city or country. The various circles of Dublin society were small enough to overlap, to be mutually aware, and to provide a forcing house for the cultivation of personality. Nothing and nobody went unremarked – the record was kept with witty malice, invention, derision, embroidered detail. At the Bailey Restaurant, in Anne Street, which is dominated by the large classical façade of St Anne's Parish Church in Dawson Street (a perpetual reminder of the Ascendancy), Oliver St John Gogarty and his fellow wits met regularly between five and seven o'clock in an upper room set aside for them, constituting an Aristophanes-like chorus to the goings-on of their city. The offices of the Gaelic League provided a late afternoon meeting-place with a more sedate atmosphere, while literary colleagues met one another, too, in the small, shabby, but much frequented Nassau Hotel. There were many societies, at whose gatherings you could see all the same people you were already meeting socially: there was the National Literary Society, the Theosophical Society, and the *Feis Coeil* (Music Festival).

A short tour of the streets lying between Abbey Street across the river and St Stephen's Green could provide a choice gallery of genius, talent, beauty and eccentricity: Oliver St John Gogarty, in a primrose waistcoat and high Edwardian jacket, arm-in-arm with James Joyce, the latter wearing a yachting cap and stopping to laugh out aloud when a joke pleased him particularly; or Yeats with Maud Gonne, he black-haired, pale, heavily cloaked, with a majestic presence and 'rich melancholy eyes', and she six foot tall, a Minerva with bronze hair and eyes, the most beautiful woman in the world according to Wickham Steed. George Moore might be seen, 'A figure with hair silver as a dandelion in summer, pink porcelain face, sloping shoulders and peg-topped trousers', carrying 'a Malacca-cane with an ivory top shaped like an egg' or Æ., large and brown-bearded, an Apostle in spectacles, with his chest-nut-haired poetess assistant Susan Mitchell. In the evenings if you were in Leinster Street you might hear George Moore whistling a motif from the *Ring* to attract Edward Martyn's attention – 'The sword motive brought the candle light glimmering down the stairs.' Then there was Endymion, a tall, moustached former employee of Guinness's Brewery whose mind had been affected through falling into a vat. Dressed in a deerstalker hat, lace jabot, knee-breeches, buckled shoes, he was equipped with two swords, a fishing-rod and an umbrella. On Trafalgar Day he wore a cocked hat, and military tabs on the anniversary of Mafeking.

It was the Dublin custom to have a fixed evening to receive friends. On Sunday's you could go to Æ's (just round the corner from Constance and Casimir and next door to Maud Gonne's house) where the street door stood open and everyone was welcome without discrimination of creed or class or sex. (Later, Yeats used to reserve some evenings for men only.) At Æ's where his selflessly devoted wife, Violet, dispensed tea and coffee, and his books and pictures lined the walls of the room where he received his guests, an atmosphere of spontanous intellectual ferment prevailed. Anyone of significance in the Irish Renaissance appeared there sooner or later to discuss their work or ideas, to read out extracts from a novel or poem, and to hear Æ's torrential, generous, inventive, inspirational monologues.

When you pushed open his door on Sunday evening, he seemed to be always inside to greet you, though how he heard your approach above the hum of talk is a mystery. Striding out to the door, with a trail of conversation still clinging around him, he wrapped it round you at once so that from the moment you arrived you were in the middle of a discussion with other guests.[3]

Later on, in the years before the First World War, the weekly at-home evenings were swelled by the hospitality of Yeats, and Padraic Colum, and Gogarty, and their wives; there was also the hospitality on Tuesday's of Stephen McKenna, the translator of *Plotinus* provided his guests talked in Irish or Greek. Above all, from 1911 onwards, there were Sarah Purser's monthly Tuesdays at Mespil House, a Georgian mansion with beautiful plaster ceilings, a small park and a lake. Here all Dublin crowded up Miss

Purser's fine staircase and on into the large drawing-room with its Seurats and Vlamincks.

The end of 1903 and the beginning of 1904 saw the temporary departure of Joyce from Dublin to study medicine in Paris, and Gogarty's temporary removal to Oxford to compete for the Newdigate Prize for English Verse. In 1903 Maud Gonne made her ill-fated marriage with John McBride; Yeats spent the autumn of that year lecturing in America. By 1903 Yeats and George Moore had quarrelled over a projected play and become only partially reconciled. At this period Æ spent every Saturday evening with George Moore in Ely Place where in fine weather they dined, outside and talked under the apple tree 'as large as a house', with the flight of swallows about them, and the scent of hawthorn in the air. In winter they used rooms made resplendent by Moore's 'beautiful, grey Manet', his 'exquisite mauve Monet and . . . sad Pisarro'.

For Constance and Casimir, Æ was the most immediately significant and the most remarkable of their Dublin friends. Constance may have met him before her marriage. John Eglinton in his *Memoir of Æ* says that when 'Count Casimir Markievicz settled in Dublin, he made the acquaintance of Æ and persuaded him to paint more in oils and to join with the Countess and himself in an exhibition of oil paintings'. John Eglinton goes on to say that this exhibition was in 1904. But, in fact, it seems that Æ exhibited with Constance and Casimir, together with W. J. Leach ARHA and Frances Baker (a Sligo neighbour) in October 1903.* It is probable that it was through the Coffey family (kinsman, as we have seen, of Constance) that the first meeting occurred. In January of 1902 there took place at the Coffey home (that same house in Harcourt Terrace where Constance and Lady Fingall had experienced their encounter with the drunken soldier) a private performance of Æ's play *Deirdre* in honour of Diarmuid Coffey's twelfth birthday, when Æ played the part of Naisi and George

*A mystery surrounds this exhibition. It is not recorded by Mr Alan Denson, editor of *Letters from Æ*, and the leading authority on the events of Æ's life. In the Markievicz family papers the catalogue is dated on the cover Monday, 11 October. Later, in ink, the year 1903 was added. By the courtesy of the National Library, Dublin, I was able to consult a *Handbook of Dates* edited by C. R. Cheney, which yielded the information that 11 October only fell on a Monday in 1897 and 1954. In the former year Constance and Casimir had not even met; in the latter they had both been long dead. It is possible that the printers of the catalogue made an error, since the circumstantial evidence seems to point to the year 1903.

Coffey that of Fergus. No doubt it was from the Coffey's that Æ heard of Constance's future move to Rathgar. Perhaps he even suggested the district, since he lived there. It was he, after all, who found George Moore the house in Ely Place. He was ever ready to help his friends. Five years previously Æ, much encouraged by Yeats, had taken the important decision to accept Horace Plunkett's offer of helping him run the Irish Agricultural Organization Society. He travelled all over the country and proved amazingly successful – for one who had been 'magnificently happy' for six years in earlier days living on from thirty to sixty pounds a year – organizing the Raffeisen banks, which through their loans saved thousands of farmers from destitution. A visitor to Dublin in later years described Æ as by far the greatest Irishman of the present generation. 'Poet, painter, politician, mystic, editor, man of business, organizer, his life full to overflowing. So great is his genius for friendship that men of directly opposite political beliefs find in him their ideal man.'⁴ Gogarty described him as 'the Angelic Anarchist, his great Johnsonian body clothed in a brown tweed ... his kind eyes shining more than the lenses of his glasses shone.' George Moore recalled him in grey tweeds, 'his wild beard and shaggy mane of hair' and wrote of 'the sweetness of his long grey eyes'. Mary Colum remarks in her autobiography that he had all the qualities which the Russian philosopher, Berdyaev, summarized as the marks of an aristocrat (although by birth he came from a middle class family), 'he was magnanimous, he was unenvious, he was courageous, he had no prejudices, he was a free being'.

The periodical edited from 1906 by Æ, *The Irish Homestead* bore the unmistakable imprint of his personality and of his metaphysical views, which proved strange bedfellows with the strictly quotidian, informative, or agricultural content of the main items. In his office, first in Lincoln Place, later in Merrion Square (where he painted the walls with magic forests and fairy princesses and two desks 'rose like rocks out of a sea of newspapers and literary clutter'), Æ was aided by his devoted assistant, the witty Susan Mitchell – she who George Moore never forgave for her mock biography which consisted of a collection of jokes against him. Visitors flocked to Æ's office as they did to his home, from Lady Betty Balfour, wife of the Chief Secretary, to Arthur Griffith the founder of *Sinn Fein*, from poets and playwrights to booted farmers and horsemen. Here, too, could be found Sir Horace Plunkett, founder of the Agricultural Organization Society, he of whom Lady Betty Balfour (wife of the Chief Secretary from 1895–1900) once said, 'He came young, gay and rich to Ireland. He lost it all', and Father Tom Finlay, Sir Horace's loved collaborator, with 'his russet-coloured face, withered like an apple'.

Æ's first biographer, and friend, John Eglinton, mentions that he regarded his painting as a minor activity in his life. Æ had a great love for the County of Donegal, with its mountains – flat-topped Muckish, and cone-shaped Errigal – its hills, its offshore islands, and its lonely silver strands.

Owing, apparently, to the persuasive powers of Casimir and Constance, Æ exhibited forty-four pictures at the Leinster Lecture Hall, Molesworth Street from 11 to 23 October 1903. The prices asked were from three to six guineas. Many of the pictures were of Donegal scenes. Constance exhibited twenty-seven pictures of subjects such as *Moonlight, Gorse, Study of an Apple Tree, A Lonely Cottage, A Misty Garden*. Casimir exhibited twenty-four pictures, nearly all of which were Polish land and townscapes. The catalogue cost threepence. The following year, on 23 August, at the same place sixpence entrance was asked, in addition to the price of the catalogue, for 'Pictures of Two Countries' by Constance Gore-Booth, Casimir Dunin-Markievicz, and George Russell (Æ). Casimir put in eighty-five pictures, Constance, seventy-six (including several painted in Poland, which presemably were either not unpacked, or not ready the year before) and Æ, sixty-three. It was altogether a more ambitious affair. Casimir exhibited *Amour* (for which picture he was asking £330, his portrait of Æ, (now in the Municipal Art Gallery) priced at £150, and a portrait of his Honour Judge Seymour Bird, for which he was asking the same amount. Constance's large oil *The Conscript* painted from life, and showing a peasant family in the Ukraine sitting sadly with their son who has been called up, was exhibited, also priced at £150. (The young man was killed in Manchuria in the Russo-Japanese war.) This picture was in the possession of the late Mr Joseph McGrath.

On the literary and dramatic front in Dublin the year 1902 had seen the first productions of Æ's play *Deirdre* (as opposed to the private performance in the Coffey's garden) and of Yeats' *Cathleen ni Houlihan*. Many Irish men and women have acknowledged the effect of the latter play on their emotions and convictions. It was one of the first folk plays, and it was important not only for the flames it kindled, but also as the most successful and famous forerunner of the new school of realistic drama based on Irish peasant life, which became identified with the Irish National Theatre (whose home was the Abbey Theatre). Yeats persuaded Maud Gonne to play the part of the mysterious old woman who appears to the hero, Michael Gillane, on the eve of his wedding in the troubled days of 1798 and causes him to abandon all human happiness for the sake of Ireland. No one who saw Maud Gonne in the part ever forgot the climax of the play when Michael follows the old crone out, and when his father asks him if he has seen an old woman going down the path, replies, 'I did not. But, I saw a young girl and she had the walk of a queen.' Yeats wrote of Maud Gonne, 'She made Cathleen seem like a divine being fallen into our mortal infirmity.' On the nights of the three performances early in April St Theresa's Hall was crowded out with working-class men and women. Out of the play The Irish National Theatre was born, with past and future intimates of Constance on the committee (Yeats, Æ, Padraic Colum, Maud Gonne, Seamus O'Sullivan).

Yeats had been in trouble with the clergy a few years previously over his play *The Countess Cathleen* which was thought to have shown an inadequate knowledge of the doctrines concerning salvation, since the heroine, Countess Cathleen, sells her soul to the devil to save her peasants from starvation, and yet is eventually redeemed. There were many cross-currents in Dublin, both then and later. Mary Colum recalls that both orthodox Catholics and Protestants thought the 'whole Abbey and literary group to be irreligious. What was called the Castle set and the anti-Nationalist set, known in Dublin as West Britons, pronounced the literary movement distinctly Fenian in tendency, and the rebel things Yeats had done with Maud Gonne were brought up against him ... it was said of Æ that he worshipped pagan Gods and of George Moore that his immorality made him an outcast.'[5]

For several years the Markieviczs' kept a foothold in all the worlds available to them. They knew the Gaelic League and Abbey Theatre circles through their friendship with Yeats and Æ; Casimir, when not painting, quickly made a niche for himself in Bohemian drinking circles; at the same time he and Constance frequented the castle, particularly after the Aberdeens came in 1906. There is no record of how much they saw of the Trinity College dons, who made up a powerful clique, unforgettably, endowed with intellect, scholarship and athleticism. The formidable scholar and wit Mahaffy was on friendly terms with Constance, judging from a note he wrote her concerning a social engagement.

King Edward and Queen Alexandra visited Ireland in 1903 and 1904. In spite of the efforts of Maud Gonne's *Inghini na h'Eireann* (Daughters of Erin) and other Nationalists, the King, according to Lady Fingall, was 'much moved by his reception'. He praised the good breeding of the Irish crowd 'that was content to cheer at a distance', adding, 'I have never had a better reception anywhere'.

The important political event of 1903 was the passing of the Land Act, brain child of George Wyndham, Chief Secretary from 1900 to 1904. He and his measure were much discussed in Constance's home, since both he and one of its early sponsors were linked with her through kinship. George Wyndham had married the widowed Lady Sibell Grosvenor, a cousin of Lady Gore-Booth's. A cousin on Sir Henry's side in the shape of Lord Dunraven was chairman of the important Land Conference of 1902 which provided the ground work for the act. (In 1903, too, Lond Dunraven caused a furore by creating the Irish Reform Association which advocated a gradual devolution to Irish control of her domestic affairs. His ideas infuriated his fellow Unionists, and failed to please the Irish parliamentary party.)

Of all the political questions the Land issue was the one nearest Constance's heart. Writing in the Republican newspaper, *Eire*, many years later she recalled how she received her first political inspiration from her own 'desolate home county' and from the 'dispossessed people' she grew up amongst. She wrote, 'It was the struggle for the land that first interested me, while the heroic spirits that generation after generation went out to carry on the fight and fought and died with arms in their hands, took my heart and imagination by storm.' At the same time she recorded that, 'No one was interested in politics in our house. It was rare that anyone mentioned them, everyone accepted the *status quo* . . . it was there just as the mountains and sea were, and it was absurd to try and alter it, for that led nowhere and only made trouble.'* Constance was referring to her mother and father. Her brother, Sir Josslyn, far from thinking that to try and alter things led nowhere was one of the first to make this land available to tenants, selling over 30,000 acres to about 1,200 tenants. According to family tradition he was much criticized by his less liberal-minded members of the Kildare Street Club for doing so.

George Wyndham's Land Act incorporated a 'bonus' to induce the landlords to sell. (One of the main problems was that very rich landlords did not wish to sell because they were content as they were, and very poor landlords were so heavily mortgaged they would derive no benefit either.) This bait cost the British treasury £12,000,000. The act was conceived by George Wyndham in a spirit of idealism. As the great-grandson of Lord Edward Fitzgerald, for whom he had a cult, he was far from unmindful of the claims of *Cathleen ni Houlihan*. His act caused the beginning of the end of landlordism in Ireland. The tenant farmers came back into their own at long last, and Ireland gradually became, like France, a country of small proprietors. It is interesting to note that Lenin, writing of the act, and referring to the tenants' terms of payment to be spread over sixty-eight years said that the Irish peasant 'is paying, and will continue to pay for many and many a long day, millions and millions of pounds of compensation to English landlords as a reward for having robbed him of his land for many centuries and for having reduced him to continual starvation'. The Land Act in its results formed the theme of one of Padraic Colum's best known plays *The Land* in which the father and the older men who have fought all their lives for the land and who are about to buy their holdings, are in bitter opposition to the son who wants to emigrate to the United States.

In September 1904 Constance was noticed at the Horse Show dressed in black, with a large leghorn hat trimmed with a pink ribbon. The Dudleys reigned then at the Castle (a daughter was born to Lady Dudley during that Horse Show week). 'Both young, extraordinarily good looking, rich, enthusiastic, charming. She had the beauty of an Eastern queen more like Esther than Rachel.'

* In this context there is a story current with her Nationalist friends that she once, when a girl, called a strike of her father's tenants in order that they should cease to pay rent. When asked the reason for her extraordinary behaviour she replied, 'Well, after all, father, they need the money more than we do.'

wrote Lady Fingall. With this glamourous couple at the Castle, and the delightful Lady Sibell at the Chief Secretary's lodge, those whose lives revolved round the British Raj were well catered for in every sense of the word. In 1905 the dazzling Dudleys departed, but not before giving a particularly splendid 'Empire' Ball at which Constance wore a high-waisted satin dress with an orange train lined with gold tissue, and gold ribbons in her hair. Casimir wore a light brown coat and salmon coloured knee-breeches. So pleased were they with these outfits, they had themselves photographed wearing them. The Dudleys went (Lady Dudley leaving a legacy of compassion in the organization of country nurses bearing her name) and the earnest Aberdeens took over early in 1906. The year before the Aberdeens came Casimir painted a large picture of the investiture of Lord Mayo as a Knight of St Patrick. Ironically enough, in view of later events, in the painting Constance is shown sitting next to the future Queen Mary.

Lord and Lady Aberdeen (known to the flippant as Jumping Jack and Blowsy Bella, owing to his predilection for the Canadian polka and her figure) were intelligent, liberal-minded, convinced Home Rulers, determined to leave Ireland better than when they found it. The Aberdeens, because of their humanitarianism, were dogged by an erroneous story that they dined habitually with their servants and played games such as Hide-and-Seek with them. This canard was never completely scotched, and Queen Victoria and King Edward successively inquired as to its truth. Constance was present at the new Viceroy's first drawing-room in 1906 (where she presented a great friend, Mrs O'Connell Fitz-Simon) wearing ivory satin with flowered chiffon and gold lace. The apartments were filled with daffodils, white lilac and tulips, and Lady Aberdeen was soberly resplendent in grey mousseline satin with 'an overskirt of satin and chiffon and a veiling of very handsome pailleted tulle embroidered in pearls and jewelled roses'.

Strange to relate, Constance was frequently at Castle functions in this year and the next, when at the same time her sympathies and loyalties were veering irrevocably towards Nationalism. Arthur Powell recalls her in his memoirs as 'tall, and distinguished and handsome' and remembers her reply to an acquaintance who remarked she had not seen Constance at the Castle lately. 'No, I want to blow it up.' No doubt she continued to go to the Castle for some time after her sympathies lay elsewhere, for Casimir's sake. When she finally ceased to obey the Viceregal commands to attend this or that Casimir went without her.

The Markieviczs were present at the first State Ball in 1906, at an afternoon party, and at Lady MacConnell's (wife of the Under-Secretary of State) dance in March, where Constance looked 'picturesque in purple chiffon'. Later in March the well-known beauty, Lady Weldon (wife of the State Steward and Chamberlain), gave a musical party, at which Casimir sang Polish songs (he took his singing seriously enough to have lessons from Maestro Esposito, a well-known teacher) and Constance accompanied him. Lady Weldon had the charming and unusual talent of a *siffleuse*. Those who remember her say her whistling was clear and silvery as a bird's song. Casimir's Polish songs and Lady Weldon's whistling were reinforced by the twin Miss Arnotts (daughters of the owner of *The Irish Times*) playing violin and 'cello duets, and by Sir Anthony Weldon reciting. Lady Aberdeen was there in a 'dark blue toilette' and Constance was 'picturesquely dressed as usual'.

In April of this year Constance, wearing black, had a stall at the *La Floralia* fête in connection with the Irish Horticultural Sociey Spring Show. The twin Miss Arnotts helped her, dressed in 'pretty white costumes and hats'. Also presiding over a stall, draped in crocus mauve draperies, was Lady Weldon, wearing a 'pink mauve tulle toque'.

On 30 January 1907 Constance's future sister-in-law, Miss Mary L'Estrange Malone, was presented by Lady Hawkesbury. Miss L'Estrange Malone was a cousin of the Gore-Booths, and, in fact, met Sir Josslyn in Constance's house. Casimir and Constance went to the State Ball in 1907, when Lady Aberdeen had a heavy cold, there were several polkas for Lord Aberdeen (played by the current most popular band, Clarke-Barry's) and six hundred guests came, in spite of the fact that as a contemporary society journal remarked, 'the Unionists do *not* love the party in power – small blame to them'. This year Casimir sang his Polish songs at an afternoon party given by the Vicereine, supported by Constance's accompaniment and the Miss Arnott's violin and 'cello duets. On 5 March there was a Lace Ball (to encourage the Irish lace industry). Lady Aberdeen, wearing blue chiffon velvet lavishly trimmed with Irish point lace made in Youghal, had to be wheeled in, for she was suffering badly from rheumatism. Constance wore 'a striking toilette of Russian green chiffon entirely covered with a robe of Limerick lace, the corsage draped *en suite* and finished off with a sash of black panne and diamond ornaments'. She and Casimir danced in the fourth and fifth sets of the eight handed reels. Ten days later Constance was noticed at an afternoon party 'looking very pretty in stone grey with a bright cerise toque'. Constance wore her purple chiffon dress again at the State Ball for St Patrick's Day, which was held on 15 March, when a thousand guests came; the women wore plumes and lappets, the men magnificent uniforms; and Lord Aberdeen was in full Highland dress with the Order of the Thistle and of St Patrick. The Irish reels of the Lace Ball were repeated.

This, then, was the pattern of the Markieviczs' formal social life. The big balls and the small musical parties, the occasional Anglo-Irish inspired charity effort. It was all a long way from Yeats and Æ and the Gaelic League; a long way, too, from the activities of Maud Gonne and her Daughters of Erin. Far from going to the Castle, Maud Gonne had succeeded in defeating the proposal that Dublin should present an Address of Loyalty to Edward VII during his 1903 visit. Miss Helena Molony, a future close friend and colleague of Constance's, was so inspired by this achievement of Maud Gonne's that she immediately joined *Inghini na h'Eireann*. It was she a few years later who had the idea of starting a monthly woman's paper *Bean na h'Eireann* (with which Constance became prominently associated) 'advocating militancy, separatism and feminism'. James Stephens in his poem *The Red Haired Man's Wife* expressed the feminist feeling in words that could also and were no doubt meant to apply to Ireland and England.

> I am separated still,
> I am I and not you,
> And my mind and my will,
> As in secret they grew,
> Still are secret, unreached and untouched,
> And not subject to you.

In 1904 Arthur Griffith's famous series of articles for his paper *United Irishman* were published in pamphlet form. In them, with particular reference to Ireland, he analysed the resurrection of the Hungarian nation through the statesman patriot, Francis Deak's policy of abstention from the Austrian Assembly. Griffith argued that just as Deak had based his argument on the Pragmatic Sanction and the Laws of 1848, so Ireland should take her stand on the provisions of the Renunciation Act of 1783. These allowed the right which was claimed by Grattan's Parliament to be still operative and binding: to be bound only by laws enacted by the King and the Parliament of Ireland. Griffith argued that the Act of Union with Britain was invalid because the Irish Parliament had no legal right to abolish itself. The Irish people should follow Deak's example and insist on a return to the terms of the Renunciation Act. One method suggested was the abstention of the Irish Members of Parliament from Westminster and the setting up of a Parliament at home. It was not until 1918 when the *Sinn Fein* candidates swept the polls that they were able to put Griffith's ideas into practice, when Constance was one of the Ministers who carried out his policy.

Arthur Griffith was a man remarkable for his purity of intention, austerity and determination. He lived for nothing but the salvation of his nation. He was master of the pithy phrase: 'Let England take her right hand from Ireland's throat and her left hand from Ireland's pocket.' P. S. O'Hegarty, a close colleague and a member of the Executives of *Sinn Fein* and the IRB, writes in his *Victory of Sinn Fein* of the first time he went to Griffith's office.

There was just enough room for a desk and a couple of chairs, one window, very dusty, walls very dusty, dust everywhere. But the visitor never saw those things at first. Sitting at that desk, on a chair that was most rickety, was a small man, modest in appearance and demeanour, unobtrusive, not remarkable until he looked full at you, and then you forgot everything save that powerful head, those hard, steadfast, balancing eyes ... Here was a man who was all brain and all good.

St John Ervine, in *Craigavon: Ulsterman*, says Griffith's 'mind was incorruptible, but his heart was stony and his spirit juiceless as a dried apple'. Kevin O'Higgins, the Free State Minister, admired Griffith for his manly and devoted qualities, but thought him a bad judge of character. O'Higgins thought the same of Cathal Brugha, Free State Minister of Defence, and used to say, when an applicant for a post brought him a recommendation signed by the latter, 'Now if only that had been signed by Arthur Griffith as well, we could be certain it was safe to refuse.' Constance, who first met Griffith at Æ's, and who later worked closely with him, found him very reserved and standoffish. She wrote of him that his personality was a tower of strength, and that with 'his mastery of the English language he might have achieved a great position in English journalism, but he chose to work in poverty for Ireland'. She admired him, but they never really got on. It is hardly surprising. He must have found her puzzling and unpredictable, in addition to the twin disadvantages in the eyes of an austere Irish Nationalist of her sex and breeding. She wrote many years later that she never trusted or understood him.

Below the famous inn, Lamb Doyle's, near the village of Balally there stood a low, double white-washed cottage belonging to Constance's friends the O'Connell Fitz-Simons. In 1906 she decided to take the smaller half, consisting of two rooms, at the modest rent of a shilling a year, where the poet, Padraic Colum, lived for a time. Today her part of the dwelling is derelict and the area is built up, but sixty years ago it was a green solitary place, backed by Kilmashogue Mountain, and with a wide, illimitably spreading view to the north-east over Dublin Bay, Howth, and the far-away island, Ireland's Eye. Constance wanted a retreat where she could paint, roam about in solitude, live on milk, bread, and eggs, and where her stepson, Stasko, could run wild amongst the rocks and gorse and icy streams. She became a familiar and loved figure to the local children, arriving on her bicycle laden with sweets. It was here in this cottage, where hung a bronze plaque of Arthur Griffith, that she came upon a pile of old numbers of *The Peasant* and *'Sinn Fein'* left by Padraic Colum, and began to read them. The lightning struck at last. She read about the death of Robert Emmet, whose face was familiar from prints on cottage walls, but whose doomed insurrection, arrest and execution, were not; she read about the other patriots and heroes of the submerged Ireland she barely knew. In a flash, she says, she decided to join up. Soon after this, she recalls, 'chance threw Mr Griffith across my path at Æ's house one Sunday night. I told him quite frankly that I had only just realized that there were men in Ireland whose principles did not allow them to take an oath of allegiance to the foreign King, whose power they were pledged to overthrow.' Griffith received her confidences very coolly, and advised her to join the Gaelic League. She afterwards realized that he suspected her of being an *agent provocateur* used by the Castle. In spite of

Griffith's suspicions, within two years she was deep in Nationalist counsels.

It was during the period following the awakening in the cottage that Constance caused pain to the faithful Ellen Banks by ceasing to lead 'a lady's life' and becoming 'very foolish with her money'. Beggars were always at the door and they did not leave empty-handed. It was Banks' opinion that Casimir did not approve of these goings on. Banks also reproached Constance with taking no interest in her house, and received the reply 'Life is too short to worry.'

The smallest incident shows the directness of her feeling about life, as again when reproached by Banks, this time for putting Maeve and Stasko into an apple tree to shake down the fruit, when she was unmoved by Maeve's spoilt silk dress and half of Stasko's blouse left torn on a branch – 'boys will be boys' – or during a heat-wave when she allowed Stasko and Æ's sons to run naked on the lawn while she played a hose over them regardless of what the neighbours might say. She is remembered vividly by Charles Duff,* who was a visitor as a boy to Lissadell during these years. He was struck by her total lack of self-consciousness, her colourful and often flamboyant clothes, and the fact that of all the Gore-Booths she was the only one who bothered to sit down and talk to him. She was particularly interested in the lessons he was taking in Gaelic, questioning him closely about his teacher, the books he used, where his lessons took place. When the cross-examination was over she slapped him on the back saying, 'Good boy. We'll make a rebel of you yet.'

The Dublin years between 1903 and 1908 crystallized the respective attitudes of Constance and Casimir. Each year brought evidence of their fundamental disunity. He looked on politics with ribald detachment. She was a born political woman. He loved good living and quickly acquired a formidable reputation for tippling, having as boon companions Martin Murphy, the Gaiety stage manager and carpenter, and Dubronsky, a Polish tailor. These three – the huge Count, the tiny tailor, and the convivial carpenter – were familiars of Dublin night life. Constance, on the other hand, apart from the fact that no respectable woman was ever seen in a Dublin public house, was virtually teetotal, and disapproved

* Author of *Six Days to Shake an Empire*.

generally of alcohol. For Constance, life had to be whole with everything in it conducing to the one chosen aim. She needed to dig deep into existence, whereas Casimir preferred to drift along its surface. She was often without him. Even in the early years he spent every summer in the Ukraine. But in spite of all the difficulties the thin ice beneath their marriage held until the claims of *Cathleen ni Houlihan* swallowed Constance up. Painting was still a bond. Their departures from the cottage at Balally on bicycles festooned with their latest canvases piled on the handlebars and carriers, and even tied on to the sides of the rear wheels were long remembered by their neighbours. In 1905, an event which gave pleasure to them both was their part in the founding of the Dublin United Arts Club, together with Æ, Yeats, and Mrs James Duncan. The Arts Club became a new centre for those Dubliners who were lively and enlightened. The Markieviczs were often seen there. Beatrice Glenavy the painter, remembers Constance arriving with her coat on inside out and when this was pointed out to her, replying that she knew, but it would be unlucky to change it. George Moore is remembered talking to William Orpen about the fuller life. 'Fuller of what? . . . Fuller of rot.' Susan Mitchell is remembered for the topical rhymes she made up. Her chief victim was George Moore. She made him the subject of a series of sarcastic ballads with titles such as 'George Moore becomes High Sheriff of Mayo', 'George Moore eats a Grey Mullet', 'George Moore becomes a Priest of Aphrodite'. The monthly club dinners were a great feature of club life. Given in turns by the members, they were enlivened by ballads, or perhaps Percy French playing his banjo:

> If you long for things artistic
> And you revel in the nebulous and mystic
> And your hair is long
> And your ties all wrong
> And your speech is symbolistic
> If you're highly democratic
> And your mode of life is essentially erratic
> From no fixed address
> But you sleep in someone's attic
>
> (*Chorus*)
> Join the Arts Club, Join the Arts Club,

Where the souls so congregate
And the observances of convention
Excites such fierce dissension
In the Arts Club, in the Arts Club
You may sit and dissertate
If your coat tails sag and your trousers bag
You'll probably be hailed as great . . .

It was outside the Arts Club that Casimir once accidentally dropped a sovereign in a puddle of mud. Yeats was with him. When Casimir left the club several hours later he observed with sardonic glee that Yeats was standing talking to a friend by the same puddle, stirring it all the time with his stick in the hopes, Casimir was convinced, of finding the coin for himself.

During these years Constance became discouraged in her professional painting ambitions, but she never ceased to draw and sketch right up to the year of her death. She has been unjustly accused by some who have written about her (particularly Sean O'Casey) of turning to politics because she had got tired of painting. Painting as a career gave her up, rather than she it. In the early years Casimir had made good use of the studio that was added on to the dining-room at St Mary's, if she did not. He undertook a respectable number of important commissions. It was only gradually that a new interest began to grip him: theatricals. This was an activity they shared for many years. The theatre eventually replaced painting as Casimir's work.

It all began modestly enough with Constance playing a small part in the revival of Æ's *Deirdre* at Christmas 1906, and Casimir writing and playing in a little piece written in collaboration with Seamus O'Kelly called *Lustre*. The subject was an Irish boy, corrupted by life in the army, who tries to steal his mother's lustre and thereby causes her death (it seems that Casimir was not immune, then, from Nationalist propaganda). Constance, of course, had frequently organized and acted in amateur theatrical performances of the kind of plays that made the round of country houses in her youth; light, innocuous drawing-room comedies, skits, mild satires, on subjects such as Bluebeard. The next venture was equally remote in concept and feeling from the realistic folk plays of the Irish National Theatre, being a production of *The Pirates of Penzance* in 1907 given by The Irish Theatrical Club in aid of the Institute for the Industrious Blind, and under the patronage of the Viceroy and Vicereine. The Chamberlain, Sir Anthony Weldon, took the part of the Sergeant of Police, and the role of the Pirate King was shared between the eight performances (six nights and two matinées) by Casimir and Lord Farnham. Casimir enjoyed every moment of the experience, and he was thenceforth a man of the theatre.

CHAPTER 8

The Harp and the Drum

One rainy night in 1908 some members of the oganization The Daughters of Erin met to discuss their new magazine – *Bean na h'Eireann*. Their aim was to raise their readers' tastes above the current standard of women's magazines; they planned to advance the causes of militancy, separatism, and feminism. 'The Daughters', as they came to be affectionately called in Dublin, had been founded by Maud Gonne on Easter Sunday, 1900, after twelve o'clock Mass. When Maud Gonne first arrived back in Dublin to live as a young woman on her own, determined to work for Nationalism, she was annoyed to discover that the Celtic Literary Society did not admit the other sex. With her usual spirit she at once declared her intention of starting a society for women, which, she told the men, their wives and sweethearts would inevitably join. Her stated aims were to 're-establish the complete independence of Ireland; to encourage the study of Gaelic, of Irish literature, history, music and art . . . to support and publicize Irish manufacture; to discourage the circulation of low English literature, the singing of English songs, the attending of vulgar English entertainments . . . and to combat in every way any English influence'. 'The Daughters' got off to a flying start by collecting the money for a vast bun-fight known for ever after as 'The Patriotic Children's Treat' which was given to twenty thousand children, who were thus persuaded to boycott Queen Victoria's treat given at Viceregal Lodge during Her Majesty's visit. Victoria, 'the Famine Queen', as Maud Gonne called her, had only fifteen thousand children at her treat; years afterwards middle-aged men and women would come up to Maud Gonne (who was as easily recognized in Dublin as Mary Pickford in Hollywood) saying, 'I was one of the patriotic children at your party when Queen Victoria was over.'

Now in 1908, 'The Daughters', after an unbroken record of hostility to all things English, had spread their wings further. One of them, Helena Molony, whose initial idea it was to start the magazine, had read a speech of Constance's and decided to invite her to join the Daughters' confabulation. But Helena Molony, disciple of Maud Gonne, Abbey Theatre actress, future 'doughty lieutenant' of James Connolly, and labour organizer, was amazed and shocked on that rainy night in 1908 when the new recruit swept into the room in full evening dress, with a short train, furs round her shoulders, diamonds in her hair – apparently straight from the dreaded Castle. Unmollified by Constance's informality in taking off her shoes and putting them to dry by the fire, the Daughters decided to be very cool indeed towards her, immediately suspecting her of being 'one of the Castle set' and of coming to do propaganda for Lady Aberdeen. Somehow she managed to melt them and get herself taken on to help with their cause. She left the meeting with a young member called Sydney Gifford (later well known as the writer and journalist 'John Brennan') who walked with her to the tram. Constance, in her usual heedless way, allowed her train to drag on the muddy pavement, but when her companion pointed this out to her she gathered up her dress, saying that she would have little time in the future for wearing fashionable clothes. The younger woman was also amused to see that when it came to paying the tram fare Constance fished absentmindedly in her purse and offered the conductor half-crowns instead of pennies.

Casimir once told his son that he well remembered the very last time that he and Constance were together at the Castle at a great ball on St Patrick's night in 1908 when they danced Irish reels. This would have been in March, and the last ball of the season. It is tempting to suppose that the two occasions link; the last Castle appearance remembered by her husabnd, and the first appearance remembered by her new friends. It would have been in keeping with her dramatic sense to have combined the two. But it seems unlikely. The gardening notes she undertook to do for *Bean na h'Eireann* first saw the light in February 1909 – eleven months after her last ball at the Castle. Then, too, if it is supposed that the Daughters of Erin were planning their new magazine as early as March 1908, and since it is known that the first number came out in November of that year it would appear that seven months' gestation was a long time for a modest periodical consisting of a handful of pages and costing one penny. But Constance did draw the heading for the cover page.* It seems the most likely that she came to the meeting from some smart, non-Castle function (although there were not many of them) in the autumn of 1908, never thinking that her finery would instantly indentify her with one place only.

Where the month of March 1908 was indisputably a milestone can be found in her last Castle appearance recorded by her husband and her first public appearance with *Sinn Fein* ten days later, and recorded by the newspaper of the movement. This occasion was a large *Sinn Fein* demonstration in the Rotunda on 28 March, when she is the twenty-first name in a non-alphabetical list of those 'on the platform or in the hall'. Since it is not possible to know how large the platform was it is also impossible to judge or guess whether Constance could have been put in such a conspicuous place immediately on joining the movement. But wherever she was, whether up on the platform or down in the hall, this act of being present at all at such an occasion put her once and for all on the other side of the fence. There were many shades of opinion in the Ireland of her day, but between Griffith and the Castle there was a gulf never to be bridged.

Griffith was implacably hostile even to Lady Aberdeen's well-meant personal efforts to find a common mean. He wrote of her in '*Sinn Fein*' on February 1 of that year,

The most enthusiastic of her adherents need not be surprised or shocked when we oppose or even decidedly attack her. We understand perfectly well that her mission is one of conciliation. That she seeks to understand the faith of extreme Nationalism. And in the face of this we who desire to preserve the National faith cannot accept for our people gifts or help or healing from her hands.

Griffith goes on to explain that this is because in the old days in Ireland to take gifts meant to render homage. In the same article he proves himself a relentless non-forgetter when he accuses Lady Aberdeen of having avoided interviews with evicted tenants in Donegal fourteen years before.

It would have been out of the question for Constance to

---

*With the lack of an extant first number it is not possible to say whether Constance's design was on it.

frequent the Castle as well as being a *Sinn Feiner*. The castle and the Gaelic League, yes, but this was different. She had made a choice as clear as marriage. It was noticed by a shrewd and perceptive observer, Padraic Colum, that she changed greatly after she entered Nationalist politics. She ceased to be restless and at random; she began to turn into the single-minded and dedicated woman of her real maturity.

Constance's first mentor in her new life was a young man called Bulmer Hobson. He was born in Belfast of a Quaker family; his father, a Gladstonian Liberal, travelled in tea; his mother was a Yorkshirewoman. Bulmer Hobson, who had a small private income, became an organizer for the Nationalist cause. He was a Vice-President of *Sinn Fein* in November 1908. He arranged for Constance to join the Drumcondra and Glasnevin branch of *Sinn Fein*. He went further the next year, and, to the annoyance of Griffith, got her chosen as the Drumcondra delegate to the annual *Sinn Fein* convention, where, on 4 September 1909, she was elected to the Resident Executive Council by twenty-four votes. Now she was really in.

Bulmer Hobson, together with his two close friends, Dr MacCartan and Sean MacGarry, set out to educate the new recruit, lending her books and, so she wrote sardonically in later years when friendship had turned to political emnity, explaining 'all the intricacies of such simple things as organizations and committees'. Now, in 1908, Bulmer Hobson opened the gates of her new world to her. She seized on the experience like an elixir, but she was shrewd enough to see and deplore from the first the divisions and suspicions that bedevilled the cause of Ireland's salvation. All were agreed on the broad aim, but when the large, vague, hopes and dreams narrowed to clear priorities and methods, men's differing ideas were so savagely debated and tenaciously clung to that it was like with the Fathers of the early Church and the doctrine of the Trinity.

Among Irish patriots of the century it might be said that orthodoxy was represented by John Redmond and the Irish Parliamentary Party, whose members sat in the English House of Commons, and unorthodoxy by the Trades Union organizer, James Connolly, who was a Marxist. Between these poles stood the creator of *Sinn Fein* – Griffith – dedicated, intolerant, incorruptible (called by Churchill 'that rare phenomenon, a silent Irishman').

In 1908 Redmond was fifty-two, Connolly was the same age as Constance – forty – and Griffith was thirty-six. Each of these four beings dedicated their life to Ireland, and not one saw their allotted span; dying, in the case of Constance, Griffith, and Redmond, rejected by a large section of the nation in whose service they had literally worn themselves out.

The Irish Parliamentary party had been disastrously split by the fall of Parnell. After his death, Redmond, who had remained loyal to his leader, took his place, but it was not until 1900 that he became chairman of an uneasily united party. He remained faithful to the cause of Home Rule, but always in the context of loyalty to England and the Crown. Redmond came of a prominent family of Wexford Catholics, a family which was one of the few in Ireland that continued to prosper through trade with Europe even under the penal laws. Redmond was bred in a tradition of service to his fellow-catholics, and loyalty to family, friends, and colleagues. Magnanimous in temperament and majestic of presence (Wilfred Scawen Blunt describes seeing him in Hyde Park, 'an imposing personage with the face and figure of a Roman emperor, seated on a huge dray horse'), Redmond was a fine speaker of the sonorous declamatory school, a shrewd parliamentary tactician, and, as Wickham Steed wrote of him, he was 'conscious of being armed with the mandate of the Irish race'. Where he made an error was in underestimating the importance of what small but influential sections of the Irish race were up to.

Sinn Fein, meaning 'we ourselves', had evolved in its final form and simplified name (*Sinn Fein* instead of the Sinn Fein League) from the amalgamation of the Dungannon Separatist clubs, founded by Bulmer Hobson and Denis McCullough and named after the Volunteers' Convention at Dungannon in 1782, and an organization set up by Griffith in 1900 called *Cumann nan Gaedheal*. Within *Sinn Fein*, as Constance soon found out, there was enmity between Griffith and Bulmer Hobson. The younger man was a member of the important militant secret organization, the Irish Revolutionary Brotherhood (IRB) founded in 1858. The IRB worked closely with the powerful Irish-American secret society, *Clan na Gael*. It was with the encouragement of the latter organization that Hobson made the decision to work for a merger between Griffith and the Dungannon clubs. Once this was achieved, there was a very apparent, constant, and unremitting conflict between the two men. In later years Constance accused Bulmer Hobson of using her as a pawn in his battles with Griffith – but this was at the period in her life when anyone who was not with the Republican cause was anathema. At the time she was immensely taken up with this new friendship and all it brought her in purpose and enlightenment. Since Hobson's ideas, as an IRB man, were more revolutionary and extremist than Griffith's it came only too naturally to her to back him against the older man. Besides, we know that she sensed Griffith's hostility towards her from the first. Whatever she may have come to feel about Bulmer Hobson, he made her free of this new world in which she began as an ignoramus and an outsider. She started twenty years later than Maud Gonne, and for a man such as Griffith, she must have possessed an ineradicable taint of the big house and landlordism. She had always liked to excel. Small wonder now that she threw herself with such fervour into politics.

The core of the *Sinn Fein* doctrine, as is well known, is separatism, and the suggested means to achieve it the setting up of duplicate Irish-run departments, which would, in fact, end by usurping the British administration. But unlike most Nationalists, Griffith was not against the monarchy, and, in fact, would have accepted a dual monarchy, as the Hungarians had. That is to say the monarch would have been King of Ireland under another hat.

James Connolly, Irish by race, Edinburgh born, self-educated, scratching a living where he could, was working and organizing labour in America in 1908. He was mistrusted and underestimated by both Redmond and Griffith. Of all the remarkable men who shaped Ireland's destiny in these years, when ideas worked like yeast in the dough that was a repressed nation, Connolly's mind reached furthest into the future. He was not only a socialist and dedicated humanitarian, but a political thinker whose books are still read today. Connolly had an admirable character as a man and a leader; he was honourable, fearless, lucid, consistent, and tenacious. Sean O'Casey has left an unforgettable description of his physical appearance at a slightly later period.

. . . a tiny group of men followed Connolly through the streets . . . a large slouch hat covering Connolly's head, a large round head, fronted by a rather commonplace face, its heaviness lightened by the fine, soft, luminous eyes; the heavy jaws were jewelled with a thick-lipped, sensuous mouth, mobile and a little sarcastic, bannered peacefully by a thick and neatly-trimmed moustache. His ears were well set to the head, the nose was a little too thick, and gave an obstinate cast to the bright eyes, and a firm fleshy neck bulged out over a perfectly white hard collar. The head and neck rested solidly on a broad sturdy trunk of a body, and all were carried forward on two short pillar-like legs, slightly bowed, causing him to waddle a little in his walk, as if his legs were, in the way of a joke, trying faintly and fearfully to throw him off his balance. Silent, he walked on, looking a little grim and surly . . .[1]

Connolly revealed once and for all the basis of his political attitudes when he wrote,

Ireland as distinct from her people is nothing to me; and the man who is bubbling over with love and affection for 'Ireland' and can pass unmoved through our streets and witness all the sorrow and suffering, the shame and degradation wrought upon Irish men and women – aye, wrought by Irish men and women – without burning to end it, is a fraud and a liar in his heart, no matter how much he loves that combination of chemical elements he is pleased to call 'Ireland'.[2]

This was the man who attached to himself Constance's fervent devotion. She became his disciple and comrade. His work became her work; but this close association no more harmed his happy marriage than a somewhat comparable relationship: that of Lenin with Inessa Armand, affected Lenin's serene relationship with his wife.

In 1908 Connolly was a veteran in political organization. He had worked and campaigned in Scotland, Dublin and America. Back in the 1890s he wrote his first important political essay, *Ireland for the Irish*, which attacked the concept of Home Rule on the grounds that if this were achieved it would merely confirm the Irish middle classes in their exploitation of the peasant and labouring classes. But neither did he believe in the cosy, utopian ideal of a peasant proprietary (such as Horace Plunkett and Æ attempted to foster through their Agricultural Co-operative Organization). Connolly boldly came out with his arguments in favour of land nationalization, declaring that 'the days of small farmers, like small capitalists, are gone'. (This was a far cry from the spirit in which Horace Plunkett, when travelling abroad, seeing black goats dotted over the Swiss mountains murmured, 'I wonder we never thought of goats for the congested districts'; and thereupon imported Swiss goats to supply nourishing milk to impoverished Irish mothers. The goats, intoxicated by Ireland, devoured everything in sight, even the thatch on the cottages and the clothes drying on the lines.)

In the larger field, Connolly, in an article written in 1898, vehemently attacked the doctrine that British socialism should first achieve its own revolution and then, and only then, grant Ireland freedom.

In 1896 Connolly founded the Irish Socialist Republican Party. He hoped to combine Socialists and democratic Nationalists. In 1898 he decided that since the Home Rule press was hostile to his ideas, the ISRP must have a newspaper of its own. By dint of doing virtually all the work himself, he therefore produced a weekly, *The Worker's Republic*. The paper had its vicissitudes, summed up by Connolly: the first series that came out was 'so weekly that it almost died', and the second appearing 'whenever it was strong enough to get out'.[3]

Connolly and Griffith first met when the latter returned to Dublin from South Africa in 1899 and founded his Nationalist paper the *United Irishman*. The Boer War broke out the same year. Much passion was engendered between English and Irish socialists. Connolly was accused by a prominent British Fabian of stampeding with a mob through the streets brandishing the Boer flag and shouting for an Irish Republic and for the defeat of Britain in the Transvaal. By 1901, when Connolly had become a member of the Dublin Trades Union Council and been adopted as Labour Candidate in the Wood Quay ward of Dublin, he was bitterly attacked by the priests. He was condemned as anti-Christ from the pulpit, and Catholics were forbidden to vote for him under threat of excommunication. It was said he sent his children to a Catholic school only so as to camouflage his atheistic beliefs. He did not win the seat but he increased the labour vote.

Connolly's first stay in America, which took place between August 1902 and January 1903, and where he was received with immense enthusiasm, came as a vindication of the harsh years of struggle. Connolly fought another election in Wood Quay ward on his return from the United States in 1903. He again lost. In the autumn of that year he returned to America where he spent seven years both earning his living and organising labour. He returned to Ireland in July 1910 and soon felt confident enough of his prospects to send for his wife and children. He wrote to his wife, 'You are not returning to the misery you left.'[4]

The General Election of 1906 brought a great change to the political scene. The Liberals got in with a majority of more than a hundred over all other parties. Since Gladstone's retirement in 1894 (having seen his Home Rule Bill of 1886 thrown out by the House of Commons and that of 1893 by the House of Lords), the Home Rule question had been shelved by a series of Conservative governments. For the Liberals the issue had proved a shirt of Nessus, but they were the party pledged to it, and all the evidence seemed to point to the fact that until there was a reformed House of Lords the Bill would continue to be thrown out. In 1907, in an attempt to find a compromise solution (never popular in Ireland) the Government decided to return to the plan evolved by Constance's cousin, Lord Dunraven; that is to say the 'Devolution' plan formerly so badly received that it had caused George Wyndham's resignation in 1905. Now, two years later, it was revived in the form of a Bill which proposed the setting up of an administrative council with an elected majority; subject, however, to the veto of the Lord Lieutenant. This council would be responsible for the chief Irish departments. The proposed Bill was badly received in Ireland, and Redmond's motion at a National Convention that it was 'inadequate in scope and unsatisfactory in detail' was passed unanimously. The Irish Parliamentary party appeared to be impotent, since the Liberals had such a large majority that they did not need the Irish votes. In 1909 and 1910 English parliamentarians were rent over the budget and the crisis caused by its rejection by the Lords, followed by the Parliament Bill which denied the Lords the right to amend or reject a Finance Bill and curtailed their power of veto over ordinary legislation to the span of two years and one month. 1910 brought the death of Edward VII and two General Elections. It was the consent of George V to the creation of sufficient peers to provide a Liberal majority in the House of Lords, with a diminished Government majority in the House of Commons, that put Redmond in a position strong enough to press his cause. But by this time other forces were gathering which made inevitable the violent conflicts of the future. The violence was contained and implicit in the dramatically opposed aims of Irish Nationalists and Ulster Unionists.

In 1908 Constance had her first taste of political campaigning when she went to Manchester to help Eva and Miss Roper in a by-election. Eva had now been living and working in Manchester for eleven years. She and Miss Roper and Miss Reddish were greatly concerned with organizing women textile workers with a view to improving their conditions and wages, but they also worked intensively for women's suffrage. In addition Eva was, for a time, on the Manchester Education Committee, and she became a joint secretary of the Women's Trade Union Council. Public work did not kill her writing career. She continued to publish poetry and prose; she made herself a niche amongst the poets of the Irish Renaissance. Her thought was imbued with the legendary figures of Gael, with her love of her native Sligo,

> At Clitheroe through the sunset hour
> My soul was far away:
> I saw Ben Bulben's rose and fire
> Shining afar o'er Sligo Bay.

Through Eva's poems there vibrates a spirit akin with Æ's. She is a poet of mystical union with nature, of the oneness of opposites,

> I have found the hidden beauty where the river finds
> the sea,
> Or the dark cloud finds the rainbow, or the desert
> finds the rain,
> Where the night sails out on the Dawn Wind and the
> darkness ceases to be
> Or the Spirit builds a rainbow from whirling rings of
> pain,
> I have found the Hidden Beauty where the river finds
> the sea.

Her poems echo the beliefs of Theosophists,

> A jelly-fish afloat on the bright wave –
> A white seagull – a great blue butterfly –
> A hunted hare – a wolf in a dark cave;
> All these I was; which one of these was I?

After Eva's death, Miss Roper's brother, Reginald, wrote of her that her spirit had 'the power of clear water *molto utile, et pretiosa, et casta:* it could quench a thirst, fall lightly on a blade of grass, or drive a tremendous dynamo of light or power'.

The new trend in Constance's life brought her closer to Eva's path, although much farther from Casimir's. Now, in 1908, Constance journeyed to Manchester to assist in fighting for the rights of barmaids. (In this alone, one presumes, Casimir would have sympathized with her.) The Government had introduced a Licensing Bill, one of whose clauses spelt the downfall of bar-maids. The by-election, which was marked by many suffragette demonstrations, was fought by Winston Churchill, and William Joynson-Hicks, who was the Conservative candidate. The Lancashire and Cheshire Women Textile Workers' Representation Committee (of which Eva and Miss Roper were secretaries) took a deputation of women to Winston Churchill to ask him to per-suade the Government to withdraw the barmaid clause in the Bill. He refused. Eva and Miss Roper therefore decided to bring their forces into play to oppose him, both in the interests of barmaids and women's suffrage of which he was not a noticeable supporter. Constance, besides canvassing and making speeches, is remem-bered best in this by-election because she drove a coach and four horses down a street in the middle of a large election crowd. When challenged by a man in the crowd with the words, 'Can you cook a dinner?' she shouted back, 'Yes. Can you drive a coach and four?'

Winston Churchill lost the by-election, Constance went back to her activities in Dublin. She had designed the title page for *Beau na h'Eireann* (a Joan of Arc figure holding up a streamer-like device bearing the name, and backed by a rising sun). Her other main contribution was her gardening notes. These apparently most innocent by-products of journalism were much used by Nationalist ladies as a cloak for propaganda: slugs, weeds, pests representing the British, and flowers, birds, trees, enslaved Ireland. Once the public got the knack it must have been hard not to see the British behind every paragraph. 'It is very unpleasant work killing slugs and snails but let us not be daunted. A good Nationalist should look upon slugs in the garden in much the same way as she looks on the English in Ireland.'

Constance also devised a more charming and poetic way of reminding her readers of politics. In July 1909 she writes that she saw a crimson rose which brings her 'straight back to the reality of July '98 ... the petals of Roisin Dubh lay as red and strange then on the green hillsides of Wexford – scattered a crimson shedding over the land from little Arklow to the shores of Lough Foyle, from the sea-bounds of the Atlantic to among the dusty streets of Dublin – everywhere in Ireland had the soil been consecrated by the blood of our noblest and best'.

Lavender makes her think of Robert Emmet because he loved the flower. The month of December reminds her of 'the wild Christmas Eve long ago when Red Hugh and the two other lads slipped down the Castle wall to face the bitter gale and blinding snow that lay between them and the work they had to do for Ireland'. In January she compares Ireland to 'a poor wee bulb buried in the dust and dirt of English rule and English influence and struggling to gain the light and air'.

Other contributions were more forthright, 'A "Moral Force" movement, i.e. a movement that stops short of shedding blood, and therefore forbids you to make the last sacrifice – that of your life – cannot be taken very seriously, and must end in contempt and ridicule.' And again, 'Learn to discipline and be disciplined, learn to shoot, learn to scout, learn to give up all for Ireland. Twenty years would not be long to prepare in, and, God knows, shall we have twenty years?' *Bean* was capable of switching from this sort of thing to clothes, 'How perfectly lovely are the hats this season', to nurses' conditions, Nationalist schools, *Sinn Fein*, and the divisions between labour groups. Katherine Tynan wrote a serial for it, and Æ contributed a poem.

Constance took her turn in all the work of 'The Daughters', from arranging chairs and benches for meetings and addressing envelopes, to correcting proofs and taking the paper out on the streets to sell. She had a drama class, too, for girls, but she found she preferred dealing with boys. Her success with boys' classes under The Daughters of Erin undoubtedly gave her the confidence for one of the most successful and significant projects of her life: her arms-drilled boy scouts, the *Fianna*.

In March 1909 Constance happened to read a newspaper account of how the Viceroy had formed a number of Boys' Brigades and Boy Scout Troops. They were reviewed at Clontarf, and addressed by the Lord Lieutenant. This event caused Constance's Republican blood to boil. She wrote later in the *Fianna* Magazine:

Surely nothing sadder could be seen than the sons of men who had thrown in their lot with the Fenians, whose forbears had been out in '48, suffered with Emmet, taken the word of command from Tone, cheered when Sarsfield, or Owen Roe O'Neill led them to victory – nothing could be sadder than to see these boys saluting the flag that flew in triumph over every defeat their nation has known, and from that day it was planted in their country has stood for murder, pillage, injustice and treachery.

For Constance emotion and action went hand in glove, so she immediately started to plan what to do about the Viceroy's scouts. It happened that a precedent lay near at hand. This was the work done in Belfast by her friend Bulmer Hobson when he was National Organizer there. Making use of huts which had been built for British soldiers during the Belfast riots, Bulmer Hobson formed classes of boys and girls for the study of the Irish language, and Irish history; he also encouraged the Gaelic game of hurling by forming a junior hurling league. (Cricket and Rugger or Soccer were banned by the Gaelic League as foreign games.) Bulmer Hobson christened his organization *Na Fianna Eireann*, after the 'hero army of ancient Ireland'. The Belfast *Fianna* prospered for a while and then lapsed. Constance now decided to re-create this project in Dublin. It was to 'weld the youth of Ireland together to work and fight for Ireland . . . An organization that would be broad enough, through love of country, to include all workers for Ireland, in whatever camp they might be . . . All that will count in the end is their willingness to undertake a life of self-sacrifice and self-denial for their country's sake'. In the words of Padraic Pearse these boys were to be trained to work for an Ireland 'not free merely, but Gaelic as well, not Gaelic merely, but free as well'.

Having decided to create her *Fianna*, Constance then had to work out how to get it started. Republicans like her first educators Bulmer Hobson, Dr MacCartan and Sean MacGarry were enthusiastic, but when, using her position on the Executive of *Sinn Fein*, she put the idea up to Griffith he received it coolly, as he had her first approach to him in Æ's house. She had now infiltrated her way too far for his liking in the organization he still sought to control. (She accused him in her reminiscences of 'always coming to the meeting with his mind made up' and only being concerned 'with forcing his own point of view on his colleagues and carrying his point'.) His objections to her plan were, perhaps, inwardly personal, since she must have been little but a thorn in his flesh through her support of his opponent, Bulmer Hobson, and others whom he thought of as hotheads. But he had more cogent reasons. Constance fully intended her boys to be taught to fight for Ireland, and Griffith was completely opposed, then, to physical force. Constance wrote of him that he 'did not want anyone to begin to talk of fighting for Ireland's freedom. In fact, the only difference between himself and the "Party" [ie the Irish Parliamentary Party] were [sic] his disapproval of men going "hat in hand to Westminster" . . . The *Sinn Fein* programme contained no provision for organizing an army.' When Constance asked for provision for a rebel boy scout organization to be included in the *Sinn Fein* programme she was 'gently but firmly turned down'.

Undaunted, Constance spoke at every *Sinn Fein* meeting in the next few months and asked for support for her idea. Little came. She and Helena Molony had many discussions as to the means of making dreams reality. One of the difficulties was that they knew no boys. Then Constance had the inspiration of finding a sympathetic schoolmaster who would surely find recruits. With her usual insouciance she approached the only schoolmaster she knew, who was a staunch Unionist. Constance asked him to give her the name of any colleague of the other creed who would help her. Very obligingly he gave her the name of a Nationalist – a teacher at St Andrew's National Schools in Brunswick Street – Mr O'Neill. Constance had some difficulty in convincing him that she was not 'an emissary of Lady Aberdeen', but once reassured he agreed to hand over eight pupils whom he thought the most suited for the work. Mr O'Neill asked all his pupils to do their exercises as a display for Constance and Sean MacGarry, who had accompanied her, after which he called out the chosen eight and introduced them to her.

It was a small beginning, but it led to one of her most significant achievements for Ireland – and it was virtually her own brain-child. These boys, as she pointed out to a critic, were soon to become men, and, going much further than Bulmer Hobson had in Belfast, she created a disciplined force, trained in the use of arms. A colleague of these days has said, 'The real value of the *Fianna*, with their thorough training, only became apparent when the Irish Volunteers started. Except for ex-British soldiers – who were viewed with great hostility and suspicion – there was no one who could drill or handle firearms. But the *Fianna Eireann*, whose original members were by this time young men of seventeen to twenty years, formed a valuable nucleus of ready-trained officer material.'[5]

At first she saw the scheme in terms of small troops based on the Baden-Powell boy scouts. She invited the first eight boys to St Mary's and called the troop 'The Red Branch Knights'. She and the handful of faithfuls who turned up regularly to help – Helena Moloney, Dr MacCartan and Sean MacGarry – tried to teach the boys signalling, drill, scouting, and other lore bewildering to the young Dubliners. These first occasions were not a great success, and it looked as though her cherished plan was going to die on its feet. One can imagine the gently subversive Casi,* whiskey glass in hand, guffawing at the window while Constance and her friends sweated it out on the lawn. He was devoted to 'his floating land-mine' as he called Constance, but nothing would stop him laughing at her. He grumbled in later days to his boon companion, the Gaiety Theatre stage manager, Martin Murphy that the 'sprouts', as he called them, 'sprouted under the bed and they sprouted over the bed, and the little devil-sprouts drink whiskey, Martin, even locked whiskey'.[6] On another occasion he called in on Martin Murphy saying that the 'sprouts' had drunk all his whiskey. His friend gave him the keys of his desk and told him there were two half pints in it – 'and you know where the water tap is'. In ten minutes Casi was back having drunk the lot.[7]

If Constance was to make a success of her scouts it was time for another inspiration. 'The brilliant idea came of having a camp.' She knew nothing of camping, so she wrote afterwards (one doubts this with her Lissadell past) but she was given a little garden tent, she bought a scout tent, 'the Fitzgerald boys volunteered a pony and car', food was bought, bedding collected as well as books, cushions, rugs, saucepans, sketching materials – and one morning Constance, Helena Molony, and six boys set out for 'a little valley' on the side of Three Rock Mountain. Constance's description (written for the *Fianna* magazine Christmas number of 1914) is worth giving in full, for its atmosphere is so characteristic of her. She never lost her boyish side (not for nothing was she sarcastically called 'a Rosalind in green tights' when she came to wear uniform.) In her burned the fire of Shakespeare's spirited heroines. She was Rosalind in the Forest of Arden, Beatrice

* I have followed Constance's own spelling of Casimir's nickname, rather than the more frequently used Cassie.

at the moment when she cries 'Kill Claudio!', Henry vi's fiery Margaret on the field of battle. She was also a boy scout. Here is what she says about that first *Fianna* camp – the forerunner of so many more.

When we left the road for a rough boreen we felt we had almost arrived, and started gaily up the rugged way. We lifted the wheels over big stones and pulled them through narrow ruts, helping and easing the gallant little pony in its struggles; sustained by the thought of the cool little stream and the soft green sward so far up the hill. After long hours of pushing, pulling, resting and pushing again we arrived at the last gate at the end of the track. A few minutes more saw us in the valley, kneeling on the soft green sward and bathing our dusty faces in the little stream. We dawdled over a most delicious tea and dragging out poetry books and sketching things we lazily drowsed away the evening.

Twilight woke us to the necessity of fixing up things for the night. We started to pitch our tents on a grassy slope where the hill slid down to the stream. It took a long, long time.

Tents are very hard to pitch if you don't know how, especially at night. Whenever you trip over a rope in the dark the peg comes out, you probably fall on to the tent, and it collapses. Anyhow the peg flies out and is lost. Next comes the task of trying to disentangle jam from blankets, frying pans, cushions, poetry books and all other indispensable articles that we had brought. Candles were the only important thing we had forgotten. But at last everything had found a place, the boys were comfortably settled and we turned in and drifted into dreamland . . .

We woke very early to find a bright, pleasant morning with a cheerful sun shining through the flaps of the tent. Early as we were, the boys were still earlier, and one was already improving his mind with Yeats' poems. The others were mostly blacking their boots, and quite ready for breakfast. I didn't wonder that they looked so fresh when at last I found my soap and towel – a brown dripping rag, wrapped round a sticky mess.

It was the only towel in the camp. After long experience I have come to the conclusion that the only thing you can be quite sure that every boy will bring to camp is boot polish.

After breakfast the boys went to Mass, we put things straight and settled ourselves snugly to read. Suddenly some heavy drops of rain sent us scurrying into the tent. We hastily grabbed all the blankets, coats, rugs and cushions that we had spread around us in the sun to air. We piled them into a snug nest, from which we defied the elements. Down came the storm, the thunder crashed above us, sharp blades of lightning cut through the rain beside us, menacing our fragile shelter. The boys came rushing up – and then – oh horror – we had not thought of digging a ditch round the tent, which was pitched on the side of a hill. The rainshed poured right through the fragile wall over the ground sheet. Our snug nest was one soppy sponge.

Luckily the rain stopped as suddenly as it began. The sun came out and did its best to dry our things . . .

The boys anyhow slept in dry coverings that night, and no one took cold. The next evening saw the end of our holiday. We had some trouble in capturing the pony. A kind neighbour had allowed us to turn it into his park and graze with his own cattle and young horses. The pony found camp life just as much to his taste as we did, and would not allow himself to be caught and harnessed into bondage again. Whenever we got near him, off he went with the other horses, dancing and kicking, and dodging in and out of the trees. It took hours to secure him. He succumbed to a feed of oats in the end.

The experience of this camp convinced Constance that she could make a success of the scouts, but, she decided, they would 'have to be run more on the lines of a Boys' Republic and an army. There would have to be a hall taken and an organization formed more on the lines that Irishmen were accustomed to work in.' She thought that the 'English loose system of organization by sections and patrols would not work'.

At this point she asked Bulmer Hobson to join her. He agreed, and she records that it was at his request that 'The Red Branch Knights' became *Na Fianna Eireann*, in memory of his Belfast boys and girls. Bulmer Hobson became president of the *Fianna*, Constance and Padraic O'Riain secretaries, Constance offered to find and pay for a hall. She really felt she was getting launched at last. The hall she found was the cold, draughty place in Lower Camden Street where the forerunner of the Abbey Players, the Irish National Theatre Society, had shivered through rehearsals.

A date was fixed for the first meeting, and the Committee advertised for any boys 'willing to work for the Independence of Ireland'. A boy was posted outside holding a large flag as a decoy. But she need not have worried. Dozens turned up. Bulmer Hobson took the chair. All was going swimmingly when one of the older boys got up to say that since this was a 'physical force assocation' it was no place for women. Indicating Constance, enthroned as secretary, and Helena Molony, the only two women in the room, he suggested they should leave. The Chairman, Bulmer Hobson, came to the rescue and managed to smooth things over. Little did the anti-feminists in the hall know that Constance was the one person connected with the organization most qualified to teach them how to fire the guns. She discovered that she could get round the prohibition on the use of firearms through the clause which allowed a householder to use them 'inside his own compound'. She openly trained the boys with firearms on the land surrounding her cottage. She bought rifles including, later, two of her stepson's. She designed a badge, a white sixpence-sized circle enclosing a green circle and a yellow sun crossed by a sword. New branches of the organization quickly sprang into being largely due to the efforts of a recruit – Liam Mellowes – who ranged the country on his bicycle for the *Fianna*. The first two branches were near Dublin at Drumcondra and North Rock. Through her visits to the homes of the *Fianna* boys Constance won the hearts of the ordinary Dublin folk. Of the people of submerged Ireland she had only known peasants until now; the urban poor, or semi-poor were a new experience. Their privations and wrongs grew in her mind like a mustard seed. It was as though she was unconsciously preparing herself for James Connolly's tenents; first of all through militant Nationalism, then through direct contact with the working people of the city. She was of the breed of crypto-socialists from the leisured classes who come to socialism through the heart.

In the days when Constance was still feeling her way to her proper role amongst the Nationalists – 'the dark and obliterated path where I was wandering', so she wrote of herself later – one of the first milestones, she says, was her meeting with the Fenian, Tom Clarke. Born of an Irish Protestant soldier and a Catholic mother, Tom Clarke became a Fenian through his observation of the results of the famine, of the land war, of evictions, and all the wrongs he saw inherent in English rule. He emigrated to America where he prospered; but his membership of *Clan na Gael* (the Irish–American extremist organization) involved him in rebels' work. His activities landed him with a life prison sentence at the time when it was the British policy to treat Irish political prisoners with calculated savagery. (It will be remembered how Maud Gonne fought for the Irish prisoners whose conditions shocked her so greatly.) Tom Clarke was half starved and constantly burnt by the heavy molten bars he had to handle. The opportunity came to him to obtain release from a life which, he wrote, outdid in its horrors the worst his imagination could have pictured beforehand; but the condition of his freedom was the betrayal of Parnell. Tom Clarke, and another prominent Fenian, John Daly, were offered money together with their release if they would give evidence against Parnell at the time when Richard Piggott's series of forged letters, bought by *The Times*, were at issue in the courts. They both refused, Tom Clarke saying, 'I would rather rot in prison than dishonour myself.' He was taken at his word. Nine more years went by, five of them in Portland, the worst of all prisons, before a long Amnesty campaign finally got him released as a 'ticket-of-leave' man. This he remained until his execution after the Rising. He took a small shop, which soon became almost a Nationalist reading-room and meeting-place as well as a shop. Constance was first taken there by Bulmer Hobson. She, with her painter's eye for physical characteristics, was immediately struck by Tom Clarke's bright, alert eyes: 'You did not see that they were brown because they seemed so full of light; they were like a searchlight turned on you, and only afterwards you noticed the colour and found how kindly they were and how they softened the fierce, bushy eyebrows under which they were closely set.' From this man who had suffered so much, Constance, and all his friends, received nothing but kindness and encouragement. He was one of the few peacemakers in the movement. 'What you got from him', Constance wrote, was 'interest in your schemes, encouragement for your hopes, support in your hours of despair'. From behind the counter in his shop Tom Clarke wielded a benign influence over the conflicts of the champions of Erin.

Another significant figure came into Constance's life in these years; a scholar and idealist whose name rang round the world in 1916. This was Padraic Pearse. As with many of those who came to fight England for Ireland, Pearse was half English. His father was a Devonshire man; his mother's family came from Co Meath. Pearse again, like many Nationalists, learnt the old, sad, stories of woe and wrong at the knees of an elderly woman whose thoughts were rooted in the past: in this case his aunt. Pearse, although he was so identified in thought with the Gaelic past, and with separatism, for many years held aloof equally from *Sinn Fein*, Labour, Constitutionalists, and the IRB. He founded a school – St Enda's – dedicated to the teaching of all things Irish. Although he was reserved, solid in looks and personality, studious and refined, at the same time he was full of fire. In 1910 he startled a Freedom Club meeting, whose members accused him of being a moderate, with a fiery speech defending the Gaelic tradition as being part of Separatism, and ending with the cry, 'Give me a hundred determined men and I will free Ireland.' These words did not go unnoted by the secret, extremist IRB organization.

Within *Sinn Fein* there was much dissatisfaction and controversy in the years 1909–11. Constance records in her memoirs that Griffith was criticized on the one hand by the Separatists for advocating policies which might lead to civil war and yet failing to make provision for this eventuality; and on the other he was blamed by the moderates for his incessant criticism in the columns of his newspaper of Redmond and the Parliamentary party, for whom there was much support in the country.

In December 1909 a storm occurred in the councils of *Sinn Fein* which seems to typify the shifting alliances and loyalties between the various Dublin factions. At the time, so Constance wrote later in *Eire*, 'all Gaelic Dublin was assembling for the *Aonoch* when we received notices to attend a special convention of *Sinn Fein*. It was not stated in the notices what the meeting had been called to consider.' But rumour took over where fact was absent. It was said that the special council meeting was somehow connected with the breakaway association formed by William O'Brien MP, The All for Ireland League, in opposition to Redmond's United Irish League. It was said, too, that Griffith intended to merge *Sinn Fein* with The All for Ireland League and that the first activity of the newly merged organization would be to fight Redmond's candidate in the South Dublin election, and back another candidate, Mr Brady. Griffith faced a hostile section of the Council, headed by Bulmer Hobson, Constance, and P. T. Daly, who were bitterly opposed to the idea of working actively with any section of the Parliamentary party. Griffith tried to be non-commital, but Constance and her friends were determined, as she puts it, to 'Kick him off the hedge'. He was pressed for full information as to what he had been up to, but as the evening wore on he only became 'more and more silent and angry'. His proposal was defeated in the end, and those present at the meeting pledged themselves to secrecy. Constance went to Lissadell for Christmas. She was horrified on her return to find that at the next *Sinn Fein* meeting she was met with a 'freezing and suspicious atmosphere'.

She was hurt and bewildered. At the end Mrs Wyse Power got up (Constance records 'It was an awfully straight and plucky thing for her to do') and said, 'Before we break up, I want to ask you something that none of the men have the courage to ask you. You are being blamed for giving an account of the secret meeting to the press.' Constance continues, 'I was dumbfounded, and the more so, when it was told me that I had given it to Mr Ryan of *The Peasant*, in Tom Clarke's shop.'

Constance was able to establish her innocence. The *Sinn Fein* movement did not benefit from these events. Members drifted away either into the newly born Socialist Party of Ireland or they supported the Parliamentary party. Two events pointed the way ahead: one was the Cork dock strike in the summer of 1909. This spread into a general strike, but it was beaten by the well organized and well financed Employers' Federation; thus, with the aftermath of over-confidence on the part of the employers and bitterness on the part of the employees, creating the climate for the savagely fought Lock-Out Strike in Dublin in 1913. The other event was the return of James Connolly from the United States in July 1910, after which he took over his vital part in the Labour, Nationalist, and Trades Union movements.

CHAPTER 9

Stage and Platform

Wholehearted in all she did, once Constance joined *Sinn Fein* she no longer looked on herself as a loyal subject of King Edward VII. She refused to stand up in public places for the National Anthem, and, further, when staying in England with her sister Mabel's in-laws, the rich, conventionally patriotic Fosters, she scandalized them by declining to drink the King's toast, which they were accustomed to do nightly at the end of dinner. It was decided to discontinue the toast while she was staying in the house. With Casi's drinking habits and Constance's politics they must have been rather trying family guests. But in spite of her identification with *Sinn Fein* and, later, her *Fianna* movement, she continued to play a large part in Casi's theatrical plans and projects. It could be doubted how much of an asset he found her in their newly formed dramatic group, The Independent Dramatic Company. It is said that their discussions at rehearsals with Casi as producer and Constance as leading actress often became extremely heated. In Casi's first full-length play, *The Dilettante*, Constance, as the heroine, Lady Alathea, has to tell her husband that she loves another. Her conception of the scene was to play it with agitation and passion. Casi wanted it taken quietly. They argued at length. Finally he exclaimed, 'Constance, you are quite wrong! When my first wife leave me she come to my room and say "Casimir, I leave you, I love another." '

Casi's first play written for The Independent Dramatic Company, a comedy – *Seymour's Redemption* – was produced in March 1908. It won qualified praise in the columns of the newspaper 'Sinn Fein'. The critic disapproved of both the subject and the characters, but that said, the play was commended for its irony: 'Count Markievicz has shown himself a fine and fiery satirist of the

English boudoir blossom. Is it an impertinence to ask him to cast his eye about him in Dublin for some more familiar folly to satirize?'

Evidently it was, since the next full-scale play – *The Dilettante* – produced for the first time at the Abbey Theatre in December 1908, concerns the effect of a dreamy, frigid, artist-poet, Archie Longhurst, on the married Lady Alathea Dering, and on his private secretary. Lady Alathea becomes widowed during the course of the action, and thus freed, she, so one critic put it, 'presses her suit upon Archie in a fashion that any self-respecting woman in this world would scorn to lend herself to'. (No wonder the same critic said Constance, as Lady Alathea, was successful in a somewhat difficult part.) The scenes were laid in a Scottish shooting-lodge, the library at Longhurst Park (scenery *Louis Quinze*) and the parlour of 'Mrs Watts' cottage'. It all seems far removed from the spirit of the Gaelic League and the plays of peasant life connected with the name of the Abbey Theatre – almost as far as Casimir's first stage appearance in *The Pirates of Penzance*. The one concession Casimir made to the current fashion for plays of the people was a one-act comedy he wrote with a member of The Independent Dramatic Company, Nora Fitzpatrick – *Home Sweet Home* – about a working-class family in Belfast whose daughter brings home a snobbish English fiancé.

At Christmas of the same year Constance showed she still kept unconscious links with her past when she and Casimir organized on the most conventional Anglo-Irish lines the Christmas carnival in Sligo, in order to clear the debt on the Gillooley Memorial Temperance Hall. *The Dilettante* was given, with the original cast, and a play called *After the Fair* (the scene laid in Whirligig Hall). There was also a historical play with Pizarro in Peru as its subject, *The Magnificent Tragedy of Pizarro*, performed by the members of the Sligo Catholic Institute. *Home Sweet Home* was given; there were *tableaux vivants*, songs from the Glee Club, and many side-shows. Not a word of Irish was spoken on stage or platform throughout the week of entertainments. But it is unlikely, given the distance of Sligo from Dublin and the Gaelic League headquarters, that the many local ladies on the committee felt aware of any incongruity.

Constance and Casimir were probably more at ease together at

Lissadell than anywhere else by now. There were no congenial pubs for him to visit, so she saw more of him, and no Nationalists to occupy her time and energy, so he saw more of her. About this time he painted the five life-size, full-length figures on five columns in the dining-room, which remain there today. He painted a self-portrait, his brother-in-law, Mordaunt, the butler, Mr Kilgallon, the keeper, Mr Woods, and the Forester, Mr Campbell. Constance's gentle pretty sister-in-law reigned in her mother's stead. There were many projects on hand inspired by the Agricultural Co-operative movement, blessed by Æ, and of which Constance could not but have approved. There was a bulb farm; there were market gardens growing tomatoes, strawberries and peas; there was a farm specializing in early potatoes; a poultry farm; a dairy; and a school for lace-making and needlework supervised by young Lady Gore-Booth.

By the summer of 1908 Maeve was living with her grandmother. Old Lady Gore-Booth had moved out to make way for the bride. She lived first of all in a rented house, Ballytivnan, before moving to her permanent home, Ardeevan. The year Maeve came to live with her, Lady Gore-Booth engaged a governess, Miss Clayton, to cope with the 'fiery little girl'.

A few years later, when Constance was deeply involved in the sort of politics which at the least completely disorganized normal domestic life, and at the most involved actual physical danger, it does not seem strange that she should have thought her mother's home a better environment for Maeve than Dublin. (There were the *Fianna* boys, as well, swarming over the house.) But in 1908, *Fianna* was a year away, *Sinn Fein* was non-militant and the faithful Banks was still in charge of St Mary's. It is possible that Maeve's education was the problem. She was now seven, and a handful. Stasko had been at a boarding-school since the previous year, so she lacked his companionship and elder-brotherly eye on her at home. No doubt old Lady Gore-Booth pleaded for her favourite grandchild's presence.

It is not surprising that Constance has had her critics in Ireland – the land of the family – for her apparent lack of maternal feeling. In her defence Maud Gonne (no respecter of persons whose integrity she doubted) has stated her conviction that Constance made a deliberate choice between enjoying Maeve's company at home, and the work she felt she had to do for Ireland.

Constance loved children and it was a *great* sacrifice when she sent Maeve to be brought up by her mother because life's evolution had made things too strenuous for the child at home. I have heard people criticize Con for this and speak of her as being a neglectful mother. Nothing could be falser than that, but she was so unselfish she sacrificed everything for Ireland, and in this case did what she thought best for the child. Only people who knew her very closely and intimately knew how deeply she felt, for with all her open exuberant manner and frank way of speaking she was very reserved about her personal feelings and kept things deep hidden in her heart.[1]

Maeve's governess, Miss Clayton, who became through the years like a second mother to her charge, remembers vividly the long journey to her new post. It was August, and she was sitting in the railway carriage waiting for the train to start for Sligo when a lady and a boy hurled themselves in at the very last minute. The boy helped arrange the luggage and soon afterwards stretched himself out and fell asleep. Kind-hearted Miss Clayton, chilly herself in the Irish summer morning, saw that neither the boy nor the lady had an overcoat or rug so she unrolled her holdall and put her own rug over him. Tongues were loosened, and it soon came out that the boy was none other than her new pupil's half-brother, Stasko, while his companion was Mrs Baker of Ballysadare, who was to be his hostess for a fortnight before he went on to his step-grandmother.

On arrival at Sligo Miss Clayton found no one to meet her, so she engaged a jaunting car driven by 'the handsomest and most talkative driver' she had ever known. He told her, amongst much else, that he always read and recited *Hamlet* whenever he was waiting for a customer. Her arrival at the cottage coincided with an invasion of luncheon guests from Lissadell and Classiebawn. During this first lunch Miss Clayton's new charge, in the true tradition of her mother in the dining-room at Lissadell twenty-eight years before, subjected her governess to a 'battery of embarrassing questions, which the grown-ups tried in vain to stem'. However, Miss Clayton quickly became a favourite, and she and Maeve settled down to a 'happy, lively (sometimes turbulent) schoolroom routine'. After a few weeks Constance and Casimir arrived on a visit to see their daughter. The first morning, Miss Clayton, having gone to her room by the time they arrived late the previous evening, was waiting for breakfast in the dining-room when she heard a great commotion in the passage. Constance and Casimir and Maeve burst into the room accompanied by a chorus of barking dogs. Constance silenced the din, walked up to Miss Clayton, and said, 'So you are the hated Sassenach, are you? If you think you are going to have any influence over my daughter you jolly well are not!* Alas, for Constance, it did not need Miss Clayton, who was completely ignorant of Irish politics, to turn Maeve against her mother's activities. The adoring grandmother was a quite sufficiently strong nucleus of anti-rebel opinion.

The rest of this visit, the pattern of many, was filled with picnics and expeditions, including climbing Knocknarea in order to place stones on Queen Maeve's cairn. Maeve recited Eva's poem,

I have seen Maeve of the Battles wandering over the hills
  And I know that the deed that is in my heart is her deed,
And my soul is blown about by the wild wind of her will,
  For always the living must follow whither the dead would lead –
I have seen Maeve of the Battles wandering over the hill.

Miss Clayton photographed the party with her Brownie camera. She noticed how much Constance was loved by everyone at Lissadell, and how effortlessly she played her part in all the typical local events smiled on by the big house: choir teas; parties for the schoolchildren; servants' balls. Constance's roles as 'Miss Con' and the beloved 'Madame' of the Dublin poor were not so far apart, after all; each demanded goodwill (the *bonté* characteristic of her and for which we have no word in English) and the imaginative courage to join in the lives of those whose deprivations might have seemed a constant reproach.

A friend and colleague of later years, the writer, Maire Comerford, says that Constance was unique in her power to draw the poor and the uneducated into her own life without the smallest strain on either side. She discovered and fostered hidden talents especially in the plastic arts, she made anyone who wanted a holiday free of her cottage at Balally. She encouraged city dwellers to garden, and in order to make the first steps in flower-growing easy she gave all beginners cuttings of white Arabis, which she knew would grow and ramp under the worst conditions. She had chosen so well that soon her protégés' gardens were choked with the plant,

* Private information from Miss Clayton.

and enough Arabis was grown in Dublin and Belfast back streets to cover the Crystal Palace. Although she appeared to some observers to be erratic and scatter-brained, she was, in fact, perfectly consistent all through her life in her humanitarianism and her love of the arts and of nature. The woman who gave Arabis cuttings to city dwellers who had never gardened was not far removed from the girl who spent the whole of an April afternoon in 1892 planting coloured hyacinths amongst the Arabis at Lissadell. The woman who worked long hours for many weeks to feed the families of Connolly's strikers in 1913 was close to the girl who took food from the well-stocked Lissadell larder when the coast was clear in order to give it to the sick or hungry.

At Balally she was much loved by the country people, who said of her 'she may be quare, but the Count-éss is a rale lady'. The son of her great friend, Mrs O'Connell Fitz-Simon, to whom I am indebted for the Balally peoples' comment, also remembers Constance leaving his parents' house barefoot on the many summer evenings she spent dining there. She would wake him by her singing, which she maintained was essential in order to placate the fairies and the leprechauns who haunted the woods.

Here at Lissadell in 1908 charades were a great feature of house-party life, as in the past. Acting was another of the strands which persisted in Constance's life. It is sad, in view of her tenacity, to relate that none of those who remember her on the boards or in the drawing-room can say that they found it possible to admire her performances. Miss Clayton recalls that Maeve as she grew older was a better actress than her mother. Constance was unable to sink her personality in her roles; she did best when she could identify herself naturally with the character like with her part as Norah in Casi's later play, *The Memory of the Dead*.

In surviving photographs of Casimir's first ambitious play, *The Dilettante*, there can be seen the glossy, black, form of a peacefully sleeping cocker spaniel. He was the first of a line of much loved dogs – the consolation for the lack of horses. Jack, which was the cocker's name, came into Constance's life when Casimir was painting a view from Viceregal Lodge over Phoenix Park, for Lord Dudley. (Jack, therefore, was pre-revolutionary period.) The Under-Secretary of State's wife, Lady MacDonnell, gave Casimir the tiny puppy for Constance. He arrived home with it in his pocket where it celebrated its arrival by making a mess. Soon after Jack had a companion in Goggles, a large mustard-coloured bulldog, who belonged to Casi. Jack followed Constance everywhere, and this included her frequent sorties on her bicycle in and around Dublin. Jack met a sad and early end through a heart attack from over-exercise combined with over-eating. Perhaps a fitting death for a Castle dog. He was replaced by Poppet, a brown cocker who became very well known in Dublin.

Casimir was of the stuff of which anecdotes are made. There is the one about when Constance took him to a reception where only tea and coffee flowed. Casi stood it for some time, but finally went up to her in the crowd and said, 'Constance, tell them I *drink*'. And there is the one about the Dublin School of Art fancy-dress ball when he arrived as a French revolutionary with his shirt thrown back in order to show his large, bloodstained chest. The secretary of the school objected and asked him to leave. Constance saw there was trouble, so she left her partner and tried to placate the outraged secretary by fastening Casi's shirt together with a safety-pin. But *pudeur* was still unappeased. A major scene then developed. The secretary continued to ask Casi to leave. The secretary of the actual dance (a student) intervened at this point. He stopped the band, called the dancers together and made a short speech explaining the problem. He suggested that Casimir or the school secretary should be asked to leave and that the company should choose by vote. Needless to say Casi won overwhelmingly, to general acclaim.

A play, *Rival Stars*, written by Casi in the following year shows that he was more sensitive than he chose to appear to his cronies. The subject is a young artist who is drifting apart spiritually from his wife – a reflection, surely, of his own marriage. There is also a speech given to the hero, and later cut from the play, which reveals another sort of sensibility in the writer – this time in his other profession of a painter.

When one paints a life's picture as I have done, one lives in one's studio a life with it. Then it's gone from the studio and it leaves behind the sort of feeling that people must have when the coffin of someone dear to them is taken out of the death chamber. One's picture is taken to be shamelessly exposed to the indifferent, unsympathetic gaze of the crowd who aimlessly throng the exhibition halls. In the studio one dares not cast one's eyes towards the familiar corner of the studio, where the dark silhouette of the empty easel, like a gallows, is drawn against the glare of the window; in such moments one feels a kind of stupidity and irresistible weariness overpowering one, and one begins to ask one-self why should one paint at all.

Besides painting, playwriting and tippling, Casimir founded a very exclusive fencing club in Dublin. He brought a fencing-master over from France. Small, dapper, fiery Monsieur Dain still to be seen in Casimir's striking portrait of him – thick of hair and mous-tache, dashing in appearance with his dark eyes and air of control-led vigour – had a tragic death. He arrived in Dublin with his mistress and was surprised to discover that her position would be equivocal in Catholic Ireland. Casimir arranged their marriage, which benefited Monsieur Dain since his bride brought him a small factory as dowry. The fencing club collapsed in due course, chiefly because the wives of the members, headed by Constance, thought too much time was spent in drinking as well as fencing. Monsieur Dain went back to France with his wife and took charge of the factory. One morning he assembled all the workmen in the yard, shook hands with each, and dropped down dead. He had taken poison because he thought his wife had betrayed him[2].

Casimir's best-known play *The Memory of the Dead* came on at the Abbey theatre in April 1909. The subject was after Constance's own heart, and since the play was a complete departure from Casimir's previous ironic comedies it seems likely that her influence had been at work in it. The story is of the effect of the abortive '98 rising on a country family. The heroine, Norah, a role tailor-made for and played by Constance, has two suitors, one a hot-headed Nationalist orator and the other a cool, cautious mili-tant. Norah marries the cool militant, Dermot, who takes her into his counsels before going off to meet the French. He does not return, but a fleeing French officer comes to the farmhouse seeking a guide to Donegal. Norah offers to go herself. On the journey, by one of those coincidences allowed to an author at the time, she meets her husband who takes the officer on the rest of his way. Dermot vanishes, is suspected of treachery by the neighbours (but not by Norah) and finally returns as an escaped prisoner of the English and dying from wounds dealt by pursuing soldiers. Over his dead body his wife passionately proclaims her resolution to bring up their child in the Nationalist creed of his father. It was an openly propagandist play, well received by the critics and the audience at the time. Constance came in for a good deal of attention. For once she had found (or created for herself) a part into which she could pour all her own emotions. Her interpretation of it was found to be full of grace, earnestness, sensibility. She was thought to be 'a charming boy guide' (a feat at the age of forty-two). 'Countess Markievicz made a very winning Norah Doyle,' wrote another critic, 'emphasizing that mixture of womanly tenderness and love, and yet, at the same time, able to be up and doing when duty and patriotism called.' A few years later a critic wrote that she possessed 'a voice with tears'. In 1909, only the paper *Irish Society* put out a paw to scratch. After praising the versatility of Casimir in writing such a play at all the notice goes on to remark, 'Countess Markievicz took a small part, which, in her hands, attained a prominence not given it by the author.' Another frank critic, in a letter to the newspaper '*Sinn Fein*', held that she had a very good idea of the part but was 'all fits and starts'.

In the same week a satiric comedy on middle-class hypocrisy by Casimir called *Mary* was produced. Constance had no part in this play.

In the same year as these theatrical ventures took place, Constance began to sever her ties with gracious living by letting St Mary's. She never lived there again. The pretty house, the lawn and greenhouse, the stables, the studio built on for Casimir – all were let for ninety pounds a year. Constance took another house in Rathgar – 9 St Edwards Terrace – for sixty pounds a year. It seemed a good transaction to her for she owned St Mary's freehold, but for the sake of thirty pounds a year she lost all the benefit of the many improvements she had made to St Mary's. A few months after the move she plunged into a new experiment in living which caused great amusement to the Dublin wits.

It all began with the written word. Bulmer Hobson lent Constance the account by E. T. Craig of how as a young man he had helped an Anglo-Irish landlord, Arthur Vandeleur, turn his poverty-racked estate of Ralahine in Co Clare into an agricultural co-operative society run for the mutual benefit of landlord and tenants. At first all went well; Ralahine even achieved a modest renown. By the end of three years the formerly derelict estate of

618 acres produced 6,000 stones of wheat, 3,000 stones of barley, and quantities of oats, butter, pork and beef. Then one morning the community was appalled to read in the newspaper that its landlord had fled, having lost his fortune at the gaming-table. A distant cousin obtained a bankruptcy order against the estate, and the courts refused to acknowledge the rights of the commune to own property. Craig nearly had a nervous breakdown. In the years that followed two of Vandeleur's daughters died of TB and ten years later his wife died of a broken heart.

In spite of the débâcle in which the experiment ended, Constance was fascinated by the idea of the Ralahine Commune. It became a main topic of conversation between herself and Bulmer Hobson, Sean MacGarry, and Helena Molony. In amongst their *Fianna* work they played with the idea of starting up such a community themselves. At first it seemed to Helena Molony, who was the youngest of the group, just a joke since none of them had any land or money. But Constance, becoming more and more bitten with the idea, pointed out that she had £350 a year, that she was tired of living in Rathmines (Casi was away) and that because she had given up all social life she was exactly ready to launch into any project that would help her *Fianna* boys. She would find a house to rent with some land and all would follow as summer succeeds spring. Bulmer Hobson suggested they should have a co-operative market garden, Helena Molony offered the portion of money she was expecting to get from the sale of a small estate of her mother's through the Land Court. It was decided to have a paid helper, a graduate of Glasnevin Agricultural College. All that remained was to find the house.

Rash schemes are seldom endangered by the lack of opportunity to undertake them. A house was duly found: Belcamp Park in the district of Raheny.

The house, and its present 120 acres, lies on the landward side of the main Dublin–Malahide Road from Raheny, which is now a built-up area round the core of the old village. Here the inhabitants can still walk under the shade of ilex trees, and smell the sea in their streets. Belcamp Park stands in gentle, wooded country, like Berkshire; it is only when you look towards the humped silhouette of Howth that you know you are in Ireland. The house itself, a sober, elegant, Georgian building, colour-washed pink, stands in a district of eighteenth-century gentlemen's residences, their parklands planted with the limes and beeches and chestnuts that remind the Anglo-Irish of their fellow landlords' demesnes across the Channel. Opposite Belcamp Park is Belcamp House, colour-washed yellow, with its two shallow bays on the front facing the brick piers which flank the entrance drive to its neighbour. A mile down the road is an earlier dwelling associated with Dean Swift, built of narrow bricks and with four small chimneys and a square roof lantern. A few miles away in the other direction at Balgriffin the painter Nathaniel Hone lived in another sober, elegant, Georgian mansion, and used to entertain the Markieviczs to dinner when they were reputed to have eaten like wolves.

At first sight the house and its seven acres must have seemed a feasible proposition. There were upwards of twelve bedrooms, there was the compact stable yard, there was a large walled garden; the district was calm, rural, secluded, and yet within easy reach of Dublin. The only puzzling factor is exactly how Constance equated herself, her friends, and the *Fianna* boys with the work-hungry labourers of Co Clare for whose benefit the Ralahine experiment was started.

The move took place in July, when the country was at its most verdant, with bird song and ripening fruit in the walled gardens, and the spell of the long summer evenings of Ireland, which when they are windless are an enticement to dreaming and indolence because the light seems so suspended between the poles of day and dark that the world is as translucent as a mirror painting. Constance's hopes were high, but disillusionment set in early. The long neglected land was unmanageable, the work in the under-furnished draughty house interminable. The *Fianna* boys made complication through their city-bred notions that anything in the country was there for the taking including milk and hens. The bewildered Stasko arrived back in Dublin for his summer holidays and was told that Constance had moved out 'somewhere at Raheny'. Casi's return from the Ukraine in the late autumn caused a crisis in the new-born community.

I have great trouble to find this house but at last I find it and I send away the cabby. I find the house at the end of the avenue, all dark, all silent. I knock and knock but not a sound. I go around the back and I call out Constance! No sound. I come around to the front and I knock and call out Constance! After a while a dirty little ragamuffin puts his head out and say 'Who da?' I say 'I want to see Countess Markievicz'.

He go away and I wait. No sound. I knock again and I call 'Constance!' Another window go up and another dirty little ragamuffin say 'Who da?' I say 'I am Count Markievicz and I want to see the Countess Markievicz'. He go away and I wait. No sound. Another window go up and another dirty little ragamuffin say 'Who da?'. I say 'I am Count Markievicz and I want to see Countess Markievicz.' I hear much scuffling and running and at last the door open. It is all dark but I see Constance. 'It's very dark, Constance,' I say. 'We have only one lamp,' she says, 'and the gardener is reading with that.' We go into the drawing-room and there I find the gardener with his legs on the mantlepiece, and he is smoking a dirty, filthy shag tobacco. He does not stand up when I go in. I say, 'I am hungry. Cannot I have some food?' And they scuffle and they whisper again while I talk to the gardener. At last they bring me cold meat and bread and butter. That is how I return to my home.[2]

Casi was extremely put out to find Helena Molony, and the 'gardener' (Donald Hannigan, a graduate of Glasnevin Agricultural College) as part of his household. The Arts Club, where he immediately repaired, rang with his stories. But he did more than crown Constance with a dunce's cap. He badgered Donald Hannigan so persistently about the lack of financial return, it is said, that, rendered desperate, the hapless gardener felled a mature holly tree and sold it in Dublin for thirty shillings. Constance was subsequently asked by the landlord to pay five pounds compensation for this transaction.

Casi enlisted Æ's help in order to kill the scheme before all was lost. Briefed by Æ, Casi turned mealtimes at Raheny into series of inquisitions as to details of the running costs and profit and loss. At first Constance refused to take him seriously, but Bulmer Hobson did. It was not long before he opted out of what he now saw to be a labour of Sisyphus and went back to Belfast. Constance began to lose heart. Donald Hannigan left. Constance implored Helena Molony to stay in the house and help her carry on until she could dispose of the three-year lease (at £100 a year). They had only been there three months.

Once the scheme was dead and Bulmer Hobson, one of the original guarantors, had retired from it, there were some painful financial discussions to be undergone. Helena Molony found herself responsible for half instead of a third of the liability, which included Donald Hannigan's wages, and the cost of removing Constance's furniture from Rathgar. Helena Molony eventually managed to get rid of the rest of the lease (which by this time had a year to run) making the total liability £220. In July 1911 Constance moved into furnished rooms at 15 Lower Mount Street where she lived until 1912 when she took Surrey House – which soon became notorious as a hornet's nest of Nationalists and was a regular port of call for the British Secret Service 'G' men.

Life went on in spite of the fiasco of the Raheny experiment. During the months based at Belcamp Park *The Memory of the Dead* was produced in Castlerea, Castlebar, Kilkenny, Westport, Roscommon, and repeated in Dublin at the Queen's theatre. It was the best remembered of all Casimir's productions, and Norah was the role in which Constance was thought to excel.

In December 1911 The Independent Dramatic Company put on a new, poetic play of Eva's, *The Buried Life of Deirdre*, also the charming comedy, *Eleanor's Enterprise*, by the Reverend J. O. Hannay, rector of Westport, County Mayo, better known as George A. Birmingham. Constance took the part of the heroine, Eleanor, just down from Girton, who sets herself to elevate the lives of some Connaught peasants. Eleanor is a Shavian girl entangled in a Somerville and Ross cats-cradle. Constance enjoyed the part, but her candid friends thought she was better as Norah. Very early in the run the audience was treated to one of those contretemps which make amateur theatricals so enjoyable. Casi, ever a realist in his productions, had introduced a small (but obstinate) donkey into the second act, when Eleanor has moved in to live with the family she plans to help and reform. One of the leading actors was irked by the donkey's presence, and having failed to get Casimir's permission for the donkey to be banished from the production, he decided to lead it off the stage himself. The donkey resisted, the bridle came away in the actor's hand and the actor fell down in the wings, to the intense delight of the audience. Casi watching backstage remarked, 'Damn good actor, donkey. Only one ass on the stage now.'

So far as politics and the *Fianna* were concerned the months at Belcamp showed a proliferation of Constance's activities. She was not the woman to be discouraged by a setback. In the first August of the ill-fated Raheny experiement she held a large *Fianna* camp where Gaelic sports were played and a 'thorough Irish National atmosphere throughout was maintained'. Later in the same month she presided over the first full-scale annual conference of the *Fianna* – in the Mansion House in Dublin, by kind permission of the Mayor. It had taken her only a year to achieve official status for her lonely enterprise, ridiculed or frowned upon at the outset by colleagues who had a hundred reasons for discounting her sincerity and value as a human being. Try as she might to sink her Anglo-Irish identity in the troubled sea of Nationalism, it was not until she, too, suffered at the hands of the British, as had the native Irish, that she could achieve the serenity of the accepted. She must be seen now as that most isolated of beings – a rebel from her own class who had not yet been given the opportunity to prove her ultimate worth. Irish political relationships were bedevilled by suspicions of those who had come over from the other side of the fence. Even Maud Gonne had once been accused by a smear journalist of being in the pay of the Castle. (Arthur Griffith horse-whipped him with a sjambok and got sent to prison for it.) Erskine Childers, another notable English convert to Irish Nationalism, was always mistrusted by Griffith, who even went so far as to suspect him of being in the English Secret Service and an *agent provocateur*. Constance herself, when her Republicanism had carried her to extremes which involved total hostility to Griffith, chides him in an article for ever suspecting Childers' good faith, when his own grandfather was supposed to have come from Wales.

While Constance was still living at Belcamp Park she came under a new influence which led her straight to James Connolly, and with him the thoughts and actions which drew her energies, her idealism, her pluck, to one true end. As with the first illumination in the cottage at Balally, the means was a newspaper. She read, she says, in her recollections, about a man – a man with an idea which filled her with 'hope, admiration, sympathy and delight'. The man was the labour leader Jim Larkin, and the idea was that Irish Labour should not be controlled from England. Constance wrote,

Here was a man who had the brains and the courage to demonstrate by his actions that International Socialism does not stand for the merging of our identity with that of England . . . but stands for free nations or national units who, on a basis of absolute equality, associate together for the purpose of obtaining and holding for the people nationally and for the nations internationally a noble civilization that should be based on National Governments by the people and for the people . . .[3]

The fact that Constance only had to read a newspaper item about Larkin to be filled with so much enthusiasm that she thereupon decided to bicycle into Dublin to attend a meeting planned in his honour shows that she was already thinking as a socialist. Through her Daughters of Erin and *Fianna* contacts she must have been brought face to face with the miseries of the Dublin poor. The poor she had always known but the rural poor with all their deprivations had the wider setting of the countryside to assimilate them. There was the sheer factor of space and the always recurring beauties brought by the passage of the seasons; for a country-woman like Constance it must have seemed less horrible to be poor in sight of the sea and the mountains, of forests and streams, of spring and harvest and the still frosts of winter when the turf fires never went out, than the total, unredeemed squalor of city conditions. The poor of Dublin lived in their beautiful city like woodlice under a statue. The soberly, elegant façades of those run-down squares and streets which had been abandoned by the respectable and well-heeled, housed an accumulation of hopeless degradation unmatched in Europe. Twenty thousand families in Dublin owned only one room – and the family could be up to eleven in number. The honorary treasurer of the NSPCC described in a report a family background typical of many.

One room, measuring about 16 feet square, with a small closet off it, contains absolutely no furniture. The family of nine (7 children) sleeps on the floor, on which there was not enough straw for a cat, and no covering of any kind whatever. The children were poorly clad; one was wrapped in a rag of a kind, and his only other clothing was a very dirty loin cloth. The utensils were a zinc bucket, can, a few mugs and jam pots for drinking. Rent 2/3. Wages in late weeks 4/6. Maximum for some time past 12/– . . .
In another house is a room 12 feet by 15, one window, very bad light and air. It has a small closet. The family consists of a widow and six children. Bed, stretcher and a few sticks of furniture. Rent 2/9 . . .[4]

James Connolly's daughter, Nora in *Portrait of a Rebel Father*, described her experience of housing conditions when she was electioneering.

How can people bear to live in such places? Why don't they burn them down? I went up pitch black stairs, my feet slipping and squelching in the filth on them; some wide, some of them with steps missing. And the smell . . . the smell . . . one woman had six children, all too small to help her so her husband had to carry every drop of water up and down.

The infant mortality rate was the highest of any city in the British Isles. Those who survived ran wild in the streets, married young, and perpetuated the dreadful cycle of ignorance and prostration. If the children went to school they arrived fasting and left fasting, since there were no school meals. (In the winter of 1910 James Connolly approached Maud Gonne and the Daughters of Erin and Mrs Sheehy Skeffington, founder of the Women's Franchise League, to start a campaign to give school meals to necessitous children.)

Labour in Ireland was dominated by its ties with the English Trades Union movement. Little support had been given to Labour by *Sinn Fein* because it was not separatist, and because Griffith personally did not think on socialist lines. There was, too, the factor of the Belfast labour organizations which had strong ethnical and religious links with England. It was Larkin and Connolly – the demagogue and the thinker – who saw that Irish Socialism must stand for something more dynamic than internationalism, and loyalty to the British Trades Union movement. In the summer of 1911 Connolly wrote,

The ILP in Belfast believes that the Socialist movement in Ireland must perforce remain a dues-paying organic part of the British Socialist movement . . . whereas the SPI (Socialist Party of Ireland) maintain that the relations between Socialism in Ireland and Great Britain should be fraternal and not organic, and should operate by exchange of literature and speakers rather than by attempts to treat as one, two people of whom one has for 700 years nurtured an unending martyrdom rather than admit the unity or surrender its national identity. The Socialist Party of Ireland considers itself the only international party in Ireland, since its conception of internationalism is that of a free federation of free peoples, whereas that of the Belfast branches of the ILP seems scarcely distinguishable from imperialism, the merging of a subjugated peoples in the political system of their conquerors.[5]

On that 'scorching' Sunday in October 1910 when Constance bicycled in to Dublin to add her voice to Larkin's welcome, he had just been released from prison after serving three months of a year's sentence. His sentence had come as a result of his action in breaking away from the English Transport Workers Union and collecting fees and dues from Cork dockers for the aid of Dublin Carters, who were affiliated with the Irish Transport Workers Union in Dublin. He was brought to court for handing over dues to the Irish instead of the English. His imprisonment made him the hero of the hour.

When Constance arrived at the scene of the welcome meeting she was recognized in the crowd by a friend of hers – Mr McGowan – who invited her on to the lorry where the speaker stood.

Sitting there listening to Larkin, I realized that I was in the presence of something that I had never come across before, some great primeval force rather than a man. A tornado, a storm-driven wave, the rush into life of spring, and the blasting breath of autumn, all seemed to emanate from the power that spoke. It seemed as if his personality caught up, assimilated, and threw back to that vast crowd that surrounded him every emotion that swayed them, every pain and joy that they had ever felt made articulate and sanctified. Only the great elemental force that is in all crowds had passed into his nature for ever.

Taller than most men, every line of him was in harmony with his personality. Not so much working man as primeval man . . . a Titan who might have been moulded by Michaelangelo or Rodin . . .[6]

They became friends. From then on the *Fianna* shared quarters with the ITWU first of all in Beresford Place, and later in the more grandiose building taken over by Larkin – Liberty Hall, near the Customs House and looking on to the Liffey. Constance's photograph together with Connolly's portrait hangs today in the modern skyscraper which succeeded the old Liberty Hall and which is still the headquarters of the ITWU.

The occasion of the State Visit to Ireland of the newly crowned King George V and Queen Mary in the summer of 1911, brought Constance the kind of publicity which proved to her friends and her enemies that she was in deadly earnest.* The various Nationalist organizations were much concerned with the question of an anti-royal welcome. Black flags, not Union Jacks was the type of bunting they had in mind. A committee was formed representing all the Nationalist groups. It was through this committee that Constance first met Padraic Pearse, who used to arrive bursting

* She had marked her attitude towards the period of mourning for Edward VII by appearing at the theatre in a bright red velvet dress.

with suggestions, and accompanied by the voluble, mercurial professor, Thomas MacDonagh, who taught at Pearse's school, St Enda's.

One of the first points at issue was the official plan for the Dublin Corporation to meet the Royal procession at the historic boundary at Leeson street bridge, complete with mace, keys of the city, and loyal address, thereby confirming in Nationalist eyes the subjugation of a race. The Nationalists decided to ensure that the visit should have, in Constance's words, 'no adverse effect on Ireland's national spirit'. The *Fianna* owned a small, old-fashioned, printing press. A handbill was drafted calling on the citizens of Dublin to rally in protest against their corporation 'paying homage to, and humbling themselves before, a foreign King'. Helena Molony and her helpers worked all night to get the leaflets printed. A meeting of the corporation was besieged by recipients of the leaflets and by *Sinn Fein* adherents. The militants did not agitate in vain, for the corporation was in the end obliged to abandon that particular ceremony of welcome.

There was a deep division of opinion on the committee as to the most effective forms of non-welcome. Griffith was opposed in general to any form of impromptu soap-box oratory, thinking it would detract from the dignity of *Sinn Fein*. A great friend of his, recently returned from America – the O'Rahilly – a delightful man, whose attributes of humour, tolerance and sanity were much needed in the movement, once replied to Griffith when the latter said 'Really, O'Rahilly, we must stand on our dignity', 'Well, if we go on standing on our dignity much longer, we soon won't have anything left to stand on.'[7] It was the O'Rahilly's idea to make a huge scroll inscribed with the historic words 'Thou art not conquered yet, dear land', to ask for permission from the paving committee of Dublin Corporation to sink two poles at the foot of Grafton Street (the Corporation thinking, innocently, that the purpose was to celebrate the royal visit) and thus to demonstrate that celebration was not the aim of the Nationalists. The O'Rahilly, 'one of the neatest and best dressed men in Ireland' so Constance described him, crouched on the floor in the dust and pencilled out the letters himself. The scroll was secretly conveyed to where the poles were stored. It was erected in drizzling rain, and its presence made its point, before the authorities pulled it down. Constance, on her way to her cottage at Balally, scribbled a hasty note to the O'Rahilly to tell him that the masts were in the gutter, 'all the black torn off ... Can we not put them up again in *broad* daylight?'

Another activity of the Nationalists consisted of a series of meetings held at night while their Majesties were dining. Constance describes one meeting in her recollections when the retiring, youthful Sean MacDearmod spoke.

It was already dark, a perfect evening, and the torches around the brake cast orange and red lights, deepening and intensifying the look of excitement on the faces of those gathered to listen. The old House of Parliament loomed gigantic and mysterious through the wreaths of smoke. Sean stood up in the brake. His white face, high above the glare of the torches, glimmered like a pale star against the deep greeny-blue sky. Tired and wan, with his great deep-set eyes, it was almost ghostly... At all times you liked to look at his face, it was so spiritual as well as being beautiful. Standing above me in the brake I felt there was a young saint, some reincarnation of one who had suffered much, and who had known torture and death ... the crowd stopped fidgeting, caught by the spell. When he spoke his voice floated out to us tremulous with emotion. Passionately he called on the people of Dublin, in the midst of all the flaunting of flags and the tramp of marching processions to remember the mighty dead who had died for Ireland. He called to our mind Robert Emmet, who had passed that very street many a time, and who had died for Ireland not a mile away in Thomas Street. One by one he named our martyrs and heroes, and each name dropped on the expectant crowd like molten flame, penetrating deep into each heart, and touching long forgotten emotions till no eye was dry.[8]

The Nationalists had also been busy pulling down Union Jacks. After MacDearmod's moving speech that evening Constance pulled out a 'huge paper parcel' which contained one of the flags the Nationalists had captured from the lawn of Leinster House. Her aim was to burn it in public. She had cut it in two because it was too large to handle. and now she tried to light it with matches. She had not realized that bunting does not burn. Match after match spluttered out while the flag remained halved, but otherwise intact. Then the police intervened. They wanted the flag but the crowd thought they were after Constance. The police seized one end of the flag (she had tied the other round her waist) and began to pull at it. The crowd, by now thoroughly entering into the spirit of the thing, seized hold of Constance. She fell back into their midst, so they thought they had rescued her. Cheers resounded, until the police arrested Mr McArdle, which damped everyone's spirits.

Constance, undaunted as always, then asked a boy to get some paraffin. With this reinforcement she had more success with her bonfire, and the spectators, she says, were suitably impressed. But even so the bunting resisted her incendiarism and the badly charred, but still intact, fragments were cut up and distributed to the crowd at the next meeting at Smithfield.

During this meeting Helena Molony 'slipped away to look for stones' to throw at the illuminations. All through this evening there had been a conflict of opinion between those who wanted to avoid a row and those who wanted to provoke one. Constance was baulked by 'Mr Milroy and his group' from driving the brake slap through a police cordon, but Helena Molony succeeded so well with her stones that she was arrested. After some difficulty, because the police would not accept bail from a woman, Constance succeeded in getting her out of the cells. By this time it was two o'clock in the morning.

Dublin was asleep. The old grey houses stood calm and cool in the tinted twilight. Flaring torches, charging police and hysterical crowds seemed like a dream of purgatory. Peace floated in the air. We passed on the Quays, and looked down the shimmering river to where the Custom House raised its stately dome. During the summer weather the day never quite dies in Ireland. The hidden sun slips across the pole to his place of resurrection in the east, and the cool mists catch his rays and dapple the world with pale rainbow tints. It is Ireland's hour of beauty, when all the sordidness and sadness slips from her, and when she lies around us simplified and beautified in the coloured dusk. Lazy seagulls lay like pearls on the golden waters, luminous with ripples in delicate blues and mauves. We paused to give a loving look at all this beauty that is Ireland, and passed on.[9]

They were exhausted and extremely hungry, so when they saw the lights of the coffee stall in Beresford Place they thought they had found manna at last. But they were told that the stall could not serve women. It was not until those in charge knew that it was Helena Molony who was hungry after her night's work that they relented and put the best food they had before her and Constance.

There was also a division of opinion in the committee as to the best form of non-welcome on the great day itself. One school of thought headed by Griffith maintained that at all costs a riot must be avoided, another, to which Constance subscribed, held that it would be a good thing to provoke the police into attacking the demonstrators thereby associating the Royals in the eyes of the public with unpleasantness and ,violence. Griffith's group won and it was decided, in co-operation with the IRB, to organize a large expedition to Bodenstown, to Wolfe Tone's grave (the public holiday decreed for the royal visit happening to fall near the anniversary of his death) thus, it was thought by those who supported the idea, boycotting the visit in a dignified manner and denying any hotheads the chance to kick up a shindy. But The Daughters of Erin which, Constance says, was 'always in favour of the most extreme action possible' thought differently. They imagined they had brought Bulmer Hobson over to their side. The Daughters and the older members of the *Fianna* decided to print handbills and distribute them to the crowd just as the procession was passing. (Bulmer Hobson left for Belfast. When he returned on the great day, he, so Constance scathingly wrote of him in 1923, 'joined the Bodenstown crowd. He was one of those who preferred the limelight and laurels to be won by a fierce speech at a rebel's graveside to the possibility of getting a hammering from the police or being arrested.')

Constance, unlike Bulmer Hobson, did not 'join the Bodenstown crowd'.

The most adventurous among us were distributed around Trinity College, the Unionist stronghold, inside the railings of which platforms and seats had been erected; I was on the corner of Nassau Street with a young man. Most of the crowd had Union Jacks and were very loyal. We had a black flag, and as soon as the procession was audible to our listening ears we produced it and began to hand out our bills to the crowd. We timed it well, for just as the first carriage came along the row started. It was a very tame one. An irate old 'gentleman' started whacking me with the stick on which his flag was mounted, but my back is pretty stiff and the stick broke almost at once.[10]

In spite of the efforts of the Nationalists, the King and Queen appear to have been well pleased with their visit. The King sent a telegram of thanks to Lord Aberdeen from the royal yacht at Holyhead saying the 'hearty cheers of Irish people' were still ringing in his and the Queen's ears.

But perhaps Constance should have the last word,

So the King passed – passed through Dublin, through the blood-red laneways that had been built in his honour. Red streamers floated from pole to pole, and red paper flowers danced in the wind, red flags, red draperies, red carpets everywhere. But he passed, too, through sad grey slums, where the sorrowful eyes of a dispossessed people huddled together in misery, looked out and wondered; looked at all the splendour and force, and saw nothing but red. Red through a grey mist . . .[11]

CHAPTER 10

Friends and Enemies

The King's visit was over. The authorities could congratulate themselves that he left Ireland with the impression that the people were united in loyalty to him. There were a few scores to settle. Helena Molony was brought before a magistrate in South Dublin police court and charged with breaking a shop-window which contained a picture of the king. She was sentenced to pay a fine of forty shillings or go to prison for a month. According to Constance, she 'hurled defiance' at the judge amidst a 'wild scene of enthusiasm', and chose the prison sentence – thus becoming the first woman of her time to go to jail for Ireland.

That day there followed a small, practical contretemps when Helena Molony's friends wanted to get her a pot of tea, and were refused by the Four Courts Hotel, although Constance, she says, offered to buy the teapot itself. A friend stepped in and provided refreshments, after which the prisoner was borne off in a Black Maria, sped on her way by cheering crowds. She served a fortnight of her sentence, and then to her surprise (and indignation as a dedicated Nationalist) she found her fine had been paid. She accused the Lord Mayor of doing this to put a stop to 'the agitation', but she discovered later that it had been none other than Anna Parnell, who wanted her freed in order to continue her work of editing *The History of the Ladies' Land League*.[1]

On Sunday, 6 August 1911, both Helena Molony and Mr McArdle (who, it will be remembered, was arrested when the police had the tug-of-war with Constance and the Union Jack) were released. A meeting of welcome was organized to take place in the street which was the scene of many skirmishes: Beresford Place. The Socialist Party of Ireland turned out in force. It was they who provided the lorry on which perched the platform party – including Constance.

We sat in the lorry and faced the quiet, orderly crowd. The dark forms of the police hovered ominously around. Miss Molony was speaking when the police took exception to something that she said and charged the platform. I stood up from where I was sitting at the table scribbling notes, and a policeman, standing in front of the lorry made a grab at my ankles. I shuffled back, another seized me from behind; I supposed that he had climbed up on the lorry from the other side. He picked me up and literally threw me into the arms of a policeman standing on the ground in front, who luckily caught me, so I was not hurt. I never was so taken by surprise in my life, the whole attack was so sudden and unexpected. I only remember the flashing of white batons, the stampeding crowd, a couple of girl friends who stood firm and spoke to me as I was dragged by two enormous policemen across Beresford Place towards Store Street Station, and one great little *Fianna* boy, who followed me the whole way kicking wildly at the huge legs of my captors, and shouting 'Ah, you devils, ah, you brutes'. Miss Molony and I met again in the Police Station, and we found that we were the only people arrested.[2]

Constance was accused of throwing dust and pebbles at the police, but she insisted both then and later that she had only been quietly taking notes. She and Helena Molony were kept in the police station all day, cheered by the voices of the crowd outside, and stayed with presents of food, of grapes, and of two roses.

Griffith, wishing to make it a test case on the question of freedom of speech, persuaded the two women to instruct counsel to defend them. Constance wrote later that she thought it would have been far better propaganda if she had conducted her own defence, since 'Lawyers are always far too anxious to win a case, and are not of the same political opinions as oneself, and are far too much inclined to respect police and magistrates and absurd laws.'[3]

Constance was found guilty of throwing dust and pebbles at the police, and Helena Molony of 'degrading the king in speeches in Beresford Place', but no sentence was passed. It was Constance's opinion that higher authority had intervened, seeing that a prison sentence would help rather than hinder the Nationalist cause. But in any case she had won her spurs. She was now a Nationalist for all the world to see. But for Casi it was different. The more goodwill she made for herself with her militant friends the less hope he had of portrait commissions from the Castle set, or even a carefree social life. That summer he planned to take Stasko on a visit to the Ukraine, but he changed his mind when he discovered that he would have to pay a fine of four pounds for every year of Stasko's absence from Russia. Stasko was sent instead to the Fosters at Falmouth. Maeve's life was now completely supervised by her grandmother. It was obviously sensible and realistic of Constance, once she had made the decision, to give her mother a free hand, but it is impossible to imagine that a child whose mother lives permanently only a hundred or so miles away would not at moments resent the separation. Constance was not the one to keep in touch through cosy, chatty weekly letters, although undoubtedly she loved Maeve in her own way; and she was a most tender stepmother to Stasko. There is the revealing anecdote of Ardeevan when Constance had just left after a visit during which she romped, chattered and quarrelled with her daughter as though she were her elder sister. When she had left Maeve threw herself back in a chair, remarking, 'Well, that's over, she won't think of me for another year.'⁴ No doubt through her knowledge of the hopeless misery of many Irish children's lives, Constance acquired a different sense of proportion from that of the average mother. In any case, she totally lacked sentimentality – that convenient cloak for received attitudes and unrealistic emotion. Her thought cut arrow-like through any question at issue, straight to where she saw the point. Her direction can be criticized, but never her sincerity.

One unalloyed pleasure for Casi in that year of 1911 was Pavlova's visit to Dublin. He went off with Martin Murphy to greet her at Kingstown. The pier was crowded with Dublin well-knowns including the directors of the Gaiety Theatre where she was to dance. Casi had been coaching Martin Murphy in the train as to a Russian greeting; so when the dancer (then in the prime of her beauty) came down the gangway the two cronies side-stepped the Quality and crying 'Ztradswite!' kissed her on each cheek. Casi went further, and arranged a traditional Russian welcome in her dressing-room of a cloth of unbleached linen, a jug of water and plain bread.⁵

On 15 July 1910 Constance delivered a lecture to the Students' National Literary Society. In *Women, Ideals and the Nation* was contained her first full-length exposition of the ideas nurtured by the various women's movements in Ireland. She addressed herself to the young, calling on them to come forward both as women and 'Irelanders' with 'all the troubles and responsibilities of both'. She warned every Nationalist woman to pause before she joined a Suffrage Society or a Franchise League 'that did not include in their Programme the Freedom of their Nation'. Neither was it possible for a Nationalist woman to 'serve her nation through her home' – far from it. 'For each one of you,' Constance told her audience, 'there is a niche waiting – your place in the nation. Try and find it. It may be as a leader, it may be as a humble follower – perhaps in a political party, perhaps in a party of your own – but it is there, and if you cannot find it for yourself, no one can find it for you.' Touching on drunkenness as one of the great national evils for women to fight, she went on to urge her hearers to boycott any Irishman wearing the King's uniform; neither were the maidens of Ireland to take any benefits offered by the British – unlike Atalanta and the golden apples, the Irish girls must resist temptation. They must buy only Irish manufactured goods, even though they might cost a little more; above all they must remember to regard themselves as Irish, as 'units of a nation distinct from England, your conqueror'; they must arm themselves with weapons to fight the nation's cause, and fill their minds with Irish history and noble ideas.

Constance was a fluent and confident speaker by now. To return to the year 1911 we find her lecturing for the Socialist Party of Ireland and speaking (on 11 September) at a meeting held in the Antient Concert Rooms after the founding of the Irish Women Workers' Union on 5 September by Larkin and his sister Delia. In October of this year Constance was elected a Vice-President of The Daughters of Erin; in November she lectured in Belfast for *Fianna*; and in Dublin organized some ambitious and significant scouting games – the attack and defence of 'the citadel' which was four hundred square yards of Mr Jolley's land in Scholarstown.

In December, the Independent Dramatic Company took *Eleanor's Enterprise* to Belfast. This visit marked the beginning of Constance's great friendship with the Connolly family (James Connolly was then organizing labour in Belfast). Constance stayed with them on two occasions. On the second as she left, she said to Mrs Connolly, 'I hope I wasn't too much bother to you'. 'Oh, no more than one of the children,' replied her hostess, patting her affectionately on the back.[6]

In the spring of the next year, 1912, Casi showed that he was interested in stronger meat than comedy when he helped Fred Morrow produce the Russian domestic tragedy *The Storm* by Alexander Ostrowski (used by Janacek as the libretto for his opera *Katya Kabanova*). Casi designed the scenery and painted it in the basement of the *Sinn Fein* bank in Harcourt Street. He also wrote an article for the *Freeman's Journal** castigating English critics for failing to understand Russian writers, and denouncing the English theatre for its preoccupation with unreal vulgarity or false sentiment.

London does not want reality and truth – she dubs it sordid realism, and prefers to shed tears over a high 'falutin' melodrama in the East-End or the West, to wonder in horror struck whispers how many clothes 'Salome' wears, or to meet on mutual ground and howl with joy at the Widow Twankey, Polish dwarfs or any other absurdities.

In the same year – 1912 – Casi had embarked on a new theatrical enterprise in keeping with his opinions expressed in this same article. He formed, together with Evelyn Ashley, a repertory company, whose aim was to give a series of European plays of the type ignored or rejected by the commercial theatre. Casi wanted to prove that Dublin could be persuaded to be in the main stream of European theatrical work. The first play was *For the Crown* by François Coppée – a drama of political ambition and parricide set in the Balkans in the fifteenth century. (Casi was moving away from comedy with a vengeance). He may have been influenced in his choice of this play, which seems a daunting work for an amateur company to tackle, by its connection with Eric Forbes-Robertson – a friend of Constance's from Paris days. Forbes-Robertson had brought the play to Dublin himself with great success, some fifteen years before, and now agreed to send over some of the original scenery, including an enormous equestrian statue.

The new company's performance was received with charity rather than acclaim. One critic wrote,

While one is bound to admire the zeal and spirit which actuated even such a gifted company of amateurs to attack such an arduous and trying work, it is only right to express the opinion that some less pretentious

* Edited by James Connolly.

play might have been chosen, and with more effective results . . . if the lines were delivered with more energy and vivacity the play might run more freely and pall less wearily on the audience . . . otherwise the company did very well . . .

The next year, in May, the Repertory Company gave *The Devil's Disciple*. It was, in fact, Casi's biggest production; his swan-song in Dublin among the men of the theatre, who loved him and never forgot him. Fred Morrow, with whom he had produced *The Storm*, wrote to him in later years, 'all my joys in Dublin were around you and your friends'.

The Devil's Disciple entailed a large cast, and fifty extras. The crowd scenes were thought to be extraordinarily vivid, and the reason was that Casi had chosen Trinity College students to act as British soldiers, and *Fianna* boys and Nationalists for the mob. The newspapers commented that in the fight scene between the soldiery and the mob nothing so realistic had ever been seen before.

Constance and Casi gave an immensely successful party after the production. It was also a birthday party for Brefni O'Rorke (who supplied the whiskey). Constance made a huge, tiered cake with an effigy of Mephistopheles on top, and an inscription 'Long live the Devil' in chocolate icing. Casi ('the only true Bohemian' wrote Brefni O'Rorke of him after his death) provided the champagne, and Constance was responsible for the beer and the food.

At the height of the party a guest (Tommy Furlong) announced his intention of singing *God Save the King*. Constance, amused, but, one imagines, more sober than many, said if he persisted she would empty the tea urn over him. He was determined to persist, so he went home, changed into a bathing-dress, returned, raised his voice in patriotism, and was duly drenched in tea. Brefni O'Rorke then 'dropped him quietly into the front garden'.

At five o'clock in the morning the survivors got into taxis and drove off to finish the revels at another house. It will be seen, therefore, that even as late as 1913 life for Constance was not all lecture halls, committee-rooms and marching along at the head of her *Fianna* boys. Casi's role in her life, however intermittent and superficial it might now appear to be, still provided a nucleus of artistic endeavour, fun, and sophistication which she was hardly likely to find in *Sinn Fein* or the Socialist Party of Ireland.

In 1912, Constance moved into Surrey House, Rathmines (known as 'Scurry House'), which was her last home as such. Surrey House is a tall, gabled, narrow villa (joined to its twin which stands on the corner of a road leading to Grosvenor Square) built of red brick, and with a strip of garden leading to the broad stretch of Leinster Road, which it faces. For Constance, it was never a house to be lived in for itself, but a headquarters for her real activities. Friends were amazed by the disorder they found there, but they were warmed by the spontaneity of Constance's welcome, and stimulated by the conversation of the ceaseless flow of visitors. The gas might be off, there might be only bread and butter and tea on offer, there was hardly an inch of space to put your coat or hang your hat, but there was a feeling that life was lived at the heart of things. One element did not exist, and that was any privacy or comfort for Casi. It was nothing for friends who happened to be in the neighbourhood and in need of a bed to climb through a window, especially left open for them, and suddenly appear for breakfast.

A series of lame ducks and protégés came and went: delicate *Fianna* boys who needed nursing, two girls who had been sacked from Jacob's biscuit factory. Constance spent less and less on herself – her only small luxury being good shoes, which were mended over and over again. She was of the breed of givers who never count the cost. (A friend once noticed that her tweed jacket was pulled together with a large safety-pin. Since it was a warm day she inquired the reason, and Constance admitted that she had just given her shirt to a poor woman.) Constance bicycled everywhere to save the tram fares. When she looked into shop windows her eye was struck by what her friends might like, not what she would herself. She was forever buying small presents and saying to the recipients, 'I saw this and it seemed just the thing for you.' But Surrey House was more than a centre of informal, eccentric entertainment, a convalescent home for the unfortunate, a second home for the *Fianna* boys. Constance had moved in with a printing press. Stasko heard it thudding night and day in the room under his bedroom, stamping out its quota of exhortations, subversive comment, advice, and commands for the converted and unconverted alike.

Through the years of struggle for Home Rule, years which sharpened the appetites of the Home Rulers, and even more those of

men and women, like Constance's friends, who wanted sovereign
independence and did not shrink from the idea of bloodshed to get
it, there was an influential body of Irishmen with an appetite of a
different kind. By 1911 the voice of Ulster was loud in the land,
and it sang another tune from that of Dublin. Dublin's black was
Ulster's white. Ulster was Protestant, Unionist, and unalterably
opposed to Home Rule.

The oldest Ulster families had arrived in Ireland with the
'Plantations' of James 1; they were succeeded through the centuries
by Protestant and Presbyterian farming families, and, later, as
Belfast grew into a powerful centre of industry, by skilled
artisans. The weapons forged by Ulster to protect its religious and
cultural identity was the Orange Order, founded after the Battle of
the Boyne. The Orange Order made itself felt through a tough
cohesion of aims, through loyalty between its members, who were
grouped in Lodges, and through the annual 12 July celebrations
of the Battle of the Boyne – with speeches, drums, marching to
bands, and the reaffirmation of beliefs.

Ulster Unionists had always meant to kill Home Rule, but so
long as a Conservative Government was in power in England
they had nothing to fear. But now, since 1910 with the Liberal
Government determined to push the measure through, the menace
to Ulster of Catholic rule from Dublin had become very real. A
leader of revolt was needed. One was found in Edward Carson.
He was a member of the Irish Bar, the senior member for Dublin
University, a former Solicitor-General, and an immensely successful practitioner at the English Bar. He was best remembered in
London literary circles for his merciless cross-examination of
Oscar Wilde in 1895. In 1910, Carson was invited by the Irish
Unionist party to become their leader in succession to Walter
Long (a former Chief Secretary of Ireland) who had lately retired
from his Dublin constituency. Most Irish Unionist MPs happened
to be Ulstermen, but because of Ulster fears of Home Rule a distinction now arose between Irish Unionists and Ulster Unionists.
The latter were looking for more than a new official chief – they
needed someone with the dynamism to provide a rallying point
for the anti-Home Rule forces. It is one of the many ironies of
Irish politics that Carson, who became the apotheosis of Ulster's
defiance of the British Government over Home Rule, was born
and bred a southern Irishman.

In July 1911, Carson had a meeting with the Ulster Unionist Council and was accepted as their leader. His emergence in Ulster politics was originally sponsored and arranged by an Ulster Unionist MP, James Craig; a quiet, shrewd, kindly, and imperturbable man, possessed both of material wealth and spiritual determination. Carson said of him in later years, when Northern Ireland stood apart from the Republic, 'It was James Craig who did most of the work, and I got most of the credit.'[7]

Now, in September 1911, Craig organized an impressive demonstration for Carson when 50,000 men who had come from every part of Ulster marched from the Belfast City Hall to Craig's home, 'Craigavon'. Here on the broad lawns they acclaimed Carson as their leader.

By the next year, emotions both for and against Home Rule were boiling up to fever-pitch in Ireland. On 31 March 1912, there was a giant Nationalist demonstration for Home Rule in Dublin just before the introduction of the Bill. The whole of O'Connell Street was jammed from end to end with people. Four platforms were erected. Redmond, in an appeal for national unity, said, 'We have not one word of reproach, or one word of bitter feeling . . . We have one feeling only in our hearts, and that is an earnest longing for the arrival of the day of reconciliation.'[8]

Padraic Pearse, on another platform within a stone's throw of the General Post Office, where in 1916 he made a declaration of a different kind, said, 'I should think myself a traitor to my country if I did not answer the summons to this gathering, for it is clear to me that the Bill which we support today will be for the good of Ireland and that we shall be stronger with it than without it.' But he added, 'Let the foreigner understand that if we are cheated now there will be red war in Ireland.'[9] James Connolly, representing Labour opinion, looked on the Bill as a necessary first step towards independence.

Meanwhile a giant demonstration of the opposite point of view was being organized in Ulster. It was decided to hold an Ulster Day at the end of September. It was to be an occasion of solemnity and dedication. James Craig was much concerned by the problem of the form in which the people of Ulster might embody their determination not to be severed from England. One evening, he was sitting in the Constitutional Club in London trying to draft a declaration of purpose in some form of oath when he was joined by

B. W. D. Montgomery, the secretary of the Ulster Club in Belfast, who, on being told of the problem, made the brilliant and imaginative suggestion of basing it on the Scottish Solemn League and Covenant of 1643. As a result of this suggestion a new Covenant was drawn up and proposed for adoption to the Ulster Unionist Council. Those who signed the Covenant pledged themselves to 'stand by one another in defending for ourselves and our children our cherished position of equal citizenship in the United Kingdom, and using all means which may be found necessary to defeat the present conspiracy to set up a Home Rule Parliament in Ireland . . .'[10]

On 23 September there was a meeting of the Ulster Unionist Council attended by five hundred delegates. The Covenant was ratified without a single dissent. If anyone doubted that the anti-Home Rule movement in Ulster lacked popular support and was solely the repository of the desire for self-preservation of the monied and privileged, the events of Ulster Day itself should have dispelled that illusion. All observers testified to the devotional mood of the huge crowds. It was a Sunday, a Sunday of calm September sunshine, and the day began with church services. There followed the first ceremony of the signing of the Covenant. The leaders of the movement walked from Ulster Hall, where there had been a service, to the City Hall, where they were received by the Lord Mayor and Corporation in official robes. The document of the Covenant lay on a table draped with the Union Jack. Carson was the first to sign. It had been arranged within the City Hall that 540 people could sign the Covenant simultaneously; each signatory was given a copy of the Covenant he had signed. Some, remembering the Scottish Covenantors, went so far as to sign in their own blood. In Ulster altogether 218,206 men and 228,991 women signed.[11]

Two months after the signing of the Covenant the Ulster leaders formed the Ulster Volunteer Force. (Legality was able to be established by the discovery that any two magistrates could sanction the practice of military drill in areas under their jurisdiction if they thought it expedient or necessary.) Out of this new departure much else flowed. The Nationalists, watching from Dublin, summoned a great meeting at the Rotunda in order to form their own Volunteers. They met in November 1913. All bodies were represented: *Sinn Fein*, the Gaelic League, the Gaelic

Athletic Association, the IRB, and the Irish Transport and General Workers' Union. The initiative had come from a figure virtually unknown except to the Gaelic League: Professor Eion MacNeill, who, as another example of the cross-currents of loyalty and race in Irish politics, came from the Ulster county of Antrim and who was hardly a military man, being a professor of Irish history at the National University. He was backed, amongst others by Padraic Pearse, who, since a visit to America to acquire funds for his school, St Enda's, had become a member of the IRB. That organization, seeing immediately the importance for future militant action of the new armed force, also detailed Sean MacDiarmada to hold a watching brief. So unsophisticated politically was Professor MacNeill that at a meeting in Cork (that stronghold of Nationalism) he actually called for three cheers for the hated Carson, because he was the man who through his example in forming the Ulster Volunteers had brought courage to Ireland. It was not the form of reasoning to appeal to his audience. A free fight ensued.

In September 1913 Ulster announced the formation of a provisional government, declaring that if Ulster were coerced into submission to a Dublin Parliament, it would have to be ruled as a conquered country.[12] Westminster and Ulster could not agree on mutually satisfactory terms for Ulster's exclusion from Home Rule. Meanwhile, by 1914 the Bill itself had been passed twice by the House of Commons and thrown out twice by the House of Lords. Once the Commons had passed it for the third time it was bound to become law, under the provisions of the Parliament Act. In the previous year, the Ulster men had shown the seriousness of their intentions through the famous incident of the Larne gun-running, when they succeeded in landing illegally 20,000 modern rifles, and a quantity of small-arms ammunition. There was consternation in Government circles. Asquith assured the House of Commons that 'His Majesty's Government will take without further delay appropriate steps to vindicate the authority of the law',[13] but the law's only manifestation was the appearance of a few destroyers off the Ulster coast.

The Larne gun-running incident created another precedent for the Nationalists. One who was quick to seize the implication was Roger Casement who was in America. 'The news of this morning,' he said, 'shows that Edward Carson is a great Irishman! He has shown us what *we* must do. He ran those guns for the Ulstermen right under the noses of the authorities! He has shown us the way!'[14]

While through the summer of 1913 the Irish Parliamentary party was struggling in the toils of the Home Rule Bill and the manoeuvres of Ulster, the most bitter and protracted battle in the history of Irish labour fought itself out in Dublin. The chief protagonists were Constance's new friend – the 'Titan who might have been moulded by Michelangelo or Rodin' – James Larkin, who was pitted against William Martin Murphy, probably the richest industrialist in Ireland, described in a contemporary English newspaper as 'a tall, spare figure, slightly stooped at the shoulders, with a mass of silvery brushed hair framing a benevolent face in which two kindly but piercing grey eyes are set', and called by Larkin, 'the most foul and vicious blackguard that ever polluted any country'.[15] These two men: the flamboyant labour organizer, and the hard-headed employer who based his profits on a calculated state of rivalry between permanent and casual labour, came to a head-on clash in the late summer of 1913. By this year Larkin had succeeded in organizing practically all the unskilled labour in Dublin with the exception of the Corporation and the builders' labourers. Guinness's workers remained outside his net because they were too well treated by their employer, Lord Iveagh, to have grievances. The other business whose employees were outside the Larkin fold was the Dublin United Tramway Company, whose chairman was William Murphy. Mr Murphy had an ingenious system of employment which produced the maximum insecurity for the men, while providing him with complete control over them. He employed men under two categories; permanent and casual. If a permanent man was late, or absent for any reason, his place was immediately taken by the man at the top of the casual list. Meanwhile the superseded permanent man was demoted to the bottom of the casual list. It is, perhaps, hardly surprising that Larkin castigated Murphy as an 'industrial octopus' and a 'blood-sucking vampire'.[16] But in the Dublin of the day he was considered by fellow-employers as hard, but just. Compared with the grain ship dockers of Belfast, for instance, who had to work at such speeds and carry such heavy burdens that few could stand the physical strain for more than very short periods of time, or the Dublin carters who sometimes worked 112 hours a week, the conditions of the Dublin United Tramway Company employees seemed relatively favourable. At any rate, William Murphy was determined that his men should not join Larkin's Transport and General Workers' Union. Employees known to be Larkinites were dismissed and replaced by casual men (who knew that the reason for their being taken on was because they were not Union members). It was an easy game to play in a city where the working classes lived on the verge of starvation.

Larkin planned a strike of tram workers in Horse Show Week, with a view to causing the maximum inconvenience. Seven hundred men came out, but more than that number stayed in since so many had recently been taken on who were not members of the Transport Union. Larkin also sought to attack Murphy by organizing the dispatch boys employed by the latter's newspaper *The Irish Independent*. Murphy retaliated by locking out those in the dispatch department who had joined the Transport Union. Larkin then called a strike in the firm of Eason (Ireland's largest newspaper distributors) because the firm refused to drop Murphy's newspaper from their delivery service. The dockers then entered the controversy when they refused to handle any goods consigned to Eason's as being 'tainted goods'. Here the shipping companies stepped in and accused Larkin of bad faith, in view of the agreement with them he had sanctioned in the previous May. Larkin declared that he could not persuade the men to handle the goods.[17]

Given the industrial climate of the times, and Murphy's determination to rule his industrial empire exactly as he wished, he was not the man to let Larkin win by default. On 29 August Murphy called a meeting of the Employers' Federation (first formed in 1911 to fight the strikes of that year). It was evident to the employers that Larkin and his Transport and General Workers' Union must be crushed. Four hundred employers decided to lock out all employees who were members of the Transport Union. The Coal Merchants' Association also decided to lock out Larkin men; The Master Builders' Association followed suit, and locked out 3,000 men who refused to sign a pledge never to join the Transport Union. A thousand farm workers were locked out for being members of the Union; the same thing happened to Union members working for the Timber and the Cement Merchants. It was not long before 25,000 men were out of work.

On 28 August Larkin and four of his colleagues were arrested and charged with seditious libel and seditious conspiracy. They were allowed out on bail. Larkin addressed a large crowd of people in Beresford Place the next evening, saying, in an inflammatory speech (in every sense of the word), 'With your permission I am going to burn the Proclamation of the King.' He set light to the document, saying, 'People can make kings, and people can unmake them . . . I am a rebel and the son of a rebel . . . I recognize no law but the people's law. We are going to raise a new standard of discontent and a new battle-cry in Ireland.'[18] The authorities issued a second warrant for his arrest. Larkin was at Liberty Hall when the news was brought to him. He must have been in close touch with Constance through these events, because it was then decided that he would be safest hiding in her house. He wanted to avoid arrest until after he had addressed a mass meeting in O'Connell Street – a meeting planned for the next day. It is impossible to believe that the next development was not suggested and planned by Constance, for it was no less than that Larkin should disguise himself as an elderly, bearded gentleman and thus avoid the attention of the police.

Larkin went to Surrey House. (Nothing, surely, could be greater proof of how involved Constance was by this time in the Labour movement.) By a fortunate coincidence for the planners, Casi arrived back that night from his yearly visit to the Ukraine. He was met at the station by a party of his friends in the theatre world. It was decided to celebrate his return with an impromptu party at Surrey House. Thus the watching detectives were put off Larkin's scent.

The next morning was spent in turning him into an elderly, bearded gentleman. Helena Molony assisted; Casi very reluctantly lent his frock-coat and top-hat; and Nellie Gifford, who was little known in Dublin since she was a Domestic Economy instructress in Co Meath, agreed to act as the old gentleman's 'niece' and interpreter to the outside world, for it was decided that the only way that Larkin could disguise his marked Liverpool accent was to pretend he was stone deaf.

Early in the afternoon (which was a Sunday) Larkin's carriage drove up to the Imperial Hotel in O'Connell Street. The hotel, ironically enough, was owned by none other than Murphy himself. The street was crowded both by those who had come in the hopes that Larkin would keep his promise to speak, and with people returning home from twelve o'clock Mass. The authorities were also wondering if Larkin would somehow keep his promise, so the street was lined with police. The mood of the police was edgy to say the least of it, for they had experienced violence from Larkin's supporters when they were guarding trams, and then later attacking 'scab' crews.

Larkin got into the hotel without trouble, walked upstairs and into the dining-room. He opened the french window, stepped out on to the balcony and began to speak. At first he was not recognized. As soon as he was, the crowd surged forward and started cheering. The police raced into the hotel and re-emerged with Larkin under arrest. 'John Brennan', sister of Nellie Gifford, and Constance had followed in an outside car, the crowd recognized Constance and demanded a speech. She called for three cheers for Larkin. Events developed rapidly into violence and tragedy. So far the crowd had been orderly; but now the police were ordered to charge. Constance plunged into the thick of the mêlée, was attacked by a policeman, and was saved by Casi sticking his pipe into his pocket in imitation of a revolver, and, saying, 'Another step and you are a dead man.'[19] James Connolly's daughter, Nora, described in her *Portrait of a Rebel Father* what she saw next,

A lad beside me yelled 'Hey! The peelers have drawn their batons!' The next thing I knew the peelers were upon us. All you could hear was the thud, thump, crack of the batons as they fell on the heads of the crowd. There was no way to escape from the batons – there were screams and groans and yells – the peelers came steadily like mowing machines, and behind them the street was like a battlefield dotted with bodies. Some of them still lying twisting in pain.'

The trouble spread like wildfire through the streets. Now the poor and desperate took a hand – seeing a chance to get even with authority,

To the accompaniment of hoarse, ribald execrations and shrieks from the rioters, the combined police force charged up towards Tyrone Street, but had to withdraw owing to the hail of bottles and stones. Each time the police drew back, the howling rabble followed them and made havoc in their ranks with the hail of missiles that poured on them from all directions . . . Women, with dishevelled hair and looking like maniacs, were even more persistent than the men and youths in belabouring the police.[20]

On 3 September a large (and orderly) crowd attended the funeral at Glasnevin of a man who had been killed by a policeman. Keir Hardie, who had come over from England on receiving the news of the riots, was in the cortège. Larkin was in prison, and so was James Connolly. Keir Hardie assured Larkin's colleagues, William O'Brien described by Sean O'Casey as a self-important man with a 'clever, sharp, shrewd mind of white heat behind the cold, pale mask,' and P. T. Daly, who were now temporarily in charge, of Socialist Labour's support in the battle with the employers which all too evidently lay ahead. The Trades Union Congress (which was meeting in Manchester) sent over a committee, headed by Arthur Henderson. After meeting the employers' representatives, who refused to give way in their determination to lock out any man who was a member of the Transport Union, the committee decided that the locked out men should be supported in their fight.

In prison Connolly asked for a grammar of the Irish language and requested a friend that his bill should be paid at Moran's hotel. He wrote to his family in Belfast explaining that he wanted his children to understand fully what he was doing and why he was doing it, 'Many more than I will have to go to prison, and perhaps to the scaffold before our freedom is won.'[21]

On Sunday, 7 September, Connolly went on hunger-strike. There was general indignation when it became known that the magistrate who had committed him to jail was a large shareholder in Murphy's Tramway Company. On the seventh day of his hunger strike, Connolly was visited by his wife Lillie, and his daughter Ina. They were worried about his condition. But the Castle had decided to step in. Orders came from the Viceroy for Connolly's release. He was driven to Constance's house in a Vice-regal car. Here, she and her great friend, Kathleen Lynn, nursed him back to strength, until he was well enough to go home to Belfast.

Larkin was released on 12 September on bail. He left at once for England with the object of getting financial support for the locked-out men. Connolly returned to Dublin to take over in Larkin's absence. From now on when in Dublin he usually stayed at Surrey House, paying Constance ten shillings a week, although it is possible this was not a regular habit until Casi left for good in that same autumn.

Money and food ships arrived from England – contributed by

various labour movements; but the help most looked for by Larkin and Connolly – sympathetic strikes in England – was withheld. On the humanitarian and domestic front, Constance's work and achievements during the confused and tormented months which followed are for what she is most lovingly remembered. From her point of view it was a simple matter of the hungry who needed to be fed. The Transport Union's headquarters, Liberty Hall, had become an elaborate commissariat and clothing store. Larkin's sister, Delia, and Constance were put in charge of the welfare. A system soon evolved. Food packages were made up to be handed out when the men came to collect their strike pay – but it was found that the wives denied themselves so as to give more to their husbands and children. A soup kitchen was set up at Liberty Hall, and, more than that, special meals were prepared for expectant and nursing mothers. But Constance's soup was the main factor, the warmth, nourishment, and comfort for the thousands who now depended on Liberty Hall for their survival in the world. She begged bacon bones from the Co-Operative Wholesale Society; tons of potatoes were peeled daily by voluntary helpers – many of them strikers from Jacob's biscuit factory – in an airless cellar to the singing of rebel songs. Constance had got hold of some large coppers and in these the soup steamed and bubbled. The kitchens were large and extensive because Liberty Hall had once been a chop-house. Every day the delicious brew was ladled out to the queues waiting with their mugs, tin cans, porringers and old jam crocks. There is the well-known story of how a small boy in the queue was recognized as being the son of a 'scab' – a man who had taken the job of a locked-out worker. The other children pushed the boy aside, taunting him, 'Go away! Your father is a scab!' Constance, with immediate presence of mind, called him back, saying, 'No child is going to be called a scab – he can't help his father. When he grows up he'll be all right himself – won't you, sonny. And now have some soup.'

At this period Constance's whole life centred round Liberty Hall and its problems. She was remembered in his reminiscences *Up and Down Stream* by the Trades Union leader, Harry Gosling. He describes her as working all day long, her sleeves rolled up, wearing an apron made of a sack, and usually smoking a cigarette; never failing in energy, spirits, and resource. It was said that a man was kept permanently on hand at Liberty Hall whose duty it was to dash off at a moment's notice to Constance's solicitors at Ormond Quay to deliver a plea for yet another loan on her dwindling securities in order to buy more food. The friends who remember her are united in the insistence that never for a moment did she take on the attitudes of a Lady Bountiful. Even the playwright and writer of genius, Sean O'Casey, her most bitter and unrelenting critic, does not quite accuse her of that. Oddly enough he accuses her – at this period when he knew her best – of failings which are the exact opposite of the virtues extolled by those who were less prejudiced in her disfavour. He sneers at her for doing no real work (she, who so needed physical activity that when she was in prison in England she had to be moved from the sewing-room to scrubbing duties in the kitchen) and of only wielding the soup ladle, dressed meanwhile in a spotless white apron, for the benefit of newspaper reporters when they came round. He also criticized her for never understanding the workers or even trying to; for dazzling Connolly with her 'flashy enthusiasm'; for never reading a book (an unusual pursuit one would have thought in any case at busy Liberty Hall which is where O'Casey knew her); he accused her of being irresponsible; of 'trying painting' and failing; and, finally, of being a champion with a cardboard lath.[22] Sean O'Casey was an extreme example of the kind of Irishman who would never understand Constance, and who much resented her influence in extremist circles. There must have been others like him for whom she could do nothing right, who would never forgive her for being born at Lissadell. First of all, they accused her of play-acting; then when in 1916 she proved she could shoot as straight and endure as much discomfort and danger as any man, they dubbed her a Fury.

On 7 October, Æ's famous open letter to the Dublin employers was published in *The Irish Times*,

Sirs,

I address this warning to you, the aristocracy of industry in this city, because like all aristocracies, you tend to grow blind in long authority, and to be unaware that you and your class and its every action are being considered and judged day by day by those who have the power to shake or overturn the whole social order, and whose restlessness in poverty today is making our industrial civilization stir like a quaking bog. You do not seem to realize that your assumption that you are answerable to yourselves alone for your actions in the industries you control is one that becomes less and less tolerable in a world so crowded with necessitous life . . .

Æ went on to accuse the employers of being uncultivated, lacking in civic generosity, and inefficient, since their enterprises had 'been dwindling' in spite of the availability of the cheapest labour market in the British Isles, where men were always hungry and ready to 'accept any pittance',

You have allowed the poor to be herded together so that one thinks of certain places in Dublin as of a pestilence. There are twenty thousand rooms, in each of which live entire families, and sometimes more, where no function of the body can be concealed, and delicacy and modesty are creatures that are stifled ere they are born . . . The representatives of labour unions in Great Britain met you, and you made of them a preposterous, an impossible demand,* and because they would not accede to it you closed the Conference; you refused to meet them further: you assumed that no other guarantees than those you asked were possible, and you determined deliberately in cold anger, to starve out one-third of the population of this city, to break the manhood of the men by the sight of the suffering of their wives and hunger of their children . . . It remained for the twentieth century and the capital city of Ireland to see an oligarchy of four hundred masters deciding openly upon starving one hundred thousand people, and refusing to consider any solution except that fixed by their pride . . . The Fate of you, the aristocracy of industry, will be as the fate of the aristocracy of the land if you do not show that you have some humanity still among you. Humanity abhors, above all things, a vacuum in itself, and your class will be cut off from humanity as the surgeon cuts the cancer and alien growth from the body. Be warned ere it is too late.[23]

A public Court of Enquiry was held in October during which Larkin delivered a searing speech lasting for two hours. The employers refused to accept the Report of the Court as a basis for negotiations.

The hungry weeks dragged on. Later in October a scheme was set in motion from London by Mrs Montefiori, the philanthropist, to send striker's children to homes in England to be cared for. This project of mercy was killed by an alarming display of priestly bigotry in Dublin. No less a personage than the Archbishop of Dublin, Dr Walsh, wrote a letter to the newspaper *Freeman's Journal* demanding to know whether Catholic mothers had lost

* The employers' demand that the Transport Union be outlawed.

their faith that they should 'so forget their duty as to send away their children to be cared for in a strange land without security of any kind that those to whom the poor children are to be handed over are Catholics, or, indeed, are persons of any faith at all.'[24] (Perhaps the fact that Mrs Montefiori was Jewish, and her chief helper, Lucille Rand, an American, rang a subconscious gong of warning in the Archbishop's mind.)

Worse was to follow. In spite of Mrs Montefiori's assurances that the children, so far as possible, would be placed in Catholic homes, and, in any case would continue to have Catholic instruction, a party of priests swooped down on the Corporation baths, where fifty children were being washed, preparatory to departure, and removed all but nineteen. Of these nineteen, ten were captured by the pursuing priests before they reached the boat at Kingstown, and the remaining nine were persuaded off the boat before it sailed.[25]

Larkin made a speech that night from a window of Liberty Hall saying, 'I have tried to kill sectarianism, whether in Catholics or Protestants. I am against bigotry or intolerance on either side. Those who want to divide the workers have resorted to the foulest methods . . .[26]'

Mrs Montefiori and Mrs Rand were actually arrested on the charge of kidnapping. Delia Larkin took over, but her attempts to get more children away were forcibly prevented by the priests who picketed the quays (together with sympathizers), and at Amiens Street station created such a disturbance that the party of children entraining for Belfast had to be brought back to Liberty Hall, and the whole scheme abandoned.

Larkin's trial took place on 27 October. He was sentenced to seven months without hard labour. On the Sunday following his sentence a gigantic protest meeting took place at the Albert Hall where Connolly and Æ spoke, together with Bernard Shaw, George Lansbury, Ben Tillett, and Delia Larkin. The speeches were eloquent, moving, and fiery; but the men remained locked out.

CHAPTER 11

The Militant

In August 1913 at the height of the agitation resulting from the O'Connell street riots and Larkin's arrest, Galsworthy's *Strife* came on in Dublin – produced by Casi. He repeated his technique of choosing extras whose background in life gave their roles in the play the projection of their own reality. He hired real labourers for the big scene at 1/6d a night. Their interpretation of the fight was so vivid one man complained, 'I don't mind being an actor for a night or two. But be Jasus I won't be killed for one and sixpence.'[1]

In the previous year a cartoon was published in the *Irish Review* by Beatrice Elvery* showing Casi as the dominating figure in a group of Arts Club friends which included Yeats, William Orpen, James Stephens, Joseph Hone and Æ. But Casi's life in Dublin was nearly over, although he and Constance did not acknowledge it in so many words. The early events of the lock-out strike in 1913 pointed all too clearly to what the future was likely to be: discomfort at home, and the kind of publicity abroad most likely to embarrass him in his social life and what remained to him of a portrait painting career. He left for the Ukraine in the late autumn of 1913, and never lived in Dublin again. He became involved in an Albanian adventure when the German Prince of Weid seized power. (As a compatriot commented, 'It would be surprising if such a strange and inane event could take place without the participation of a Pole.')[2] The Prince of Weid returned to Germany, and Casi to the Ukraine. Here he wrote a satiric comedy *Wild Fields*, which was put on in Warsaw, and had a *succès de scandale*, in the Ukraine at any rate, because Casi had drawn freely on the local gentry for his inspiration.

Back in Ireland, one of the causes of Casi's departure – Larkin –

* Lady Glenavy.

was released after serving only seventeen days of his sentence. This remission was greatly due to Connolly who appealed to the Labour movement to work against the Liberal Government until Larkin be freed – even if it endangered Home Rule.³ So much feeling was aroused that the Liberals lost a by-election at Reading, and suffered a much reduced majority at the Linlithgow by-election. Fireworks were let off from the roof of Liberty Hall in rejoicing.

Throughout the winter, while thousands of men remained workless and dependent on what Liberty Hall could distribute in the way of strike pay, clothes, and food, Larkin's attitude became increasingly truculent towards the British Labour leaders who hesitated to commit themselves to sympathetic strikes. Matters came to a head late in November when he virtually appealed to ordinary labour supporters over the heads of their leaders to insist that they 'must stand for Trade Unionism'⁴ (i.e. to back the Dublin Transport Union in its fight, with more than welfare). In December 1913 a special Trades Union Congress met in London. After a restrained start the meetings were noticeable for the personal recriminations between Larkin and the British leaders. The Congress ended with the defeat of Larkin's and Connolly's hopes of sympathetic action in their struggle against the employers. Instead, a resolution was proposed that another attempt be made by the Joint Board of British and Irish delegates to negotiate with the employers. An amendment proposed by a Larkin supporter, Jack Jones, that unions in the transport trades should not handle Dublin traffic after a certain date, and that a monthly levy be raised to support the Dublin workers, was defeated by over two million as against two hundred votes. It was the beginning of the end. By February 1914 the Dublin Relief Fund sponsored by the British Trades Union Council was closed. Connolly wrote, 'And so we Irish workers must again go down into Hell, bow our backs to the lash of the slave-driver, let our hearts be seared by the iron of his hatred, and instead of the sacramental wafer of brotherhood and common sacrifice, eat the dust of defeat and betrayal. Dublin is isolated'.⁵

The great battle, undertaken with so much confidence by Larkin six months before, petered out in a series of defeats for the hungry, dispirited workers. Christmas passed with a children's treat for 20,000 in a marquee in Croydon Park. Delia Larkin

organized a theatre company and made a tour of Lancashire. A
Distress Fund was opened in Liverpool. But the workers slowly
trickled back. They signed the pledge against the ITGW union but
continued to belong to it; workers for firms which did not operate
the pledge had already returned to their places of employment.
But the defeat was on both sides; many of the smaller employers
were bankrupt; while sympathy had been aroused for the Dublin
workers in quarters where their plight had not hitherto seemed so
urgent as the freeing of Ireland.

The Irish Citizen Army, with whose names those of Connolly and
Constance were intimately connected, was a significant off-shoot
of the great lock-out strike. Without the Citizen Army, small
though it was, the Easter Rising of 1916 could hardly have begun.
Connolly's first biographer, R. M. Fox, writes that the idea of
forming a Citizen Army from the numbers of the locked-out men
was originally put forward at a meeting of the Industrial Peace
Committee – which had been got together in the hope of finding a
means of reconciling the men with the employers. But even before
this, the notion of arming the workers against the police-protected
'scabs' was in the air: a Civil Guard to protect civil rights. The
motion was put forward by a man who thought that to drill and
train the workers would restore their shattered self-respect. Like
Eion MacNeill of the Volunteers, this man was an idealistic native
of Ulster who had thrown his lot in with the Nationalists. But here
all resemblance ended. Captain James White DSO was the dapper,
fiery and idiosyncratic son of Field-Marshal Sir George White,
the hero of Ladysmith. When in India, so he recounts in *Story of a
Misfit*, serving in The Gordon Highlanders and reading Tolstoy,
he wrote to his father, 'I feel I am odd, and I cannot be odd without making more or less of a scandal. Will you agree to my
leaving and help me to do something else?'

His father replied, 'My dear Boy, I think you have been quite
odd enough; I should be a little less odd, if I were you, and go on
with your work.'

Captain White retired from the army. On his return to his
native land (after many vicissitudes) he found himself in sympathy
with such non-Unionist Protestants as Alice Stopford-Green,
widow of the historian, and herself a historian and the future
treasurer of the Irish Volunteers, and Sir Roger Casement.

At this Mansion House meeting, Captain White's proposal had to be ruled out of order because the committee based its existence on its neutrality. So the meeting adjourned to the rooms of the Reverend R.M.Gwynn in near-by Trinity College, where the motion was passed, and money collected to buy staves and boots. At a later meeting of the Trinity College Gaelic Society, Captain White made an appeal for the new force. A special meeting was then arranged in the Antient Concert Rooms where Captain White and James Connolly spoke. A telegram from Sir Roger Casement was read out, 'I understand you begin to drill and discipline Dublin Workers. That is a good and healthy movement. I wish to support it and I hope it may begin a widespread national movement to organize drilled and disciplined Irish Volunteers to assert Irish manhood and uphold the national cause in all that is right.'[6]

The Provost of Trinity, however, apparently did not share Sir Roger Casement's views on the 'good and healthy' movement, for he placed the meeting out of bounds for his students, who, nettled by his dictatorial attitude, marched some eighty strong to the Antient Concert Rooms in order to defy him. A month later the formation of the Irish Volunteers was called for by Professor Eion MacNeill at a big meeting in the Rotunda where practically all the Irish patriotic bodies were represented. Thus the Citizen Army found itself with a powerful rival almost from the outset. But Captain White strove gallantly, drilling in Croydon Park, training in Liberty Hall, and the *Fianna* Hall lent by Constance. He did the work of ten men, so one of his helpers, Sean O'Casey, records in *The Story of the Irish Citizen Army* (for which O'Casey earned his first money as a writer – the sum of fifteen guineas). But the events of the strike which unrolled in all their turmoil and misery during these first months, the constant arrest of the Labour leaders, the distraction for the men of strike meetings and strike actions, not to speak of the pull of the far richer and better organized Volunteers, depleted the ranks of the new force. O'Casey wrote, 'the inevitable happened; the drills became irregular, the numbers continued to decrease, and, finally, the Captain found himself reduced to the command of one company of faithful stalwarts, who, in spite of all obstacles, had remained as a sure and trustworthy nucleus of the Irish Citizen Army'.[7]

In March 1914 Captain White was badly hurt in the head in an affray with the police after a meeting, when Constance bravely defied them to tend his wounds herself. Sean O'Casey sought an interview with Captain White and suggested that the Citizen Army be organized 'into a systematic unit of labour' with a written constitution, a council, a fund for buying equipment, and a countrywide campaign to get new recruits. A public meeting was held in Liberty Hall, attended by James Connolly and Constance, and presided over by James Larkin, where the new constitution, drafted by Sean O'Casey, was read out and the four principles unanimously accepted. 'The first and last principle of the Irish Citizen Army is the avowal that the ownership of Ireland, moral and material, is vested of right in the people of Ireland.'[8]

Larkin then asked for a clause to be proposed for inclusion in the Army constitution that before being enrolled every applicant must be a member of a Trades Union recognized by the Irish Trades Union Congress. Constance proposed the clause, seconded by Thomas Healy, and it was carried unanimously. (This proviso carries with it the interesting implication that Constance must have been a card-carrying Union member unless women Citizen Army soldiers were exempt.) A committee was then elected to serve for six months with Captain White as chairman, Larkin and Francis Sheehy-Skeffington amongst the five vice-chairmen, Sean O'Casey as honorary secretary, and Richard Brannigan, yet another Ulsterman converted to Nationalism, together with Constance as honorary treasurers. Connolly, strangely enough, was not on this committee, but possibly the reason was his commitments in Belfast where he was actually living.

In April 1914, on a Sunday, Captain White, P. T. Daly, Constance and Sean O'Casey set out in Captain White's car on their first attempt to recruit a new company in a country district. They were headed for Lucan and Clondalkin, where announcements had already been posted to herald their arrival. It was a beautiful day, and in Lucan the party had 'a very pleasant tea in a local restaurant' before they moved on in the car to a suitable spot, where, slowly, a silent crowd of about five hundred people gathered to hear them. The three men spoke first, but, O'Casey relates, it was the 'passionate and nervous eloquence of Countess Markievicz' which really interested the crowd. (Perhaps they were also amazed to see a woman addressing them on such a subject.) Twenty names were taken, and these volunteers were authorized to hold a meeting to 'elect officers and arrange for drills'. The recruiting party even got a cheer as they drove away. The people of Clondalkin were more apathetic; it was several hours before enough collected to hold a meeting, which when it finally took place was presided over by the Transport Union delegate for the district.

At no time did the Citizen Army's far bigger rival, the Volunteers, show anything but hostility to a force which was connected so intimately with the Labour movement. The enmities engendered by the lock-out strike* penetrated deeply though the leadership cadres of the two forces. Behind the rank and file on the one side stood the Irish Parliamentary party and many employers involved in the lock-out struggle – besides full-blown Nationalists and *Sinn Feiners*; on the other side there was no one but the Labour leaders and their supporters.

Now there were two Cathleen ni Houlihans running round Dublin: one, like the traditional, in green dress, shamrocks in her hair, a little brian-boru harp under her oxster, chanting her share of song ... the other Cathleen coarsely dressed, hair a little tousled, caught roughly together by a pin, barefooted, sometimes with a whiff of whiskey off her breath; brave and brawny; at ease in the smell of sweat and the sound of bad language, vital, and asurge with immortality.[9]

The Citizen Army organizers found that halls suitable for use in the winter months and used by the Volunteers on certain days of the week, were denied them. Labour had not been invited to be officially represented at the initial Rotunda gathering. A suggestion of Larkin's that the Executive of the Volunteers and the Citizen Army Council should hold a debate was 'curtly refused'. There was a clear division in the Citizen Army Council over what the attitude should be towards the Volunteers. Larkin and O'Casey were totally hostile; Connolly, Captain White and Constance, on the other hand, saw the advantages of co-operation – were the Volunteers to suggest it. This inner conflict came to a head in 1914.

The new army had its own hymn of battle, adapted by Constance from an old Polish hymn – 'With the Smoke of the Fires'.

> Armed for the battle
> Kneel we before Thee,

* Constance never forgave Bulmer Hobson for failing to commit the IRB officially to the cause.

Bless thou our banners
>God of the brave.
Ireland is living!
>Shout we triumphant.
Ireland is waking,
>Hands grasp the sword.
Who fights for Ireland
>God guides his blows home,
Who dies for Ireland,
>God give him peace.
Knowing our cause just
>March we victorious,
Giving our hearts' blood
>Ireland to free . . .

There was, too, a happy bucolic side to the activities of the Citizen Army during that fateful summer of 1914. Croydon Park, which was rented by the ITGW union, was the setting for weekly jollifications on the only day available to the workers – Sunday. Concerts were held 'Dancing, singing and piping kept the night perpetually young,' O'Casey wrote, and even Jim Larkin would be prevailed upon to sing in his 'hoarse, tremulous voice, amid a tense and reverent silence, *The Red Flag* or *The Rising o' the Moon*.' At one festival the crowds were so enormous that most of the planned events had to be cancelled, but the five-mile Marathon race 'provoked the wildest enthusiasm of the onlookers . . . Bands played, artistes sang and children danced desperately at the same moment. Jim Larkin hurried frantically about the place . . . and the gallant Countess Markievicz tried frequently to be in ten places at one time.'[10]

That a worker's union should have a social and cultural side was a strong element in Larkin's concept of his work. It was his idea to rent Croydon Park – which was a house and three acres at Clontarf – in order to give the members a place for sports, and the opportunity to know a little about country life. He bought a cow and a calf, he planned to bring the gardens back into cultivation. Since 1912 Delia Larkin had been organizing choirs and dancers and a dramatic company in the Women's Workers Unions. At Christmas 1912 four one-act plays were performed on two nights running with Delia Larkin as the star. It will be noticed, therefore, that in Constance and Delia there were two able and active women among the Union leaders whose talents were identical rather than complementary.

In the Citizen Army an argument developed amongst the leaders over the question of uniforms – and this question involved the crucial one of status if there were to be armed conflict. Constance suggested a brassard, of St Patrick's blue for the men, and of red for the officers. The sporting of these brassards, it was hoped, would classify the wearers as belligerents under International Law with all that this implied in protection, and rights as prisoners. Sean O'Casey was vehemently opposed to this notion, arguing (and how rightly as it proved in the event) that whatever the Citizen Army put on in the way of brassards or uniforms the British would look on them as no more than 'decorated rebels'. He maintained that it would be far more effective (and safer) for the Citizen Army soldiers to employ the guerilla tactics of merging as civilians into the crowd when they were threatened with capture. He quoted Bernard Shaw's comparison of Ireland's fight with England as a 'perambulator against a Pickford van' the tactics of the Citizen Army should be to 'strike and dodge; dodge and strike,' he said.[11] Captain White (rather naturally as a professional soldier) took the opposite view, arguing that nothing less than proper uniforms would give the men sufficient pride and *esprit de corps* to hold them together as a corporate body. The Captain clinched the argument by announcing that he had, in fact, already gone guarantor for £50, the price of fifty uniforms, and that the men picked for the honour of wearing them had already been measured at Arnott's. The Citizen Army also acquired a flag of deep blue poplin, with a plough and stars, woven by the Dun Emer Guild where Yeats' sister Lily was embroideress.

With June came the annual pilgrimage to Wolfe Tone's grave at Bodenstown – always an occasion for a display of Nationalism. The burning question for the new Citizen Army was what their role was to be. When Sean O'Casey went to the Wolfe Tone Committee to apply for tickets he found a distinctly cool atmosphere and a strong element of doubt that the 'other Cathleen' would know how to behave herself. Here Tom Clarke came to the rescue. With all he had suffered in the cause of Ireland's freedom he was a man who could not be denied. From the chair, he declared that the Citizen Army would be welcome at the celebration, and, further, that they, as the first armed body of Nationalist Ireland, should head the procession. On 26 June the various Nationalist bodies turned out in force for the event: the Volunteers, the Citizen Army, the *Fianna* youths with Constance at their head, and the girls and women of *Cumman na mBan*. Tom Clarke gave an address from the graveside. Thanks to him this was the first occasion on which the Volunteers and the Irish Citizen Army stood together in their ranks at a public event.

In that same summer Captain White became so discouraged by the difficulties of training and drilling men who were kept tied by their varying hours of work that he resigned, and Larkin took his place.

The leaders of the Volunteers were not without their tensions during the summer of 1914. Redmond, whose prestige had been much shaken by the Larne gun-running, saw that it was essential for the Parliamentary party to get control of the Volunteers. The IRB, equally, were not blind to the significance of this new armed force, even though its avowed aims were purely defensive and protective. In May negotiations opened between Redmond, Dillon and Devlin, representing the Parliamentary party, and Professor MacNeill, Colonel Moore and Roger Casement, representing the Volunteers. The Parliamentary party was seeking equal representation on the provisional committee of the Volunteers; twenty-five of their number to join the twenty-five existing members. At that time Bulmer Hobson was the IRB representative on the provisional committee; it was on his advice that Redmond's nominees were reluctantly admitted. This action finally lost Hobson the confidence of the extremists. By July he was told to stop acting on behalf of the IRB and instructions went forth that he 'was to be kept in strict ignorance of any decision arrived at or to be arrived at in the IRB'.[12] Bulmer Hobson's influence waned as a result of the negotiations, but Redmond's was strengthened in London. Even so, Redmond's triumph was an empty one for there was a secret committee of IRB men within the Volunteers through which the IRB controlled the new movement. This committee consisted of Padraic Pearse, Joseph Plunkett, Eamonn Ceannt, Sean MacDermott, Thomas MacDonagh and Tom Clarke. In the March of 1914 there unfolded the events known as the Curragh Mutiny or Incident. Early in March Asquith reported to the Cabinet that police reports from Ireland seemed to indicate that the Ulster Volunteers might attempt to seize barracks and police stations, together with arms and ammunition. The Commander-in-Chief of the British Forces in Ireland was Sir Arthur Paget, a bluff, regular soldier, now sixty-three years of age, and not noticeable for his tact or judgement. He was an open Ulster Unionist sympathizer. In London, the Director of Military Operations in the War Office was Major-General Henry Wilson, a strong pro-Ulster Unionist Conservative. The result of the Government's attempt to contain the possible danger was that Brigadier-General Hubert Gough and sixty-four officers of the 3rd Cavalry Brigade communicated their intention to accept dismissal from the army rather than take part in the 'initiation of active military operations against Ulster.'[13] The affair got into the newspapers, *The Times* stressing the 'utmost gravity' of the crisis. The Government had to back down, and Brigadier-General Sir Hubert Gough received a document signed by Colonel Seely, the Secretary of State for War, to the effect that officers of the 3rd Cavalry Brigade would not be called upon to take action to enforce Home Rule in Ulster. It was another victory for the anti-Home Rule forces. On 24 and 25 of April that year Constance took an active part in a 'Daffodil Fête', held in aid of the Irish Women's Franchise League which had been founded by her great friend Mrs Sheehy-Skeffington. There were thirteen 'Suffrage Tableaux'. Constance appeared as a vision of Joan of Arc come to comfort a suffragette prisoner in her cell (played by Kathleen Houston, released from six months' imprisonment in Mountjoy). Constance took infinite pains with her 'armour' of silver cardboard, copied from fifteenth-century prints. In a contemporary press photograph she looks remarkably young and boyish for a woman of forty-six.

Constance was now a very well-known figure in Dublin – marching through the streets with her *Fianna* boys, or presiding over the soup kitchen at Liberty Hall, or marching with the Citizen Army in her dark green uniform with her wide hat pinned up on one side with the insignia of the ITGW Union – a red hand. Her house was constantly watched by the special police. It was not hard to imagine what her old Castle friends must have thought of her. She was now identified with everything abhorrent to the average upper class family: Socialism, Feminism, extreme Nationalism. But there were those, who had reasons for not liking her such as Lady Gregory, who yet saw what she was trying to do.

When Constance died, Lady Gregory wrote in her Journal entry of 18 July 1927:

Poor Madame Markievicz also gone . . . I knew her in her Castle days when she was rather a jealous meddler in the Abbey and Hugh's [Lane] Gallery. But her energy found a better scope when she took up the Labour movement, and then a more violent outlet in 1916 when she fought with the Boy Scouts she had trained, against the English troops, and was imprisoned. I remember one evening when I was coming from some hard hours' work at the Abbey I felt tired and jaded on the tram. And then she got in, tired and jaded also from drilling some of her *'Fianna'*, and I felt drawn to her. There was something gallant about her. We were each working for what we believed would help Ireland, and we talked together.

Against this moving glimpse of the two middle-aged warriors, weary but indomitable, finding comfort in their underlying unity of aim, however much their means differed, must be set a less happy scene a year later, when Sir Josslyn remonstrated with his sister for what he thought to be her fool's course, and a heated argument developed just before dinner in the absence of Lady Gore-Booth upstairs. If Sir Josslyn had known just how deeply Constance was entangled in subversive activities – how much more there was than the drilling and speeches, the tableaux and sing-songs – he would surely have never spent another peaceful night.

In June 1914 the Irish TUC became the Irish TUC and Labour party. The large crowds at the opening, outdoor meeting in Phoenix Park were supposed to be addressed by both Larkin and Connolly, speaking from two platforms simultaneously; the signal to begin was a trumpet blast. Unfortunately, Larkin, impatient to start, had the trumpet blown earlier than the time arranged, thus so annoying Connolly that he refused to make his speech although men had come from Cork especially to hear him. Larkin was not an easy colleague – being emotional, headstrong, and unpredictable – but Connolly was too balanced a personality himself to fail to appreciate Larkin's immense services to the Labour cause. He co-operated loyally with Larkin and refused to lend himself to the rumours of quarrels between them.

That summer Larkin shook the Transport Union to its depths by offering his resignation. He was suffering from nervous exhaustion which showed itself through increasing acerbity; there was conflict with his colleagues throughout the TUC meetings. He was persuaded by his friends in the Transport Union to withdraw his resignation. They suggested a complete change of scene in the form of an American fund-raising tour.

During this summer the Irish Labour Leaders, and particularly Connolly, set themselves steadfastly against any of the Government's proposed concessions to Ulster over Home Rule. The Buckingham Palace Conference of June between Asquith, Lloyd George, Lord Lansdowne, Bonar Law, Redmond, John Dillon, Sir Edward Carson and James Craig broke down over the question of the extent of Ulster's exclusion, and the Government was, therefore, obliged to fall back on Asquith's Amending Bill which was designed to enable any county in Ulster, including the cities of Belfast and Derry, to vote itself out of the Home Rule jurisdiction for six years. Carson and Connolly were certainly of a mind in one thing only: their total hostility to the Government's proposal. Carson said it was 'a sentence of death, with a stay of execution for six years'.[14] and Connolly wrote in *Forward* of 11 April,

The counties to be voted on the question are the counties where the Unionists are in an overwhelming majority, and where therefore, the vote is a mere farce – a subterfuge to hide the grossness of the betrayal of the Home Rule electors. Then again each county or borough enters or remains outside according to its own vote, and quite independent of the vote of its neighbours in Ulster. Thus the Home Rule question as far as Ulster is concerned, may be indefinitely prolonged and kept alive as an issue to divide and disrupt the Labour vote in Great Britain.

The effect of such exclusion upon Labour in Ireland will be at least equally, and probably more, disastrous . . . I am not speaking without due knowledge of the sentiments of the organized Labour movement in Ireland when I say we would much rather see the Home Rule Bill defeated than see it carried with Ulster or any part of Ulster left out.

In his newspaper, *Sinn Fein*, Griffith thundered on 21 March,

If Ireland were an independent country worsted in a foreign war, she might be forced to pay a heavy price, but there is one price she would never pay while there was virtue in her heart – the alienation of a square foot of her territory. If she paid that price her independence would be gone.

and on 11 April,

It is not whether 30,000 square miles or one square yard of our soil be alienated. It is whether Ireland is an entity. It is whether Ireland does or does *not* belong to the Irish. It is *whether the Irish nation is a reality or a myth*.

On Sunday 26 July 1914 the Nationalists proved that the Ulstermen were not the only ones who could run guns. The *coup* had been planned in London by Erskine Childers and his wife, Mary Spring-Rice (daughter of a Southern Unionist peer, Lord Monteagle), Mrs Stopford-Green, Sir Roger Casement and Darrel Figgis, a writer and journalist (who came to a tragic end unconnected with politics). It was planned to ship the guns (to be bought by Erskine Childers and Darrell Figgis on the Continent) in three yachts – the main consignment to be landed at Howth from Erskine Childers' yacht the *Asgard*. The Volunteers and the *Fianna* both had vital parts to play in the operation. A big parade of the Volunteers was arranged for that Sunday in the Father Mathew Park at Fairview. A company of the *Fianna* boys was also present. Many of the *Fianna* boys were summoned at the very last moment, that is to say on the Sunday morning, having no idea why they had been suddenly ordered to report at their headquarters with a day's rations. They made their way to Fairview with a closely covered and heavily loaded trek-cart. They then proceeded in the centre of the column of some seven hundred Volunteers to Howth, where they were ordered to the head of the column. Meanwhile, the *Asgard* in spite of the failure of the agreed signal from the shore (the appearance of Darrell Figgis in a small boat) was brought into harbour after some hesitation on Childers' part. The O'Rahilly was amongst those on the quay. He wrote afterwards, 'When the White Yacht, the harbinger of Liberty, suddenly appeared out of nowhere, and, on the stroke of the appointed hour, landed her precious freight at Howth, history was in the making.'[15] The *Fianna* contingent rushed forward with the trek-cart which they were told to unload at the double. They found that far from containing 'minerals and refreshments' for the Volunteers as they had been told, the cart contained nothing less than large wooden batons for the protection of the gun-running party. The coastguards realized something was extremely amiss so they sent up rockets for help. The Volunteers broke into cheers of triumph. The guns were safely distributed, the trek-cart was loaded, together with motor-cars belonging to sympathizers, and the now armed men prepared to march back to Dublin. Crowds appeared to watch them; a priest blessed them from the top of a tram. The Volunteers went ahead of the *Fianna* who were by now weary with the strain of pulling the heavy trek-cart. Nearing Clontarf the *Fianna* party saw a company of soldiers with fixed bayonets blocking their way. (This was a contingent of the King's Own Scottish Borderers brought on the scene through the medium of the Assistant Commissioner of the Dublin Metropolitan Police.) The *Fianna* swerved and went down Charlemont Road and out on to the Malahide Road. A *Fianna* member who was there wrote afterwards,

Before we were a hundred yards on the Malahide Road we knew that the first companies of Volunteers were in conflict with the military. The sounds of rifles clashing, revolver shots and shouting, made a terrific din. We got the order to 'halt', and we were told we had got to defend the ammunition at all costs. The Captain of *Cead Sluagh* drew an automatic pistol, and with some of our fellows dashed off into the fray . . . We clustered round the cart with our rifles gripped tightly in our hands. Suddenly we saw the Volunteers scatter and run. Some of the men were bleeding from the head, but most of them seemed uninjured and still clung to their rifles. As they passed us we appealed to them to stand. We shouted and called them cowards. Our commander, not knowing that they had received orders to retire and get off with their rifles, shouted 'By God! We won't run away.'[16]

The *Fianna* contingent found themselves in the middle of a police baton charge. The narrator continues,

Everything was confusion. I saw the police and the soldiers and the glitter of their bayonets as in a maze. A huge policeman with a rifle swooped towards me. I was seized with a sort of frenzy, and putting forth all my strength I made a deadly blow at his head.[17]

Ten or twelve of the *Fianna* made off with the trek-cart and left the main road. They passed two old men gossiping near a pump, who appeared quite oblivious of the affray near by. The trek-cart party turned up a lane near a big house; they decided to pretend they wanted to camp out and then to bury the ammunition until it could be safely removed. Permission was granted by the unsuspecting owners; the ammunition was buried, and so far as that group of Nationalists was concerned their day ended happily.

But nearer to the city an incident took place which added more fuel to the fires of hatred for England. As the British troops marched back into Dublin, (the Volunteers, incidentally, having got away with all their guns except for nineteen), the crowds started to jeer and to throw stones, causing injuries to a number of the soldiers. The officer in command ordered some of his men to halt and to be ready to fire. In the confusion of the moment some men thought they had received the order and fired into the crowd, killing three people, and wounding thirty-two. The Bachelor's Walk incident, as it came to be known, caused the most intense indignation in Ireland. What exacerbated the Nationalists most being the fact that Ulster Unionists, as opposed to Irish Nationalists, marched about armed, unchecked by the British. The populace seized on the event as the basis for one of the vast displays of public mourning which were always the outward expression of far more than the actual death of the mourned.

On that Sunday, 26 July, Constance was at her cottage with Nora Connolly, having held a successful *Fianna* convention there. That night Nora Connolly and her *Fianna* girls, who had come from Belfast, were just about to make a dash in the rain for their tents when half a dozen *Fianna* boys appeared in a state of great elation, waving their clubs and demanding that Constance should guess what they had been doing. 'It's too much trouble to guess,' she said, 'tell us about it and we'll know all the quicker.'[18]

The next morning Constance and the boys departed early in the sunshine for Dublin, leaving Nora Connolly and the girls to clear up. That morning, Constance's young friend, Maurice O'Connell Fitz-Simons was out for a walk with his father when he saw three cars pull up at the entrance to the grassy track which leads to the cottage. Father and son remained watching. They saw a man approach the cottage (in fact a *Fianna* captain who spoke to Nora Connolly). Soon other men came out of the cars carrying rifles and boxes of ammunition which they rushed into the hiding-place the cottage afforded. Maurice's father remarked that it was time to go home for tea, and he told his son never to speak of what he had seen. It seems likely that this consignment was all or part of the trek-cart load – since the *Fianna* member who wrote the account of the gun-running states that the buried arms were got safely away by taxi – and who but Constance would they have

1 Constance aged
five on her pony
at Lissadell

2 Constance and
Eva at Lissadell,
painted by Sarah
Purser

3 The garden side of Lissadell

4 The gallery at Lissadell

5 Constance as a debutante in 1886

6 Constance with
her brother,
Josslyn, in 1895

7 Constance in the
woods at Lissadell

8 Constance and a friend in her London studio

9 Pastel of Constance by her friend, Anna Nordgren, 1899

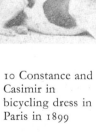

10 Constance and
Casimir in
bicycling dress in
Paris in 1899

11 Constance and
Casimir on their
wedding day: 29
September 1900

12 Casimir in the Paris flat in the Rue Campagne Première,
dressed as Maréchal Ney

13 Constance in peasant dress in the Ukraine in 1902

14 Casimir's home, Zywotowka, in the Ukraine

15 Constance with
her daughter,
Maeve, and her
stepson, Stanislas

16 Constance's first Dublin home, St Mary's, Frankfort Avenue

17 Constance and Casimir in their fancy dress
Dublin Castle Ball of 1905

18 Casimir as the
Pirate King in
*The Pirates of
Penzance* in 1906

19 Constance as
Lady Alathea in
The Dillettante in
1908

20 Belcamp Park,
Raheny

21 Surrey House,
Dublin

22 Casimir with his friends in the Arts' Club in about 1912.
Cartoon by Beatrice Elvery

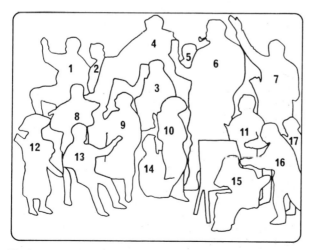

Key: 1 Roger Dickinson 2 Alan Duncan 3 Dominick Spring Rice 4
Jospeh How 5 O'Reilly 6 Casimir Markievicz 7 W. B. Yeats 8 Frank Craig
9 Frank Sparrow 10 Beatrice Elvery 11 Woods 12 Betty Duncan 13 James
Duncan 14 Conor O'Brien 15 W. Orpen 16 Richard Orpen 17 O'Connell

23 Casimir before
he finally left for
Russia in 1913

24 Stanislas
photographed
especially for
Constance before
he joined his
father in 1915

25 Constance in Citizen Army uniform with her dog Poppet in 1914

26 Constance with her *Fianna* boys

27 Constance at
the Ursuline
Convent in Sligo
after her release
from prison in
1917

28 Constance,
Maeve and Eva

first thought of as providing the safe repository for their booty? Nora Connolly and the girls took in the rifles, but they were quickly warned by a neighbour (perhaps the retired laundry-maid from Lissadell who occupied the adjoining cottage to that of Constance and acted as her caretaker) that it was most risky to have the rifles there because a retired police sergeant lived up the road. Nora Connolly sped into Dublin to get advice. She went to the Volunteer office where the star *Fianna* member, Liam Mellows, was temporarily in charge. He arranged to send out a taxi with two men to collect the rifles. The taxi travelled back with rifles, men, and Nora Connolly and some girls to sit on the rifles in order to hide them. The next day was spent in making funeral wreaths for Bachelor's Walk victims. Flowers were begged by the *Fianna* boys from sympathetic florists. Surrey House was crowded all day and humming with discussion about the funeral arrangements. The funeral was that night. All the Nationalist bodies paraded: the Volunteers and the Citizen Army, composing jointly the Guard of Honour, the *Fianna, Cumann na mBan*, and the Fintan Lalor Pipers. Nora Connolly found herself marching beside a weeping young man in British uniform whose mother had been killed by British soldiers.

Nine days after the Howth gun-running and the Bachelor's Walk incident Britain declared war on Germany. Connolly and Redmond acted swiftly according to their very different lights. Early in August, Connolly foreseeing the outbreak of war had got into touch with the chairman of the Ulster IRB and told him his intention of going to see the leaders in Dublin – remarking, 'Never mind about formalities; in times like these I am willing to take a score of oaths.'[19] Redmond, on England's declaration of war, without giving himself time to consult his whole party, pledged it and the Irish Volunteers to unconditional support of England, even going so far as to suggest that all British troops should be withdrawn from Ireland and that the Volunteers would defend their country (meaning for Britain). On Sunday, 20 September, Redmond was on his way to his country estate – Aughvanagh – when he discovered there was to be a parade of local Volunteers at Woodenbridge. He broke his journey to address them, saying,

This war is undertaken in defence of the highest principles of religion and morality and right, and it would be a disgrace for ever to our country . . . if young Ireland confined her efforts to remaining at home to defend our shores or Ireland from unlikely invasion, and shrunk from the duty of providing on the field of battle that gallantry and courage which has distinguished our race all through its history.[20]

Redmond's pledges and exhortation were most ill-received by the Nationalists amongst the Irish Volunteer committee. They decided to take action against him. On 25 September a Convention was summoned in order to 'repudiate any undertaking given by the Redmondites, and affirm the principles of the Volunteers'. A manifesto was signed by, among others, Eion MacNeill, Bulmer Hobson, the O'Rahilly, Padraic Pearse, Thomas MacDonagh, Joseph Plunkett, expelling Redmond's nominees from the committee. The result of this was that the Volunteers split into two movements, Redmond's followers being called the National Volunteers and the Nationalists retaining the name the Irish Volunteers. By far the largest number of Volunteers followed Redmond – about 168,000, as against 12,000 for MacNeill, which perhaps proves that the rank and file felt like the honorary treasurer, Mrs Stopford-Green, did about him when she wrote to Redmond that she had 'seldom seen a man more unfitted for action, and less fit to lead others in a difficult crisis.'

In this same September, in the blameless setting of the Gaelic League headquarters, a significant meeting took place, summoned by the Supreme Council of the Republican Brotherhood. Tom Clarke was there, and Connolly, Griffith, Pearse and Sean MacDermott. At this meeting the fateful decision was discussed that there should be an armed insurrection against England, at a time to be determined. The fuse was now set. It only remained to choose the time to light the match.

During the summer of 1914 the latent hostility between Sean O'Casey and Constance came to a head. She has left no record of her side of the affair. His account is chiefly to be found in his *Story of the Irish Citizen Army*. Apart from the surface irritations set up between two personalities who evidently mixed about as well as oil and water, there was the more important question of their differences over the attitude of the Citizen Army towards the Volunteers. When the Committee of the Volunteers accepted the Redmond nominees in May, Sean O'Casey considered this action to be the last betrayal. It is also impossible to avoid the conclusion that he looked on it as a stick with which finally to beat Constance for her friendship with various Volunteer leaders, such as the O'Rahilly, Padraic Pearse, Thomas MacDonagh. She was also on the committee of *Cumann na mBan* (the Women's Council), one of whose functions was to act as a military auxiliary to the Volunteers. O'Casey as Honorary Secretary summoned a special meeting of the Citizen Army Council to discuss whether or not members of the Council would be permitted to continue to have an 'active and sympathetic connection' with the Volunteer Movement. O'Casey writes that 'this thrust was aimed purposely at Countess Markievicz'.

At the Council meeting, at which according to O'Casey's list neither Larkin nor Connolly were among the fourteen men present, O'Casey moved the motion,

Seeing that Madame Markievicz was, through *Cumann na mBan*, attached to the Volunteers, and on intimate terms with many of the Volunteer leaders, and as the Volunteer Association was, in its methods and aims, inimical to the first interests of Labour, it could not be expected that Madame could retain the confidence of the Council; and that she was now being asked to sever her connection with either the Volunteers or the Irish Citizen Army.

O'Casey added that he felt it was the most honest course for him to pursue – to state frankly what he thought about her connection with an association 'with which the Irish Citizen Army differed so widely'. Five of the members 'vigorously opposed' the motion, and after a 'warm discussion' a vote of confidence was proposed and carried by seven votes to six. William O'Brien, who was present, is quoted by Dr Edward MacLysaght as saying in his memoirs (which are awaiting publication) that Thomas Foran, president of the Transport Union, who rarely attended meetings, came especially to this Council and voted for Constance, giving her her majority of one. But O'Casey says further, in *Drums Under the Windows*, that Constance voted for herself (which he failed to do for himself) and thus carried the day. It was then moved that the Secretary be called to tender an apology to Countess Markievicz (one imagines the meeting must have become very heated by this time). He refused, and instead wrote out his resignation which was accepted by a meeting of the Council a few days later.

More was to come. Larkin – probably at Constance's instigation, since she was a great one for having things out – called a general meeting of members to discuss the situation. Larkin made a statement and appealed to O'Casey to withdraw anything he had said against Constance for the sake of peace within the Army. O'Casey refused. This was the end of his connection with the Citizen Army. It is sad to think of the confrontation. The young man, delicate, poor, his genius unguessed at; and the middle-aged rebel, as isolated as he was in her way, and yet seeming to have the big battalions on her side.

Later in 1914 Larkin went to America, where he remained for eight years, leaving Connolly in control. With the outbreak of the war, many Irish extremists looked to Germany for help in the one struggle which really mattered to them – theirs against England. So imbued was Constance with the dire necessity of help from some-where, anywhere, she was as prepared as anyone to co-operate with the enemy of England. It is even said by her friends that she would point out her fine crop of tomatoes in that summer and say it was to grace the table of the Kaiser when he arrived in Ireland. (Since her most devoted friends surviving, recall that she had no sense of humour, rather a sense of mischief, it is difficult to know quite how to interpret the tomato story.) At any rate, circumstantial evidence points to her being on a secret sub-committee sponsored by the IRB with the aim of making contact with Germany. Nora Connolly recalls in her *Portrait of a Rebel Father* that late in 1914 her father, in Constance's presence, told her she was to go to America with a message so dangerous it could only be given verbally, and that were its purport to be discovered it would mean death for her-self, her father, Tom Clarke, Sean MacDermott and Madame Markievicz. Nora was met on the other side by Constance's great friend 'John Brennan'. She stayed with more friends of Constance's – Padraic Colum and his wife. Nora Connolly relates that she did not tell Larkin of her mission, and that she was asked by the famous, elderly Fenian, John Devoy, to take back to Ireland letters from Roger Casement, who was in Germany endeavouring both to get arms and ammunition for the Irish Nationalists and to raise an illegal Irish Brigade from Irish prisoners in German camps. Devoy offered to pay Nora Connolly's passage. She travelled back in the *Lusitania*.

Roger Casement was one of the most controversial of all the strange, courageous and doomed figures thrown up by Ireland's struggle to be free of England. His portrait in middle age by Sarah Purser shows a marvellously handsome man who is a mixture of monk and *conquistadore*. He was born in 1864 of a Protestant father and a Catholic mother, and brought up in Antrim. Through the interest he developed in West Africa, and his participation in General Henry Sanford's explorations in the Congo, he became appointed to the British Colonial service as Travelling Commissioner in the Nigerian Protectorate, and later Consul at Lourenço Marques in Portuguese East Africa, followed by two appointments in the Congo. He first became known (and received his baptism of spiritual fire) through his report on the Congo which with its frank and detailed revelations of the brutalities of Belgian rule caused a sensation. In the true tradition of the Goddess of Irony who appears to preside over the old Ireland, he, who was considered at his traitor's death at the hands of the British a Catholic martyr in the cause of free, Catholic Ireland, was then hounded down by the Catholic hierarchy in Belgium and elsewhere as a tool of British Protestantism. The British Foreign Office failed to give Casement the support that he felt was his due and he was indignant.

Roger Casement's health was affected by his journeys in the Congo. In a mood of deep disgust with the British Foreign Office he returned to Ireland for an extended vacation. With his intense humanitarianism and his interest in oppressed nations it is hardly surprising that he fell in with Ulster Nationalists such as Mrs Stopford-Green and Bulmer Hobson. He even went so far, although he was still in the employ of a British Government department, as to offer to assist Mrs Stopford-Green and Bulmer Hobson in the compilation of an anti-enlisting pamphlet. From 1906 to 1911 he was *en poste* in South America, where in 1910 he investigated the conditions of employees in the rubber reserves of the Peruvian Amazon Company. His exposure of atrocities inflicted on the natives brought him Foreign Office praise and a knighthood. He retired to Ireland on his pension. Through the years of absence he had not lost touch with his Nationalist friends, and during his leaves he saw much of Arthur Griffith and his circle. It was no doubt during these visits to Dublin that he made friends with Constance, and through her with Eva Gore-Booth.

Roger Casement was in the vanguard of those who looked on Germany as the most hopeful means of freeing Ireland. He foresaw the 1914 War. He was convinced that England's danger must be Ireland's opportunity. In July 1913 he wrote an article in the

Irish Review, under the pen-name *Shan Van Nocht*, in which he said,

I propose to show that Ireland, far from sharing the calamities that must necessarily fall upon Britain from defeat by a Great Power, might conceivably thereby emerge into a position of much greater prosperity.

Casement's activities, therefore, in the early months of the war were perfectly consistent with his past views and actions. It was only a step farther on from helping to write an anti-enlisting pamphlet in the first years of the century, to endeavour to suborn the, to him, deluded and misguided Irish members of His Majesty's Forces. The logic of others is a more potent source of disagreement than are their inconsistencies.

In the autumn of 1914 Constance had the disagreeable experience of being asked by the British Police authorities to register as an alien. She indignantly refused, saying she was an Irishwoman. The police replied that they meant, of course, a friendly alien, whereupon she told them that no nation that was on England's side could be regarded as friendly. It is not recorded what the Police authorities made of this, but, in fact, Constance, as Casimir's wife was a subject of the Czar and later of the USSR. A few weeks later the police raided Surrey House. Her friend, John Brennan, wrote that they:

carried off a large number of back numbers of *Munsey's*, and a disused printing press. The Countess had been prepared for their visit for many months, but happened to be out at the time it occurred. She returned just in time to see their exit and to present them with an obsolete make of rifle, which, she assured, them, would lend a colourful and dramatic touch to their visit.[21]

On another occasion, recalled by Nora Connolly, during the months of preparation for the armed insurrection, Constance was surprised by callers when she was working on plans of the Dublin streets with the key points marked for the Commandants who would have to hold them. She pushed her drawing-board away, remarking that she was drawing out a housing scheme for Mr Connolly.

With so much dangerous and secret activity in her life it is not surprising that Constance was worried about Stasko's future. He was now eighteen. He was working in the autumn of 1914 at the

Berlitz School of Languages in Grafton Street, learning French and Russian. With all her manifold projects, Constance still made time to help him with his work, reading the *Echo de Paris* with him so as to correct his diction. At one moment she had an idea he might work in the offices of the family solicitors; there was also the possibility of entering Trinity College, but Constance declared herself apprehensive that he would join the Officer's Training Corps and become identified with the enemy. In that same autumn Constance and Stasko had a family outing when they went to see Princess Bariatynska act the part of Anna Karenina. Constance was not impressed by the Princess's acting, but both she and Stasko greatly admired the 'Mazurka scene'. After the performance there was a collection for Russian soldiers. Constance disapproved of this, remarking to Stasko that Irish money should stay in Ireland.

In September of this year soon after Redmond's ill-judged Woodenbridge speech pledging the Volunteers to England, Asquith came over to Dublin to address a giant recruiting meeting. A plan was formed to use Irish Volunteers and Citizen Army men to seize the Mansion House before the meeting, but it was abandoned. What did take place was an impressive Citizen Army demonstration on the night Asquith was to speak. A brake set out from Liberty Hall, carrying Larkin, Connolly, Constance and P. T. Daly. Following it were a hundred Citizen Army men with fixed bayonets. They made a great impression. They marched up O'Connell Street and Grafton Street, then they halted in St Stephen's Green as near the Mansion House as they could get (it being cordoned off by the police). While Asquith, inside, was assuring his audience that no Irishman need be afraid of losing his identity be joining the British colours – 'we all want to see an Irish Brigade' (a fine example in the light of subsequent events of the vain promises of politicians) – the anti-recruiters outside were addressing cheering crowds who from time to time drowned Asquith's voice. At that meeting he only secured six recruits.[22]

Early in October Connolly launched the Irish Neutrality League. He became president and among the committee members were Arthur Griffith, Francis Sheehy-Skeffington, Constance, and William O'Brien. Soon after the inaugural meeting of the League, Constance gave a lecture (on 18 October) under the auspices of the Irish Labour party in the Trades Hall. Her theme was neutrality.

'The burden and suffering that would fall on the common people as a result of the present war,' she said, 'would be greater than in any other war . . . The present duty of every Irishman is to stay at home and fight, if at all, for the welfare of his own country.'[23]

Larkin departed for America on 24 October, leaving Connolly as both acting General Secretary of the union and editor of the *Irish Worker* (not, however, without some skirmishings when Larkin tried to install P. T. Daly). One of Connolly's first actions was to have a banner stretched across the front of Liberty Hall bearing the defiant legend 'We serve neither King nor Kaiser but Ireland.'[24] Sean O'Casey describes watching Connolly and Constance at a parade outside Liberty Hall. He comments that Connolly looked awkward in his new uniform and with his bow-legs 'ensnared in rich, red-brown leather leggings' which add to the waddle of his walk. But his derision was softened by admiration,

There was a dire sparkle of vanity lighting this little group of armed men: it sparkled from Connolly's waddle, from the uniformed men stiff to attention, and from the bunch of cock-feathers fluttering in the cap of the Countess. But it was a vanity that none could challenge, for it came from a group that was willing to sprinkle itself into oblivion that a change might be born in the long-settled thought of the people.[25]

Nora Connolly relates in her autobiography how she loved to visit the guardroom at night when the 'long, dimly lit room was filled with men. Stacked around the walls were the rifles, bandoliers and haversacks, and the men sat in groups busily cleaning and polishing parts of the guns, or sharpening the bayonets, while the ruddy light of the fire glinted around them.'

In October 1914 there took place an important Volunteer Convention where the crucial point at issue was between those who wanted to plan for an armed insurrection and those who did not. The situation was made more confused by the hidden influence of the secret IRB committee within the Volunteers. It was IRB influence (unknown to Connolly) which caused the rejection of his offer of affiliation between the Citizen Army and the Volunteers. Both the Citizen Army and the Volunteers paraded while the Convention deliberated. Later Connolly, P. T. Daly, and Constance held a meeting, together with Padraic Pearse, who had never before shared a platform with Connolly. At the

Convention the moderates (who included Eion MacNeill) carried the day, but authority had become sufficiently alarmed to dismiss the Volunteer's best instructor Captain Monteith from his Government post and to order him to leave Dublin. Connolly organized a protest meeting, at which William O'Brien presided, and the O'Rahilly spoke, as well as P. T. Daly, Constance, and Sean Milroy.[26]

With the close of the year the authorities suppressed the newspapers, *Sinn Fein*, *Irish Freedom* and the *Irish Worker*.

In February 1915 Constance was presented with the Illuminated Address which was the outward sign of the ITGW Union members' appreciation of her efforts to help them. This address was not presented earlier because Larkin had refused to sign – it was thought out of partisanship for his sister, Delia. The Address bears a picture of Lissadell and Liberty Hall (strange juxtaposition) and the text declares that the members and officers of the Union, wish to present Countess de Markievicz with 'a memorial of the high esteem and affection' in which she is held as a result of her 'unselfish and earnest labours on their behalf during the Great Dublin Lockout 1913–1914'.

At a time when all the forces of Capitalism had combined to crush the Workers, when the forces of the British Crown were exhibiting all their traditional brutality and hatred of the people, in ferocious batonings and murders; when the prisons were full of innocent men, women and girls, and all looked black before us, you came to our aid to organize relief, and for months worked amongst us, and served the cause of labour by such untiring toil, far-seeing vigilance and sympathetic insight as cheered and encouraged all who were privileged to witness it . . .

At the same time Constance was made an Honorary member of the Union.

In this same month Edward Dalton organized a public poll to discover who was the most popular woman in the Labour movement. One imagines that the idea behind it may have been to counteract the effect of the presentation, since Delia Larkin won the poll by a large majority. It is most unlikely that two such dynamic figures as Delia Larkin (who possessed many of her brother's characteristics) and Constance could have worked happily in harness together. That summer Delia Larkin resigned as the result of disagreements with officials in the Women's Workers Union and went to England.

On 18 February Constance engaged herself in public debate with her friend, Francis Sheehy-Skeffington, on the subject 'Do We Want Peace Now?' Mrs Skeffington recalls that the debate was 'passionate, and prolonged, both protagonists being convinced and sincere'. Francis Sheehy-Skeffington – 'Skeffy' – loved by his friends for his kindness, a don-like figure full of good works was a pacifist, so he argued for the benefits of an early peace, while Constance, as a militant Nationalist, maintained that the longer the war the better hope of Ireland's independence. Connolly was watching from the back. Just before the vote was taken he intervened with a 'strong speech' which tipped the scales in Constance's favour. When Sheehy-Skeffington mildly remonstrated with him afterwards for intervening, Connolly replied that he had been afraid the wrong side would win.[27]

In February 1915, too, the other face of Ireland showed itself when on the 12th the Aberdeens were presented with a farewell address in the Mansion House, to mark the close of their Vice-regal reign. They were told that their lives were 'models of devotion to duty' and that 'their Court gave an example and inspiration to the country ... Revered by the people, you are honoured by the Crown. Henceforth you shall not be alone Marquis and Marchioness of Aberdeen – but also – dearer to us, Marquis and Marchioness of Temair. Your new honour is rooted in the most cherished seat of our ancient Kings and heroes.' The Address was bound in St Patrick's blue morocco stamped with Celtic designs, and enclosed in a 'costly gold-mounted casket of Irish manufacture', and accompanied by a replica of the Ardagh Chalice. Lady Aberdeen told the gathering that 'on arriving in Ireland in 1886 (i.e. their first, brief tenure of the Castle) we had plighted our troth to Ireland for better or worse – for richer for poorer, till death us do part – and that we have never regretted the pledge.'[28]

In April Constance had a letter from Casi. His life had not lacked adventure, even after the collapse of the Prince of Weid's *coup*. Casi was working as a newspaper correspondent in the Balkans and Italy when war broke out. On reading of the Grand Duke Nicholas's proclamation to the Poles, Casi immediately responded by taking horse and riding 700 miles (not on the same horse, one imagines) in order to join up in an Imperial Hussar regiment. He was wounded in the winter campaign in the Carpathians, then became seriously ill with typhus and remained for many weeks in Lwow on the point of death. His brother, Jan, finally got him home to convalesce. Jan and his wife, Lena, had endured a shattering blow a few years previously in the death of their son from drowning on a school outing. Lena never recovered from her grief, and Casi on rejoining his family found her 'nervous and unaccountable'.

Stasko's future was now decided. He was to go to his father in the Ukraine. Casi sent three hundred roubles (£33). Stasko raised a little more money through selling Constance his two rifles (one of which can still be seen in the National Museum in Dublin) together with his two bicycles. He had a daunting journey ahead of him – through Norway, Sweden and Finland to Petrograd and thence to the Ukraine. Constance, with his childhood friend, Æ's son Brian Russell, saw him off on 15 June. With Stasko's departure Constance lost the last of her close family ties, apart from Eva. In Æ's words she was, indeed, to 'fight and suffer' to 'endure loneliness, the coldness of friends, the alienation of love' for the sake of 'that high and holy Eri of prophecy'.

CHAPTER 12

A Terrible Beauty is Born

On 1 August 1915 the funeral of the venerated Fenian, O'Donovan Rossa, provided the occasion for yet another Nationalist display of mourning. His body had been brought back from America for burial. It lay in state in the City Hall, guarded by both the Volunteers and the Citizen Army. He was buried at Glasnevin Cemetery after a funeral procession in which all the Nationalist organizations took part: the Volunteers, the Citizen Army, the *Fianna, Cumann na mBan*, Irish Girl Guides, National Foresters, Hibernian hurling teams. It was surely this funeral procession which Eva Gore-Booth's friend, Esther Roper, describes herself and Eva watching from a window 'about twelve months before Easter Week' when, they saw, 'Padraic Pearse in uniform and men and women of the Citizen Army and Volunteers, *Fianna* boys, women of *Cumann na mBan* and a crowd of sympathizers march by. After they had passed, Esther Roper relates that thinking 'with admiration of all those gifted people in those ranks' she said to Eva with relief, 'Well, thank goodness, they can't be planning a rising now, not with such a tiny force.'[1]

At the graveside Padraic Pearse, dressed in the uniform of a Commandant of the Volunteers, delivered the oration in words which were long remembered.

We pledge to Ireland our life, and to English rule in Ireland our hate . . . Our foes are strong and wise and wary; but strong and wise and wary as they are, they cannot undo the miracle of God, who ripens in the hearts of young men the seeds sown by the young men of a former generation. And the seed sown by the young men of '65 and '67 are coming to their miraculous ripening today.

Rulers and Defenders of the Realms had need to be wary if they would guard against such processes. Life springs from death, and from the graves of patriot men and women spring living nations. The Defenders of this realm have worked well in secret and in the open. They think they have pacified Ireland. They think that they have purchased half of us and intimidated the other half. They think they have foreseen everything, they think that they have provided against everything; but the fools, the fools! – they have left us our Fenian dead, and while Ireland holds these graves, Ireland unfree will never be at peace.

A volley was fired over the grave by the Volunteers. Padraic Pearse left the cemetery alone, then took a tram back to St Enda's School.

It was possibly during this visit of Eva and Esther Roper to Dublin that the incident took place which shows Connolly's unsleeping personal concern for the individual as well as for workers in the mass. Esther Roper relates that she and Constance and Eva were sitting at supper with Connolly 'talking about Socialism' when a woman rushed into the house in a state of great agitation, saying that 'a young girl member of the Union had left her home and disappeared into the slums'. Connolly immediately left the table and went in search of her – not returning until he had found her and taken her back to her home. He got back about midnight to continue the conversation and drink tea, instead of the supper he had left.[2]

Constance's home was now a recognized 'open house' for any Nationalist who cared to go there. Mrs Sheehy-Skeffington recalling for Esther Roper, after Constance's death, the atmosphere of those evenings when Constance would issue a last-minute invitation to the Skeffingtons wrote that Constance would say 'the gas is cut off and the carpets up, but you won't mind'. 'They would talk,' says Mrs Sheehy-Skeffington, 'round the big fire, sitting on her large divan in the big bow window, by the light of innumerable candles stuck around.'

Another familiar of the house, Frank Kelly, recalled for Constance's first biographer, Sean O'Faolain, his memories of that time,

Crowds used to gather into it at night. We had tea in the kitchen; a long table with Madame cutting up slices of bread about an inch thick, and handing them around . . . She had lovely furniture and splendid pictures. Then we used to go into the sitting-room and someone would sit at the piano and there would be great singing and cheering and rough amusements. She had lifted her lovely drawing-room carpet but had left her pictures on the walls and on the bare boards there was stamping of feet.[3]

Frank Kelly describes seeing Connolly sitting looking into the fire and speaking to no one. Then he suddenly got up and left the room. That night Michael Collins was there and recited Emmet's speech from the dock at the top of his voice. In the midst of all this coming and going, teaching and marching, speechifying and plotting, Constance is remembered by Nora Connolly as embarking on the ambitious work of embroidering four large curtains of unbleached linen in a Jacobean design.

Those who had trusted in Asquith's assurances to Irish recruits that they would never be absorbed in 'an invertebrate mass' were soon disappointed. The Secretary of State for War was Lord Kitchener, whose childhood in Kerry had unfortunately left him with an ineradicable prejudice against the southern Irish; the officer in command of the third Irish Division information was General Parsons, whose every action showed he was influenced by Kitchener and not by Asquith. The Ulster Volunteers remained a unit in an Ulster Division, and they were allowed to use the Red Hand of Ulster* as their divisional emblem. No such concession was granted to the southern Irish. In spite of Lady Mayo's school of embroidery making a flag it was returned to her. The southern Irish were refused a distinctive division. They were not even allowed a badge. General Parson also showed great reluctance in granting commissions to Irish gentlemen. He refused one to Stephen Gwynn, who was over fifty and had been MP for Galway for eight years. He was told he could join through the ranks. Gavan Duffy – a member of a well known Irish family – came all the way from Australia to join up only to be refused a commission.[4] Lloyd George, who was then Chancellor of the Exchequer, remarked that the attitude of the War Office amounted to 'stupidities which almost looked like malignancy'.[5] It was a personal tragedy for Redmond, and fuel to the fire of the Nationalists. Connolly had written in the *Irish Worker* at the end of August 1914, that the English wanted to wage war on Germany so that British and Irish capitalists should be enabled to steal German trade.

* The historical origin of Ulster's emblem is the legendary rowing race for territory between a McDonnell and an O'Neill. In order to win the O'Neill claimant cut off his hand and threw it ahead of him to the finishing point.

The British Capitalist class have planned this colossal crime in order to ensure its uninterrupted domination of the commerce of the world. To achieve that end it is prepared to bathe a continent in blood, to kill off the flower of the manhood of the three most civilized great nations of Europe ... Yes, this is the war of a pirate upon the German nation. And up from the blood-soaked graves of the Belgian frontiers the spirits of murdered Irish soldiers of England call to Heaven for vengeance upon the Parliamentarian tricksters who seduced them into the armies of the oppressor of their country.

Throughout 1915 the Volunteers and the Citizen Army marched and drilled. Connolly's men had many night marches. There were two midnight exercises, one of them based on the supposition that Dublin Castle was in the hands of insurgents and that the Citizen Army had to prevent its relief by the British. Constance, who by this time had been given a commission in the Citizen Army by Connolly, was in the forefront of this manoeuvre.

Within Nationalist councils the two tails continued to wag the dog: the moderate Eion MacNeill – Bulmer Hobson group which believed in any course short of armed insurrection, acting in ignorance of the insurrection plans of the IRB group led by Padraic Pearse, Thomas MacDonagh, and Sean MacDermott. Connolly, still ignorant of IRB plans continued in articles and speeches to press for extreme action. Early in February 1915 he had succeeded in installing a private printing press at Liberty Hall, since he rightly foresaw a series of Government confiscations of extremist newspapers. It was an old machine but it was capable of turning out 1,600 copies an hour.

At Christmas a new friend came into Constance's life when a young woman called Margaret Skinnider came over from Glasgow with some detonators. The day after her arrival at Surrey House Constance took her into the Wicklow hills where they tried out the detonators and succeeded in blowing up a wall. Margaret Skinnider recalls that during this visit Constance heard that word had come from America that a shipload of arms and ammunition would arrive in Ireland on or near Easter Sunday. It is difficult to place this incident in the tangled skein of Ireland's negotiations with Germany for arms. Perhaps Constance had received an optimistic private message from Roger Casement, although he was in a bad nervous state at the time.*

* Casement's attempt to form an Irish Brigade from Irish prisoners of war had been

The German Government were favourable to Casement's mission, but in that autumn they had received word from their High Seas Command that the plan suggested of sending a submarine to Tralee bay was impracticable because of insufficient depth of water. It was not until February 1916 that the veteran Fenian John Devoy of the American *Clan na Gael* got a message in code to the effect that the Supreme Council of the IRB had decided on the date of Easter Sunday 23 April for the insurrection.[6] They asked for arms. The *Clan na Gael*, whose coffers were empty on Ireland's behalf, negotiated with the German Embassy in Washington and succeeded in making arrangements for trawlers (which the High Seas Command considered the only feasible type of vessel for the job) to land ammunition at Fenit Pier, Tralee Bay, in County Kerry.

By January 1916 it had become clear to the IRB group in the Volunteers that Connolly would have to be taken into their counsels. Their decision to negotiate with him led to the strange incident when Connolly 'disappeared' for three days, leaving his office after lunch on Wednesday 19 January, and not returning to Surrey House until very late on the following Saturday night. A counsel of war was held on the Thursday between William O'Brien, his brother Daniel, Thomas Foran, president of the Union, Constance, and Michael Mallin (who was her commanding officer in the Rebellion). Constance apparently lost her head, for she is said to have demanded that the Citizen Army rise on its own even, apparently telling Pearse when she met him in the street that the Citizen Army was going to rush the Castle, with or without Connolly. She was only quieted by Michael Mallin's promise that he would get in touch with the IRB, whose Supreme Council was thought to be in session.[7] When Connolly emerged from what was for him an ordeal of decision as to how much he would sacrifice of Labour's programme for the sake of an insurrection, he said he had been 'through hell', but he did not disclose where the discussions had taken place. It is the opinion of Connolly's most recent biographer that in all probability the IRB had to abandon their conditions of no rising unless conscription were introduced into Ireland (as it had been by this time in

---

a signal failure – particularly because he first tried to influence NCOs of many years' service with the British colours. He was suspected by the Germans of being a British agent.

England) or that the Germans landed; and that Connolly, for his part, had to relinquish his dream of a 'revolution led by the working class and involving trade unions'.[8]

The night after Connolly's return, Surrey House was raided by the police. A *Fianna* boy had brought a quantity of gelignite to Dublin. Through a series of mishaps as to its delivery he had ended up at Constance's with it. He was later arrested, but the gelignite was never found.

On 26 March the Union Dramatic Society put on a play written by Connolly and called *Under Which Flag* (it is hard to believe that Constance had no hand in this venture), whose hero is a young man torn between the two poles of the British Army and the IRB. Needless to say he chooses the latter.

Two days before a crisis had occurred at Liberty Hall after the police had raided the premises of the Gaelic Press. Constance, who had heard the news and immediately saw the danger for Liberty Hall, rushed into Connolly's office. Nora Connolly was there. She at once began to make out Citizen Army mobilization forms. Constance, since she had left her revolver at Surrey House, borrowed one from James Connolly. News then came that the police were on their way. (Pickets had been run by the faithful from the police barracks to Liberty Hall.) The only thing that mattered to Connolly was to save his printing press. A Co-operative shop was attached to Liberty Hall from which a door led to the printing press. Nora Connolly, hurrying to the shop to give out the forms for distribution, found her father with a gun, Constance holding the Mauser she had borrowed, and Helena Molony who had succeeded Delia Larkin as secretary of the Women's Workers Union also handling her automatic. The forms were quickly slipped to a trusted Citizen Army man who delivered them to the Mobilization Officer and Michael Mallin. The police then entered the scene. They said they had come to search for and confiscate any copies of the publications *The Gael*, *The Gael Athlete*, *Honesty*, or *The Spark*, the latter paper being owned by Constance's friend Madame Perolz, and edited by Constance herself. Connolly, armed, seeing a policeman with a bundle of papers in his hand cried 'Drop them or I'll drop you'. He then with what would appear to be foolhardy courage, since he knew the regulations, asked to see the search warrant, although under the Defence of the Realm Regulations Act – DORA – this was not needed. An inspector and four plain clothes men then appeared on the scene, with a warrant, saying they had come to search for and confiscate any suppressed papers. Nora was terrified her father would be arrested. In the event the police found nothing and departed. No sooner was the danger over than the mobilized members started pouring in, having downed tools and left work on receipt of their orders. Work-stained and grimy some even soaked to the skin from having swum the canal they answered the summons loyally, a hundred and fifty of them arriving at Liberty Hall in less than an hour. Connolly decided that never again night or day would he let Liberty Hall be unguarded, so he asked a *Fianna* boy to go to Surrey House for his carbine and bandolier.

Later Constance went home and changed into her uniform preparatory to taking her turn standing guard. Nora Connolly describes her having a 'stand-up' snack in the kitchen of bread and butter and tea, wearing a dark green woollen tunic with brass buttons, tweed knee-breeches, black stockings, and heavy boots, armed with an automatic pistol and a Mauser rifle, and with a bandolier and haversack crossed on her shoulders. While Constance and Nora were standing in the kitchen two detectives knocked on the door. Constance went into the hallway and reduced the light to a glimmer, then opened the door. The detectives told her that they had come to prohibit her from entering County Kerry to speak at Tralee, under the Defence of the Realm regulations. (It seems possible she would have had other business there since it was the appointed rendezvous for the German arms ship.) The following dialogue took place between Constance and the detectives.

'What will happen if I refuse to obey the order and go to Kerry? Would I be shot?'
'Ah now, Madame, who'd want to shoot you? You wouldn't want to shoot one of us. Now would you, Madame?'
'But I would! I'm quite prepared to shoot and be shot at.'
'Ah now, Madame, you don't mean that. None of us want to die yet. We all want to live a little longer.'
'If you want to live a little longer you'd better not be coming here. None of us are fond of you, and you make grand big targets . . .'⁹

Connolly told Constance that she would be too valuable a prisoner were she arrested and suggested that Madame Perolz be asked to take her place. Back at Surrey House once more Constance settled down to write the speech. When she had finished, Nora Connolly watched her at her drawing-board working at the plans of the city – plans she was drawing out for the insurrection.

In this same month Constance's most able *Fianna* member – Liam Mellows – who had been appointed to lead the Rising in the West, was arrested and deported to England. Nora Connolly and Liam's brother, Herbert, departed on a mission to rescue him, which they succeeded in doing by the means of Herbert taking his place, while Liam returned to Ireland disguised as a priest.

While the days of April 1916 passed as fatefully as the count-down hours before space-flight, all who were in the plot completed their arrangements. On the personal level, Mrs Connolly arrived to spend Easter at Constance's cottage. Constance had a discussion with Dr Kathleen Lynn on the ever-present woman's problem of clothes. Should skirts be discarded altogether by the women warriors of the Citizen Army? In the end Constance compromised by wearing a skirt over her breeches when she was in uniform before the Rising so as not to attract too much attention.

On Holy Thursday there was a presentation to Dr Kathleen Lynn in Liberty Hall at which Constance made a speech before handing to Dr Lynn a poem she had written. Another poem of Constance's was printed in the last number of the *Workers Republic* published on Easter Saturday, 22 April, two days after the presentation.

> We are ready to fight for the Ireland we love
> Be the chances great or small;
> We are willing to die for the flag above
> Be the chances nothing at all.
>
> We have sworn by prison and torture and death
> By the faith of Emmet and Tone;
> By the martyr men of our noble race
> By the peaceful days that are gone,
>
> That to Ireland's days we'll devote our lives,
> That we'll stand where our forebears stood
> That as Ireland's soldiers we'll live and die
> In ranks with men of our blood . . .

So we're waiting till 'Somebody' gives the word
That sends us freedom or death;
As free men defiant we'd sooner fall
Than be slaves to our dying breath.

On Holy Thursday, too, Margaret Skinnider arrived from Glasgow to join the Citizen Army.

By Holy Thursday, in the outside world, Admiral Sir Lewis Bayley, C-in-C Queenstown had disposed his forces so as to watch for any suspicious vessels approaching Ireland's shores. On Holy Thursday the German ship disguised as a Norwegian trawler bearing the much-needed arms lay off Fenit Pier, flashing the pre-arranged signal and failing to elicit a response from the shore. On Good Friday the trawler was engaged by British vessels and escorted to Queenstown Harbour where at the last moment the German officer in command scuttled the ship. The British did not get the arms; but neither did the rebels. By a disastrous error and failure in communications the Volunteer officer at Tralee was not expecting the German ship until the week-end.

On Good Friday, too, Roger Casement, and the former Volunteer instructor Captain Monteith (a sworn IRB man) together with one of the few Irish prisoners of war Casement had succeeded in detaching from allegiance to the Crown, were landed by dinghy from the submarine which had brought them from Germany. They were discovered through information given by a farmer who was walking along Banna Strand on his way to pray at a holy well, and they were arrested that day by the RIC.

In Dublin confusion was growing. On the Wednesday of Easter week, Connolly told Citizen Army officers that the rising was planned for Easter Sunday at 6.30 pm in Dublin and 7 pm in the provinces. He gave them their instructions.[10] On Holy Thursday the truth burst at last upon Professor Eion MacNeill, head of the Volunteers, that an insurrection was actually planned for that week-end. Although it was late at night when Bulmer Hobson and others brought him the news, he went straight to see Pearse, who by this time, after Tom Clarke had refused the honour, had been named by the IRB as the President of the future Republic of Ireland. At St Enda's a stormy scene took place. Eion MacNeill declared that he would do anything to stop a rising short of ringing up the Castle.[11] The next day he was persuaded to change his mind. That evening the O'Rahilly entered the scene. He, like Eion MacNeill, was convinced of the futility of the proposed attempt and he acted strongly and decisively first confronting Pearse at St Enda's, then the havering leader. By this time definite news had arrived of the capture of Roger Casement and the loss of the arms ship. Eion MacNeill, now totally convinced by the O'Rahilly and his supporters, together with the plain facts of the double setback had one last abortive interview with Pearse and finally acted decisively; thereby virtually ensuring the failure of the rising. He countermanded the Volunteer orders, and went further by composing a newspaper announcement which he took himself to the *Sunday Independent* office.[12] The message, which struck total dismay into the hearts of the Citizen Army and the IRB faction in the Volunteers read,

Owing to the very critical position, all orders given to Irish Volunteers for tomorrow, Easter Sunday, are hereby rescinded and no parades, marches, or other movement of Irish Volunteers will take place. Each individual Volunteer will obey this order strictly in every particular.

Constance spent the Easter Saturday night with her friend, Mrs Wyse-Power. There she read the fateful announcement. She was, she recalls, 'stunned'. She made her way with all speed to Liberty Hall (which, incidentally, the new Viceroy, Lord Wimborne, was bent on having raided in order to round up the *Sinn Feiners*) where she found Connolly and Sean MacDermott sitting at a table in the room where Connolly worked and slept. In 1923 Constance wrote of this day,

'What has happened?' said I. 'MacNeill has cut the ground from under our feet,' said he. I began to lament and question them, he cut me short with, 'it will be all right, we are going on, it will only mean a little delay.'

When he said this he must have known that MacNeill's action had taken from us the little chance we had of winning, or even of holding out for long enough to create that public opinion that might have saved his life and the lives of other leaders.[13]

Nora Connolly was at Liberty Hall, having experienced a hazardous and difficult journey from the North. She had come for news since MacNeill's rescinding order had caused great confusion amongst the rank and file of the Volunteers. Constance wrote later that the Easter Sunday of 1916 was the busiest day she had ever lived through. The leaders were met throughout the day in Connolly's room – The Provisional Government of the Republic – so Constance called it. Tom Clarke was there, Sean MacDermott, and Pearse. Messengers came and went; the printing press rolled off the Proclamation of the Republic; new orders were sent out. As the hours passed and action took the place of dismay and disappointment, the organizers of the revolt acquired the courage and gaiety which belongs to those whose die is cast. 'Our hearts desire was granted to us,' wrote Constance, 'and we counted ourselves lucky.'

The Easter Rising was barely expected, hardly believed in at the outset, yet by the time the events it precipitated had run their full course it had gathered to itself the sum of a nation's buried aspirations. Dublin was exactly as usual that Easter Monday morning. There were many visitors for the races at Fairyhouse and the Spring Show of the Royal Dublin Society. The D'Oyly Carte opera company was about to open a season at the Gaiety theatre; Bernard Shaw had just published an article in the *Irish Times* called 'Irish Nonsense talked in Ireland'. The weather was fine, and since it was a late Easter the pleasure garden of St Stephen's Green enfolded the strollers, the children, the nursemaids, the idlers watching the ducks and gulls, in a net of young leaves.

The insurgents came early that morning to Liberty Hall for their final orders. Connolly addressed them, telling them, in his capacity of Commandant-General of all the insurgent forces in Dublin, that there was no longer a Citizen Army and a Volunteer force, but, instead, the Irish Republican Army.

Constance had been made a staff officer, together with Michael Mallin – who like all the leaders of the insurrection was not simply a politician, or a soldier; he was in fact a skilled silk weaver and a musician. Constance held the rank of Staff Lieutenant, with Mallin as her superior officer. Constance's friend, Dr Kathleen Lynn, as medical officer, held the rank of Captain.

While the unsuspecting city slept, the friends and comrades paraded that morning on the brink of the abyss that they knew was waiting for them: Tom Clarke with his long history of suffering for and faith in Ireland; Padraic Pearse, the solitary, fastidious scholar, the son of an Englishman, with his poet's conviction of Ireland's salvation through blood sacrifice; James Connolly, the valiant, seasoned fighter of the privileged, stoical in his necessary compromise over Labour's cause; Thomas MacDonagh, Greek scholar and poet, married to one of the spirited, gifted Gifford sisters; Joseph Plunkett, son of a papal Count, poet, one of the editors of the *Irish Review* and betrothed to Grace Gifford; Sean MacDermott, as delicate in health but as determined in spirit as Joseph Plunkett; Eamon Ceannt, City Treasury clerk and Gaelic Leaguer – and Constance, the only woman among the leaders, and having come a longer ideological journey than any of them to arrive at this day.

The broad plan, mainly worked out by Joseph Plunkett, was to set up a defence ring round the centre of the city and hold these points while the rising spread through the country. Connolly held the erroneous theory that a capitalist nation such as England would never destroy the buildings which were the seat of its temporal power. The insurgents had a force of only 120 Citizen Army men and 700 Volunteers. 'We are going to be slaughtered' said Connolly to William O'Brien in Liberty Hall.[14]

In spite of the fierce controversy before the rising, and the contradictory orders which ensued, there was no leakage of the secret. Once the die had been cast by Pearse and his comrades and the battle joined, both Eion MacNeill and the O'Rahilly abandoned their opposition to the venture and entered the fray. The gallant O'Rahilly was killed in a sortie when the GPO fell, Eion MacNeill was sentenced to life imprisonment for his part in the fighting.

On the Monday Constance, who had only recently learnt to drive, left Liberty Hall with Dr Kathleen Lynn in a car loaded with medical supplies for the City Hall. They drove through 'quiet, dusty streets' and reached the City Hall just as Connolly and his contingent came round the corner. A policeman tried to bar their way – no doubt with unconcern – since the Volunteers, and Citizen Army in their dark green uniforms and slouch hats were by now familiar and somewhat derisory figures marching about Dublin. But the policeman had a shock and Constance had her first sight of action, for Connolly shot him down. Excited crowds collected, but Dr Lynn and Constance were successful in getting the medical supplies into the building where the insurgents had already penetrated from the back. Constance then bade farewell to Dr Lynn, who, in fact, she did not see again until after her release from prison in 1917, and drove on to St Stephen's Green where she had to report to Michael Mallin. She was, as it happened, wearing his discarded Citizen Army tunic, which exactly fitted her except for the sleeves being too short.

When Constance arrived at the Green, Mallin told her he was so short of men that he must keep her with his unit instead of her acting as liaison officer between the different points, as had been planned. She must be ready to 'take up the work of a sniper', he told her. He took her round the 'familiar Green' with its 'unfamiliar barricades' and then left her in charge of the trench digging.

Meanwhile, the historic moment took place before the unbelieving eyes of indifferent passers-by when Connolly, Pearse, Clarke, Plunkett and the men charged the General Post Office in O'Connell Street, captured it and raised the Republican tricolour from its roof into the sunlit air. Pearse, standing with Clarke and Connolly on the plinth of the GPO read out the Proclamation of the Republic. 'Thank God,' said Connolly, 'that we have lived to see this day.'[15]

The insurgents at the Green had been faced with the problem of ejecting an indignant and bewildered public who were enjoying their holiday ease in the sun. Constance's friend, the poet and novelist James Stephens came through Merrion Row, which runs out of the Green, in the afternoon and saw groups of people staring intently in the direction of the Green. 'Has there been an accident?' he asked. 'The *Sinn Feiners* have seized the city this morning,' he was told. 'They seized the city at eleven o'clock this morning. The Green is full of them. They have captured the Castle. They have taken the post office.'[16]

In fact, the insurgents had not captured the Castle. They held Jacob's biscuit factory, which was a point of vantage, Boland's Mills, The Four Courts, and part of the South Dublin Union hospital and workhouse complex of buildings. But the Castle was intact and its offices and telephone service functioning. The attempt on it had failed through lack of pressing the initial advantage home.

It was between one and two o'clock on this first day that the page-boy of the University Club saw Constance drive up in a car, blow a whistle, then give orders to the rebels who were urging civilians out of the Green. He then, he alleged, saw her take aim from behind one of the monuments at the window of the club. (It was on this evidence that Constance was convicted after the rising.) Eva's friend, Esther Roper, quotes Constance as saying that the page could not have seen her from the place where he said he was standing, and Esther Roper, further, gives it as her personal opinion that Constance never really shot at anybody. On the other hand, Dr de Burgh Daly, who was then a medical officer in the RAMC, told Constance's stepson that he remembers standing in the window of the United Services Club talking to Mr Best (later Lord Chief Justice of Northern Ireland) when Mr Best exclaimed, 'Look out! There's a woman on the Green pointing a gun at us.' The window was slightly raised and a bullet cracked between the two men. Constance herself records that she spent her day making the rounds of the Green and 'tackling any sniper who was particularly objectionable'.

A British officer was taken prisoner that day. With what turned out to be unjustified faith in the word of an 'officer and gentleman' Mallin put him on parole and left him at large in the Green behind the barricaded gates. Considering, no doubt, that a word to a rebel was no pledge, the officer quietly observed all he could, then escaped. Other prisoners and wounded were put in the band-stand. All this day the insurgents in the Green were digging trenches. Passers-by found themselves urged to join the rebellion. Some did, including an elderly man who had served for seven years in the American artillery. During the day the bandstand had to be evacuated because the British had trained a machine gun on it from the Shelbourne hotel. This minor retreat was accomplished successfully by Constance's friend, Madeleine Ffrench-Mullen, who was in charge of Red Cross and the commissariat. One Citizen Army girl said to Constance, 'What is there to be afraid of? Won't I go straight to heaven if I die for Ireland?' During that day Mallin took the precaution of occupying the College of Surgeons. Constance walked up to the front door and rang the bell. When no one answered she blew the lock with her pistol and marched in. That day, too, Margaret Skinnider saw Constance's encounter with some British soldiers. They were marching down Harcourt Street, and Constance, together with Councillor William Partridge, watched them approach. She raised her rifle, took aim and fired into the group. Margaret Skinnider, who was bicycling up behind Constance, saw the two officers at the head drop to the ground.

Constance took aim again; the soldiers retreated the way they had come.

That evening at dusk Mallin told twenty men to go up Lower Leeson Street and hold the bridge. The night was mild and starry. The insurgents camped out, feeding themselves on bread commandeered from bakers' carts, sweets, tea, and biscuits from Jacobs factory – which was in the command of Thomas MacDonagh, aided by Maud Greene's estranged husband, John MacBride, who had come to Dublin for a wedding but could not resist joining in the fight against England. This action cost him his life.

Tuesday was a sultry, grey day that threatened rain. Rumours proliferated in the city and looting broke out on a large scale. The Dublin poor, come into their own for a few days of bullet-ridden bacchanalia, were so innocent in their first onrush of lawlessness that they looted toy shops and sweet shops, gorging themselves on chocolate, slabs of toffee, sticks of rock; or collecting armfuls of dolls and mechanical toys, or hitting golf balls with hockey sticks in the streets. Gold watches passed hands for the price of a shilling and boots and shoes went for threepence a pair. That night the wind lifted the clouds and the sky was full of stars. The St Stephen's Green contingent had to retreat into the College of Surgeons, and the Leeson Street Bridge party were ordered back again. Nellie Gifford (of the Larkin's 'niece' episode) was put in charge of a classroom which held a large grate, there was also plenty of coal, but she had nothing she could cook until she got hold of a quantity of oatmeal with which she made porridge. That Tuesday evening there took place the tragic episode of Francis Sheehy-Skeffington's arrest. He was non-militant to the last but he exposed himself to hourly danger through his self-imposed task of trying to keep order in the streets. He was arrested by British soldiers and taken to Portobello Barracks. He was questioned as to his politics. He admitted freely that he was in sympathy with the Nationalists but added that he was opposed to militarism. In the circumstances these were hardly views which would appeal to his hearers. What made it worse was that the officer in charge happened to be an unbalanced Irishman called Captain Bowen-Colthurst. In his disordered mind, the mildly eccentric, gentle, but adamant prisoner before him constituted a danger to the realm. He had Francis Sheehy-Skeffington shot. When Mrs

Sheehy-Skeffington, most alarmed by rumours, came to ask for news of her husband she was bullied and harried under Captain Bowen-Colthurst's orders, her house ransacked, her child frightened, and her husband's possessions confiscated.

In the College of Surgeons the initial confusion became arranged into some sort of order. Michael Mallin and Constance had the caretaker's two rooms as offices, and for what moments of rest they could get. Constance was a strict chaperone of the 150 men and 20 women who were under the same roof, making frequent tours of inspection. The Rosary was recited nightly by Councillor Partridge who had been wounded earlier in the week.

On Wednesday, a fine, sunny day, Margaret Skinnider was sent out with a party detailed to set fire to a house behind Russell's hotel (other accounts say she was in a party sent out to attack snipers). At any rate she was badly wounded, and brought back under fire by Councillor Partridge. A nightdress was urgently needed for her. This, surprisingly, was supplied by Corporal Liam O'Brien of the Volunteers (now Professor O'Brien) who had noticed one in the near-by flat in which he was stationed, foodless, with some comrades.

On Thursday the occupants of the College of Surgeons were much cheered by the discovery of a cache of sixty four rifles in perfect condition. But, had they known it, the news in the city was ominous. The GPO had been isolated by the British, and Connolly himself was seriously wounded. Nora Connolly, returning from Tyrone where she had been sent by Connolly with dispatches for Volunteer organizers, found her mother at Constance's cottage at Balally in a state of collapse because she had read in a newspaper that Connolly was dead. All the week Mrs Connolly had lived without news, seeing only the smoke and flames from the city, and with her nights haunted by the sound of gunfire. Great fires were spreading and the normal life of the city had virtually come to a standstill. The populace, as a whole, was infuriated by the insurgents, seeing only the bloodshed, the disruption of normality, the destruction of property and the unexpected dangers which menaced them personally. Never was a national movement less understood by its nation.

The insurgents had isolated successes born of courage against odds. Twelve Volunteers detailed by de Valera, in command at

Boland's Mills, held Mount Street Bridge for a day and an evening, inflicting casualties amounting to nearly half of those suffered by the British during the whole week. One of Constance's *Fianna* members, Sean Heuston, held out from Monday until Wednesday in his outpost of the Four Courts Garrison.

Of the Friday, James Stephens wrote in *The Insurrection in Dublin*

It is hard to get to bed these nights. It is hard even to sit down, for the moment one does sit down one stands immediately up again resuming the ridiculous ship's march from the window to the wall and back. I am foot weary as I have never been before in my life, but I cannot say I am excited. No person in Dublin is excited, but there exists a state of tension and expectancy which is mentally more exasperating than any excitement could be. The absence of news is largely responsible for this. We do not know what has happened, what is happening, or what is going to happen, and the reversion to barbarism (for barbarism is largely lack of news) disturbs us.

What had happened was that the adventure was practically over.

The news of the surrender came as a great shock in the College of Surgeons. All Saturday was spent in preparing for a possible charge by the British and these preparations involved demolishing the staircase that led to the main positions. The other great event for the hungry insurgents was the arrival of food, including a large piece of bacon.

That night, which was to be the last, there were prayers for the dead and dying. This experience was a crucial one in Constance's spiritual life. She wanted with all her being to join as an initiate in the Catholic prayers – having by now come to identify the Protestant religion with the oppressor and the Church of Rome with where her heart and soul belonged. The unquestioning faith of her comrades-in-arms amid the dire circumstances in which they found themselves, together with her own yearning for identification with the Irish people culminated in a flash of spiritual insight never forgotten. From that moment for her, so she told Esther Roper later, 'the things that are seen became temporal and the things that are unseen, eternal'.

It was not known on Saturday night in the College of Surgeons that the official surrender had been negotiated that day. The scene of negotiations was, strangely enough, Tom Clarke's shop which was one of the British headquarters. Brigadier-General Lowe, who was in command of the British forces in the city, while accepting Pearse's capitulation asked for Constance by name; he would not at first believe that she was not in Pearse's actual section.

When the news came on Sunday to the College of Surgeons there was great excitement and anger. Constance moved amongst the throng saying 'I trust Connolly. We must obey.' Suddenly, a British soldier walked into the hall 'unarmed, bare-headed, smoking a cigarette'. One of the insurgents raised his revolver. But the Countess was watching, 'Don't, Joe, don't. It would be a great shame now.'[17]

Captain de Courcy Wheeler, King's Royal Rifle Corps of the Anglo-Irish Ascendancy; married to a kinswoman of the Gore-Booths', came on Sunday 30 April, to receive the surrender of the College of Surgeons rebels. He met Michael Mallin and Constance at the side-door and had a meeting with them under the flag of truce. Constance handed over her pistol and her Sam Browne belt. Captain de Courcy Wheeler records that she 'reverently kissed' her weapon before handing it over. He also states that she surrendered her Mauser (given her by Casi) but, on the other hand, Madeleine Ffrench-Mullen relates that Constance hid this weapon, for she particularly wanted to avoid its confiscation, and that the authorities only found it later. Captain de Courcy Wheeler offered to drive Constance by car to the Castle, but she refused, saying she preferred to march with her men, since she was second-in-command. Captain de Courcy Wheeler then inspected the building, which, he states, was in an indescribable state of confusion.

So they marched to their fate. Constance discussed with an insurgent, who had once been a private in the British Army whether they were likely to be shot or hung. Many cheered (according to Captain de Courcy Wheeler) but at Trinity College an elderly servant, writes Professor O'Brien, shouted 'Shoot every bloody one of them!'

The defeated rebels were taken first to Dublin Castle, in whose hospital, inaugurated by Lady Aberdeen after the outbreak of war, Connolly lay in great pain, and then to Richmond Barracks. Here they enjoyed that apparently indispensable adjunct of Nationalist life, a cup of tea, through Madeleine Ffrench-Mullen's family being known to someone in charge. Later that evening they were moved to Kilmainham Jail, and crowded eight in a cell. Soon Constance was isolated from her comrades. They feared for her life – but she would have welcomed death.

CHAPTER 13

Aylesbury Jail

In the space of six days the rebel leaders passed from active civilian life filled with the manifold business of their various callings and interests to the claustrophobic anonymity of prison. In the Castle Red Cross hospital Connolly daily grew weaker from his leg wounds. Gangrene set in and he was under morphia. Even so when his wife and Nora visited him on Tuesday, 9 May, they learnt that he had just undergone his court-martial. Eleven of his comrades had already been shot, including Clarke, Pearse, MacDonagh, Joseph Plunkett, Michael Mallin. The Viceroy, the Chief Secretary and the Under-Secretary had resigned. The Unionist newspapers howled for the severest measures against the insurgents. William Murphy, unrelenting enemy of Connolly to the last, published in his newspaper *Independent* a photograph of Connolly with the caption 'Still lies in Dublin Castle recovering from his wounds'. The editorial the same day demanded, 'Let the worst of the ringleaders be singled out and dealt with as they deserve.'

In Ulster, the Unionists looked on both the rebellion and the punishment of the rebels with grim satisfaction. Nationalist Ireland had proved itself treacherous, and its punishment was becoming manifest for all Ireland to see. In Dublin Sarah Purser said, 'We have been put back a hundred years.' Redmond stated that the insurrection was 'the insanity of a small section of people once again to turn all her [Ireland's] marvellous victories into irreparable defeat, and to send her back, on the very eve of her final recognition as a free nation, into another long night of slavery, incalculable suffering, weary and uncertain struggle'.[1] Bernard Shaw wrote in a different strain in a letter published in *The Irish Times*.

My own view is that the men who were shot in cold blood, after their capture or surrender, were prisoners of war, and it is therefore entirely incorrect to slaughter them. The relation of Ireland to Dublin Castle is in this respect precisely that of the Balkan states to Turkey, of Belgium or of the City of Lille to the Kaiser, and of the United States to Great Britain. . . An Irishman resorting to arms to achieve the independence of his country is only doing what Englishmen will do if it be their misfortune to be invaded and conquered by the Germans in the course of the present war.

Of Constance, Horace Plunkett wrote in his journal, 'They are shooting the leaders of the Rebellion, some 8 so far, and Con Gore-Booth of long ago – the Countess Markievicz for 18 years – has been condemned to death. She is deeply dyed in blood but her motives were as noble as her methods foul. I met Powerscourt* and he was, he told me, begging the authorities to shoot her.'

Eva, in London, was distracted with anxiety. First the newspapers reported Constance's death – then that she was alive but condemned to die. She worked unceasingly for her reprieve.

Liam O'Brien of the College of Surgeons contingent, recalls how when he had been moved to Wandsworth prison he saw a lady standing alone amongst a crowd of visitors, and English sympathizers with the rebels (including Robert Lynd with a bag of oranges). The stranger so resembled Constance he went up to her, saying, 'You must be the sister of the Countess. I was with her in Easter week.' Eva turned eagerly to him. 'Tell me about her!' Liam O'Brien wrote many years later about Constance, 'Gallant the Countess was and elegant with natural grace – natural above all, there was no posing, no theatrical gesture whatever . . .' For her, he says, the Rising was 'action after preparation'.[2]

Esther Roper wrote later that in her opinion it was Asquith's personal intervention that saved Constance's life. Meanwhile, in Kilmainham Jail in Dublin the women prisoners, including Constance, lived to the dreaded sound of the execution squads. The men prisoners were lodged above the women's quarters and the women would hear the priest being brought to the cells of the condemned, and tremble, and wonder who would go next. As soon as Eva received the news that Constance had been reprieved she applied for a permit to visit her. She and the faithful Esther Roper sailed in the *Leinster* for Dublin on the night of 11 May – twelve

* Lord Powerscourt, the Provost Marshall.

days after the collapse of the Rising. The two friends arrived on a brilliant, sunny morning – a morning made for happiness and hope – but they soon saw the reality of Ireland's situation in the crowds of soldiers waiting at the foot of the gangway. The military, however, were in a relaxed mood at that time and place, seeming to Eva lethargic, or 'amiably frivolous', one calling out to some passengers who were trying to get on shore too soon, 'Stay where you are for God's sake. If I let you go over there I shall be courtmartialled and shot at dawn.' Ten minutes later the joke turned into horror for the two women when they read the posters flared with the news of Connolly's execution. Soon they knew, as all came to know, of how he had been shot sitting in a chair, still in great pain, too weak to stand; of how, when asked by the priest to say a prayer for his executioners, he had replied, 'I will pray for all brave men who do their duty according to their lights.'³

Eva and Miss Roper were driven through the shattered, still smoking streets by a surly taxi-driver, who told them that he and his family were nearly starved during the Rebellion, for he was not allowed out of his house for three days and could buy no food. He dropped them at their destination. Shortly afterwards they left with their hostess, who had been instrumental in getting the permit for the visit, and by a coincidence the same driver picked them up. When he heard where they wanted to go he became a man transformed, all grumbling forgotten, saying, as he set them down, as though the prison gates were the entrance to a 'very select paradise', 'It's little I thought this morning when I drive you from the boat it was to the prison I'd be taking you.'

Already the executions had wrought a great change in the minds of the people. Ernie O'Malley a contemporary and the author of *On Another Man's Wound* wrote,

Without guide or direction, moving as if to clarify itself, nebulous, forming, reforming, the strange rebirth took place. It was manifest in flags, badges, songs, speech, all seemingly superficial signs, it was as if the inarticulate attempted to express themselves in any way or by any method; later would come organization and cool headed reasoning. Now was the lyrical stage, blood sang and pulsed, a strange love was born that was for some never to die till they lay stiff on the hillside or in quicklime near a barrack wall.⁴

For Eva, that morning, one thought dominated all others. Did

Constance know that Connolly had been executed or would she, Eva, have to break the news?

The visitors showed their permits, crossed the yard and walked down a long corridor which led to a bleak, whitewashed, and barred room. Here the visitors had to peer across a narrow passage, patrolled by a wardress, on the opposite side of which the prisoner stood behind another, similar window grille. Constance appeared, wan, but controlled and smiling. She asked almost at once if anything was known of Connolly's fate. Eva did not answer directly, but Constance needed no further telling, since she had listened dawn after dawn to the shots which killed her comrades. For the first and last time in all her imprisonments she broke down, exclaiming, 'Why don't they let me die with my friends?' The instant form of her grief is significant; it was the realization of the kind of loneliness she would have to bear; her destiny was to be left walking the road, while those she loved best and admired most preceded her into a heaven in which she had begun fervently to believe. A phase of her existence was finished for ever; everything in her temperament would have been drawn to share in a gallant ending at the peak of experience rather than a life spent in anti-climax. Her political friend and colleague, Madame Perolz, has described finding Constance in her cell in the days following the surrender (presumably between her trial on 4 May and the confirmation on 6 May that the death sentence be commuted) saying with the happiness of a bride, 'Did you hear the news? I have been sentenced to death.' Now she knew that not only she must live, but that Connolly was dead. She quickly recovered herself, no doubt the pacing wardress stiffened her pride, and said, 'Well, Ireland was free for a week.'

The rest of the twenty minute interview was taken up with Constance's enquiries for friends, her bewilderment at the execution of Francis Sheehy-Skeffington – 'Why on earth did they shoot Skeffy? After all, he wasn't in it. He didn't even believe in fighting. What did it mean?' – and her concern for Mrs Michael Mallin, newly widowed by the execution of her husband and expecting a child any day. Eva and Miss Roper promised to find her. Of her own conditions Constance told them nothing – they could only guess at the discomfort and privations she ignored. The interview ended. Eva and Esther Roper left. They did not see her for another four months.

The two friends went on to Surrey House which had been seized and ransacked by the military authorities. The soldiers had not only searched it, but wrecked it. Furniture was broken, books, ornaments and pictures strewn everywhere. Someone had even taken the trouble to smash every single one of a collection of lantern slides. The garden had been dug in a search for arms. It was known later that the Dublin looters had finished what the soldiers began. The military were particularly suspicious of a manuscript article on Catherine de' Medici – 'Who is this woman? A *Sinn Feiner*?'

This was the finish of Constance's last proper home. From now on when she was not in prison she nested like a bird in others' houses, retaining a few of her possessions but recklessly generous always in giving away what little remained to her. A friend had only to admire an object to become the sometimes embarrassed recipient of it. If in the decade that remained to her she missed her own background: her garden, her pretty personal objects, her family furniture, she never openly expressed regret at the course she had chosen.

Leaving Surrey House, Eva was taken for Constance by the people who hung about the scene of destruction. There were many who told her that she risked her life walking about Dublin, since a soldier might fire at her in mistake for her sister because the likeness between them was thought to be so strong.

The next day Eva and Miss Roper spent hours walking through 'endless poverty-stricken streets' trying to find Mrs Michael Mallin. They passed Richmond Barracks and saw the men and women who had stood there day after day in 'a sort of hopeless, grey dejection' waiting for news that never came of the prisoners. Instead, terrible rumours spread: that the officers in the barracks had sworn to kill forty rebels for the lives of four dead soldiers, that the prisoners were without food, water or sanitation, so that when it came for their time to be court-martialled they were barely conscious. The two friends came upon a small chapel crowded with people and stayed for Mass. Afterwards they talked to the priest who spoke indignantly to them of the dreadful conditions in Richmond Barracks. He also told them that a girl was imprisoned there for waving at Constance when she marched with the other captives through the streets. The priest was able to end their quest for Mrs Mallin, since he knew some of her relations and was certain he could trace her.

With these experiences still fresh in their minds, Eva and Miss Roper while eating lunch in their hotel, heard an interchange shouted from table to table between a soldier and a Unionist. The latter complained of how a friend of his, a 'strong Orangeman' had been shot dead on opening his front door after three days shut up in his house, 'I must say your people are pretty free with their bullets.' The soldier shrugged his shoulders. 'Stupid thing to do, to put your head out at a time like that.'

Eva and Miss Roper spent some time with friends such as the widowed Mrs Sheehy-Skeffington, who showed them the 'poor little parcel returned from the barracks, containing a watch, a tie and a collar'. She told them of how her house had been fired on when she was alone there, apart from her seven-year-old son.* The bad stories were beginning to proliferate as Dubliners met and talked. The meaninglessly brutal death of the unarmed Francis Sheehy-Skeffington and the shooting of two journalists, one of whom was the editor of a strongly anti-Larkin paper, was discussed in the English press as well as in Dublin. Then there was the North King Street incident where two dead men were found buried in a cellar, and fifteen others were said to have been dragged from their houses and bayoneted by soldiers of the South Staffordshire regiment. (As is well known Captain Bowen-Colthurst, who had Francis Sheehy-Skeffington and the journalists shot, was subject to a court-martial and was shut up in Broadmoor for several years.)

There can never be any doubt that in a time of riot and revolution, crimes and, at the least, errors of judgement occur on both sides; but in the Dublin of 1916, the effect of such stories and rumours, together with the long lists of prisoners deported, and the executions 'like blood running from under a closed door' created the first stirrings of a momentous change of opinion. There were those in authority who regretted their role. General Blackadar, President of the Courts Martial, told Lady Fingall that Pearse was one of the finest characters he had ever come across. 'There must be something very wrong in the state of things that makes a man like that a rebel. I don't wonder his pupils adore

---

* This account of Eva Gore-Booth and Esther Roper's visit to Dublin is compiled from the biographical sketch in the *Prison Letters of Countess Markievicz*.

him.' The surgeon who attended Connolly in the Castle said he was one of the bravest men he had ever known.

One of the most poignant of the stories circulating Dublin was the death cell marriage of the charming young Joseph Plunkett, and Grace Gifford – talented cartoonist, Nationalist daughter of a Protestant father and a Catholic mother, and sister-in-law of the executed leader Thomas MacDonagh. On 3 May (the day Mac-Donagh was shot) Grace Gifford arrived at Kilmainham at six o'clock in the morning where she was kept waiting until half past eleven, when she saw her betrothed for the first time since the Rising, in the prison chapel. He was brought in handcuffed. She was allowed no conversation with him. The marriage was performed, and she left the prison. She was woken in the middle of the night in the lodgings she had found and a letter was handed to her from the prison Commandant, asking her to visit her husband, She was allowed ten minutes exactly with him in his cell which was, she recorded later, 'packed with officers, and a sergeant'. That morning he was shot.[5]

Æ wrote a letter to the London *Times* in which he forcibly put his opinion of the results of General Maxwell's handling of the aftermath of the Rising,

If the authorities were wanting to make Dublin a place with the bombs blazing in the street they were going the right way about it. It was Labour supplied the passionate element in the revolt. It has a real grievance. The cultural element, poets, Gaels, etc., never stir more than one per cent of a country. It is only when an immense injustice stirs the workers that they unite their grievances with all other grievances.

The Government became anxious. On 12 May Asquith himself came over to interview officials. He also visited the prisoners in Richmond Barracks, where as a Unionist observer caustically wrote, they threw off their penitence and depression at the sight of the British Prime Minister, feeling 'they had not fought in vain . . . Mr Asquith had scarcely left the prison before they were insulting their guards, throwing up their caps, and shouting victory.' Asquith himself wrote of this encounter that 'an extraordinary number of prisoners had beautiful eyes', adding 'I have no doubt they lied freely'.[6]

In Kilmainham Jail, at the time when Constance still thought she would be executed, she declared her wish to become a Catholic

– in order to feel herself closer to her comrades 'in death by a baptism of desire' if necessary. The chaplain, the Reverend Father Ryan, promised to be with her at the end if she, too, had to die. Her time had not come, but when it finally did Father Ryan, faithful to his word, was at her graveside in Glasnevin Cemetery.

When she was moved to Mountjoy Prison Constance received instruction from the chaplain, the Reverend Father McMahon, although she was not in fact received into the Roman Catholic Church until after her release from Aylesbury Jail in 1917. This was because, so she said, she did not want to have a religious ceremony in prison. Mrs Sheehy-Skeffington told Esther Roper that she remembered meeting Father McMahon at Mountjoy Prison gate and his expression of bewilderment at Constance's forthright attitude to her instruction – 'I can't understand Countess Markievicz at all. She wants to be received into the Church, but she won't attend to me when I try to explain Transubstantiation and other doctrines. She just says "Please don't trouble to explain. I tell you I believe all the Church teaches. Now, Father, please tell me about the boys." ' Her wish to be united with her dead comrades never faded as a centre in her religious feeling. From a significant remark she made to a friend in Sligo in 1927 this feeling played a large part in her unwavering attitude towards the knotty problem of the Oath and the Free State government. Now in Mountjoy with the puzzled Reverend Father McMahon she characteristically defended the devil as a 'good rebel'. The Reverend Father failed to see the joke. Mrs Sheehy-Skeffington adds that Constance as a Catholic, belonged to the Church of St Francis of Assisi rather than that of St Paul.

It is hardly possible that Constance did not expect Connolly's execution, since she knew that was happening to the other leaders in Kilmainham Jail. But perhaps because of his wound she hoped against hope that he would be reprieved. When the blow fell she gave vent to her feelings in a poem which reveals the depth and intensity of her feelings for him. It is unlikely in the highest degree that there was anything physically intimate in their relationship. They had a close-knit working life; there was his appreciation of her loyalty and devotion to his work; there was her need for a focal point on which to centre her idealism. They were both supremely honourable people in a time when that word had not lost its meaning. Their life was spent in a crowd of helpers and colleagues. Nora Connolly, who adored both her mother and her father, was an intimate of the house. But, given all this, it would seem that Constance lived the rest of her life as a loving woman might live in the shadow of an admired husband, determined to continue his work, determined, in this case, to leave nothing undone to achieve the free Ireland and the workers' republic Connolly had striven for.

> You died for your country my Hero-love
> In the first grey dawn of spring;
> On your lips was a prayer to God above
> That your death will have helped to bring
> Freedom and peace to the land you love,
> Love above everything.

> You died for your country and left me here
> To weep – No! my eyes are dry
> For the woman you found so sweet and dear
> Has a sterner destiny –
> She will fight as she fought when you were here
> For freedom I'll live and die.

> On your murdered body I'll pledge my life
> With its passionate love and hate
> To secret plotting and open strife
> For vengeance early and late
> To Ireland and you I have pledged my life
> Revenge for your memory's sake!

The poem was neatly copied on a piece of flimsy paper, and given by Constance to a wardress as a souvenir before she was moved to England.

At the end of a week, Eva and Miss Roper returned sadly to London to wait for news. Constance had been given permission to write a letter, so on 16 May she gave full, practical and detailed instructions to Eva about letting Surrey House, storing her remaining possessions, paying tradesmen, and helping servants and friends. This is the letter of a truly responsible person who remembers the smallest debt or obligation in circumstances when she might have been forgiven for forgetting everything but her own plight. Constance was still worried about Mrs Mallin, since

Eva had not been able to get any news into the prison. Constance added as regarded herself,

It is very economical living here. I feel half glad that I am not treated as a political prisoner, as I would then be tempted to eat, smoke and dress at my own expense . . . Everybody is quite kind, and though this is not exactly a bed of roses, still many rebels have had much worse to bear. The life is colourless, the beds are hard, the food peculiar, but you might say that of many a free person's life.[7]

While in London, Eva was inquiring in vain as to Constance's fate in Ireland, General Maxwell was equally concerned about her – for other reasons. On 19 July 1916 he wrote to the Home Office,

It appears to be desirable that the Countess Markievicz should be removed from Mountjoy Prison, Dublin, to some prison in England. From censored letters it appears that sympathizers know how she is getting on in prison and that in some way information is leaking out. This would be quite possible through the Visiting Justices. There are sixteen Visiting Justices to the Prison, eight of whom are elected by the Dublin Corporation, which, it is well known, has strong *Sinn Fein* sympathies; four are elected by the Grand Jury for the County of Dublin, and four others from adjoining Counties.

It is obvious that the Dublin Corporation members would be most likely to attend and inspect the prison.

A short time ago a book containing the poems of the late Thomas MacDonagh was handed in at the gate of the prison for Miss Giblin [*sic*] Gifford who was at that time a prisoner. On the book being examined, between two lines of a poem was found written in pencil the words, 'The prison was attacked on Sunday.' The meaning of these words is not obvious as no attack was made on the prison, but it is possible that some of the wilder spirits may have contemplated such. The book was submitted to the Visiting Justices and they directed that it should be given back to Miss Gifford . . .

In addition to the Visiting Justices there are certain lady visitors who are allowed to visit the female prisoners, including Countess Markievicz.

This lady is the only prisoner convicted for rebellion who is now in Ireland.

One hot Sunday afternoon in June, Eva and Miss Roper were sitting in the flat they shared, talking about Constance, of whose whereabouts they were still ignorant, when Miss Roper had a sudden irrational impulse that she must go to Euston Station to meet the Irish Mail. In the face of Eva's surprise she was unable to explain why, but the feeling was too strong to be denied and in the end Eva decided to go as well. When they arrived at Euston there was nothing to make them feel their presence was justified, but since they had arrived they decided each to go to different ends of the platform. Eva chose the farthest. Esther Roper at her end felt no surprise at seeing a few policemen and detectives come along and an officer with staff tabs. The train came in and drew to a stop. Eva, at her end, looked into the carriage window opposite her and saw Constance. The door opened, Constance rushed into Eva's arms and kissed her in spite of the protests of the officer in charge and the presence of the soldiers accompanying her. Miss Roper still waiting at her end and having seen several passengers unknown to her already pass through the barrier, then beheld approaching 'the strangest little procession ever seen by my astonished eyes. First a brown cocker spaniel, well known in Dublin as "The Poppet", then a couple of soldiers with rifles, then Eva and Constance together smiling and talking hard. Lastly an officer with drawn sword, looking very agitated.' Constance was hurried into a taxi, all information being refused as to where she was being taken. But Eva heard a detective tell the driver to go to Holloway Prison. Poppet jumped in after his mistress unchecked, so Eva called to Constance to send him to the flat if (as in the circumstances it must have seemed most likely) 'they won't let him in'.

During their brief walk down the platform, Constance had managed to hand over to Eva the document concerning her trial which gave all the information Eva had vainly asked for in the past weeks. Her Court-Martial had taken place on 4 May. The schedule was signed by General Maxwell and Brigadier General Blackader. The accusation was that Constance Georgina Markievicz

1. Did an act to wit did take part in an armed rebellion against His Majesty the King, such an act being of such a nature as to be calculated to be prejudicial to the Defence of the Realm and being done with the intention and for the purpose of assisting the enemy.

2. Did attempt to cause disaffection among the civilian population of His Majesty.

The page-boy of the University Club, Walter McKay, aged

seventeen years, gave evidence, and Captain de Courcy Wheeler described Constance's surrender of her arms.

She was found guilty on both counts and sentenced to be shot, with a recommendation to mercy only on account of her sex. The sentence was commuted to one of penal servitude for life. [7]

An hour after Eva and Miss Roper had returned to their flat on that June afternoon in 1916, the door-bell rang and Poppet was brought in. Apparently he had rushed on to the boat at Kingston at the last minute – brought, one can only assume, for his mistress to have a glimpse of him by someone tipped off about her journey. Constance told Eva later that she had greatly enjoyed the trip. Her escort was daunted by the fear of seasickness, so Constance lay undisturbed beside a sunny open porthole and felt the fresh breeze on her face. She saw a big airship and felt she would love to fly (or alternatively dive in a submarine).

Somehow, under 'huge difficulties' Constance managed to smuggle out a letter telling Eva she was going to Aylesbury Jail. 'I shall be quite amiable,' she wrote, 'and I am not going to hunger-strike, as I am advised by comrades to do. It would suit the government very well to let me die quietly.'

So the gates of Aylesbury closed behind her and Constance became an inmate of the cold, damp, ramshackle prison, convict number twelve, dressed in convict's clothes, and at the mercy of wardresses who were underpaid, disagreeable, also not above framing a prisoner who got into their bad books. Constance was prepared to face everything uncomplainingly, but what she had not been able to imagine in her blackest moments was an especial feature of the Aylesbury cells which, she admitted, nearly drove her mad in the first week. This was a carved and painted eye in the centre of every cell door, realistic to the last detail – pupil, eyelashes, eyebrow – and provided with a sliding disc on the outside, so authority could substitute its real eye for the artificial one. If a prisoner defaced the eye or covered it she was punished. Constance was now stripped of the last vestige of her last remaining prerogative: privacy. A fellow-prisoner who got to know and love Constance for her courage ('No kind of hardship ever fazed her') a tough Irish-bred gangster's moll, known as Chicago May wrote of this painted eye, 'You can get used to nearly anything, but you never quite got over the horror of being constantly watched and of your privacy being invaded. Whether you were staring at it or not it was useless to try to persuade yourself that there was not a real eye looking at you.'

The day began at 6.30 am. Prisoners washed and dressed and ate their breakfast of six ounces of bread and one pint of tea (usually cold) in their cells. Then work began. Hard labour, soft labour, or no labour at all, depending on your sentence. Constance, sentenced to hard labour, was given, together with the other hard labour women, two ounces of cheese and a small piece of bread at ten o'clock. Lunch was at twelve and consisted of two ounces of meat, two ounces of cabbage, one potato, thick flour gravy and six ounces of bread; this was varied on Thursdays, when there was hard, cold, suet pudding with black treacle, and on Fridays, when the prisoners ate boiled fish. Supper at about 4.30 pm was a pint of cocoa or tea and six ounces of bread. Constance, so she is reported as having told an American newspaperman, went from eleven to seven and a half stone. (The only thing that is hard to believe is that she was ever eleven stone.) Sanitary conditions were bad, the sick neglected. No one dared to complain because the prisoners were convinced that those who did risked being certified and sent to Broadmoor. Constance, never daunted, wrote, in a smuggled letter to Eva, that visitors should make a point of asking awkward questions; that the Trades Union should have an inspector at Aylesbury to inquire into conditions. She wrote,

> 'These questions should be asked me and all political
> prisoners at a visit:
> What do you weigh? What was your normal weight?
> What do you eat? Can you eat it?
> How much exercise do you get per day?
> Are you constipated. Can you get medicine?
> What temperature is the room you work in?
> What is your task? How much do you do in a week?'

Once Constance was shut in her cell for the night at 5.30 pm, she had nothing to occupy the uneasy hours spent beneath the gaze of the ever-watching eye until Eva, after much badgering, persuaded the Home Office to allow the prisoner paper and pencil for drawing. Constance's life was one of total isolation from her own kind. Her companions were female criminals; the ignorant and the uneducated. The male Irish rebels in the various prisons were permitted some 'association' and were able to combine to better their lot, but Constance had no contact with any other political prisoner in Aylesbury. She alone was treated as a convicted murderess. Once Constance met a Mrs Wheeldon in the passage, who had been convicted (unjustly some thought) of an attempt to assassinate Lloyd George. Constance greeted her warmly, saying, 'Oh, I know you, you're in for trying to kill Lloyd George.' 'But I didn't,' protested Mrs Wheeldon, as she was hustled away from dangerous contact with the Irish rebel.

In her first officially permitted letter from Aylesbury, Constance tells Eva that it is 'queer and lonely' after Mountjoy, because there she saw sea-gulls and pigeons, which she tamed; there were 'Stop Press' cries, and 'little boys splashing in the canal and singing Irish songs . . . there was a black spaniel, too, with long silky ears, and a most attractive convict baby with a squint, and soft Irish voices everywhere.' Here, in Aylesbury she had to console herself with the sight of some well grown hollyhocks, and a good crop of carrots, round which she and her fellow lags walked like 'so many old hunters in a summer'. She signed herself with a characteristic flash of derision Con (vict) 12.

Eva got permission for a visit in late August or early September, and Constance wrote afterwards to say how pleasing it had been to see the 'soft dreamy colours' Eva and Miss Roper were wearing. 'Moral: always visit criminals in your best clothes, blue and grey for choice, if it's me!'

In a confidential report of this interview made by the Governor of Aylesbury it is stated that Constance told Eva that she had smuggled a message out of Mountjoy hidden in a glove. She talked much of Madame Perolz and asked Eva to give her a certain dress, and that Madame Perolz was to wear it like 'Elijah's Mantle'. Madame Perolz was to 'keep things going and keep the clique together'. According to this report, Constance told Eva that Connolly had gone away for a fortnight at the time of his negotiations with the IRB, and that if he had not returned, she, Constance, would have started the Revolution herself. She begged to see Maeve. She also asked Eva to contact Devoy in America if help were needed.

Meanwhile in Ireland, Sir Josslyn had been given official permission to administer her property. 'The convict's property,' stated the solicitor's report to London, 'is badly in need of administration, and is subject to much loss . . .' Constance gave her permission in writing to her brother's appointment. Recklessly generous as she was, Sir Josslyn took on a thankless task as controller of her affairs. There was even a danger at one time that she could be classed as a felon and her property administered under the Forfeiture Act of 1870.

On 26 January 1917 Constance was visited by Esther Roper and Lady Clare Annesley. In conversation with them, according to the Principal Matron's report, she said that she had been accused of being in command of 'the Army that attacked Dublin Castle' but that this was totally untrue. The Army was divided into sections and her section did not go to Dublin Castle at all.

An unexpected visitor was her admirer from long past days – Sir John Leslie, with whom she had walked in the moonlight at Castle Leslie, eaten grapes, and skittered about the lake in the velocipede – who brought her drawing materials. At the time of her arrest he was serving in Ireland as an officer in the British army. In view of the aversion and rancour displayed towards her by most of her former kind it is pleasant to note the equable affection with which he wrote of Constance at that time, recalling the 'charming high-spirited girl he used to know', and hoping the prison authorities would find some work that might suit her 'clever artistic fingers'. He added: 'I don't know what the dear child would say if she knew I was commanding the garrison here, defending bridges and controlling the district.'[9]

Constance was first put to work in the sewing-room, which was considered the plum posting by the other prisoners, being the warmest, driest place in that damp, cold prison. Constance was set to make the prison nightgowns and the prison underwear of heavy, unbleached calico. But she found the work too inactive, so she asked to be moved. She was then put to cleaning the prison kitchens. (Long after she told her friend, Eithne Coyle, that the wardresses took pleasure in throwing dirt all over a floor that she had just scrubbed clean.) There is the scrubbing anecdote regarding the occasion when Mr Byrne, later Lord Mayor of Dublin, came to visit Constance and found her absent from her cell. When he tracked her down finally he found her with her pail and brush, and she asked him gaily if he had guessed that she would know how to scrub. A less cheerful visit was that of the Dowager Duchess of St Albans, a friend, like Sir John Leslie, of Constance's youth, but one with more of a sense of duty than affection. The

Duchess inquired if Constance said her prayers. Constance related to Eva that she 'really felt a bit insulted, but I thought I would get my own back without showing my feelings, so I opened my eyes wide and replied, "Of course; why, don't you?" '

Friends who were less smug than the Dowager Duchess of St Albans – friends such as Captain White and Alfred Byrne (never forgetting Eva and Miss Roper) – plagued the authorities through petitions and questions in Parliament because Constance was the sole Irish political prisoner to be denied the recently granted privilege of association with comrades. This was because she was the only Irish political prisoner in Aylesbury Women's Jail. The authorities (rather naturally in the circumstances) did not see their way to forming a special woman's wing in Lewes Jail, whither the male Irish politicals had been moved, so that Constance should enjoy the privilege of association. On the other hand, the argument that Constance had little to complain of since she was rated as a 'Star Class' prisoner, and therefore only met prisoners in this category, seems a little thin in the light of a list of these prisoners together with their offences. Out of a list of twenty 'Star Class' prisoners (excluding Constance) twelve were in for 'Wilful Murder', three for Manslaughter, and one for wounding. These twenty women were employed in the kitchens where Constance also worked (by her own request, as the authorities rightly pointed out). But no amount of official gloss could hide the fact that she was being treated as a common criminal, and not as a political prisoner.

On 17 February 1917 the Irishwomen's International League sent a petition to the Home Secretary,

The late Home Secretary had promised to accord to the Irish men and women imprisoned for participation in the insurrection of last Easter, the privileges of political prisoners. We understood that such privileges would remove Madame de Markievicz from enforced association with criminals and would entitle her to a considerably increased number of visitors and to other advantages in the way of food, clothes and books. We learn, however, from her sister that she is still in a convict prison under the same discipline and treatment as the lowest type of criminals and is placed in close association with prostitutes of infamous character. In the name of justice and humanity we feel compelled to protest against the infliction of this punishment upon a woman whose motives were pure and whose moral character was unblemished, however serious her political offences . . . We therefore beg you to fulfil the promise already made to this prisoner and to grant her without further delay the ordinary privileges given to political prisoners . . .

Constance had been entered in the records as Roman Catholic, so she was allowed to do the flowers in the chapel. The chaplain, Father Scott, won her affection and respect for his goodness to the most degraded and apparently hopeless of prisoners, and for his perceptive thought for others, such as when she was unwell and he came to see her bringing a large bottle of eau de cologne whose contents he sprinkled about for he knew how hard she found the prison smells to bear. Another solace was embroidery. She devised this by drawing out coloured threads from the rags she was given for cleaning and keeping any white pieces of material to embroider on. She got up early before the prison bell went in order to sew in peace.

Constance suffered in health from the coarse, badly cooked food. With immense difficulty Eva obtained the concession for her sister of a glass of milk a day. Like the other prisoners Constance was always hungry. Once said to Miss Roper, 'The only thing that prison does for people, as far as I can see, is to teach them to use bad language and to steal. I was so hungry yesterday I stole a raw turnip and ate it.'

Constance wrote an article about her Aylesbury experiences which was published in the *San Francisco Examiner* of 7 December 1919. She describes the then Governor – a woman – Dr Fox, as possessing neither heart nor imagination. 'A more unsuitable person to control a jail,' wrote Constance, 'it has never been my misfortune or experience to come across.' Constance went on to relate that,

The chief thing that strikes you . . . is the extreme dirt concealed under a parade of cleanliness.

Every bit of brass is immaculate, the floors are scrubbed unceasingly, but the baths were constantly so dirty that we refused to use them until they were washed. Vermin was constantly crawling over one.

Every evening they served us out with porridge with a huge tin ladle from a can, then the ladle was left for the night in a dirty pail with the brush which was used to sweep the lavatory . . .

The mattress I was given on my entry was so dirty that I cannot describe it. I had to put up with this until the very day I was released. I was given some old clothes which had been discarded by another convict who had left the prison. The shoes were full of holes, which let in the wet and snow.

There was one horror always hanging over our heads, and that was the fear of catching loathsome diseases. One section of the prison was called the Borstal* and contained some 150 'girls'. We cooked and washed up for that number. The food was served in tins, many of them old and musty. The 'girls' tins often came down to us in a state too disgusting to be described and there was neither sufficient water, vessels, or labour employed to keep them really clean . . . fifteen tins were marked with a 'D'. We were told to keep them separate from the rest.

About a week later fifteen more tins were marked. No care was taken outside the kitchen and they were always getting mixed up with the others in spite of our protestations, and shortly we were told it did not matter and not to mind about separating them . . .

While I was there one of these 'girls' tried to kill herself by cutting her throat; another set fire to her cell and she nearly died from burns. Several tried to hang themselves with ropes used in the making of mailbags, and more swallowed buttons and huge needles. Poor girls! It seemed so wicked and futile to drive them to this.

All who loved Constance wanted to do what they could to brighten her first Christmas in prison. Eva wrote and illustrated a poem as a Christmas card.

> Do not be lonely,
> Dear, nor grieve,
> This Christmas Eve,
> Is it so vain a thing
> That your heart's harper, dark Roseen,
> A wandering singer, yet a queen,
> Crowned with all her seventeen stars
> Outside your prison bars
> Stands carolling?

These words, and the illustration, which showed a long-haired lady harpist playing her instrument below a barred window where the head of a woman can be seen, made such an impression on the overwrought authorities that they told Constance, who was eagerly awaiting Eva's promised card, that it had, indeed, arrived, but could not be given to her without the approval of the Home Office. 'What *can* you have put on it?' she wrote to Eva. In spite of this delay, Constance had more cards than ever in her life before (46).

* In 1918 Aylesbury Jail became solely a female 'Borstal' prison.

She felt that with them came 'the world of Art and life and hope' into her cell. She seized on any crumb of comfort that her observation and love of nature brought her. 'The one thing I am learning here is to watch everything closely, whether it is trees or black beetles, birds or women.' She watched the starlings quarrel on her sill over the remains of her food. She noticed 'a wedge-shaped flight of wild geese over us as we were exercising, making their weird cackling cry, and they brought me home at once'. Eva's poems transported her to a beautiful world of 'dim sunshine and pearly waves'. Another solace was the especial time each day when Eva and she by arrangement sat silently and thought of each other. Constance's frame of mind, expressed in a letter to Eva of 29 December 1916, shows an extraordinary degree of acceptance of her isolation and obscurity (she might have fallen into an oubliette for all the contact she had with the outside world) for one who was thought by her critics to be avid for sensation and publicity. If it was an audience she was supposed to crave she had none now but thieves, prostitutes and their brutalized gaolers. She wrote, 'All my life in a funny sort of way seems to have led up to the last year, and it's all been such a hurry skurry sort of a life. Now I feel I have done what I was born to do. The great wave has crashed up against the rock, and now all the bubbles and ripples and little me slip back into a quiet pool of the sea.' She tells Eva not to make herself miserable on her account. 'I am often afraid that you are much more unhappy than I am. I feel a quiet, peaceful, a "nunc dimitis" sort of feeling.' What she never apparently felt was regret for her life with Casi. Her thoughts, refined and sharpened by deprivation flew straight to Eva, Lissadell, nature, art; or to her Nationalist friends.

Without Eva, Constance would have been alone indeed: Casimir and Stasko were in another world now, fraught with new problems for them. Maeve was estranged in spirit through indoctrination and absence. The immediate family, apart from Eva, was appalled, concerned, or totally disapproving. Family friends, such as Lord Powerscourt, as has been seen, openly expressed their conviction that she should have been shot. Militant political women have never had a good press in a man's world and Constance had now crossed the rubicon that lies between words and deeds. While in the past her reputation had rested on conventional courage (in the hunting-field) and acceptable public outlets (art and the stage) her whole soul was now directed towards righting the wrongs she thought intolerable. Her good name was at the mercy of outraged conservatives who had known her in different times. Little wonder that she clung to her political comrades and Eva. Comrades would not have been enough. In Ireland, the country of close-knit clan and family feeling, no comradeship could quite replace the love of kith and kin. The outside observer is constantly struck by this factor: the mutual devotion of the Gifford sisters; the love Padraic Pearse had for his brother Willie, Kevin O'Higgins for his sister Kathleen. Here, Eva's role was unique and irreplaceable. It was more than her sympathy, resource, tenacity in giving help, it was also the knowledge that all this came from more than loyalty and love: she believed in the cause. The relationship between the sisters was penetrated by what was outside and greater than themselves: that for which they fought and endured. Constance knew that she was secure in Eva's approval of her chosen life. They both expressed thoughts through action, although their immediate aims and methods differed. Constance had always been brave, but Eva gave her more courage. It is significant that she only survived Eva by one year.

Although her life was lonely in jail, Constance certainly did not live in moral isolation from the other women prisoners. She became especially interested in a woman serving seven years for shooting her lover. The circumstances made the crime understandable by Latin if not Edwardian England's standards, since on her telling her lover that she was pregnant by him he announced his intention of marrying another woman. This prisoner was entirely cut off from her child (a boy) who had been removed from her at a year old because no child was allowed in prison between the ages of one and fifteen years. Through Constance's and Eva's intercession a philanthropist, Mrs Cobden Saunderson, achieved the almost impossible feat of getting the mother released under her supervision, after which she worked in a small hotel. Another prison friend, the Chicago May mentioned earlier, who wrote a vivid account of life in Aylesbury Jail in her autobiography, had a certain kinship to Constance through her Irish horse-riding country childhood on a farm, and tomboy exploits. Her career after childhood held fewer similarities. She ran away to America at thirteen, fell in love with a safe-cracker and cattle-rustler, married, and was widowed at fifteen through her beloved's death in a hold-up. After various colourful criminal adventures, another marriage, several lovers, and an involvement in a shooting incident she was jailed in 1907 for fifteen years. She and Constance became great friends. They saw themselves as two Irish women determined not to be got down by the British. Doubtless Constance found qualities to admire in May: her courage, panache, lack of self-deception. May whole-heartedly admired Constance. Writing of her friend after her death she stated, 'She was a real Irish patriot, sacrificing money, position, health and freedom for liberty.' The two met again by chance after they were both free. It was in Philadelphia in 1922 when Constance was touring as the star figure of the Republican Delegation. Constance spotted May across a room in the Belleview Stratford Hotel and ran across to greet her. They 'had quite a long chat, to the amazement of the swells' who did not know who May was, and, who, surely, would have been even more amazed had they known.

Those who loved and understood Constance were only able to express their feelings through poems. Æ wrote a tribute to the rebels and had it printed for private circulation.

> Their dream had left me numb and cold
> But yet my spirit rose in pride,
> Refashioning in burnished gold
> The images of those who died
> Or were shut in the penal cell.
> Here's to you Pearse, your dream not mine,
> But yet the thought for this you fell
> Has turned life's waters into wine
>
> The hope lives on age after age
> Earth in its beauty might be won
> For labour as a heritage.
> For this Ireland lost a son.
> This hope into a flame to fan
> Men have put life by with a smile.
> Here's to you, Connolly, my man,
> Who cast the last torch on the pile.
>
> Here's to the women of our blood
> Stood by them in the fiery hour,
> Rapt lest some weakness in their mood

Rob manhood of a single power.
You, brave on such a hope forlorn,
Who smiled through crack of shot and shell,
Though the world cry on you with scorn,
Here's to you, Constance in your cell.

Eva wrote a play in verse *The Death of Fionavar* for which
Constance drew the delicate and charming page decorations in
prison. It was as though all her frustrated love of the beauty of
nature expressed itself in the borders she designed of wild roses
and leaves, of berries, butterflies, caterpillars and twined black-
thorn. The play, in Eva's words, was 'a symbol of the world-old
struggle in the human mind between the forces of dominance and
pity, of peace and war'. The dedicatory poem was written in
honour of the rebels.

Poets, Utopians, bravest of the brave,
  Pearse and MacDonagh, Plunkett, Connolly,
Dreamers turned fighters but to find a grave
  Glad for the dreams' austerity to die.

And my own sister, through wild hours of pain,
  Whilst murderous bombs were blotting out the stars
Little I thought to see you smile again
  As I did yesterday through prison bars.

Oh bitterest sorrow of that land of tears,
  Utopia, Ireland of the coming time,
That thy true citizens through weary years
  Can for thy sake but make their grief sublime!

In August 1916 the committee and members of the Woman's
Council, *Cumann na mBan*, showed their appreciation of Constance's
work for Ireland by electing her their president at their annual
convention. She had disappeared from everyday life, but she was
not forgotten. Father Albert of the Franciscan Capuchin Friars in
Church Street, Dublin, wrote to Eva a few months later saying
that when she obtained her release she must first spend some time
in the Church Street district 'because there is no place in Dublin
where she has such friends'. He also wrote of her remarkable
influence over the men and boys she worked with, 'There was not
one of those – and I have met hundreds of them – that would not

die for her.' Eva together with her Irish friends such as the widowed Mrs Pearse and Madame O'Rahilly and Mrs Eamon Ceannt still organized petitions on Constance's behalf setting out the facts of her isolation from any other Irish political prisoners, and her treatment by the authorities as a common criminal. Unknown to her, while she suffered and endured, news of her and of the other Irish prisoners trickled and spread in secret amongst the people – a knowledge which, for her, grew into the explosion of joy and love and gratitude that engulfed her on her release.

In the early days of Constance's imprisonment her friend, Sir Roger Casement, was put on trial in England and condemned to death. Eva, as always the loyal friend to the last, was present at one of the Court's sittings. Casement caught sight of her and his 'face lighted up with a rare and beautiful smile'.[10] Needless to say Eva, and Esther Roper were shocked and horrified by the stories of the notorious 'black diaries', but they dismissed them as lies circulated by 'relentless foes' in the seats of power. These two women were never content merely to sympathize with friends in danger or distress. Benevolent action was the mainspring of their lives. They set about helping to organize a petition, and on the evening of 2 August they, together with Casement's cousin, Gertrude Bannister, Mrs Stopford-Green, Mr Nevinson, and Mr Philip Morrell, took it to Buckingham Palace. But, so they were told, the King was not in a position to use his prerogative of mercy since it was now vested in his Ministers. He could only inform them of the appeal. Roger Casement was executed as a traitor. Today his body has been returned to Ireland, and those who go to Glasnevin Cemetery to visit Constance's grave – a narrow plot surrounded with box and bearing no headstone – are told that one day her grave will be part of a monument erected by the Irish nation to Casement and others who died for Ireland.

In December 1916 a new coalition Government was formed with Lloyd George as Prime Minister, with the enemy of Home Rule – Carson – as Minister for the Navy and another anti-Home Ruler in Bonar Law as Chancellor of the Exchequer. In the same month six hundred untried internees were released from Frongoch Camp (in Wales). Their return was the first occasion given to the Irish people to show how public opinion had changed towards the events of Easter week. As Sean O'Casey wrote, Easter Week 'became the Year One in Irish History and Irish life'. Among the Frongoch Camp internees was a young man from County Cork who had acquired great influence over his fellow-prisoners. He came quickly to the front in the re-grouping of leaders of militant Nationalism which took place as the surviving rebels and their sympathizers were gradually released from their prisons. This young man was Michael Collins. Prisons everywhere that held any large number of captives from Easter Week became virtually forcing houses for *Sinn Fein* and Republican doctrine. In place of the dead leaders who were unknown to few but members of their own organizations there sprang a new group of able men to take over the work: Eamon de Valera, Michael Collins, Kevin O'Higgins; and with the events of the Rising, a new spirit in Ireland as a whole rose to enforce their ideas.

The by-election of Roscommon in this year was more than a straw in the wind. For the first time the militant Nationalists decided to run a candidate against the Redmondites who had held the seat for nearly forty years. The candidate chosen was Count Plunkett, father of the executed Joseph. He was not a political figure, being scholarly and retiring, so it was all the more of a triumph that he won by 3,022 votes against the Parliamentary Party Candidate's 1,708. The result of the poll was a bitter blow to Redmond. He felt his position was becoming intolerable.

In April 1917 America came into the war. The question of American feeling as regards Ireland could never be disregarded by the British Government because of the strong anti-English element among Irish-Americans, who had arrived the other side of the Atlantic through the failure of English rule to give them the means to keep alive. In May, another by-election showed the Government that Roscommon was possibly the beginning of the deluge. *Sinn Fein* put up a candidate who was actually in prison, and although South Longford was a stronghold of the Parliamentary Party the *Sinn Fein* candidate won by a small majority. (*Sinn Fein* candidates, if elected, refused to take their seats at Westminster, since this would have been a contradiction of what *Sinn Fein* meant.)

Meanwhile men of goodwill, hopefully but ever less hopefully, were still seeking a compromise acceptable to all: to Ulster, to *Sinn Fein*, to the Parliamentary Party. They called for a National

Convention to be attended, it was hoped, by representatives of all shades of Irish opinion. Unfortunately *Sinn Fein*, also organized Labour, were dissatisfied with the planned proportion of representation so they refused to attend.

On 10 June a large protest meeting on behalf of Irish political prisoners was held in Beresford Place. Count Plunkett addressed the crowd, together with Cathal Brugha. A few days later the Government, wishing to create a favourable atmosphere for the Convention, decided to release all the prisoners. As de Valera left the gates of Pentonville he was handed a telegram which told him that he had been chosen as the *Sinn Fein* candidate for the pending by-election in East Clare – a seat left vacant by the death in action of Redmond's brother, Willy.

On the day of Constance's release, 17 June, she was met at the gates by a welcome party which had travelled to Aylesbury consisting of Eva, and Esther Roper, Helena Molony, Marie Perolz and Dr Kathleen Lynn. They were allowed in to help her dress in the summer clothes they had brought her. They travelled to London together, when the Irish contingent sped their way back to Dublin to help prepare the public welcome. Constance spent the day in London where with true bravado she had tea and strawberries and cream on the terrace of the House of Commons with Eva, Esther, Mr Byrne, and Captain Jimmy White resplendent in top-hat and spats. Constance, it is said, graciously acknowledged the bows of such political enemies as the late Viceroy. The next morning she and Eva and Esther left on the boat train. Even as soon as this the welcome Ireland was preparing began, with Irish men and women singing patriotic songs on the platform. On the boat she was brought grapes and peaches. Boarding the boat when Constance called out, 'Which is the right side for us to get on?' a grimy face thrust itself out from the engine roon, and a voice shouted, 'It's always the right side if you're on it.'[11] At Kingstown Harbour there were so many cheering people the party was hardly able to make its way to the train. On arrival at Westland Row Station Constance drove in Dr Kathleen Lynn's car – the same one she had used in Easter Week – to Liberty Hall, but drive is hardly the word to describe the slow progress through the multitude that had come on that hot June day to welcome the prisoners. Work was given up and the traffic diverted. Constance, as the last of the prisoners to arrive, received the accumulation of the crowds' rapture. She was, too, the best known of the rebels, almost the only survivor of the leaders of the actual Rising. In her beautiful new hat, and a much older looking cardigan suit, she, who had left Ireland under the cloud of the public's dislike for what the rebels had done to Dublin, now returned to the role of the heroine this same public had transformed her into. She had come home to the submerged Ireland whose heart she had been sueing all these years. No one who has seen the news film of her progress through the streets could fail to be moved by it. One thing only remained, and that was to be received into the religion of the people – the Roman Catholic faith.

Constance went straight from the welcome ceremonies to the house of Dr Lynn, who cared for her until she had recovered from the effects of prison life. She was short of money so the Union told her that she could draw on their funds. When her brother got in touch with her and asked her if she needed money, one can imagine that she took pleasure in replying that the ITGW Union was looking after her.

On 24 June, a week after her arrival back in Ireland, Constance was received into the Roman Catholic Church at Clonliffe College. She received the baptismal name of Anastasia. She had taken the final step now in her identification with Ireland.

CHAPTER 14

Madame Minister

All of politically conscious Ireland watched the East Clare by-election. The circumstances were interesting. The dead member, Major Willie Redmond, was the brother of the leader of the Parliamentary party. The man, who in the name of *Sinn Fein* had been chosen to oppose the party's choice as Major Willie Redmond's successor was one of the very few surviving rebel leaders. De Valera was unknown apart from his command at Boland Mills in the Rising. (It was unknown, too, that it was John Redmond who had intervened to get de Valera's death sentence commuted to one of life imprisonment.)[1] The Parliamentary party's candidate, Patrick Lynch KC, was prominent locally, de Valera a stranger. De Valera began his campaign boldly by quoting the Easter Week Proclamation of the Republic. Throughout his electioneering he delivered an uncompromising message of Republicism. When the poll was declared de Valera was the victor by more than twice the number of votes given to his opponent. The result was a startling victory for *Sinn Fein* and a public set-back for the Parliamentary party. A month later another by-election was won by a *Sinn Fein* candidate, also a survivor of the Rising – William Cosgrave. The revived movement was becoming the voice of awakening Ireland. Meanwhile the IRB was under reorganization by the able and energetic Michael Collins, aided by Diarmuid Lynch and Thomas Ashe.

The next large public demonstration of defiance was the funeral of the same Thomas Ashe, who had been imprisoned in August for making seditious speeches. He died in September of cold, hunger-strike and forcible feeding. All the now proscribed uniforms of the extremists appeared in the procession, including Constance in her Citizen Army uniform raising a cheer from the crowd. A guard of Volunteers fired a volley over his grave (completely against Dublin Castle regulations). Michael Collins, at the head of the grave pronounced a valedictory in Gaelic, and in English, he said, 'That volley which we have just heard is the only speech which it is proper to make above the grave of a dead Fenian.'

Meanwhile the National Convention, in spite of sitting under the benevolent twin influences of Horace Plunkett and Æ, was bedevilled by the absence of *Sinn Fein* representation and by the suspicions of the Ulster delegates. The leaders of *Sinn Fein* were engaged in negotiations far more momentous to them. In October 1917 the annual meeting of the governing body of *Sinn Fein* – the *Ard-fheis* – met in Dublin. It was a meeting of crucial importance, because from it de Valera emerged as the new leader of a re-thought *Sinn Fein* movement, which now reconciled Republicanism with its own essential doctrines. Since Griffith was connected in the minds of many Republicans (including the Irish Volunteer movement) with a tendency for compromise over the question of Ireland's relations with the monarchy, it was evident he would not be acceptable to all as President (a position he had held for six years). He stood down. De Valera was elected in his stead by a unanimous vote. A new Constitution was accepted which declared the movement's intention to deny the right of the British Parliament or Crown to legislate for Ireland, and to make use of every means available to render England's power impotent. Constance was re-elected one of the twenty-four members of the Executive Council. In the next month de Valera was elected President of the Volunteers, thereby achieving power in the two main Republican organizations. His stated aim was simple and clear: to 'make English rule absolutely impossible in Ireland'.[2]

For Constance, the months after her release from prison were filled with meetings and the reception of Welcome Addresses. In July she was photographed in a group with William Cosgrave after his victory at Kilkenny – presumably, therefore, she had been electioneering for him. Red-bearded Darrell Figgis (of the Howth gun-running) is in the photograph, as well as de Valera and white-bearded Lawrence Ginnell, called the stormy petrel of the House of Commons. No one could look less like a rebel leader than Constance does in this photograph. She is wearing a long silky coat with a softly draped white fichu collar; she is hatless, holding a bouquet, and her whole air is gentle, feminine and appealing. In another snapshot of this period she is dressed like a *femme fatale* in a large, dramatic black hat. She was evidently one of those women who vary between two extremes in dressing. When not in uniform, she was either totally shabby, and uncaring about her appearance, or she dressed up to the nines like a girl for a party.

In August 1917 Constance received the Freedom of Sligo. (One wonders what Sir Josslyn thought about that.) Constance was met at Ballymote railway station by a young girl, Baby Bohan, who with her sister, Doty, became a great friend and ally.* Baby Bohan was on the station in order to present Constance with a bouquet, which she duly did, amongst the cheering crowds. But there was nearly a terrible hitch after Constance had made a speech and was leaning, bouquet in hand, out of the carriage window to wave farewell. A 'separation woman' – that is to say the wife of an Irishman serving in the British forces – was, rather naturally, incensed by Constance's speech, and she rushed forward to snatch the bouquet away. Constance, with her unfailing presence of mind, swept it back just in time and threw it behind her in the carriage.

The next day, too, the other element showed itself when a 'gang of Britishers' started pulling emblems and colours off the coats of 'quiet, inoffensive people'. The Committee of Welcome asked the local company of Irish Volunteers to take control. Armed with wooden batons they marched to the Town Hall and thus peace was restored. Constance received the freedom of her native town and signed the roll of honour. Afterwards she was asked by the parish priest of Keash to come and speak in his district on 'Garland Sunday'. She was evidently then travelling about speaking in many different places, possibly with the party of the Kilkenny photograph since she told the priest she was not in control of her own arrangements, so she could not make a definite promise. Meanwhile Constance's Easter Week comrade-in-arms, William Partridge, had died as a result of privations in prison. He was buried at Ballaghdereen which was within reach of Ballymote. Constance went to his funeral, and from thence came once more to Ballymote on her way to speak at Keash. She was then in her Citizen Army uniform, and wearing, so she told Baby Bohan, the

---

* I am indebted to Miss Baby Bohan for the account of this occasion.

executed Michael Mallin's tunic (which she had worn through
Easter Week). Constance spoke in Ballymote and after going to
Mass the next day and being entertained by the nuns in the convent she was taken in an outside-car to Keash. There were sports,
there was lunch in the priest's house, the sun shone, she was
enfolded in admiration and affection. She spoke to the younger
women about her life and her work; she showed them the rosary
William Partridge had given her when she was taken prisoner
and which she wore always round her wrist. Later she made
a speech and held the rapt attention of four thousand people.
In 1917 Constance held meetings in Trim, Clonakilty, Ennis,
Rothfarnham, Castlewellan, Bantry, and Listowel.

On Sunday, 21 October, Constance received a truly overwhelming reception in the remote town of Athea in County Limerick. It
was the home town of Con Colbert, one of her most outstanding
Fianna boys who had been executed for his part in the Rising.
The crowds (and bands) who had poured in from miles around
were so packed in the wide main street that one spectator wrote
afterwards he felt the houses themselves might give way under the
pressure. There was an open-air meeting in a field by the river, in
which the crowds must have participated through intuition rather
than knowledge since in the absence of loudspeakers only those on
or near the platform could hear what Constance said. Afterwards
she was the guest of honour at a luncheon given in Con Colbert's
home, Gale View. In the evening she spoke again in Mullane's
Hall. Another eyewitness of the event wrote of her speech that
'her address was characterized by terseness and lucidity, and was
punctuated at various points by deafening roars of applause from
the vast multitude gathered around the platform ... this lady
certainly has the courage of her convictions, for even her most
pronounced political opponents never ventured to doubt her
sincerity of motive and singleness of mind.'[3]

In these months Constance was always on the move speaking
for *Sinn Fein*. She spoke in Clonmel, in Carrick-on-Suir, in
Cookstown, where she also bought her dog licence. *Sinn Feiners*
were constantly being arrested and there was much bitterness over
the authorities' refusal to treat political prisoners as such. Hunger-
strikes were frequent but forcible feeding was abandoned, mainly
as a result of the inquiry into Thomas Ashe's death. Instead, what
was known as the 'cat-and-mouse' method was put into force. By

this hunger-strike prisoners were released as soon as they became weak and were rearrested after they had regained strength out of prison.

In March 1918 John Redmond died, worn out with a lifetime of political work which had ended for him in a series of crippling disappointments. He was spared the last of all when the National Convention broke down, from which, in any case he had retired in January. His son, Captain William Redmond, contested his father's seat against a *Sinn Fein* candidate and won by five hundred votes. In April the Government introduced a Bill which empowered them to enforce conscription in Ireland. In spite of the Irish Parliamentary party voting against it to a man it was passed on 16 April. In order to soften the bitter pill the Government proposed at the same time to introduce a new Home Rule Bill.

The whole of non-Unionist Ireland was united in opposition to the Conscription Bill (few were impressed by the sop of the promise of imminent Home Rule). The Irish MPs walked out of the House of Commons; de Valera convened an anti-conscription meeting and drafted an anti-conscription pledge; he even succeeded in getting a denunciation of conscription out of the Irish Bishops, then in session at Maynooth. A twenty-four-hour General Strike was called which brought all Ireland to a standstill, except for Belfast. But the Government, too, meant business. The army was desperate for men. Field-Marshal Lord French was appointed Viceroy, and he saw his task clearly. 'Home Rule will be offered and declined,' he said to Lord Riddell, 'then conscription will be enforced. If they will leave me alone I can do what is necessary. I shall notify a date before which recruits must offer themselves in the various districts. If they do not come, we will fetch them.'[4] The Field-Marshal, for all his despotism, was quite unable to control his sister, Mrs Despard, a militant feminist and Republican who vociferously stated her case in the Dublin streets during his tenure of office.

Lord French quickly displayed his zeal. In April a shipwrecked man was rescued off the coast of Galway by the police whom he told he was a member of Roger Casement's illegal Irish Brigade. On this incident the Castle authorities (obviously fidgety about what action *Sinn Fein* might take at any moment regarding the detested Conscription Bill) decided there was a 'German Plot' and proceeded to round up the *Sinn Fein* leaders. On 17 and 18 May more than seventy-three arrests were made. Their number included Constance, whose many 'seditious' speeches had been duly noted by the authorities, Maud Gonne (recently returned from France to live in Ireland) Mrs Clarke, the widow of Tom Clarke, Arthur Griffith, Count Plunkett, de Valera, and William Cosgrave.

So began Constance's second prison term. This time she was not isolated; her companions were her friends instead of the ignorant and the depraved and desperate. In August Mrs Sheehy-Skeffington joined the select group on their especial floor in Holloway. She had been arrested outside the offices of the Irish Women's Franchise League after a tour in America where she had addressed 250 meetings on the subject of Easter Week and Ireland's fight for freedom, and handed the President the Irish Women's plea for Independence. After a happy reunion with Constance, Maud Gonne, and Mrs Clarke, and talk lasting until the cell doors were locked she immediately went on hunger-strike. She was released after a few days.

In Holloway Maud Gonne was tormented with anxiety about her young son. She had to live with the dreadful memory of his running after the Black Maria which took her away when she was arrested. She was not permitted to sign a cheque in order to provide for him. Mrs Clarke, so Constance wrote to Eva, was in a very weak state as a result of the shock of her husband's execution; she was constantly worrying about her sons. Judging from Constance's letters to Eva at this time she must have been by far the most cheerful of the prisoners. She, after all, was the experienced jail-bird of the party (as she did not fail to make clear, rather to the annoyance of her companions). She had faced and accepted long ago the absence of her daughter from her life. But she did worry—about Casi and Stasko. 'Poor Casi hated wars, revolutions and politics,' she wrote in a letter to Eva, 'and there he is – or was – in Kiev, or in the Ukraine', and in another, 'Poor Stasko! I'd hate him to be killed or wounded. He did love life . . . when you get back, try and find out through any and all agents.'[5] After her release, through the means of William O'Brien she approached Maxim Litvinoff, then Representative of the Russian Soviet Republic in London, in an attempt to get in touch with Casi.

Apart from the lack of visitors because the Irish prisoners

refused to sign an undertaking not to discuss politics with them* – apart from censored letters and the locked cell door at night, life in Holloway must have been like a very bad boarding-house. Constance was allowed her painting materials, and books, and food from outside. She cooked 'savoury messes' over a gas-ring, rejoiced when she was sent sweets or cigarettes, and during her time there painted over forty water-colours, which were later exhibited in Dublin. It was fortunate for her that she was the best adjusted to imprisonment because in the end she was left alone, Maud Gonne and Mrs Clarke being released on the grounds of ill health. Between July and October, 1918 Constance was offered the Freedom of the City of Limerick as a protest against her imprisonment. It is interesting to note that Yeats signed the document in spite of his disapproval of her politics.

In November 1918 there was a General Election. *Sinn Fein* decided to contest every constituency in Ireland, whether or not the candidate was in prison. Constance's name was put forward for the Dublin St Patrick's Division. She managed to send out an election address (dated 11 November).

It is with great pleasure that I have been accepted as SF candidate for St Patrick's constituency. As I will not procure my freedom by giving any pledge or undertaking to the enemy, you will probably have to fight without me. I have many friends in the constituency who will work all the harder for me. They know that I stand for the Irish Republic, to establish which our heroes died, and that my colleagues are firm in the belief that the freeing of Ireland is in the hands of the Irish people today ... There are many roads to freedom, today we may hope that our road to freedom will be a peaceful and bloodless one; I need hardly assure you that it will be an honourable one. I would never take an oath of allegiance to the power I meant to overthrow ... The one thing to bear in mind is that this election must voice the people of Ireland's demand to be heard at the peace conference ... We are quite cheerful and ready for anything that comes, ready to stick on here, certain that things are going on just as well without us, and that our voices are even louder than free men's.

Miss May Power wrote to Constance on 9 November that the

* Constance wrote to Eva, 'They want us to promise not to talk about politics. Today life *is* politics. Finance, economics, education, even the ever-popular (in England) subject of divorce is mixed up with politics today. I can't invest my money without politics; buy clothes without politics.'[6]

Catholic Bulletin had offered a prize for the best essay on 'my favourite heroine'. A great many were written about Constance, and the first prize was won by a boy who had chosen her as his subject.

Constance wrote to Mrs Sheehy-Skeffington on 12 January 1918,

My dear Mrs Skeffington,

Many thanks for your card received some days ago. I have received so few letters since the Election Campaign began that I begin to think the Censor is holding them up. I don't even know if my Elec. address was let pass. One letter I had written previously was not allowed to go. I don't know why they keep the letters they have a fancy for these days. One cannot but laugh at the delightfully fair way that this election is being managed, our opponents are making full use of the opportunities that are being lavished on them, to misrepresent us in the press, and we are gagged and cannot answer them. Luckily our people have no delusions with regard to the truthfulness of the subsidized daily press. With this long delay between the voting and counting any villany [*sic*] may be tried also these 'absent voters' seem to me to give unlimited scope for trickery. It would look very funny if *Sinn Feiners* only won when unopposed! . . . I never feel that it matters much what happens to us [i.e. the prisoners] and I have such a sure conviction that things are going all right for Ireland, we are only pawns in the game. Its been so good for the country having no leaders. They have all had a chance and learnt how to think and act. Leaders can be such a curse! I see that you and yours have been doing splendid work for me . . . I am full of schemes and ideas. And now good-bye and good luck, love to yourself and remember me to my friends in your league.

Yours in Ireland's Cause,
Constance de Markievicz IRA

In the same month there is a moving glimpse of Nationalist Ireland to be found in a letter to Constance from C. F. Stafford. He tells her how hard he is working for her in her adopted constituency,

Last night at 10 o'clock we knocked at the door of a top back room and a voice said come in, and inside was a very old man and a little Irish Terrier guarding him. He told us he had lived 88 years always looking forward to Ireland Free and Independent and he said he felt God would not take him until he saw it Free . . .

In this month also, Constance wrote to Mrs Daly trying to reassure her,

I heard from Ag: that you were very ill, mainly owing to my imprisonment preying on your mind, now I am sure if you knew how very much harder such news makes that imprisonment, you would make the same brave effort to get well and live, that you did when your only son was murdered by the same power that now imprisons me . . .

I am not ill treated in any way, it is not the cruel inhuman thing Uncle John and Tom had to endure, so there is really nothing to fret yourself about, look at what a satisfaction it is to me to know that my imprisonment is helping on the cause I love and for which so many of our countrymen have suffered and died for. I could ask the favour of a visit home to see you on parole but I want no favours from the British Gov. I shall ask none, not if every one belonging to me died. You I know would be the last to wish to me do so.

Another letter of 15 January shows her aims for her constituency,

I am full of plans to start all sorts of things in St Patrick. If I ever get out of this I intend to live there and to show the people that they did right to trust me and prove to them, that a member among them working for them is more use than one living in a foreign country.

In a letter to Mrs Wyse Power of 31 January 1919, Constance wrote,

I've such heaps of money nowadays. Jail is so economical. The other thing I love is spending so for goodness sake look after everyone and send me the account, a few ten pound notes are all the same to me. I'm sure Billy Brian would like a change this Spring .

The new leader of the Irish Parliamentary party, John Dillon, declared its intention of fighting *Sinn Fein* with all the resources at its disposal. But in spite of the open hostility of the party, in spite of the repressive measures taken by the Castle against all Republicans, in spite, too, of forty-seven out of seventy-three of the candidates being in jail (possibly, on the other hand, because of it) the election resulted in a great victory for *Sinn Fein*. Constance, whose name had gone forward for the Dublin St Patrick's Division, was swept in on the tide thus becoming the first woman to be elected to the British Parliament, although from that point of view it was an empty distinction since in accordance with *Sinn Fein* policy she could not take her seat. The Viceroy's sister, Mrs Despard, standing as a woman's suffrage candidate in North Battersea was defeated, as were the seventeen other women candidates in England. The Irish people had made their choice; although a powerful *Sinn Fein* supporter, the priest Father O'Flanagan remarked, "The people have voted *Sinn Fein*. What we have to do now is to explain to them what *Sinn Fein* is'. Of 105 candidates returned for Ireland, 73 were Republicans. *Sinn Fein* with its avowed aim of 'making English rule absolutely impossible in Ireland' now felt it had the mandate to do so.

Early in February when she was still in Holloway, Constance received her summons to attend the new Parliament on 11 February. On the 20th of the month Lady Gregory noted in her Journal that she had met Mrs Cobden-Saunderson (she who had helped Constance rescue the *crime passionel* murderess in Aylesbury Jail) who was 'full of excitement' because she was going to a reception the next day held in honour of Countess Markievicz, newly released from prison. During this time in London, when Constance stayed with Eva, and Esther Roper, she visited the House of Commons incognito to see the cloakroom peg with her name upon it – the sole outward and tangible sign in England of her electoral victory.

In March she returned to a welcome that a 'queen or a president might envy', so said the *Irish Citizen*, in a Dublin, red in the glow of sunset and torchlight. Her *Hymn of Battle* was sung, also the *Red Flag* and *Soldiers Song*. The streets were jammed, the Volunteers and the Citizen's Army paraded, and bands played far down the quays of the Liffey.

In the same month that Constance was released from Holloway a daughter was born to Yeats. In a poem written to commemorate her birth the poet expresses all his distaste for militancy in women – every line can be read as a rebuke for the life-pattern of Maud Gonne, and also Constance. Nothing could be less like the effect made on others by his great love, Maud Gonne, and his dear friend of the past, Constance, than the wish that his daughter may 'become a flourishing hidden tree, That all her thoughts may like the linnet be.'

> I have walked and prayed for this young child an hour
> And heard the sea-wind scream upon the tower,
> And under the arches of the bridge, and scream
> In the elms above the flooded stream;
> Imagining in excited reverie
> That the future years to come

Dancing to a frenzied drum,
Out of the murderous innocence of the sea . . .

Have I not seen the loveliest woman born
Out of mouth of Plenty's horn,
Because of her opinionated mind
Barter that horn and every good
By quiet natures understood
For an old bellows full of angry wind?

Constance returned to an Ireland which now had its own Parliament – self-instated. The first *Dail Eireann* met on 21 January in
the Mansion House. Invitations had been sent to every elected
member of an Irish constituency, but the non-Republicans did
not attend. The president of *Sinn Fein* was in prison, so was the
man who had first created the movement out of the fabric of his
thoughts and dreams and aspirations for Ireland – Arthur Griffith.
If the Rising was the necessary blood sacrifice foreseen by Pearse
before Ireland could be free, Griffith's was the imaginative leap
into a new concept of national resistance. Without it the blood
victims would have left no structure through which their successors
could make manifest the ideals for which they had died.

The assembly opened its proceedings with a prayer read in
Irish by Father O'Flanagan. The members reaffirmed Pearse's
Easter Week Declaration of Independence and adopted unanimously an exemplary series of resolutions regarding their future
conduct of the nation's affairs. The session lasted two hours. It
had been watched by many journalists and visitors from the gallery
who were impressed throughout by the 'orderly and dignified'
proceedings.

The first *Dail* had met; in the following days its Ministry showed
its determination to function actively by applying for representation at the Peace Conference, sitting at Versailles. But the *Dail's*
President was still shut up in Lincoln Jail.

Early in February the British Government was disturbed to
receive the news that de Valera was free, together with two other
Sinn Fein prisoners. The escape was directed by Michael Collins
and Harry Boland from outside the prison while de Valera himself,
through the means of a wax impression of keys stolen from the
prison chaplain, organized the getaway from inside.

De Valera was obliged to stay in hiding in England until March when the Government, chiefly for extraneous reasons, decided to release all Irish political prisoners. On his return he formed his ministry. He appointed Arthur Griffith for Home Affairs, Cathal Brugha for Defence, Eion MacNeill (forgiven now for calling back the Volunteers from the Rising) for Industry, Michael Collins for Finance, William Cosgrave for Local Government, and Constance as Minister of Labour. She wrote to him 'I can give you all my time for Ireland.'[7]

So began the unique and extraordinary history of the shadow administration, first advocated by Arthur Griffith, which took over the proper functions of government from the occupying power. But ideas are never enough in temporal affairs; money was needed as well. De Valera went secretly to America in June on a fund raising tour (a plan he had already conceived in Lincoln Jail); in Ireland a National Loan was floated by Michael Collins. At this time one of the able new men of the troubled future came into the administration as William Cosgrave's assistant. This was Kevin O'Higgins, a native of Queen's County, described by Winston Churchill as 'a figure from the antique cast in bronze', recklessly brave, argumentative, loyal, and toughly realistic.

Constance had received her reward – her recognition amongst her peers – but she barely tasted its fruits before she was arrested again. Since she was arrested as the result of her supposed presence in a town proscribed to her and as she had gone to elaborate means to avoid the proscription, the story is an example of how determined the authorities were to get her. On Saturday 17 May, Constance came to Mallow on her way to Newmarket – the town forbidden to her by the British authorities – and was met by jubilant crowds who had feared the dauntless Countess might fail them. It was decided to get round the proscription by holding the meeting that night instead of Sunday as arranged. In her speech she repeated Swift's cry, 'Burn everything British but its coal' to the usual enthusiastic applause. Once the meeting was over the problem remained of avoiding the inevitable arrest the next morning, since the town was filled with RIC men and the military. A plan was devised whereby a brave young lady undertook to masquerade as Constance for that night. At a pre-arranged rendezvous the girl, Miss Madge McCarthy, dressed herself in Constance's clothes and proceeded very openly to the local hotel which was being closely watched by the RIC. Here she spent the night. Meanwhile Constance, dressed as a man, was driven through the RIC patrols, and spent the night at Drominorigle. The next day the RIC sergeant asked for Constance at the hotel. He was not deceived by the conspiratorial bewilderment of the proprietress who said she had not seen the Countess. Having searched the building he remembered that the RIC and the military had been fooled under their very eyes. At this time Constance was addressing a large meeting in Drominorigle. The problem then arose as to how Constance was to be reunited with her clothes. It was decided that Madge McCarthy should smuggle them out of the hotel under her own coat and take them to the original rendezvous in Newmarket. This was accomplished successfully. But nemesis was not to be cheated. When Constance was arrested afterwards in spite of her denial of being in the hotel, the sworn testimony of the RIC and military that they had seen her address a meeting and enter the hotel secured her conviction. But, even so, she had saved herself from the ignominy of being carted off then and there by the local police – and the incident became local legend.

When the news came out of Constance's sentence to four months' imprisonment the *Irish Citizen* accused the Castle of getting her shut up because of her importance as a witness before the Neutral Committee of Inquiry into the conditions existing in Ireland, as disclosed in the report of the American Delegates. Dublin Castle officially denied this. Constance, in a letter from prison to Nellie Gifford mentioned that she was so pleased to think she had not missed the visit of the American delegates, 'They are so splendid, three "Knights of Valour" '; but she seemed unaware that there was any reason for her arrest other than her appearance in Newmarket, Co Cork. At her trial, which was held in private with the maximum security arrangements, she was accused of saying at Newmarket that '*Sinn Feiners* should treat the children of the police as spies, ostracize them, treat them as lepers, and refuse to sit near them in church or school'. She emphatically denied this; it certainly seems most out of character. (In a later term of imprisonment she even defended the wardresses to a co-prisoner, maintaining they were only doing a job like anyone else.)

Constance wrote to Eva that Cork Jail was the most comfortable prison she had yet been in. There was a lovely view over the River Lee, a garden full of pinks, constant meals sent in by local friends, and at night the company of the most beautiful moths fluttering against the bars. She took her third incarceration with admirable calm, even making a rock garden for the Governor. She was amused by her escort to her trial in Mallow: an armoured car as well as RIC and soldiers 'armed to the teeth'. On the political side, so she told Eva, she felt that her imprisonment had the good effect of bringing diffident women workers out into the open in her constituency in her absence. She wrote Eva long letters discussing the books she was reading. She was deep in Mitchel and Lalor, Chesterton and Georges. Her mind ranged from whether Maeve's musical talent had a spark, to the slave trade, the English attitude to the Kaiser, 'People would not hate the Kaiser if they saw that he was only a sad and dignified old man and not a Minotaur'; from Kickham on evictions, to the question of the effect of Mrs Fitzherbert on Catholic emancipation. In a letter to Nellie Gifford (Mrs Donnelly) she spoke of her amused gratification that the 'Enemy' had to employ so many armed guards for her (an Irishman who was a boy in Cork during her imprisonment well remembers the impression made on him by the sight of an armoured car, and being told it was there to guard the Countess). Her exercise was taken alone, with a Senior Officer in constant charge. Constance wrote to Nellie Gifford that she was studying History and Economics 'which together spell politics'. She only allowed herself one wistful comment that the 'worst thing she has missed' is the 'summer with its roses and the ripe corn of autumn'. Nora Connolly paid her two visits during this time. In spite of the cheerfulness Constance showed in her letters to Eva, when Nora Connolly and her companion left her the second time they had the impression she was very lonely.

It was borne in on us very much how dreadfully lonely she must be with not a single associate, with no one to talk to, a very small courtyard to exercise in, barbed wire entanglements under her window, soldiers in trench helmets and war apparel, tanks, etc. We echoed the saying of the woman near the jail when she saw all the activity of the military: 'Yerra, God help ye, all that turnout for one lone woman'.[8]

Release came early in October. On Saturday, 5 October, Constance was present at a reception and concert given to celebrate her release by the Irish Women's Franchise League. She was given the very practical present of a pair of driving gloves; she appeared to be in 'radiant spirits' and overjoyed to be amongst her friends again.

That same autumn the Viceroy banned the annual *Cumann na mBan* Conference (of which organization Constance was now president, it will be remembered), which was to have been held in the Mansion House. The resourceful ladies of the Council successfully held their meeting in the Gaelic League Hall while the soldiers guarded the Mansion House in vain. In November 1919 Dublin Castle made an unsuccessful attempt to get Constance deported to Poland as an alien.

Now began a strange, hunted period for Constance, which reflected the troubles that were gathering throughout the country. It was a hunted and shadowy time, yet one of amazing achievement in Government. It is only possible to catch glimpses of Constance through a stray letter or reference, because all that she and her colleagues undertook in their administration was under the ban, and therefore the constant and expert surveillance, of the Castle organizations. By the time Constance was out of jail the Viceroy had proclaimed *Dail Eireann* an illegal association; the activities of the Volunteers in the countryside against the RIC were becoming more and more like guerilla warfare; Michael Collins as Director of Intelligence in the IRA was perfecting his system of counter-espionage; Republican newspapers were suppressed; and more ominous for the future than any other event, by the extension of recruitment for the RIC to the British Isles early in 1920 the way was made open for the Black and Tans. But the *Dail Eireann* met regularly and as openly as possible without risking the arrest of all its members.[9] Constance is said never to have missed a meeting except when she was in prison. The next glimpse we have of her is through a police directive of 14 January 1920.

Superintendent D. Division.

The Countess Markiewicz has, according to the newspapers, made two appearances at unannounced meetings in the City. One last night, the other a few days ago. I must again impress on all who superintend the grave importance of securing this woman's arrest, and, to this end, force sufficiently strong to secure her arrest must be held in reserve at each Divisional Headquarters tonight and tomorrow night. The moment an unannounced meeting is discovered a message must be sent by the quickest method available to the nearest Divisional Headquarters and to the G. Division, Dublin Castle. The police on the spot must act firmly and promptly, as the Countess never remains at a meeting for more than a few minutes and may possibly be heavily veiled, and, therefore, difficult to recognize.

A motor van will be kept in waiting at the Castle and will be sent out promptly if her arrest is reported.

Superintendents will have at least three cyclists on duty in their Divisions to look out for suddenly convened meetings and the presence of the Countess or other suspects. They will report at once to their Divisional Headquarters and the Castle any information obtained.

Signed W. E. Johnstone
Chief Commissioner,
Jan 14th 1920.

In January and February 1920 under the initials C.M. Constance wrote two items for The *Irish Citizen* (founded by Francis Sheehy-Skeffington). One concerned the necessity for a decent home for every family – and how to this end she loved 'to go round and get working women to form a procession of hundreds and hundreds to march to the Authorities and demand that proper homes be provided for the workers of Dublin – not just Better homes but Best homes'. The other article comments on the difficulty of justice being done in cases of criminal assault on children. She describes how she has attended most of the criminal assault cases in Dublin in the past years, and that although the officials are kind and conscientious, yet the children are put at a great disadvantage through the officers of the law being entirely men. She writes of a particular case involving three little girls.

A man doctor had examined the little girls. A big official offered a little testament to the first wee girl . . . After the poor child had taken her oath she was asked to be seated, and give her evidence, which by the very nature of the case, is most painful and revolting. The sergeant, who had charge of the case, helped the child out with her horrible evidence, and when finished the clerk read out the evidence, and the child signed her name . . . The prisoner pleaded guilty to common assault, and the magistrate brought in a verdict accordingly with a fine of £5. One left that court with the feeling that something was very wrong somewhere, and one knew that the something wrong was the lack of women dealing with these little children . . . The poor little witnesses must be terrified with so many enormous policemen surrounding them, and will give almost any answer to suit the case . . . Let women be appointed as magistrates and solicitors to deal with children's cases.

Constance disappears from view until March of this year when she came, heavily disguised as an old woman, to stay with the O'Carroll family, where she remained for eight months, known to the children as 'Auntie'. She is remembered by the family for the amount of gardening she did and the time she devoted to improving her Irish. It appears that she must have been in too much danger then to be actively running her department because Mrs O'Carroll records that after 'some months' she threw off her disguise and started to 'work in earnest'. 'She worked unceasingly,' Mrs O'Carroll adds. (Mrs O'Carroll also remembers seeing Constance give a large silver coin to an obviously drunken woman, saying, 'Poor thing, its probably the only enjoyment she gets in life.') On 1 March of this year Constance wrote a letter asking for support for the Republican Loan.

A Chara,

I enclose leaflets for your perusal dealing with the Republican Loan.

You will see by reading these the purpose for which Ireland's Representatives desire to raise this Loan. You will realize its importance when you consider that the whole force of the British Government is concentrated on preventing the People of Ireland from subscribing to it.

The people collecting it are in constant danger of imprisonment. Those already arrested ungrudgingly pay the penalty and accept the suffering that comes to them in Ireland's cause.

They trust you to carry on and believe that you will take up the task that they have had to lay aside for a while. Do your share by subscribing generously and making it as easy as you can for those engaged in the work of collecting subscriptions.

On mutual trust and mutual help our Republic is being built up – a trust founded on our mutual love of Ireland and sanctified by our mutual participation in the Great Awakening when the Republic was proclaimed from the GPO in Easter Week 1916.

Remember: Each Bond subscribed for is a bullet fired straight into the heart of British Tyranny, and give what you can in the name of those who gave all.[10]

These were the months when Constance moved around Dublin in her role of *Charlie's Aunt*, with her bonnet trimmed with bobbing cherries, recognized by tram conductors, newsboys, basket women, but never betrayed. Mrs Sheehy-Skeffington told Esther Roper that she 'had the freedom of the city literally'.[11] Mrs Skeffington emphasized that her voice instantly gave her away. It seems strange that she, an actress, was not able to slip into an Irish accent, since most Irish bred people, however Anglo-Irish their background, acquire the lilting brogue as a second language. There are many anecdotes of her *Charlie's Aunt* days – taking the Connolly children to school; getting helped across the road by an unsuspecting policeman and dancing a little jig of delight when she was safely over; going to the Abbey Theatre; visiting Liberty Hall.

In May of this year, 1920, Constance wrote to a friend,

My latest news regarding myself is that I have just received what is commonly called a 'Death Notice from the Black Hand gang in the police'. On paper that they had taken the precaution to steal from us they had typed

> An eye for an eye
> A tooth for a tooth
> Therefore a life for a life.

I think that there is no doubt that they are plotting to murder us, and before doing so they are taking precautions to manufacture evidence to prove that we assassinated each other. No action is too mean and low for the present Government and its officials. Luckily we are not nervous, and have the strength to go on just the same as before. One is a little more careful to try and be ready to die and that is all.

We held our *Fianna Aeroght* on Sunday – the annual commemoration of our *Fianna* Martyrs, and it was a tremendous success ... The boys made Aunt Sallies in the form of hideous caricatures of Police and soldiers painted on boards – these were a great attraction as well as being an educational form of amusement. It gives a boy a great sense of his own capabilities to shy sticks at a Peeler, even if its only a wooden effigy.[12]

Constance wrote to de Valera, who was still in America at about this time,

Just a few words to wish you luck and congratulate you. In spite of everything we go on just the same, and if they are clever we can always manage to go one better. The situation has brought such splendid boys to the front, such courage, brains, and discretion, a rare combination.

You've done wonders. I expected great things but your tour has been beyond my wildest imaginings. We've all just received death notices from the police, on our stolen note paper too; but no one seems to mind much.[13]

Eva, on the other hand, minded very much indeed. She and Esther

Roper were in Italy this year, both recuperating from serious illnesses due to overwork. They spent some time in Rome staying with the solicitor Gavan Duffy who was *Sinn Fein* representative there, and who had acted for Roger Casement at his trial. Eva was aware that Constance's friends in Ireland were alarmed for her very life at the hands of the Black and Tans; they had begged Eva to obtain an audience with the Pope so as to intercede with him on her sister's behalf.

In Esther Roper's account of this incident she states that Constance's friends were both frightened for her safety, and dissatisfied with her treatment in prison. It hardly seems possible that Constance could have been in danger of her life in Cork, where she made a rock garden for the Governor and lived on the food sent in by her friends. This, therefore, would place Eva's courageous plea to the Holy Father at the end of September when Constance was first imprisoned in Mountjoy. Her friends asked Eva to make an attempt to get a rosary blessed by the Pope for the prisoner. Not without difficulty, as a non-Catholic, Eva obtained permission to attend a public audience. The Pope made his round of the audience chamber to give his individual blessings to the kneeling crowd. Eva seized her opportunity when her turn came and addressed him in fluent Italian about her 'sister's danger'. He listened patiently to all she had to say and blessed the rosary. The unusual pause in the proceedings attracted the attention of the attendants; also of an Irish Chamberlain in a resplendent uniform.

During this year there was labour trouble at Lissadell. Alderman Jinks of Sligo had organized the farm workers into the ITWGU. There was a dispute about conditions and a strike was called. Constance, rather tactlessly, wrote to her brother telling him to remember that he came from a family of 'tyrants and usurpers'. Sir Josslyn, meanwhile, was far more concerned with the present plight of his dairy cows who were in great suffering through not being milked. He milked them himself until his hands bled. Finally in desperation he went to the Union headquarters in Sligo and demanded that the animals should not be allowed to suffer. As a result the cows were relieved of their milk, but it was poured into the grass.

By the middle of this summer of 1920 two forces had clearly emerged. One of hidden, patient, construction; the other of ever more savage destruction. The secret government of *Dail Eireann* grew steadily in influence, particularly in the departments of Home Affairs, Local Government, and Labour. The clandestine administrators proved themselves to be both fair-minded and efficient; thus their influence grew amongst the people. But the other side of Ireland's fight for freedom was manifest in the dark annals of the Black and Tans and the even more dreaded Auxiliaries. One account of the avowed policy of terrorism which was initiated to counter the guerilla tactics of Michael Collins, and all who might be friends of *Sinn Fein*, is relevant to this biography, since the incident involved Constable Jeremiah Mee RIC, who later became an assistant to Constance in her Ministry of Labour. The incident concerns the notorious speech made by Colonel Smyth, Divisional Commissioner of Police for the Munster Area, as a result of which fourteen RIC men resigned. They went further and sent an account of Colonel Smyth's speech to the *Freeman's Journal*. In June 1920 Colonel Smyth had visited the RIC barracks in Listowel in company with General Tudor, Inspector General of Police and the Black and Tans for Ireland, together with other police chiefs. Colonel Smyth is quoted as saying,

Well, men, I have something of interest to tell you, something that I am sure you would not wish your wives and families to hear. I am going to lay all my cards on the table, but I must reserve one card for myself. Now, men, *Sinn Fein* has had all the sport up to the present, and we are going to have sport now . . . We must take the offensive and beat *Sinn Fein* with its own tactics. Martial law applying to Ireland is coming into operation shortly. I am promised as many troops from England as I require; thousands are coming daily. I am getting 700 police from England . . . what I wish to explain to you is that you are to strengthen your comrades in the out-stations. If a police barracks is burned, or if the barracks already occupied is not suitable, then the best house in the locality is to be commandeered, the occupants thrown out in the gutter. Let them die there, the more the merrier . . . Police and military will patrol the country roads at least five nights a week. They are not to confine themselves to the main roads but make across the country, lie in ambush, take cover behind fences near roads, and when civilians are seen approaching shout: 'Hands up!' Should the order be not obeyed, shoot, and shoot with effect. If the persons approaching carry their hands in their pockets or are in any way suspicious looking, shoot them down. You may make mistakes occasionally and innocent persons may be shot, but that cannot be helped, and you are bound to get the right persons sometimes. The more you shoot the better I will like you; and I assure you that no policeman will get into trouble for shooting any man and I will guarantee that your names will not be given at the inquest. Hunger-strikers will be allowed to die in jail, the more the merrier . . . An emigrant ship will be leaving an Irish port with lots of *Sinn Feiners* on board. I assure you, men, it will never land. That is nearly all I have to say to you. We want your assistance in carrying out this scheme of wiping out *Sinn Fein*. A man who is not prepared to do so is a hindrance rather than a help to us, and he had better leave the job at once.

Each man was then asked individually if he were prepared to carry out the orders. Constable Mee (who had previously been appointed spokesman, since there had been rumours of what might occur) then stepped forward, saying to Colonel Smyth 'Sir, I take it by your accent that you are an Englishman who in your ignor- ance forgets that you are addressing Irishmen.' He removed his cap, belt, and bayonet, and laying them on the table said 'These too are English, and you can have them. To hell with you! You are a murderer!'[14]

Colonel Smyth instantly ordered Mee's arrest. The Corporal's comrades surrounded him and swore that the room would run with blood were the order carried out. Colonel Smyth retired into another room, and according to one account, barred himself in for several hours. Fourteen of the unmarried RIC men resigned as a result of the incident, including Corporal Mee, who later came to the Labour Party offices in Dublin to be interviewed. (Colonel Smyth was shot dead by the IRA in the Cork County Club in July.)

When ex-Corporal Mee came to the Labour Party offices one day at the end of July 1920 he found quite a large gathering waiting to question him. This included Constance, Michael Collins, William O'Brien, Martin Fitzgerald (of the *Freeman's Journal*) and Tom Johnston. Mee was closely questioned about the events which had led to his resignation and especially as regards the chances of further resignations from the RIC. He was, so he wrote in later years, greatly impressed by Constance's 'dignified bearing and direct, business-like manner'. After he left an argu- ment broke out between his hearers, Michael Collins being of the opinion that he was a dangerous spy who had told his audience a pack of lies, and Constance maintaining that the British Government were capable of any crime against the Irish nation. She went so far as to give the ex-corporal an appointment at her office at 14 Frederick Street. Having satisfied herself as to his sincerity she took him on as an assistant. His is one of the very few eyewitness accounts of Constance at work.

The office was on the second floor of the building. It was camouflaged by a sign 'Apartments to Let'. Should prospective tenants arrive much innocent pleasure was derived by the staff in fobbing them off with demands for an impossibly high rent. Mee relates that Constance was a martinet as regards security; in his opinion it was no coincidence that hers, so he believed, was the only *Dail Eireann* government office not raided by the authorities. Not more than one person at a time was ever allowed to leave the premises. No member of the staff was allowed to approach the office should they notice anyone who appeared to be on the watch in the street. Every evening all important documents were taken away and hidden in a pre-arranged place. Mee relates that there were 'several pianos' in the office with rolls of music displayed, so that in the event of a surprise raid the lady members of the staff could masquerade as teachers of music. Planks were placed against the windows at the back of the office to facilitate a quick getaway. One evening in November 1920, Mee recalled, there was a false alarm when two armoured cars and two military lorries drew up at the front door of the office building. The emergency plans were at once put into operation and the staff disappeared as swiftly as flying monkeys by means of the planks.* But it was discovered that the convoy had only stopped in that particular place because one of the armoured cars had broken down. There is another better-known anecdote of how, when having received warning of a raid Constance bundled all the papers into a trunk and set off in a cab with the trunk perched on top. The next problem was where to go. She was driven hither and thither through Dublin by the bewildered cabman until she decided on the bold expedient of having the trunk placed in the window of a second-hand shop which was situated directly opposite the Black and Tan Headquarters. The owner of the shop was a friend, so she had no difficulty in persuading him to put such a large price on the trunk that no one would buy it.[15]

The question of RIC men resigning from the force was one

---

* Mee describes Constance sliding down the rope like an acrobat, but in fact by November 1920 she was shut up in Mountjoy. The false alarm must have taken place earlier.

which much concerned the authorities. Jeremiah Mee relates that his first task on joining Constance was to countersign circulars addressed to the RIC appealing to them to leave and 'throw in their lot with the Irish people'. Mee implies that this was Constance's own idea, and certainly judging by the rage this manoeuvre aroused in British circles it was an effective one. In September Constance issued another signed circular in connection with RIC resignations.

At the present moment a large number of RIC men have left the Force owing to their repugnance to the outrages that are taking place and in which they are required to take part. Some of these men have narrowly escaped with their lives. In one case, of which I have the details, a man was dismissed for refusing to participate in sacking a town, and was fired at on leaving the barracks.

These men whether they were dismissed for refusing to carry out instructions or whether they resigned as a protest, are now without any means of support.

I am addressing this to you as I believe you to be one who would object on principle to the outrages on the people that are taking place, and that you would view with horror the burning of creameries and homesteads, and burning and looting towns, and the daily terrors the people have to suffer from the callous shootings from which so many have lost their lives.

In expectation of your being willing to come to the aid of men victimized because they would not allow themselves to be used for such work, I write to ask you to co-operate with me in finding work for these men, and I would ask you if there are any vacant jobs under your patronage for which they would be suitable, to communicate with me.

The majority of these men seek employment as clerks, agricultural workers, stewards, watchmen, agents, motor drivers, caretakers, etc.[16]

The death-roll mounted with such incidents, this same September, as the sacking by Black and Tans of the small town of Balbriggan in revenge for the death of a comrade in a public house brawl. Danger spread like a poisoned growth over all Irish people, whatever their convictions. The innocent and the guilty, the involved and the non-involved – all were at the mercy of the ambush, the night search, the bullet in the street, the burning of the home. Jeremiah Mee recalls how when Constance received news of the death of a Republican she would become very depressed and sad. She would sit in her office chair, smoking cigarette after cigarette in silence and then, evidently with a supreme effort, she would pull herself together, and carry on as if nothing had happened.

In this summer of 1920 Constance risked her life in the streets after curfew in order to save the lives of nine Republicans. She came to the house of her old friend Alderman (later Mayor) Byrne, who spent much of his time travelling between Ireland and England in order to help political prisoners. Alfred Byrne had just arrived home when he heard a gentle tap on his window. With some apprehension he asked who was there. 'It's me, Constance,' came the reply. He let her in, noticing that she was wearing a heavy cloak and that she had two revolvers stuck in her belt. She handed him a roll of music. She told him it was vital to get it to London immediately, for it contained a message of warning to nine of 'our boys' that they were about to be arrested. The courageous Alderman immediately set out for London and succeeded in reaching the men just before the police did.

On 26 September Constance herself was arrested when returning from a trip in the Wicklow Hills with a friend in his car. She described the arrest herself to a friend in a letter written from Mountjoy in October where she was kept for two months pending trial.

The police stopped us at about 11.30 for having no lamp.* When they found we had no permit they got suspicious. One lit a light in my face and then went and telephoned for the military and held us up until they came. They are now occupied in raiding all my lady friends to try and find some proofs that I am linked up with something for which they can bring a charge against me. They have also stolen my handbag with my nightie and a few necesssities. They're probably considering if they will 'plant' anything in it.[17]

The next month Constance wrote to her friend May Coughlin who had offered to send her in food parcels.

If you want to give me pleasure send anything you have – if you can find a way – to some of the unfortunate sufferers of Balbriggan, Granard† or elsewhere, wherever it would be handier. How my heart bleeds for them, especially the little children. It's awful when the enemy makes war on them ...

* Tail lamp.
† Granard, in County Longford, was sacked in November by 'men who arrived in eleven lorries with bombs and petrol.' *The Irish Republic* Dorothy Macardle p 403.

Constance added that she had been finally charged with conspiracy against DORA. She was sentenced to two months' hard labour.

Constance's arrest brought her work as Minister of Labour to an end. Her detractors tend to give credit for the Ministry's solid achievements to her deputy, the late Mr Joseph McGrath. Her defenders hold that this is yet one more proof of how difficult it is for a woman to be valued for a man's work in a man's world. A brief chronological survey, together with Jeremiah Mee's recollections would appear to show that credit could perhaps be evenly divided.

Constance was released from Cork Jail in early October 1919. Since she appears to have been constantly shadowed by the police all that winter, and as it could be supposed that the infant Ministry had not then got into its stride, it seems that her real activity must have started after she 'threw off her disguise' some months after March 1920, according to her hostess, Mrs O'Carroll. Given the fact that she was arrested again in late September 1920, this leaves possibly four months of active administration. The historian of the Irish Republic, Dorothy Macardle, states that the Ministry of Labour did 'a great deal of successful work' in the autumn of 1920. During September and October it was instrumental in settling twenty-eight strikes, lock-outs and disputes. The October successes cannot be laid at Constance's door, since she was in prison, after which Joseph McGrath became acting Minister in her place. For this reason hers cannot be the credit for any further achievements. One of the easiest forms of denigration is to debit the victim with the reverse of their qualities. Constance was brave, resourceful, unselfish, gallant through any ordeal – but every thoughtful observer who knew her bears witness to her love of action, and impatience with inaction (hence the true heroism of her patience in prison). It does not seem likely that the intricacies of industrial bargaining were her forte. On the other hand, there is no doubt she inspired her Ministry with her fighting spirit, and proved herself a vigilant guardian of its secrets. Surely it could be said that both she and Joseph McGrath played vital parts in their country's secret development.

CHAPTER 15

The Rift in the Lute

In Mountjoy Constance's first thought, as always, was for Eva. She wrote to Mrs Wyse Power asking her to send a picture post-card to Eva in Florance to say that she, Constance, was well and cheerful. In December she wrote to Eva saying 'jail is the only place where one gets time to read'.

Don't bother about me here. As you know, the English ideal of modern civilization always galled me. Endless relays of exquisite food and the eternal changing of costume bored me always to tears and I prefer my own to so many people's company . . . I don't mind hard beds or simple food: none of what you might call the 'externals' worry me. I have my health and I can always find a way to give my dreams a living form. So I sit and dream and build up a world of birds and butterflies and flowers from the sheen in a dew-drop or the flash of a sea-gull's wing.[1]

In another letter of December 1920 she tells Eva she in engrossed in her studies of the Irish language. 'If I can go on for two years I *will* be master.' She notes that there is no verb 'to have' which proves, she feels, that 'we are not a covetous and aggressive race'. The Irish language 'seems to have developed along the lines of the softest and most subtle sounds and to be capable of very definite and subtle expression and shades of thought'.

After Constance had been in Mountjoy Prison for two months she was joined by a fellow-Republican – Eithne Coyle. The younger woman vividly remembers how Constance gardened (in June Constance wrote to Eva telling how her 'cooking peas are covered in bloom and the sweet peas are in bud, pansies very bright, carnations in bud and it's all come out of a desert'.)

Constance showed herself a true gardener by her comments to Eva about the necessity of 'digging deep' and also in the incident of the Visiting Justices. It was part of the duties of the Visiting

Justices to inquire as to the needs of the prisoners. When Constance was asked, she demanded dung for the garden. The Visiting Justices were so shaken by her request that they failed altogether to visit Eithne Coyle. Some time later Constance was sitting in her cell when Eithne Coyle called to her, 'Santa Claus is here'. 'What do you mean?' asked Constance. 'Come out and see. I want it to be a surprise.' The surprise was several sacks of manure, which Constance insisted on carrying on her back (although the wardresses offered to help) saying that she was as well able to carry a bag of dung as any man. Apart from gardening and learning Irish – she was in the fifth book of Growney when Eithne Coyle arrived – Constance worked at embroidery for the prison chapel altar.

During this imprisonment Constance read the lives of Tolstoy and Danton, also *Eothen* and the *Conquest of Peru*. 'It's so modern,' she comments. 'All those atrocities were done in the name of Christianity and of all noble virtues – just like today. A nation of quiet, peaceful people was wiped out and their civilization destroyed because the Spaniards wanted gold.'[2]

Eva was still in Italy, and Constance wrote wistfully of how she envied her sister in the 'land of flowers' and recalled how much she had loved Florence in the far-off days with the devoted 'Squidge', when Constance tormented her by tearing across the hedges and ditches at Fiesole to catch butterflies.

In his poem *On a Political Prisoner*, Yeats expressed his reluctant admiration for Constance's fortitude; but no amount of the sterner virtues displayed by both Constance and Maud Gonne could reconcile the poet to their politics.

> She that but little patience knew
> From childhood on, had now so much.
> A grey gull lost its fear and flew
> Down to her cell and there alit,
> And there endured her fingers' touch
> And from her fingers ate its bit.
>
> Did she in touching that lone wing
> Recall the years before her mind
> Became a bitter, an abstract thing,
> Her thought some popular enmity;
> Blind and leader of the blind,
> Drinking the foul ditch where they lie?

When long ago I saw her ride
Under Ben Bulben to the meet,
The beauty of her countryside
With all youth's lonely wildness stirred,
She seemed to have grown clean and sweet
Like any rock-bred, sea-borne bird:

Sea-borne and balanced on the air,
When first it sprang out of the nest
Upon some lofty rock to stare
Upon the cloudy canopy,
While under its storm-beaten breast
Cries out the hollows of the sea.

Release came in July with the Truce. Eithne Coyle had become
so devoted to Constance she cried for a week after her departure
and was comforted by a friendly wardress with libations of hot
milk.

Constance scribbled a jaunty note to Mrs Wyse Power. 'Just
been thrown out of jail and tried to find you. Hope to see you
tomorrow.' Her last link with the past had gone when Sir Josslyn
was obliged to sell St Mary's to raise money to meet her expenses.
From now on she made her home with the Coughlin family at
Frankfort House Rathgar, where the atmosphere of carefree
informality was after her own heart.

Because of her imprisonment, Constance had missed the direct
impact of such events as the death from hunger-strike of Terence
MacSwiney, scholarly, Republican, Lord Mayor of Cork, which
occurred on 25 October 1920 a few weeks after her arrest. In
the next month public opinion was again profoundly disturbed
and shocked by the execution of an eighteen-year-old student
called Kevin Barry (whose sister later became a great friend of
Constance's). The young man was captured after taking part in an
ambush. The historian of the Irish Republic states that there was
no evidence that he fired one of the fatal shots when six soldiers
were killed.[3] The result of his execution was that many of his
indignant fellow-students joined the IRA. In December of this
year came the burning of Cork city by Black and Tans and
Auxiliaries. The damage was estimated at between £2,000,000 and
£3,000,000.[4]

In 1921 Lord French was replaced as Viceroy by Lord FitzAlan, who became the first Roman Catholic to occupy the seat of power. Constance's old acquaintance, Lady Gregory, noted in her Journal of 10 June 1921, that Lord FitzAlan had admitted that 'crimes, horrible crimes had been committed by members of this force' (i.e. the Black and Tans). Another friend of Constance's past, Lady Fingall, described the perfect summer weather of 1921 which made more horrifying the village searches when men and women, old and young, the sick and the decrepit were lined up against walls with their hands up, questioned and searched. 'No raid was ever carried out by these ex-officers without their beating up with their butt ends of their revolvers at least half a dozen deople.'[5]

These things happened in beautiful summer weather. It was a wonderful and unforgettable summer, that of 1921. Such long evenings over the quiet country where there was a Curfew now at 11 o'clock and motor Curfew at 7 o'clock, so that the country seemed to belong to the lambs and birds, who were not bound by Curfew, and did not recognize it. But people were ill at night, and babies frequently choose to be born during those hours, knowing nothing of Curfew, either. The Doctors drove in fear, and messages summoning them must be carried on foot by the poor, who have no telephone. And such messengers made terrifying journeys and were sometimes shot 'by mistake'.[6]

In the January of this same year Robert Lynd wrote in the *Daily News*,

England is now ruling Ireland in the spirit of the torturer. How many Englishmen realize that the bloodhound and the thong are in use in Ireland as they were in the Slave States of America? I was taught that under the Union Jack all men were free and that the deliberate infliction of physical and mental torture on men, women and children was under that sign impossible. But human nature is much the same everywhere and the Irishman 'on the run' is in some respects in a worse plight than the negro slave.

There is no borderland to which he can fly. Were he not sustained by an invincible faith in God and a love of his country that counts life well lost for her he would be a man without hope. He can no more be defeated by persecution than the Scottish Covenanters would be defeated by persecution. The most tragic figure in Ireland today is not the persecuted but that of the persecutor.

The new Viceroy came into office on 19 May. In this month an election took place. It was virtually the election of the second *Dail Eireann*, since even the Irish Parliamentary party agreed not to contest Republican candidates. In the twenty-six counties a Republican candidate was returned unopposed for every county and borough.⁷ Equally in the six counties of Ulster every Unionist candidate was elected.⁸ The result of the election crystallized the mutually exclusive aims of North and South. Under the new Government of Ireland Act Ulster now had her own parliament, blessed by the Government and the Crown, while the official Southern Irish Parliament, which consisted of four non-Republican members representing Trinity College and fifteen Senators nominated by the Governor-General, met, elected a speaker, and dissolved for ever.⁹ Throughout these summer weeks, while violence continued to rule the land, de Valera was in negotiation with Ulster and with England. (De Valera and his colleagues marked their electoral triumph by burning the finest building in Dublin because it was the repository of the British archives – the Custom House.) The Government of Ireland Act held a new menace for the Republicans, since the Act laid down that unless a certain proportion of the elected members took the Oath of Allegiance, Southern Ireland would be ruled by Crown Colony government.

But at the official opening of the first elected Parliament of Ulster, the highest voice in the land, that of the King, spoke in a vein of generosity and concern which brought a new element into the troubled situation.

Few things are more earnestly desired throughout the English-speaking world [he said] than a satisfying solution of the age-long Irish problem, which for generations embarrassed our forefathers, as they now weigh heavily upon us.

Most certainly there is no wish nearer to my heart than that every man of Irish birth, whatever his creed and wherever be his home, should work on loyal co-operation with the free communities on which the British Empire is based . . .

I speak from a full heart when I pray that my coming to Ireland today may prove to be the first step towards an end of strife among her people, whatever their race or creed. In that hope, I appeal to all Irishmen to pause, to stretch out the hand of forbearance and conciliation, to forgive and forget, and to join in making for the land which they love a new era of peace, contentment, and goodwill.¹⁰

The King's speech brought de Valera and Lloyd George together in negotiation. The most immediate public effect was the Truce which came into force on 11 July. It was received with unqualified gratitude by the ordinary people of Ireland; but there was a feeling among the military that they had the IRA on the run and with the cessation of hostilities their chance had gone to settle the problem once and for all according to their own lights. There were those, too, in the IRA who felt their cause would be betrayed in 'the meshes of diplomacy'.[11]

The second *Dail Eireann* met in August 1921. Constance was re-appointed Minister of Labour. De Valera became President, instead of Prime Minister.

About this time Constance received a letter from Casi. He was now settled in Warsaw, working as Legal Adviser and Commerical Counsellor to the American Consulate General in Warsaw. The family home – Zywotowka – had been burnt down by the Bolsheviks, and the family itself was scattered. Stasko had seen five years' service with the Imperial Marine Guards, followed by two years as 'a hostage of the Bolsheviks'. He was repatriated in the following year.

Since Casimir's letter is not in existence, it is not possible to know what it contained or did not contain to evoke such a stilted reply. No greater contrast could be imagined between the almost school-girlish reticence of this epistle, compared with the loving intimacy of Constance's letters to Eva, and the unaffected warmth of those written to her Republican friends.

Mansion House

My dear Casi,

I was very glad to see your writing on an envelope. I don't suppose I should have got your letter except that it arrived in the time of the Truce. It is the first I have had from you since 1916. You ask me 'what are my plans?' Well, I have none, in fact its quite impossible to make any at a time like this. Everybody here remembers you. I have come across a great many of the old acting crowd lately and everyone besieges me with questions. Jacky O'C., I met at Mrs Kennedy Cahils (I don't know if you know that Frances Baker married your friend the Actor) also [illegible] and *they* are full of affectionate inquiries. Since the Truce we have all become popular. Its a funny world. I met Nora and P. J. in Grafton Street, I hadn't seen them since I stayed with them, and they stopped me and asked me to spend the evening. They are just as nice as ever and full of inquiries about you and told me to remember them to you and give their love. Poor Nesbit is shut up in a camp. I'm sure I don't know why.

He always used to ask after you. I never go anywhere that someone does not want to know have I heard from you. 'Sink' is always wishing for you back. I met him at a fête a few nights ago.

I am so glad that you have been successful with plays, and only hope that you are fairly comfortable. I've often been very unhappy thinking of all you and your people must have suffered. Did they lose everything at Zywotowka? Is Babshia alive still? and what happened to Stanislas:* I'm so sorry about Stas.† I wonder why anybody considers it wrong to marry the girl you love. Surely it was not political, he hated politics so. Do write and tell me.

Most of the pictures and some of the furniture is safe up to this. Lots of things were stolen and destroyed in 1916.

A one-act play of mine was played last night with great success . . . If this Truce goes on you ought to come over for a bit. I know a lot of Irish now, you will be surprised to hear. Now goodbye for the present. Do write to me again soon.

Yours ever,
Constance de Markievicz[12]

On 11 October 1921 began the Anglo-Irish Treaty negotiations which were to result in a tragic and bitter division between Irish patriots, which in its turn led to a civil war equalling in savagery anything that had gone before.

De Valera, who had conducted the initial negotiations with Lloyd George, refused to go to London as a delegate. He sent Arthur Griffith, Michael Collins, Robert Barton, together with Eva's friend from Rome, Gavan Duffy, and Eamon Duggan. Erskine Childers (hated by Griffith) was one of the four secretaries taken to London by the delegation. On the British side the chief figures were Lloyd George, Austen Chamberlain, Lord Birkenhead (a well-known Ulster sympathizer) Winston Churchill, Sir Hamar Greenwood, Chief Secretary for Ireland, Laming Worthington-Evans, and the Attorney-General, Sir Gordon Hewart.

The course of the negotiations has been described by many able commentators; the denouement when the delegates returned to Ireland on 6 December with the Treaty signed will continue to be argued for many years to come. As with all compromise solutions of a problem whose basis is totally opposed convictions, no one

* A brother-in-law.
† Her stepson.

was pleased with it except, perhaps, some of the exhausted delegates (although Collins remarked that he had signed his death warrant).

Through the Treaty, Southern Ireland was granted Dominion Status; with England claiming only a modified Oath of Allegiance. In Ireland, as with the Truce, the Treaty was acclaimed by the ordinary people and regarded with mixed feelings by the politicians. 'There was a spirit of general acquiescence in the *fait accompli*,' wrote Collins' friend and biographer, 'grumbling acquiescence on the part of the Separatists, enthusiastic acquiescence on the part of the general public.'[13] In England, Unionists looked on it as abject surrender on the part of the Government.

De Valera, his hands untied by any part in the negotiations, soon made his position clear. In a letter to the press on 9 December he said,

A Chairde Gaedheal – You have seen in the public Press the text of the proposed Treaty with Great Britain.

The terms of this agreement are in violent conflict with the wishes of the majority of this nation as expressed freely in successive elections during the last three years.

I feel it my duty to inform you immediately that I cannot recommend the acceptance of this Treaty, either to *Dail Eireann* or the country. In this attitude I am supported by the Ministers of Home Affairs and Defence.*

A public session of *Dail Eireann* is being summoned for Wednesday at 11 o'clock. I ask the people to maintain during the interval the same discipline as heretofore. The Members of the Cabinet, though divided in opinions, are prepared to carry on the public services as usual.

The Army, as such, is, of course, not affected by the political situation and continues under the same orders and control.

The great test of our people has come. Let us face it worthily without bitterness and, above all, without recriminations. There is a definite constitutional way of resolving our political differences – let us not depart from it, and let the conduct of the Cabinet in this matter be an example to the whole nation.[14]

If the signs of a mature society are co-operation, reason, and pragmatism, Republican Ireland from now on proved itself to be still in its birth-throes rather than ready to enjoy the fruits of its past struggles. But growth is usually painful. Ireland had much to

* Austin Stack and Cathal Brugha, both extremists who were not sent to London.

forget before she could divest herself of a past in which she had always been the loser. The Treaty debates make melancholy reading – and the speeches of the militant women the most melancholy of all.

The meeting of *Dail Eireann* to discuss the Peace Treaty began in the Council Chamber of University College, Dublin, on 14 December 1921. De Valera opened the debate by arguing at length about the plenary powers of the plenipotentiaries and the rights of the rest of the Cabinet not to sign the Treaty. Here there had been an initial, fatal, lack of clarity since through the delegates' first terms of reference it was possible to argue that they were empowered to sign a Treaty on behalf of the Cabinet; on the other hand de Valera argued that through a subsequent clause (3) written on 7 October in his own hand, he stipulated that a 'complete text of the draft treaty about to be signed will be . . . submitted to Dublin and a reply awaited'.[15]

On the afternoon of 19 December, Michael Collins bluntly stated that in his view 'Rejection of the Treaty is a declaration of war until you have beaten the British Empire.'

Rejection of the Treaty means your national policy is war. If you do this, if you go on that as a national policy, I for one am satisfied. But I want you to go on it as a national policy and understand what it means. The Treaty was signed by me not because they held up the alternative of immediate war. I signed it because I would not be one of those to commit the Irish people to war without the Irish people committing themselves to war . . . Now summing up – and nobody can say that I haven't talked plainly – I say that this Treaty gives us, not recognition of the Irish Republic, but it gives us more recognition on the part of Great Britian and the associated states than we have got from any other nation.[16]

Erskine Childers replied to Collins in a lucidly argued speech. He wished to make it clear to the Assembly that: 'this Treaty does not give you what is called Dominion status.'

The Minister for Finance (Collins) passed lightly over this clause concerning the occupation of our ports . . . Clause No. 6 in effect declares that the people of Ireland inhabiting the island called Ireland have no responsibility for defending that island from attack . . . This clause declares that Ireland is unfit, or, for we know the real reason – too dangerous a neighbour to be entrusted with her own coastal defence . . . Clause No. 7 declares that permanently and for ever some of our most important ports are to be occupied by British Forces.

Childers went on to argue that the Treaty itself depended upon the Act of the British Parliament and that nobody knew what form that Act would take.

That same day Kevin O'Higgins made his position plain.

I do say [the Treaty] represents a broad measure of liberty for the Irish people and it acknowledges such a large proportion of its rights, you are not entitled to reject it without being able to show them that you have a reasonable prospect of achieving more. 'The man who is against peace' said the English Premier in presenting his ultimatum, 'must bear now and for ever the responsibility for terrible and immediate war.'

In direct contradiction to Erskine Childers, O'Higgins went on to say that in his view under the terms of the Treaty Ireland 'has the right to maintain an army and defend her coasts'.[17]

Another delegate, Robert Barton, rose to say that in signing the Treaty he did not seek to shield himself from the charge of having broken his oath of allegiance to the Republic. He defended Arthur Griffith as having repeatedly sought in vain to have the final decision referred back to *Dail Eireann* in the face of Lloyd George's insistence that the delegates were fully accredited plenipotentiaries and that they must accept or reject the Treaty terms in the space of two hours: that it was a question of peace of war.

20 December brought with Mrs O'Callaghan the first of the women's speeches, with their emotional references to past suffering and adamant refusal to compromise over what they conceived as first prinicples.

On the next day Gavan Duffy spoke 'very reluctantly' in favour of the Treaty, because he saw no alternative.

I have no sympathy with those who acclaim this partial composition as if it was payment in full, with compound interest; nor have I any sympathy with those who would treat this agreement as if it were utterly valueless . . . I tried to look at it fairly, and it must be realized that the Irish people have an achievement to their credit in this respect at least, that this Treaty gives them what they have not had for hundreds of years; it gives them power, it puts power of control, power of Government, military power in the hands of our people and our Government . . . The vital defect of this Treaty is that it inflicts a grievous wound upon the dignity of this nation by thrusting the King of England upon us . . . and I do not want to minimize for a moment the evil of that portion of the Treaty.

Gavan Duffy concluded his speech with a plea 'Ratify it with the most dignified protest you can, ratify it because you cannot do otherwise, but ratify it in the interests of the people you must'.[18]

This same day, 21 December, brought Mary MacSwiney to her feet (sister of Terence MacSwiney Mayor of Cork who had died of hunger-strike) for three hours of vituperation and exhortation. Through this she showed a particular concern for the social aspects of the Treaty in the sense of the sinister social temptations implicit in the person of a Governor General and his entourage. 'Under the Constitution of the Irish Free State,' she said, 'you have no right to call any girl a shoneen* because she walks into a dance at vice-regal lodge.'[19]

The next day Arthur Griffith expressed concern at the length of Miss MacSwiney's speech. She countered his remarks with the irrefutable emotional appeal that what she went through for seventy-four days in Brixton Prison gave her the right to speak for the honour of her nation.

It was not until 3 January that Constance made her speech. 'I rise today,' she said, 'to oppose with all the force of my will, with all the force of my whole existence, this so-called Treaty – this Home Rule Bill covered with the sugar of a Treaty'. Constance, faithful to the principles of Connolly, particularly objected to the idea that Southern Unionists should be invited to have full representation in the Parliament, 'for that class of capitalists,' she said, 'have been more crushing, cruel and grinding on the people of the nation than any class of capitalists of whom I have ever read in any other country, while the people were dying on the road-sides.' She declared that the Oath of Allegiance was a dishonour-able oath. 'It is an oath that can be twisted in every imaginable form ... Now, personally, I being an honourable woman, would sooner die than give a declaration of fidelity to King George or the British Empire ... Of course you may want to send the Black and Tans out of this country. Now mind you, there are people in Ireland who were not afraid to face them before, and I believe would not be afraid to face them again. You would be labouring under a mistake if you believe that England, for the first time in her life is treating you honourably ... Can any Irishman take that oath honourably and then go back and prepare to fight for an Irish Republic or even to work for the Republic. It is like a person

* Fraternizer with the British.

going to get married plotting a divorce.' (It is sad to relate that Constance repeated the absurd rumour that Princess Mary was to break off her engagement to Lord Lascelles and marry Michael Collins who would be appointed first Governor of the new State.) Constance wound up what appears to have been a highly over-excited discourse with the old appeal for blood sacrifice,

O'Connell said that Ireland's freedom was not worth a drop of blood. Now I say that Ireland's freedom is worth blood, and worth my blood, and I will willingly give it for it, and I appeal to the men of the *Dail* to stand true. They ought to stand true and remember what God has put into their hearts and not be led astray by phantasmagoria. Stand true to Ireland, stand true to your oaths, and put a little trust in God.[20]

James J. Walsh spoke directly after Constance in favour of the Treaty. There could be no more striking example of two opposed ways of thought than the almost cynical realism with which he presented his theme of the inevitability of gradualness, compared with her blind faith in the spirit of the past. This inability to develop with the changing situation was shown by all the women who spoke; it was as though their souls were transfixed by the memory of past violence and personal loss. They nursed the thought of their dead; and with the fatal simplicity of the politic-ally innocent their love and loyalty knew no lesson but the slogans buried in the dust.

The year 1922 opened ominously with a Proclamation by President de Valera on the front page of the newspaper *The Republic of Ireland* on 5 January.

Fellow Citizens:
You are in danger. Influences more deadly to a nation faced by an enemy than a plague in the ranks of its army, are at work amongst you.
The instinct in you for peace and repose . . . is being played upon. If you give way you are undone – all you have gained will be lost, and all the sacrifices you have made will be in vain . . .
To the utmost limit to which they could go, our Delegates had gone to arrive at an agreement such as this nation could freely accept . . . By the threat of war they were dragged beyond that limit and the circum stances will ever be remembered by Irishmen as the crowning act of infamy of England's rulers against Ireland in this period.

On 7 January the vote was taken on the motion by the Minister for Foreign Affairs (Griffith) 'that *Dail Eireann* approves of the

Treaty'. The result of the division was sixty-four for approval and fifty-seven against, thus giving the supporters of the Treaty a majority of seven.[21]

In the first moment of this knowledge Michael Collins made a generous appeal for co-operation. He said,

In times of change . . . when countries change from peace to war or war to peace, there are always elements that make for disorder and that make for chaos. That is as true of Ireland as of any other country; for in that respect all countries are the same. Now what I suggest is that – I suppose we could regard it like this – we are a kind of majority party and that the others are a minority party . . . if we could form some kind of joint Committee to carry on . . . I make the promise publicly to the Irish nation that I will do my best, and though some people have said hard things of me . . . I have just as high a regard for some of them, and am prepared to do as much for them, now as always. The President knows how I tried to do my best for him.

President de Valera: Hear, hear.

Mr M. Collins: Well, he has exactly the same position in my heart as he always has.

As he spoke the words Collins stretched out his hand to de Valera.

In the seconds which passed when de Valera might or might not have met this token of conciliation the whole future hung in the balance: whether the people of Ireland, weary with strife, should have peace or civil war. But the voice of Mary MacSwiney intervened. 'I claim my right,' she said, 'before matters go further, to register my protest, because I look upon this act tonight worse than I look upon the Act of Castlereagh . . . I maintain now that this is the grossest act of betrayal that Ireland ever endured.' She concluded her indignant tirade with the words: 'I tell you here there can be no union between the representatives of the Irish Republic and the so-called Free State.'[22] Her speech was decisive. The opportunity for peaceful co-operation hovered, and passed, never to return.

Michael Collins made one further plea for an arrangement between the two sides. The President spoke of the 'glorious record' of the past four years, then broke down. The House adjourned.

The result of the Treaty split was a new government. Griffith was elected President. The chief members of his cabinet were Collins, Cosgrave, Gavan Duffy, Kevin O'Higgins, and Richard Mulcahy who succeeded Cathal Brugha as Minister of Defence. A distressing scene had taken place in the last *Dail Eireann* session of 10 January when de Valera had walked out of the chamber followed by all his supporters to cries and counter cries of 'Deserters all! . . . Oath breakers and cowards! . . . Foreigners-Americans-English! . . . Lloyd Georgeites!'

On 10 January Constance ceased to be Minister of Labour. On 16 January the new Government of Ireland (hereafter called the Free State) formally took over Dublin Castle. Meanwhile de Valera had already formed a new political group, *Cumann na Poblachta* (the Republican Party).

In this same month Constance attended the Irish Race Convention in Paris, where she saw a great deal of Maud Gonne. In February she was re-elected President of *Cumann na mBan*. The Women's Council rejected the Treaty by 419 votes to 63; supporters of it were asked to resign. Soon after this Constance made a stay of several weeks in London with Eva and Esther Roper. She addressed meetings around London and in the Midlands in order to explain the position of the Republicans. At one meeting in the Midlands she was nearly arrested, but friends spirited her away by a back door. Esther Roper recorded that her 'great desire was the removal of the Oath for the members of the Dail'.[23]

On St Patrick's Day she was with Erskine Childers, speaking 'from a little cart in a south-west outskirt of Dublin', heard by Henry Nevinson, who recounts how he remembered her on an earlier occasion, just before the Curragh Incident, 'dressed in brilliant light blue, while with impassioned gaiety she distributed bread to starving workers'.

During this spring Constance was honoured by de Valera by being chosen to be one of the chief speakers in a tour of America under the auspices of the American Association for the Recognition of the Irish Republic (as opposed to the Free State). It could be supposed that the decision was not unconnected with the presence of a Free State Delegation in America at that time. One party followed hot on the heels of the other – one to defend the Free State, the other to attack it. Austin Stack, former Minister for Home Affairs, led the attack together with J. J. Kelly, Editor of the *Catholic Bulletin* and President of the Gaelic League.

Constance was chosen to go, no doubt because her vivid personality, together with her history, was bound to appeal to a people who set a high value on spontaneity and guts. (Ironically enough, before the split Collins himself had intended sending her.) The fourth member of the party was the young and able Miss Kathleen Barry – sister of the executed student, Kevin Barry and an active member of *Cumann na mBan*.

When Constance and Kathleen Barry sailed on 1 April, Austin Stack and J. J. Kelly were already in the United States. The two women travelled in the *Aquitania*. Amongst their fellow-passengers was Prince Maximilian of Hohenloe, and a Mrs Peter Cooper Hewitt, who kept to her suite the whole voyage and on arrival refused to comment on the slander suit filed against her by her late husband's nurse.

Constance had no need to avoid the reporters. Fifty journalists and photographers took to the water in a US Revenue Cutter and boarded the *Aquitania* at the quarantine station. Constance – 'Joan of Erin' – sat at a writing table and took them on with complete aplomb. She opened her luggage with 'youthful alacrity' which pleased the Customs officials, who found nothing explosive except literature. A woman reporter on the *New York Evening World* wrote of her, 'Despite her martial achievements she is not a martial looking person – frail, rather, and almost deprecatory except when she is talking about the Irish Republic. Very tall and slender she has the stoop characteristic of so many women of her height. Her soft, waving ash-brown hair is done in the quaint psyche knot at the crown of her head, her eyes behind the eyeglasses are clear blue, and there is a dash of pink in her thin cheeks. Her smile is charming. Back of everything she says one feels emotion like a flame.'

The Irish party was welcomed vociferously at the Cunard pier. They were then driven to the Waldorf Astoria, where Constance was enchanted with the food and with American coffee – but she was not so pleased with American central heating, telling a reporter that in her own bedroom at home she had never had a fire in her life. Remarking that the air blew straight from America to Lissadell, she gave the reporters who visited her the following morning a lively account of her sporting childhood and her later exploits. Her expressed Amazonian tastes and her martial achievements were found to be in marked contrast with her physical being. One reporter described her as pale and fragile 'with light fluffy hair and wide blue eyes, obviously one of the soft, sweet unyielding sort'. But she was also found to be 'quixotic and shrewd mystical and wayward, a figure to kindle the imagination'. She was compared to the Russian heroine, Sophia Perooskaya. Kathleen Barry's smile was described as slow and sweet; her accent captivating.

While based in New York, as well as being invited to a secret *Clan na Gael* meeting, Constance went to visit Jim Larkin in Sing-Sing, returning to report that she had been given roast chicken for lunch.

The four Irish Republicans first addressed a small meeting in Lexington, then large meetings at Laurel Garden in Newark, and in Jersey City. Their theme was put across with simplicity and directness in every city they visited – the necessity of a free, independent Republic, the impossibility of accepting partition, the lack of support in Ireland for the Free State, the insuperable difficulty of the Oath of Allegiance, since to take it and having taken it to set out to achieve a Republic would be a perjury. The theme was coupled with appeals for financial support for the Republicans.

The two women arrived in Philadelphia at four o'clock in the afternoon of Good Friday; Mr Stack was already there, staying with his sister, and Mr Kelly did not come until Sunday. However, Constance was found to be a host in herself. Broad Street station was thronged with enthusiasts. She was photographed in her handsome coat of grey Irish tweed, fur collared and cuffed; the kind, quietly dressed matron hiding the revolutionary. But the fire was always ready to spring up. When a reporter, unversed in the finer points of current Irish politics, asked her if she sympathized with the Provisional Government, she leapt from her chair, shouting 'My God, man!', then controlled herself, smiled, and lifting a huge sheaf of American beauty roses to her face, apologized, acknowledging that Americans could not be expected to know all about Irish politics.

On arrival in Philadelphia Constance immediately asked if Mr Joe McGarrity (prominent and influential both in IRB Irish-American circles) was at the station. She requested to be photographed with him, saying he was her oldest friend in America. The first time Constance and Joe McGarrity had met was in Dublin when he came unexpectedly and unknown to a *Fianna* meeting at a time when she was struggling for sympathy and support. He got up at the back of the hall and subscribed twenty-five dollars.

On Easter Saturday Constance had a day off and was shown historic places in the city including Valley Forge. She wanted especially to 'walk in the hallowed footsteps of Washington'. She was always observant and she particularly admired those public buildings that were constructed in classical forms.

Constance dined at the Art Allegiance; she was greatly interested in the conversation of Colonels Gates and Meehan, and Major Gardiner. On Easter Sunday she and Kathleen Barry were escorted to church in state by the five-hundred-strong Irish Volunteers and their magnificent brass band. This was the beginning of a full day. They lunched with Miss Catherine Day in Spruce Street, where as 'a delicate compliment' to Constance, Mr Frank Lee sang her Battle Hymn. After a long lunch they were taken on to the Irish American Club where they were the guests of honour at a reception, ate 'a lovely Irish tea' and Constance afterwards delivered a stirring address. Constance explained to the Philadelphians that part of her mission was to tell Americans that the Republican movement did not merely consist of fanatical followers of Mr de Valera, but it existed, rather, out of a profound conviction that Ireland 'must and will be a Republic'. She added, 'We want moral and financial support.'

On Easter Sunday there was a mass meeting at the Academy of Music under the chairmanship of Mr Joe McGarrity. 'Countess Markievicz wins all hearts with a moving appeal' said the headlines in *The Irish Press*. The aptly named Peter Golden (Irish orator and poet) achieved subscription pledges worth 50,000 dollars. Following the President of the American Association for the Recognition of the Irish Republic, and Austin Stack, he made an impassioned appeal for support of the Republican ideal. 'Oh men and women of Ireland, I ask you will these people be defeated? No, God forbid. You see my hands uplifted – that's where Ireland's face is – uplifted to the dome of heaven. Will you, children of the race, stand by and see that dead face beaten back again. Don't. Don't.' Constance in her turn spoke of how the star-spangled banner had been an inspiration – 'your stars on their blue ground; stars shining to us in the dark night of our trouble tell us how you have suffered for freedom.' The audience responded.

It is interesting to note that at this stage in the stormy history of the Irish Free State it was still possible for Austin Stack to defend Griffith from the platform at a Republican meeting and praise him as a man for whom he had the greatest respect; and for Constance to tell reporters that there was no real bad blood between the Free Staters and the Republicans; nothing more in the way of incidents than skylarking between young people. She was less mild regarding the British, announcing to her audience that 'we, like you, in Dublin in Easter Week, learned the joy of looking along a gun at the heart of an English soldier'. She had, indeed, travelled far since the café conversation in Paris when (according to him) she told the Pole Krzywoszewski that the Irish were not able to appreciate the benefits bestowed on them by the British. (When she was asked in New York why Ireland did not adopt the Ghandi programme of non-co-operation, she replied with spirit that 'the Ghandi programme was copied from us. I have not a stitch on me of anything that was made in England. The blouse I wear was made in the White Cross shops established with American money. The skirt I wear was made in the Co-operative tailoring shop in Abbey Street in Dublin.')

On Tuesday, 18 April, the party now without Austin Stack, who had gone East, reached Detroit where, so Constance told Eva, they found the first pear trees in white and pink bud in the apple orchards. There were in a land of great lakes and pine forests. Peter Golden came with them, together with Father O'Flanagan, Vice-President of *Sinn Fein*. A mass meeting was held at the Danceland Auditorium on the 18th; the next night the delegation attended a banquet in the Knights of Columbus Hall, given by the Kevin Barry Club and the Gaelic Club of Detroit.

On the 20th the delegates made a quick dash into near-by Canada for a trip to Windsor. We do not know if any of the Canadians Constance met reacted to her statement as reported by the Philadelphia *Public Ledger* to the effect that she expected America would eventually take over Canada and thereby abolish the border.

The party then travelled southwards to Akron, Ohio. They arrived on 21 April, the same day that the Bishop in Cleveland, Ohio, received a telegram of thanks from Michael Collins for his assurance of no support for the Republican delegation. The week previously *The Akron Beacon Journal* had come out with a leader praising the Free State Delegates, General Beaslai and Counsellor Forrestal, remarking that it was hard to see what Mr de Valera could gain by holding out for an Irish Republic when Ireland had already gained a position as regards Great Britain comparable to Canada's. Constance and Kathleen Barry found themselves in this somewhat cool atmosphere without the support of either Austin Stack or Father O'Flanagan because the party had split, Mr Stack and Father O'Flanagan following a different schedule. It was in Akron that Constance was told by the organizers of her visit that they had been warned against her by the Beaslai delegation in such shocking terms they could not bring themselves to repeat the accusations. She presed them to tell her. They finally revealed that the unmentionable charge was that she was virtually a Communist. She laughed this off without difficulty. In Akron there was an afternoon meeting in the Marian auditorium, a reception and a banquet beginning at six o'clock, followed by another meeting. The delegates went on to Cleveland, in spite of the Bishop. After Cleveland, St Paul, north-westwards in Minnesota was the next stop. (The *St Paul Dispatch* mentioned in the caption underneath a photograph of the delegates that it was the second Irish delegation to visit St Paul within a week.) The Republicans were given an official lunch 'under the auspices of the St Paul Central Council of the American Association for the Irish Republic'. In the evening they held a meeting in the People's church. From St Paul the delegates went to its 'twin city', Minneapolis. Speaking in the Minneapolis auditorium, Constance compared the Battle of Bunker Hill with Easter Week, 'You learned freedom – you hunted every last Saxon like rats into the Atlantic. We have learned the same lesson – to stand up to the foe with gun in hand – and we have not forgotten the lesson so bitterly earned.'

She saw the Mississippi 'and a lovely waterfall, by the side of which great piles of unmelted snow lay, melting slowly in the shade of the cliff crowned by flowering cherry trees and shrubs in full leaf'.[24]

In all towns that they visited, Constance and Miss Barry found it was considered a necessary honour to be shown the prison, including the condemned cells. During one of these prison visits Constance showed her totally practical outlook on every level by asking for details of the make-up methods used by jailed prostitutes, since she held that they were experts in this field.

Continuing their journey across the lands of the North-West the delegates arrived at Butte in Montana on the 27th. They were met by the Pearse and Connolly fife and drum band at the head of a large delegation of Irish sympathizers who formed an escort so far as the Thornton Hotel. The reporter of *The Butte Miner* wrote that Constance was a living paradox in that she was 'born and reared in luxury' and yet she was the woman who was promoted to the second highest command in the Irish Army for valour in action. This reporter went on to give a detailed description of her clothes and appearance. She was wearing 'a very fetching hat, small and many coloured. Her feet were encased in small suède grey slippers. Trim grey silk stockings. A dress mostly black, but trimmed in red braid with a fancy design worked in red thread round the edges of sleeve and collar . . . She is rather sharp featured, clear and yet some [*sic*] tanned of complexion, and a person of much nervous energy.' Kathleen Barry was found by the Butte reporters to be 'A winsome Irish lassie, with dark blue eyes, the matchless skin of her soft climate, white teeth well set behind a mobile mouth and a wealth of brown hair that her black sailor hat did not half conceal.'

There was a snowstorm which caused the delegates to arrive late for their meeting in Anaconda the next night. The enthusiasm of the audience was undiminished. When Constance arrived the whole assembly greeted her by standing, remaining standing until she reached the platform. Two days later, on Sunday 30th, there was a meeting in the Butte High School Auditorium. Here in Montana the Irish party found themselves in the centre of a mining district. Constance would not have been Constance had she not visited a mine. It was an official visit, but she made searching and awkward inquiries as to conditions of work and the high incident of vocational illness. She received the miners' leaders privately.

The party moved on across the Rockies and the 'waste lands of Montana' to the Pacific seaboard States of Washington and Oregon where they held meetings in Seattle and Portland. By this time they had traversed the whole breadth of the United States. They then travelled south into the orange groves and warm skies of California, arriving in San Francisco on 6 May to be met by a deputation dressed in ancient Gaelic dress. Here it was 'Roses,

roses all the way'. The party was driven slowly from the Ferry building up Market Street, Constance carrying a 'small, drooping bunch of Californian poppies' which had been tossed into her lap by a woman leaning over the rail of a passing street car. A young man ran alongside Constance's vehicle, saying 'Countess, do you remember the terrible fighting of Easter Week. . . . I was one of those who got away alive. I came all this way.' 'Ah, indeed I do, lad,' she replied clasping his hand.

At San Francisco the delegates received word that they were to cut short their proposed four-month tour so as to return to Ireland in time for the Pact Election. They held a meeting in the Exposition auditorium on Sunday, 7 May. The next day Constance was guest of honour at a lunch given by the Chamber of Commerce. The day after the party arrived in Los Angeles, and had a meeting in the Trinity Auditorium. Constance wrote to Eva that it was like the tropics, 'Great palm trees lining the streets and aloes scattered like thistles through the waste stretches of country.'

At some point in this tour Constance remarked to Kathleen Barry that she noticed how happy those who chewed gum appeared to be at meetings. She thought she would try it. Soon she was rarely seen without a piece of gum tucked in her cheek; so much so that her friends had to ask her to moderate her new habit.

After Los Angeles the party made the five-day journey by the Santa Fé route across 'the desert land' of Arizona, and on east to Springfield, Massachusetts where lilac and syringa was in bloom. Here they were piped to their meeting in the auditorium by the Brian Boru pipers; they received pledges of two thousand dollars for the cause of the Republic.

After Springfield, Massachusetts the delegates looped their way back to Cincinnati, which city they reached on 16 May. Then came Chicago; then back to the East again, arriving in Boston on Sunday, 28 May. This was the farewell week. It was heralded the day before by a leader in *The Boston Telegraph* which opened with the words,

Tomorrow a remarkable woman will visit Boston. While there has been, unhappily, division of opinion as to the better method for Ireland to adopt in securing her freedom, no one has ever disputed the intellect or ability or vision or valour of Countess Georgina Constance Markievicz . . . Men may differ with her in opinion, but no one can deny that history will recognize her as one of the great women in the world's history. Rightly she has been termed Ireland's Joan of Arc . . . Men and women and children who have the opportunity to see this woman tomorrow should not let it pass, for in future years those who have gazed on the face of Countess Markievicz will proudly boast of that distinction.

The week began with a reception and tea in the Coply-Plaza Hotel, and continued that evening with an address to the members of *Cumann na mBan*. There was a meeting every day: in New Bedford, Lynn, Norwood, Lawrence, Full River, Worcester, and in Maple Street playgrounds, Holyroke. Finally, in New York there was a monster farewell meeting in Madison Square Garden.

And then it was all over. The immense journeys through the fabulous, unknown land; the sight of new cities, of small towns and raw, half finished hamlets; the myriad attentive faces in the auditoriums; the bouquets of American beauty roses; the reception committees and pipe bands; the applause and praise and comment. It was the last public place in the sun for Constance. And there is no doubt that she enjoyed the role of a public woman. She had two clear personalities; the private, 'thoughtful, gay, interesting and interested in the young' recalls Kathleen Barry, and the public. Unconsciously she would switch from one to the other, particularly on this trip, assuming on arrival at the stations – where waited the receiving committees, the bands, the bearers of bouquets – the gestures and bearing of the heroine they had come to see. She was confident, extrovert, happy to be there, so the crowds were happy to see her. Once her ship sailed from New York she was journeying to the shadows. There was still work to do, danger, the love of loyal friends; but always in the twilight world of politicians on the run.

While she was in St Paul, Constance began a long letter to Stasko, which she finished in the train. I quote it in full, because it proves how deep and constant were her affections, and how true her concern for her own, as well as for the poor, the hunted, and dispossessed.

My dear Staskou,

I have just received your letter forwarded to me from Ireland via New York to this place, St Paul, it is called, and its in the wilds of Minnesota. I am on a tour visiting all our Irish centres in the us.

I never wrote to you because I was afraid of compromising you, but I sent you many messages by Eva. She gave me yours. Do you remember you wrote her asking for some articles of apparel? I was getting them for you and my daughter-in-law when I was again shut up. You know I've had a pretty stiff time of it, about three years and a half, and some of it was awful. I did what I could to help you and I think that some of the people whom I got to intercede for you may have been a little help. I did not know how it was with you for a long time and when I first heard I could find out nothing. Father just mentioned that you were locked up for no reason. Some of your 'mixers' old friends found out all about you for me and have been doing all they could to get influential men among your captors to see a little reason and let you out. I do long to see you again. You were always as dear to me as if you had been my own son. Also dear Casi, I hate to think of him having to work on a job. Of course, we are all frightfully poor just now, for money won't buy anything. I wonder if he got the money I sent him from Ireland. He never wrote, at least I never got the letter. Do send me a photo of your wife. Eva showed me one long ago – When you have time write and tell me all about yourself and what happened at Zywotowka. I got a letter from Michael Flick, a fellow sufferer of yours, who is awfully fond of you. I was getting it copied and was sending it to Jim Larkin who had already promised to try and get certain Bolshie friends of his to try and get you set free. He is in prison here, I think because he was too revolutionary and made wild speeches. But he's awfully decent and promised to do all he could to get you out. . . . You rail against the Bolshies. I know little about them, but one thing I do know that our people suffered far worse from the English; and what I begin to believe is that all governments are the same, and that men in power use that power for themselves and are absolutely unscrupulous in their dealings with those who disagree with them. I am finishing this letter in the train. We are now in the Rockies, en route for Butte, Montana. The scenery is beautiful, wild and rugged with patches of snow everywhere, and real cowboys rounding up cattle in the fields . . . Again I must say how glad I am that you are out, and how I pray that all your troubles will soon be over. Of course if we get things fixed right in Ireland, I am sure we shall want men like you, who know languages, and that I could get you a good job.

Now good-bye darling boy, and much love from your loving Mother.[25]

During this trip Constance spoke often to Kathleen Barry of Maeve, whom she apparently had not seen since before her imprisonment in Cork Jail. (An undated letter placed by Esther Roper in the section of the *Prison Letters* before the Cork Jail period mentions that Constance thinks Maeve is 'fit and well and looking lovely though thin'.[26] Constance bought many presents for 'my little daughter', including Hudson Bay furs in Seattle. When the two women finally reached London, Constance spent her first day with Eva, returning to her hotel about ten o'clock. Kathleen Barry went to bed soon after Constance's return. She was disturbed by a chambermaid who came to tell her that a lady wanted to see the Countess, but there was no answer from her room. Miss Barry thought Constance must be asleep, so she suggested that the visitor should come again the next day. Behind the chambermaid appeared the figure of a very tall, robust, young woman who said she must see the Countess. Kathleen Barry demurred. After some conversation the stranger revealed that she was Maeve, who through absence from home had failed to receive Eva's message about her mother's arrival. Miss Barry immediately went to Constance's room, but found she was not there. She suggested that Maeve should look for her mother downstairs; there was a hesitation and Maeve confessed she was not certain what her mother looked like now. Miss Barry supplied a description. Maeve went downstairs, but, still hesitant, came back to say that she had seen a lady resembling Miss Barry's description having coffee with two friends. Miss Barry encouraged her to return. The lady was indeed Constance. Thus was accomplished the reunion between two beings whose natural love for one another was interrupted and almost irrevocably spoilt by the overmastering claims of *Cathleen ni Houlihan*.

CHAPTER 16

In the Shadows

A photograph of Constance in *The Graphic* of 24 June 1922 shows her making a tour of her constituency during the 'Pact Election'. She is wheeling that invaluable accessory to her life – her bicycle – and she is surrounded, very fittingly, by the ragamuffin children whom she knew so well how to comfort and help. But of the former impetuous charmer there is no trace. She might be any earnest committee woman on her rounds. From now on it is apparent from the comments of her first biographer, the distinguished Irish writer, Sean O'Faolain, that the young intellectual Republicans who met her during these last years of her life found it hard to penetrate the mask of tense exhaustion, the gum-chewing, the chain-smoking, the shabby clothes, in order to perceive the exceptional being that still lay behind the ruins of her beauty and her physical élan. Her assistant and devoted adherent from her Ministry of Labour days, Jeremiah Mee, wrote of her that when he first knew her in 1920 she was 'handsome, athletic, bright-eyed and keen' but when he saw her four years later at a meeting in Sligo she 'was a careworn woman, broken, dispirited and sad'.[1] No one could live with Constance's character, as the present biographer has done for over three years, without wishing her the forgetfulness of 'old, unhappy, far-off things, and battles long ago' … an 'old age serene and bright, and lovely as a Lapland night'. But as she was shaped and changed by the troubles of her country, so her last years reflect the torments still to be undergone before peace came at last.

In this year, while skirmishes, murders, and acts of arson increased between Protestants and Catholics, the 'Pact Election' came about as the result of an agreement between Collins and de

Valera regarding the distribution and proportion of candidates as between the pro-Treaty and anti-Treaty factions. At the same time Southern Ireland waited for the publication of the constitution arising from the Treaty itself. Unluckily for the future, the Treaty had been so framed that it was 'capable of two interpretations, one so narrow that Lloyd George had been able to appease with it the English Conservatives, one so wide that Michael Collins had been able to persuade half the nation that it gave Ireland a Republic in all but name'.[2] The constitution was not published in the Irish press until polling day itself, so it could hardly be said that the electorate had a chance to study it. When the polls were declared there were found to be 58 pro-Treaty members, 36 Republican (anti-Treaty), 17 Labour members, 7 of the Farmer's Party, 6 Independents, and 4 Unionists, representing Trinity College.[3] In other words, 466,419 electors voted for the Treaty, and 133,864 against it.[4] (Constance was among the Republican candidates defeated.) Such were the complications of the situation that it was possible for the two main parties to interpret the result differently. But before time could prove whether in the circumstances a coalition government was possible or workable, violence transformed the situation. First Field-Marshal Sir Henry Wilson (Director of Military Operations during the Curragh incident and prominent Ulster sympathizer) was assassinated in London on 22 June by two members of the London battalion of the IRA. It has never been established on whose orders they acted.[5] Six days later came the event which made civil war inevitable: the bombardment on Collins' orders of the Dublin Law Courts – the Four Courts Building – which was occupied by Irregulars (who had kidnapped the pro-Treaty Deputy Chief of Staff General J.J. O'Connell, as a reprisal for the arrest of an IRA officer, Leo Henderson). Two days later the Four Courts garrison surrendered when the building caught fire; but the battle continued because the Provisional Government troops turned their attention to the headquarters of the Dublin Brigade of the IRA. The garrison finally withdrew into the Hamman Hotel. Constance is remembered as being in the thick of the fighting here. She took up a highly dangerous position on the roof and engaged the Provisional Government snipers, who were on the roof tops of Henry Street, until she had silenced them.[6] As in 1916 the women of *Cumann na mBan* worked like Trojans as accessories to the men. Constance followed orders as a soldier; and as a soldier on Cathal Brugha's orders she surrendered her arms.

In this fighting there began the long toll of lives that Ireland could ill spare. Cathal Brugha was killed because he bravely and defiantly refused to surrender. Liam Mellows, one of the most able of Constance's ex-*Fianna* boys, was arrested. He was later executed. Two days after Cathal Brugha's death, Harry Boland, former intimate friend of Collins, now a de Valera adherent, was shot by Provisional Government troops when they came to arrest him. The next month – August – brought the death of Arthur Griffith at the age of fifty from a cerebral haemorrhage. Like Redmond before him, he was worn out long before his time; he found half his colleagues had become his enemies, his motives impugned, his life-work threatened by chaos and anarchy. Worse was still to come. On 22 August, ten days after the death of Griffith, news came to the Government that Michael Collins had been killed in an ambush by a party of Cork Irregulars, who did not recognize their eminent victim. Well might Kevin O'Higgins, speaking later of that time, say that the Provisional Government was 'simply eight young men in the City Hall standing amidst the ruins of one administration with the foundations of another not yet laid, and with wild men screaming through the keyhole'.[7]

Government had to continue whatever the danger to those who governed. William Cosgrave was elected President in succession to Griffith. The newly elected *Dail* met in September. A cabinet was formed. The constitution was debated, and finally enacted. The Provisional Government became the Government of the Free State. All the time the violence grew. De Valera, the principal public figure on the anti-Treaty side, was quoted afterwards as having seen himself as 'condemned to view the tragedy through a wall of glass, powerless to intervene effectively'.[8] The Republicans had constituted themselves as a *de jure* Government, with de Valera at its head, but the IRA leaders in this government appear to have retained the effective power of strategy.

On receiving the news of the Four Courts fighting and the subsequent imprisonments of Irregulars, Maud Gonne gave up her position in Paris, where she was Irish Representative, in order to help the wives and children of the prisoners. She was remembered by the writer R. M. Fox as a tall 'queenly figure, robed in black, moving gracefully among the children'.

In the months that followed, Constance and other political women flung themselves into the fray with a loyalty which did not count the cost. For her, as for her friends, the actions which endangered her freedom and even her life were undertaken for the sake of the ideals of 1916. For Constance the supreme allegiance was to the teaching of Connolly. In this she was perfectly consistent. Warm hearted as she was it is impossible to believe that she did not suffer through her knowledge of the savagery which grew between her compatriots, but she soldiered on without complaint until she dropped in her tracks.

She was in Carrick-on-Suir in March and April with the Irregular Forces, and later on in that summer in Clonmel and Tipperary. There is a local tradition that she was in command at Carrick-on-Suir when the town was taken after heavy fighting in September. It is certain that she delivered an address from the Town Hall steps in Carrick, calling the townspeople 'my fellow rebels'. There was a strong labour movement in this area at the time, which must have appealed to her. Workers' Co-operatives had taken over creameries and factories. At Carrick, the Red Flag flew at one end of the town and the Tricolour at the other.[9]

In the late summer and early autumn of 1922 she produced a Roneo paper in the Republican interest. She wrote most of the copy, drew the political cartoons, printed and circulated the paper. In October or November her Roneo duplicator was seized in a raid.[10] She then went to Glasgow where she helped to edit the Republican newspaper *Eire*. In Scotland she addressed many meetings besides doing her work for the newspaper. She remained chiefly based in the North of England for nearly a year.

In late September 1922, the Government took the crucial step of granting especial powers to the army. These powers gave the right to set up military courts, and to 'inflict punishment of fine, imprisonment, deportation or death'.[11] In December, two Deputies on their way to the Dail were shot at – one fatally. As a reprisal the Government executed four political prisoners. These included Liam Mellows, and Rory O'Connor, who had been best man at Kevin O'Higgins' wedding the year before.

It is sad when contemplating the months of bitter in-fighting which marked the years 1922 and 1923 to remember Constance's words written from Cork Jail in 1919, 'Easter Week comrades don't fall out: they laugh and chaff and disagree.'[12] In the November of the same year, 1922, another comrade had already met his death by the orders of former comrades. Erskine Childers, who had been in Munster holding the position of staff officer to the Republican Army, was captured by Free State troops in the house of his cousin, Robert Barton. He was executed on 23 November. 'I die full of love for Ireland,' he wrote; and again, 'I die loving England and passionately praying that she may change completely and finally towards Ireland.'[13]

Maud Gonne relates in her autobiography how the Women's Prisoners' Defence League organized a protest meeting against the shooting of the four prisoners, outside the house of the Commander-in-Chief and Minister of Defence, Richard Mulcahy,

The Free State soldiers were drawn up inside the railings; some shots had been fired over our heads; a woman's hat had been pierced by a bullet. I heard an order given and the front line of soldiers knelt down with rifles ready – some of the young soldiers were white and trembling. I got up on the parapet and smiled contempt at the officer. He had curious rather beautiful pale grey eyes and a thin brown face. We gazed at each other for a full minute. The order to fire was not given. Later I was told I was brave and had saved many lives.[14]

In December, the veteran Irish Nationalist, Tim Healy, whose past reached back to Parnell and the Land League, was installed as the first Governor-General of the Free State. Cosgrave issued his list of thirty Senate nominations. These included well-known names from the past such as Yeats, Sir Horace Plunkett, and Oliver St John Gogarty. Among the thirty elected members were Mrs Stopford Green, Colonel Maurice Moore, brother of George Moore, and Constance's great friend, Mrs Wyse Power.

On 27 December *The Irish Times* published Æ's open letter to Irish Republicans,

If I intervene in a conflict, my natural desire is to take part with the underman. If I do not do so now, it is because you are where you are only by reason of a mentality which may be changed. You are not like the poor in the slums – held there by inexorable pressure from a social order not yet beneficent enough to secure comfort for all in the national household. You have only to speak a word and active hostility against you is ended. Can you say that word without dishonour? I believe you can . . . No ideal, however noble in itself, can remain for long lovable or desirable in the minds of men while it is associated with deeds such as have been done in recent years in Ireland. I believe that Christ in his Kingdom would have been execrated by humanity if his followers had sought to impose their religion on the world by a warfare such as has been waged in the name of Irish freedom . . . I do not like to think of you that the only service you can render Ireland is to shed blood on its behalf . . . can you name those, who, if you were all killed, would have left behind, as Pearse or Connolly, MacDonagh or Childers did, evidence of thought or imagination?

Æ's words were ignored by the Irregulars. The homes of Senators now became a favourite target. One of the most cruel cuts of fate was the burning of Sir Horace Plunkett's house at Foxrock, when his fine collection of modern Irish paintings was destroyed. He had spared nothing of his time, energy, fortune, and faith for Ireland. In January of 1922 and February of 1923 the houses of the thirty-seven Senators were burnt, including the loved home of Oliver St John Gogarty-Renvyle in Connemara. In February, too, came the murder by Irregulars of Kevin O'Higgins' father, the much respected Dr Higgins – on a Sunday evening, in his own house.

When Constance wrote to Stasko late in 1922 she mentioned none of these occurrences. She spoke of trying to send him ten pounds for Christmas, and of helping to find him work in America, for, she wrote,

I believe that if you got a start somewhere, you would come out on the top; and I could give a great account of your powers of work for I saw the way you tackled Russian; and also of your very high standards of honour and honesty, and these are two qualities that help a man to success.[15]

From February of 1923 onwards Constance was always on the move; speaking at meetings which were designed to woo back to the Republican cause those Irish ex-patriates who were bewildered by the events following the split between the Irish leaders after the Treaty debates. Her theme both in speeches and articles was that the Free State had stolen the sacred symbols of the true Republican Ireland; the tricolour flag, the green uniform of the Volunteers, the very names *Saor Stat* and *Dail Eireann* – and that this Free State was nothing more than a vassal of English Imperialism, a betrayal of the heroes of Easter Week. Reading the speeches and articles Constance produced during this year one is struck by the simplicity of an extremist attitude: to be entirely blinkered to an opposing point of view and to the subtle conflicts and strains which have produced a given situation, endows the blinkered one with the strength of fanaticism. On a lower level, the servants of the opposing sides, continuing the all too familiar pattern of savagery, made daily martyrs of the captives.

Constance held meetings in Scotland in February, in London in March. On the anniversary of the Easter Rising she spoke at Dumbarton and moved her audience to tears with her accounts of the sufferings inflicted on Republican prisoners by Free State jailers. In April and May she spoke in Hamilton, Uddingston and Glasgow. During this time there occurred the worst episodes relating to the women Republican prisoners who used hunger-strike as a weapon for better conditions or release. In Kilmainham were Mary MacSwiney, Dorothy Macardle – future historian of the Republic – Maire Comerford, and the neice of the O'Rahilly, Shiela Humphries. On the nineteenth day of Mary MacSwiney's and Mrs O'Callaghan's* hunger-strike, the Governor decided to move eighty-one prisoners to the North Dublin Union, if necessary by force. The women were deeply concerned about the physical condition of Miss MacSwiney and Mrs O'Callaghan. They held an emergency meeting; they decided unanimously to tell the Governor they would resist the proposed move unless Mrs O'Callaghan and Mary MacSwiney were released. He grimly told them that their resistance would not worry him, since he had beaten his wife. Later, stretcher-bearers appeared but only Mrs O'Callaghan was taken away. The women held a council of war. They realized their best strategic position was the top gallery, caged in with iron bars, and from which a narrow iron staircase descended to the ground floor – where Mary MacSwiney lay in her cell.

Our officers gave us our instructions; we were to resist, but not to attack; we were not to come to one another's rescue; no missiles were to be thrown; above all, for the patient's sake, whatever was done to us, no one must cry out. Then we knelt and said the Rosary. There was no sign of an attack. We stood three deep, arms locked, and sang, as we do every evening, some of Miss MacSwiney's favourite songs.[16]

* Mrs O'Callaghan was one of the T Ds who had spoken against the Treaty in the debate.

Ten minutes later an agitated matron came up the darkened stairs with a lighted taper; she begged the girls to give in. She warned them that it was not the military who were coming for them, but CID and military police. 'God pity you, girls,' she said, 'you are going into the hands of men worse than devils.'

The attack when it came was 'violent but disorganized', wrote Miss Macardle. The girls clung to the iron bars. The men rushed up the stairs; they used every method such as kicking, thumb-twisting, head bashing, in order to force the girls down the stairs. Many of the wardresses were in tears, but the prison doctor, wrote Miss Macardle, seemed more amused than anything else; he did nothing to help the girls who were injured. The ordeal was not over, because now came the macabre farce of being 'searched' in the surgery by drunken women brought in by the CID. Another eyewitness account described some of the girls being kicked about like footballs; others were seen being dragged down the stairs by their hair or their feet. A wardress who intervened because of the rough handling of the prisoners got a cut on her face for her pains. In all it was five hours before the prisoners scheduled to be moved were finally loaded into the waiting lorries.

The next afternoon Mary MacSwiney was released; so the girls felt that they had proved their point.

On 24 May 1923 the Civil War ended. It was estimated that it had cost the Free State Government £17,000,000. At this time the Government had the right, due to the state of war, to hold prisoners without trial. It was estimated that 11,316 were so held, including about 250 women.[17] The Government felt it was necessary to keep these people in prison so they rushed through a Public Safety Act in order to legalize the situation.

In August a General Election took place. Constance returned from Scotland to take part in the campaign. She won her seat back. The Republicans, as *Sinn Fein*, put forward eighty-seven candidates, although, as in the past with the British Parliament, their election negated itself. They could not take their seats in a Free State Parliament because of the stumbling block of the Oath of Allegiance. The election resulted in a victory for the Government party. During the election de Valera was arrested at Ennis. He remained in solitary confinement, without trial for nearly a year.

During this autumn there was much agitation for the release of the political prisoners. Many of the women prisoners were in the North Dublin Union, including Constance's friend from Ballymote, Baby Bohan, and Shiela Humphries, together with Miss Humphries' cousin, the daughter of the O'Rahilly. Here the women lived their limbo life – crowded into the former workhouse dormitories where the iron beds had two grey blankets each, where parcels from home alleviated the monotonous prison food, where they drilled under a fellow-prisoner who was a gym instructress, and where the days passed chiefly in sewing and knitting and reading. News came to the women that the men were on hunger-strike in order to obtain their release. After a few days the women made the decision to go on hunger-strike as well in order to back up the men.

Constance spent her days speaking in the streets on behalf of the prisoners. Miss Bohan's family became extremely worried about her health on hunger-strike, so her sister Doty was sent to try to get news. As Doty Bohan was walking along the streets she came one day upon a large crowd gathered round a dray. 'It's the Countess,' said a man standing beside her, 'she's holding a meeting for the release of the prisoners.' Constance was asking everyone to go to the City Hall to sign the public petition. Doty Bohan recalls that she could not get near her then, but that her heart swelled with pride at the sight of 'our own Sligo heroine'. A few days later she was asked at Republican Headquarters to join Constance in her rounds and help to hand round leaflets. Inevitably Constance was arrested after one of her speeches from her dray. That day, 20 November, Mrs Sheehy-Skeffington was with her, together with several members of *Cumann na mBan*. Maud Gonne and Mrs Sheehy-Skeffington went anxiously to the police station to hear if Constance had been charged, and if so with what offence, also to find out if she wanted food or clothes. Constance sent them a message accepting the clothes, but announcing her intention of also going on hunger-strike. Soon after her arrival at North Dublin Union, she heard that her friend Baby Bohan was so ill after thirty days that she had been Anointed by the priest and given the Last Sacraments. Of her own hunger-strike Constance wrote to Eva that the worst part was taking the decision:

I always rather dreaded a hunger-strike, but when I had to do it I found that like most things, the worst part was looking forward to the possibility of having to do it. I did not suffer at all but just stayed in bed and dozed and tried to prepare myself to leave the world. I was perfectly happy and had no regrets . . . I am telling you this because you have such a horror of hunger-strike and I want you to realize what it was to me.[18]

With the realism that never deserted her Constance added that her hunger-strike had cured her rheumatism, and that many sufferers from stomach trouble were also cured. 'Most of those who were on for a fortnight seem to be none the worse. Of course some of those who were on for a month or longer have been very bad. One girl, Baby Bohon [sic] from Ballymote, will probably never be the same again.'

The men gave up their hunger-strike (but not before two of them had died). The call-off was in time to save Baby Bohan. She recalls that no one could have been a more tender and devoted nurse than Constance. She cooked for her; she spent hours sitting on the sick girl's bed supporting her with her own body to ease the patient's backache; she gave her mittens to Baby Bohan to protect her starvation-shrivelled hands from the cold. (Baby Bohan afterwards sent Constance a pair of black cashmere mittens in return; Constance wrote to say that she thought she had had the best of the exchange.) Doty Bohan remembers that when she first saw Constance in the North Dublin Union when the hunger-strike had been called off, she asked eagerly if anyone had continued the rounds on the dray. She expressed great disappointment to hear that no one had taken her place.[19] Another friend remembers that unlike the other political prisoners Constance wanted to do some active work, and that the sight of her scrubbing floors, skirt tucked into her blue bloomers, somewhat scandalized the Free State soldiers. Another glimpse of her at this period (after her release in time for Christmas) is given by R. M. Fox who remembers her sitting on the edge of a wooden table in the temporary hospital run by Maud Gonne for the released hunger-strikers, 'swinging her legs' and suggesting making a propaganda display by hanging Red Cross flags from the window.

One of Constance's first public appearances after her release was to deliver the oration at the grave of her ex-*Fianna* boy, Liam Mellows, on the first anniversary of his death. She said that she was there in her official capacity as Chief Scout of the *Fianna*. He was, she said, 'one of the most loyal and honoured Commandants. He was a great soldier, as brave as could be found.'

In April 1924 a 'largely attended' meeting of *Cumann na mBan* took place with the intention of devising a plan whereby the organization would continue its military training and at the same time fit itself for other spheres in the national life.

Constance, as President, in the chair, said, 'We meet here in this time of truce to get together and take council together to consider ways of reorganizing *Cumann na mBan* and of carrying on the work. In a time like this when there comes, as it were, a pause, we cannot afford to sit still and do nothing.'

She went on to urge all members to fresh endeavours, bidding them to feel encouraged by the assurance of 'ultimate success in this our own time', pointing out the weak position of the corrupt Free State Administration . . . 'Peace is beautiful,' she said, 'and we want peace; but we cannot shirk the fight if it is the only way to win.' She concluded with an appeal to the members to 'study and master the Irish language. They might not find it easy in the beginning, but most things that are worth doing are not easy'.[20] It will be seen that the Civil War had not really ended for *Cumann na mBan*.

Some time in 1924 (probably the spring or early summer) Casimir came to London on a Diplomatic Corps mission and from thence travelled to Dublin to see Constance. We can only imagine what this meeting was like after a separation of eleven years, since neither of the two people concerned have left any record which still exists. But friends recall that Constance was excited and full of joy at the prospect of the reunion. Casimir, the *bon viveur* and lover of women, must have been shocked by the deterioration in his wife's physical appearance. He had left a woman who still looked young enough to impersonate Joan of Arc; he came back to find this same woman, now aged fifty-six, worn out prematurely with work and privation – with no home in which to welcome him, and surrounded by friends with whom he could not possibly have been in sympathy. She, in turn, must have felt that their mental and spiritual separation now equalled the geographical one. But, no doubt, since she never lost her capacity for animation, and he his charming, gentle manners; since there were still friends to visit who inhabited neutral ground, they somehow managed to avoid the dangerous truths of a failed relationship.

After Casi's visit Constance wrote to Stasko, again full of

concern about his future. She described how bad things were in Ireland for ordinary people,

All the small businesses here are heading for ruin, and the farmers are in a bad way. The list of bankrupts is something appalling. The list of highly paid officials for whom jobs are made by those at present in power is daily increasing. To meet these expenses the old age pensioners have been docked 1/– per week of their pensions, as well as their bag of coal per fortnight. Taxes are awful, and food prices are daily rising and rents are wicked.[21]

She concluded by telling him that his father had found most of the old gang scattered. 'This is rather a doleful letter, but it will just let you know that I have not forgotten you, and that you will always be one of those whom I love most, for you really became like my own son, and I loved you for your honourable and upright character.'

In July Constance returned to her political life when she went with de Valera to Sligo to a monster meeting to celebrate his release from prison. She had a happy reunion with the Bohan sisters, saying affectionately of Baby Bohan 'Look at her now, and she didn't seem worth threepence halfpenny.' There was a *Ceilidhe* in the Town Hall where Constance danced 'several times' claiming that she felt rejuvenated.

In December 1925 Constance resigned from her position as President of *Cumann na mBan* because of her adherence to de Valera's new party *Fianna Fail*. De Valera had now reached the point when he contemplated entry into the Free State Dail under terms which remained to be decided upon. Without Constance, according to Shiela Humphries, the *Cumann na mBan* meetings were never quite the same again. Constance was not an ideal chairwoman, tending to draw caricatures when bored, and to brighten only when it was a question of direct action; but she was so much loved and respected by the members of the organization that her resignation seemed an unbearable loss. They could not even bring themselves to arrange a presentation because it seemed the proof of severance.

In this same year, in a letter to Stasko Constance admitted that she had been 'very sick', but in the same breath she reassured him as to her health being wonderful. In the letter she shows how her love of painting persisted to the last. She tells Stasko that she has bought a second-hand Ford car which she keeps in an old stable in the garden of Frankfort House. She spends most of her spare time driving out into the country and sketching,

I have been struggling to teach myself water-colours these last few years, and am just beginning to express myself in them. Oils were too expensive for me to continue, unless I gave up politics and tried to earn money by them, also they take more time and are more trouble to cart around. I began water-colours when I was in prison in England, and it would not have been possible to work in oils there, because of the smell, and being in such close quarters with other prisoners one of who was very delicate and so I did not like to even suggest inflicting the smell of oil on her.[22]

In January 1926 she wrote again to Stasko recommending Joseph Conrad's novels to him, and telling him that she has cut off her hair, 'I don't see why old women should not be as comfortable as young.' She goes on to tell him that because of the new fashion for wearing Russian boots she has fished out the red boots that his aunts obtained for her at Zywotowka so many years ago – that they are the smartest boots in Dublin. As regards her family, she says that Eva is the 'only real relation' she has left. She never sees her brother, Josslyn, and never wants to. (Her mother, in fact, kept in touch with her throughout the troubled times by means of assignations at Mespil House, home of Sarah Purser.) Constance added that she considered her family to be no worse than others, 'I suppose its very embarrassing to have a relation that gets into jail and fights in revolutions that you are not in sympathy with.'[23]

Constance now had only one more year to live. She was still a figure who could not be ignored in the Ireland that she had helped to shape – in spite of her rejection of its present rulers. She filled her days with work, as she had always done. She wrote several plays. She supported the movement for getting the State Pension Scheme for Necessitous Mothers. She tried to rebuild her *Fianna* movement, having, so she wrote to a friend, 'to start again from the very beginning with nothing'. She still took part in public occasions such as when in 1925 she went with Mr and Mrs de Valera to greet Dr Mannix, Archbishop of Melbourne, at Dun Laoghaire. As the member for Dublin Borough South, she was among the signatories of the Republican Declaration of Protest against Partition (which was confirmed by the Free State *Dail* in December 1925). In 1926 she was elected to the Rathmines Urban District Council, thus adding to her official duties. She was also closely connected with the work of St Ultan's Infant Hospital, where her friend, Dr Kathleen Lynn, was Vice-Chairman, and another friend, Madeleine French-Mullen, Secretary. In the same year, 1926, there originated one of the best known of the many stories connected with her name. This was her work for the poor in the Strike of 1926, known as the coal strike. Constance made many sorties in her rackety car into the country to collect turf; and not content with that she carried the heavy bags herself up the dark tenement stairs of the aged and feeble.

In June 1926 came the bitter blow of Eva's death. In this connection she made a remark which reveals as nothing else could her isolation from the roots of her past. When her friend, Eithne Coyle, asked her if she was going to the funeral of this sister who had become the being dearest to her on earth, Constance replied, 'I simply cannot face the family.'

There remain a few revealing glimpses of Constance in the last phase of her life. Through them can be seen the alterations of defiant gaiety and involuntary gloom which she now presented to the world outside her inner thoughts. There is the defiantly gay image she presented to her admirers, the street-traders of Moore Street, ardent Republicans and feared hecklers, known as 'Madame's Wans'. There were the hilarious trips in the ramshackle Ford with the Coughlin children. There was the quiet country day she spent in the company of the present Minister of Defence, then a youth. He drove her to a Holy Well in Meath where she sketched for several hours, often pausing to sit in silent thought. Mr Hilliard remembers her beautiful eyes and her distinguished bearing. There is the more sombre picture given by that sensitive and acute observer, Mary Colum. The wife of the poet relates how she saw Constance at one of Æ's crowded gatherings, 'sitting in her usual place on the couch in the corner, a brown dog lying at her feet,'

But now, as she sat there, she whom I remembered as a beautiful woman, only second in beauty to Maud Gonne, was haggard and old, dressed in ancient demoded clothes; the outline of the face was the same, but the expression was different; the familiar eyes that blinked at me from behind glasses were bereft of the old fire and eagerness, she gave me a limp hand and barely spoke to me . . . I had known Constance Markievicz in her vibrant maturity, at the height of her youth and her courage, when she was engaged in masculine activities ... Now I saw her she was obviously a dying woman, sunk in dejection resulting either from imprisonment or from the loss of her hopes. What she had fought for had not really come into being; maybe nothing on earth could have brought it into being, so romantic and heroic was it.[24]

The experience of the last eyewitness of this time proves that Mary Colum was right in her analysis: that Constance was heartsick. Had she lived it is not possible that she could have understood the processes of thought by which her leader, de Valera, finally decided to take the Oath of Allegiance and enter the Dail. She was consistent to the last – her political attitudes had become forever fixed through her humanitarianism which was reinforced by Connolly's teaching. The spirit of compromise was not in her nature. For her, it had ever been all or nothing. Through giving all she gained much; and at the end she was mercifully released before she could experience the anguish of choice between loyalty to past ideals and the bleak necessity of compromise. The words she spoke to Baby Bohan when they spent what was to be their last day together in Sligo are the proof of how much she was spared. The younger woman asked her, 'How anyone could think of going into the Dail and taking an oath to the British King?' Constance replied, 'I will never take that Oath. How could I ever meet Paddy Pearse or Jim Connolly in the hereafter if I took an oath to a British King?' For her it was as simple as that.

There was still one more election to fight. Constance undertook the campaign with her usual energy, although there were those among her friends who feared for her health. She broke her arm, cranking her old Ford. She was attended by a doctor to whom she declared her intention of going on with her political meeting, 'It's lucky it's only my arm. I can still talk.' She was re-elected. She walked with de Valera and the other Republican Deputies in an attempt to enter the Dail without taking the Oath. But there was little time left to her now.

At the end of June she became so ill that she was ordered into hospital by Dr Lathleen Lynn. She chose to go into a public ward in Sir Patrick Dun's Hospital. She was operated on for appendicitis by Sir William Taylor. Dr Kathleen Lynn, feeling confident of her recovery, went on holiday. She was shocked when Mrs Sheehy-

Skeffington accompanied by the son of Erskine Childers came to Wicklow to tell her that Constance was gravely ill. Constance underwent a second operation on 8 July. She developed peritonitis.[25] She lay, desperately ill, but alert and yet calm, surrounded by roses, in the public ward where her awed and loving fellow-patients hardly spoke for fear of disturbing her. Throughout the Saturday night on which Dr Kathleen Lynn arrived back in Dublin some of Constance's most devoted friends – Helena Molony, Mary Perolz, May Coughlin, and Florrie O'Connell, together with Esther Roper, undertook a vigil, praying for her in the hospital Board Room. Miraculously she rallied. (A patient discharged from the Ward said to her as she left, 'Please God I'll meet you again in Dublin, but if not there, in Heaven, Madame dear.') The surgeon told Esther Roper the next morning: 'It's a miracle but I think she will recover. I never expected her to live out the night.'

Shiela Humphries came to see Constance wearing a new pink dress she had bought in Paris, knowing how she loved to look at pretty things. In the streets where Esther Roper was out doing errands for Constance, strangers came up to ask about the Countess. 'Ah, what would the people in the slums do without her,' said one woman with her eyes full of tears. 'She's given up everything for us and she thinks what's good enough for us is good enough for her. Please God she'll get better.'

Three days after the vigil night, Casimir and Stasko arrived from Warsaw. 'This is the happiest day of my life,' she said. They ordered roses for her. When they arrived Esther Roper was with her. Constance insisted on opening the package, although her hands were shaking with weakness. She read the loving inscription on the card, and with a flash of the old fire – a last flicker of the admired beauty who had once said to Mary Colum, 'I'm not interested in men, for I have had the pick of too many men', she exclaimed. 'Look! Don't they know how to do things?'

There were two days left; but these days were filled with consolations for one who did not fear death. 'It is so beautiful to have this love and kindness before I go,' she said. And for the first time she admitted her deep weariness of spirit when she said 'I sometimes long for the peace of the Republican Plot,'[26] She died on 15 July. Five days before, although she did not know it, one of the main figures among those she opposed, Kevin O'Higgins, had been brutally assassinated on his way to Mass. 'Madame's dearest wish' remarked one of her Moore Street fanatics; but it is impossible to believe this in the face of her Republican women friends' opinion that her kind heart warred with her politics. At any rate, although she herself died in peace and love, at the same time, in death as in life, the divisions of her country intervened. Half Dublin mourned O'Higgins, and the other half the Countess.

Her body lay in state in the Rotunda (the use of the City Hall or the Mansion House having been refused by the authorities). Her funeral was as vast a demonstration as any that she had witnessed or taken part in during her lifetime. Flowers were expensive in Dublin, but there were eight lorry loads of them. Even more after her own heart was the tribute of three fresh eggs brought in fulfilment of a promise, when it seemed that she might live, by an old countrywoman. Thousands lined the streets; the official organizations marched: *Sinn Fein, Fianna Eireann, Inghinidhe na bEireann, Cumann na mBan, Fianna Fail,* ITGWU, Irish Citizen Army. At Glasnevin her Irish Citizen Army uniform was lowered into her grave. At Glasnevin, too, there were Free State soldiers armed and ready to prevent a volley being fired over her grave. Her old friend from Mountjoy, Father Ryan, was there, faithful to his word to be with her at the end. Sir Josslyn was there, and Casimir and Stasko. Mr de Valera pronounced the oration,

Madame Markievicz is gone from us. Madame the friend of the toiler, the lover of the poor. Ease and station she put aside and took the hard way of service with the weak and downtrodden. Sacrifice, misunderstanding and scorn lay on her road she adopted, but she trod unflinchingly. She now lies at rest with her fellow champions of the right – mourned by the people whose liberties she fought for, blessed by the loving prayers of the poor she tried so hard to befriend . . . We know the friendliness, the great woman's heart of her, the great Irish soul of her, and we know the loss we have suffered is not to be repaired. It is sadly we leave, but we pray High Heaven that all she longed and worked for may one day be achieved.

These were the public tributes. The private voice spoke through a previous poem of Eva's: Eva the confidante of her life's hopes, dreams and sorrows.

> The dogwood's dead and a mantle red
> Over the corpse is flung

Bow down, O willow your silver head,
Summer's silver and winter's red
Glory and grey and green have fled,
All winds are silent, all sorrows said
And all songs sung.

FINIS

Genealogy of the Gore-Booth Family

Captain Paul Gore came over with Essex in 1598 and was made a commander of a troop of horse. He was charged by Mountjoy with the responsibility of escorting the last two Irish chieftains (Rory O'Donnell and Sir Donough O'Connor) to submit to Queen Elizabeth and got them safely to Athlone. He was granted lands by the Queen and later by James I and created a Baronet of Ireland in 1621. He married Isabella, daughter of Francis Wickliffe and niece of Sir Thomas Wentworth Earl of Strafford. They had six sons and seven daughters.

Sir Paul Gore's fourth son, Francis, Knight of Ardtarman, was the founder of the Gore-Booth family. He co-operated with the Cromwellians, yet reconciled himself with the Royalists when the time came. He married Anne Parker, a Co Leitrim heiress, and was granted more land at the Restoration. He had nine sons and four daughters, and is remembered for his courage as a Commissioner of the High Court of Justice in 1652 in refusing to concur in the death sentence passed on young Lord Mayo.

Sir Francis was succeeded by his son Robert, who was made Knight of Newton, and married Frances Newcomen, daughter of Sir Thomas Newcomen, Knight of Sutton. Sir Robert had seven sons and four daughters.

Sir Robert was succeeded by his eldest son, Nathanial Gore who married Letitia only daughter and heiress of Humphrey Booth – a Cromwellian, Titulado of Sligo town. Nathanial had two sons and three daughters.

Nathanial was succeeded by his eldest son, Booth, who was made a Baronet of Ireland in 1760. Sir Booth Gore married Emily, daughter of Brabazon Newcomen, and had two sons and a daughter.

Sir Booth Gore was succeeded by his son Booth, who died unmarried. He lived at Lissadell and at Huntercombe House Bucks.

Sir Booth Gore the second was succeeded by his younger brother Robert Newcomen Gore-Booth who assumed the additional surname and arms of Booth. He married Hannah, daughter of Henry Irwin of Streamstown, Co Sligo. Sir Robert had two sons and a daughter.

Sir Robert was succeeded by his eldest son Robert who first married Caroline, daughter of the first Viscount Lorton. She died, and Sir Robert married secondly Caroline, daughter of Thomas Goold of Dublin, a Master of Chancery.

Sir Robert was succeeded by his second surviving son Henry, who married Georgina Mary daughter of Colonel John Hill of Tickill Castle, Yorkshire.

Sir Henry was succeeded by his eldest son Josslyn, who married Mary Sibell, daughter of the Reverend Savile L'Estrange-Malone.

Sir Josslyn was succeeded by his son – the present Baronet.

The Seven Cartrons Incident

An account of the Palmerston and Gore-Booth evictions is given in the chapter on emigration in the collection of studies edited by Professor Dudley Edwards and Professor Desmond Williams and published under the title *The Great Famine*.* The author of the emigration section, Oliver MacDonagh MA PhD, records† that although the number of tenants whom Sir Robert Gore-Booth sent to New Brunswick was very great, the vessels were well supplied with food, and 'no other group of Irish emigrants was so well cared for in the province'. The people were not abandoned on arrival; arrangements were made to find employment and lodging. What did cause high indignation at St John in Canada was the unsuitability of many of Sir Robert's former tenants. The chief emigration officer at St John declared that Sir Robert should be publicly condemned for 'shovelling out the helpless and infirm'. Back in Ireland the landlords and their agents thought it only natural that they should send away the poorest, the oldest, and the worst of their tenants. But Sir Robert Gore-Booth, in the light of his times, was acknowledged to be a good landlord, and one who had given his serious attention to the subject of assisted emigration.

As regards the local tradition of the lost ship, a search for any reference to it in those contemporary newspapers which are available has failed to produce any evidence.

* Published for the Irish Committee of Historical Science by Browne and Nolan, Dublin 1956.
† PP 338–9.

Bibliography

Aberdeen, Lord & Lady: *We T'wa*, London, 1925

Asquith, Cyril: see Spender, J. A.

Barry, T.: *Guerilla Days in Ireland*, Dublin, 1949

Bashkirtseff, M.: *The Journal of Marie Bashkirtseff*, L., & with an intro by Mathilde Blind, 2 vols, London and Melbourne, 1890

Beaslai, P.: *Michael Collins and The Making of a New Ireland*, 2 vols, London, 1926

Blunt, W. S.: *The Land War in Ireland*, London, 1912

Blunt, W. S.: *My Diaries*, London, 1919

Boyd, E. A.: *Ireland's Literary Renaissance*, New York, 1916

Boyle, J. F.: *The Irish Rebellion of 1916*, London, 1916

Caufield, M.: *The Easter Rebellion*, London, 1964

Colum, M.: *Life and the Dream*, London, 1947

Colum, P.: *My Irish Year*, London, 1912

Colum, P.: *Arthur Griffith*, Dublin, 1959

Connolly, J.: *Labour in Ireland*, Dublin and London, 1917

Coxhead, E.: *Daughters of Erin*, London, 1965

Coxhead, E.: *Lady Gregory*, London, 1961

Craig, E. T.: *An Irish Commune*. The History of Ralahine Adapted from the narrative of, Dublin, 1920

Curtis, E.: *A History of Ireland*, London, 1936

Denson, A., (ed.): *Letters From Æ.*, London, 1961

Digby, J. F.: *Sir Horace Plunkett*, Oxford, 1949

Edwards, R. D. and Williams, J. D.: *The Great Famine*, Dublin, 1956

Eglington, J.: *A Memoir of Æ.*, London, 1937

Ervine, St John: *Craigavon: Ulsterman*, London, 1949

Ervine, St John: *Parnell*, London, 1936

Fergusson, J.: *The Curragh Incident*, London, 1964

Fingall, Elizabeth Countess of: *Seventy Years Young*, London, 1937

Fox, R. M.: *Rebel Irishwomen*, Dublin and Cork, 1935

Fox, R. M.: *James Connolly, The Forerunner*, County Kerry, 1946

Glenavy, B.: *Today We Will Only Gossip*, London, 1964

Godley, A.: *Life of an Irish Soldier*, London, 1939

Gogarty, O. St John.: *As I Was Going Down Sackville Street*, London, 1937

Gore-Booth, E.: *Selected Poems* London, 1933

Gibbon, M., (ed.): *The Living Torch*, London, 1937

Greaves, C. D.: *The Life and Times of James Connolly*, London, 1961

Gwynn, D.: *The History of Partition*, Dublin, 1950

Gwynn, D.: *The Life of John Redmond*, London, 1932

Gwynn, D.: *The Life and Death of Roger Casement*, London, 1930

Gwynn, S., (ed.): *Scattering Branches*, London, 1940

Gwynn, S.: *John Redmond's Last Years*, London, 1919

Haslip, J.: *Parnell*, London, 1936

Holt, E.: *Protest in Arms*, London, 1960

Hone, J.: *W. B. Yeats*, London, 1942

Hone, J.: *The Life of George Moore*, London, 1936

Horgan, J. J.: *Parnell to Pearse*, Dublin, 1948

Inglis, B.: *The Story of Ireland*, London, 1956

Jeffares, A. W. and Cross, K. W. C.: *In Excited Reverie*, New York and London, 1965

Joy, M., (ed.): *The Irish Rebellion and Its Martyrs*, New York, 1916

Kirby, S.: *The Yeats Country*, Dublin, 1962

Larkin, E.: *James Larkin*, Boston and London, 1965

Leslie, S.: *The Irish Tangle*, London, 1946

Lyons, F. S. L.: *The Fall of Parnell*, London, 1960

Macardle, D.: *The Irish Republic*, London, 1937

MacBride, M. G.: *A Servant of the Queen*, London, 1938

MacDonagh, J. C.: *History of Ballymote*, Dublin, 1936

Magnus, P.: *Gladstone*, London, 1954

McCarthy, J.: *Irish Recollections*, London, 1911

Maloney, W. J.: *The Forged Casement Diaries* Dublin and Cork, 1936

Moore, G.: *Hail and Farewell:*, 2 vols, London, 1911–1914

O'Brien, B.: *Dublin Castle and the Irish People*, London, 1909

O'Brien, N. C.: *Portrait of a Rebel Father*, Dublin, 1935

O'Casey, S.: *Sunset and Evening Star*, London, 1954

O'Casey, S.: *I Knock at the Door*, London, 1939

O'Casey, S.: *Pictures in the Hallway*, London, 1942

O'Casey, S.: *Drums Under the Windows*, London, 1945

O'Casey, S.: (Pseud. p. 6 Cálthasaigh): *The Story of the Irish Citizen Army*, Dublin, 1919

O'Casey, S.: *Inishfallen Fare Thee Well*, London, 1949

O'Casey, S.: *Rose and Crown*, London, 1952

O'Connor, U.: *Oliver St John Gogarty*, London, 1964

O'Faolain, S.: *Constance Markievicz*, London and Toronto, 1934

O'Hegarty, P. S.: *The Victory of Sinn Fein*, Dublin, 1924

O'Malley, E.: *On Another Man's Wound*, London, 1936
O'Rorke, Archdeacon: *History of Sligo*, 2 vols, Dublin, 1890
Orpen, W.: *Stories of Old Ireland and Myself*, London, 1924
Pakenham, F. A.: *Peace by Ordeal*, London, 1935
Pope-Hennessy, J.: *Lord Crewe*, London, 1955
Robinson, L., (ed.): *Lady Gregory's Journals*, London, 1946
Roper, E., (ed.): *Prison Letters of Countess Markievicz*, London, 1934
le Roux, L. N.: *Patrick H. Pearse*, Dublin, 1932
Sharpe, M. C.: *Chicago May*, London, 1929
Solomons, B. A. H.: *One Doctor and His Time*, London, 1959
Spender, J. A. and Asquith, C.: *Life of Herbert Henry Asqnith, Lord Oxford and Asquith*, vol 2, London, 1932
Stephens, J.: *The Insurrection in Dublin*, Dublin and London, 1916
Street, C. J. C.: *Administration of Ireland*, London, 1921
Tansill, C. C.: *America and the Fight for Irish Freedom*, New York, 1957
Wade, A., (ed.): *The Letters of W. B. Yeats*, London, 1954
Wedgewood, C. V.: *Thomas Wentworth, Earl of Strafford*, London, 1935
White, T. de Vere: *Kevin O'Higgins*, London, 1948
Whyte, J. H.: *The Independent Irish Party*, Oxford, 1958
Woodham Smith, C.: *The Great Hunger*, London, 1962
Wright, A.: *Disturbed Dublin*, London, 1914
Yeats, W. B.: *Collected Poems*, London, 1950

Official Report on the Debate on the Treaty Between Great Britain & Ireland, London.

NEWSPAPERS AND PERIODICALS
Files of: The Capuchin Annual, Eire, Fianna, The Homestead, Bean na h'Eireann, Irish Citizen, Irish Times, Sinn Fein, New Ireland, Sligo Independent

Notes

CHAPTER I

1 *Gladstone* Philip Magnus p 193.
2 *Seventy Years Young* Elizabeth Countess of Fingall p 37.

CHAPTER 2

1 *Seventy Years Young* Elizabeth Countess of Fingall p 25.
2 *The Great Hunger* Cecil Woodham Smith pp 71, 73.
3 *My Irish Year* Padriac Colum pp 14, 15.
4 Cecil Woodham Smith *op cit* p 364.
5 Padraic Colum *op cit* p 14.
6 *History of Ballymote* J. C. MacDonagh pp 167, 171, 172.
7 Miss Brigid O'Mullane interviewed by Count Stanislas Dunin-Markiewicz.
8 *A Servant of the Queen* Maud Gonne MacBride p 41.
9 Family Papers.
10 *Ibid.*
11 *History of Sligo* Archdeacon O'Rorke p 17.

CHAPTER 3

1 *Memoir of Æ* John Eglinton p 8.
2 *Life of an Irish Soldier* General Sir Alexander Godley p 16.
3 *Seventy Years Young* Elizabeth Countess of Fingall p 121.
4 *Ibid* p 191.
5 *Ibid* p 192.
6 *A Servant of the Queen* Maud Gonne MacBride p 116 *et seq.*

CHAPTER 4

1 *The Journal of Marie Bashkirtseff* p 266.

CHAPTER 5

1 *Constance Markievicz* Sean O'Faolain p 46.
2 *The Letters of W. B. Yeats* Edited by Allan Wade p 243.
3 *Hail and Farewell* Vol I *Ave* George Moore p 34.
4 *W. B. Yeats* Joseph Hone p 86.
5 *Sligo Independent* 31 March 1894.

CHAPTER 6

1 *A Long Life* Stefan Kryzwoszewski: extract translated by Stanislas Dunin-Markiewicz
2 *Constance Markievicz* Sean O'Faolain. p 54.

CHAPTER 7

1 Article in *Kurjer Warszawski* by Kornel Makuszysnki translated by Stanislas Dunin-Markiewicz.
2 *Oliver St Gogarty* Ulick O'Connor p 76.
3 *Dublin Fifty Years Ago* John Brennan, *Irish Independent*, 19 May 1951.
4 *A Memoir of Æ* John Eglinton p 102.
5 *Life and the Dream* Mary Colum p 98.

CHAPTER 8

1 *Drums Under The Windows* Sean O'Casey p 8 *et seq.*
2 *Socialism and Communism; writings of James Connolly*, Edited by Desmond Ryan p 20.
3 *Ibid* p 91.
4 *Ibid* p 108.
5 Private Letter to Stanislas Dunin-Markiewicz from Helena Molony.
6 *Constance Markievicz* Sean O'Faolain p 123.
7 *Ibid* p 66.

CHAPTER 9

1 Private letter from Maud Gonne MacBride to Count Stanislas Dunin-Markiewicz, 14 May 1931.
2 *Constance Markievicz* Sean O'Faolain p 131 *et seq.*

3 *A Few Memories* Constance de Markievicz, published in the Republican Newspaper *Eire* 16 June 1923.
4 *Disturbed Dublin* Arnold Wright p 29 *et seq.*
5 *James Connolly* Desmond Greaves pp 209–10.
6 *A Few Memories op cit*
7 *Memories* Constance de Markievicz, *Eire* 21 July 1923.
8 *Ibid* 21 July 1923.
9 *Ibid* 28 July 1923.
10 *Ibid* 14 July 1923.
11 *Ibid* 28 July 1923.

CHAPTER 10

1 *Rebel Irishwomen* R. M. Fox p 123.
2 *Memories* Constance de Markievicz – Republican Newspaper *Eire* 4 August 1923.
3 *Ibid.*
4 *Daughters of Erin* Elizabeth Coxhead p 87.
5 *Constance Markievicz* Sean O'Faolain p 81.
6 *The Green Jacket* Philip Rooney *Sunday Press* 1 September 1960.
7 *Protest in Arms* Edgar Holt p 35.
8 *The Life of John Redmond* Denis Gwynn p 201.
9 *John Redmond's Last Years* Stephen Gwynn p 63.
10 *Craigavon; Ulsterman* St John Ervine p 222.
11 *Ibid* p 236.
12 *Ibid* p 245.
13 Denis Gwynn *op cit* p 306.
14 *The Jerome Connexion* Seymour Leslie p 76.
15 *James Larkin* Emmet Larkin p 119.
16 *Ibid.*
17 *Ibid* p 121.
18 *Ibid* pp 123–4.
19 Article by Stanislas Dunin-Markiewicz in *Irish Press* 4 February 1938.
20 *Disturbed Dublin* Arnold Wright p 136.
21 *Portrait of a Rebel Father* Norah Connolly O'Brien.
22 *Drums Under the Windows* Sean O'Casey p 249 *et seq.*
23 *Letters from Æ* Edited by Alan Denson p 85 *et seq.*
24 Emmet Larkin *op cit* p 138.
25 Arnold Wright *op cit* pp 222–3.
26 Emmet Larkin *op cit* p 139.

CHAPTER 11

1 *Constance Markievicz* Sean O'Faolain p 79.
2 Article in *Karjer Warszawski* by Kornel Makuszyznki, translated by Stanislas Dunin-Markiewicz.
3 *James Larkin* Emmet Larkin p 142.
4 *Ibid* p 146.
5 *Ibid* pp 156–7.
6 *James Connolly* R. M. Fox, p 153.
7 *The Story of the Irish Citizen Army* Sean O'Casey Pamphlet.
8 *Ibid*.
9 *Drums Under the Windows* Sean O'Casey, St Martin's Library edition, p 609.
10 Sean O'Casey Pamphlet *op cit*.
11 Sean O'Casey *op cit* p 610.
12 *Patrick H. Pearse* Louis N. le Roux, p 272.
13 *The Curragh Incident* Sir James Fergusson p 86.
14 *Craigavon: Ulsterman* St John Ervine p 250.
15 *The Irish Republic* Dorothy MacCardle p 113.
16 Article by Corporal Willie Nelston in *The Fianna Christmas* December 1914.
17 *Ibid*.
18 *Portrait of a Rebel Father* Nora Connolly O'Brien p 178.
19 Louis N. le Roux *op cit* p 307.
20 *The Life of John Redmond* Denis Gwynn p 484.
21 *The Irish Rebellion of 1916 and its Martyrs* Edited by Maurice Joy p 358.
22 *The Life and Times of James Connolly* C. Desmond Greaves p 292.
23 *The Irish Worker* 24 October 1914.
24 C. Desmond Greaves *op cit* p 294.
25 Sean O'Casey *op cit* p 647.
26 C. Desmond Greaves *op cit* p 296.
27 Article in *The Press* by Hanna Sheehy-Sheffington, February 1940.
28 *We T'wa* Memoirs of Lord and Lady Aberdeen, Vol II, p 262 *et seq*.

CHAPTER 12

1 *Prison Letters of Countess Markievicz* Edited by Esther Roper pp 13, 14.
2 *Ibid* p 13.
3 *Constance Markievicz* Sean O'Faolain p 209.

4 *The Life of John Redmond* Denis Gwynn pp 405, 406.
5 *Protest in Arms* Edgar Holt p 62.
6 *America and the Fight for Irish Freedom* Charles Callan Tansill p 191.
7 *The Life and Times of James Connolly* C. Desmond Greaves pp 315, 316.
8 *Ibid* p 316.
9 *Portrait of a Rebel Father* Nora Connolly O'Brien p 259 *et seq.*
10 C. Desmond Greaves *op cit* p 325.
11 *Ibid* p 326.
12 *The Easter Rebellion* Max Caulfield. Four Square Edition p 61.
13 *A Memory* Constance de Markievicz *Eire* 26 May 1923.
14 C. Desmond Greaves *op cit* p 330.
15 *Ibid* p 332.
16 *The Insurrection in Dublin* James Stephens. Septer Edition p 17.
17 Article by Professor Liam O'Brien in *Capuchin Annual* 1966.

CHAPTER 13

1 *The Life of John Redmond* Denis Gwynn p 480.
2 Articles by Professor Liam O'Brien in the *Capuchin Annual* 1966.
3 *The Life and Times of James Connolly* C. Desmond Greaves p 340.
4 *On Another Man's Wound* Ernie O'Malley p 45.
5 *Rebel Irishwomen* R. M. Fox p 76 *et seq.*
6 *Life of Herbert Henry Asquith, Lord Oxford and Asquith* J. A. Spender and Cyril Asquith, Vol II, p 216.
7 *Prison Letters of Countess Markievicz* Edited by Esther Roper pp 139–40.
8 *Ibid* p 24.
9 *Ibid* p 42.
10 *Ibid* p 75.
11 *Ibid* p 72.

CHAPTER 14

1 *The Life of John Redmond* Denis Gwynn p 562.
2 *The Irish Republic* Dorothy Macardle p 235.
3 Private letter to Count Stanislas Dunin-Markiewicz.
4 Dorothy Macardle *op cit* p 252.
5 *Prison Letters of Countess Markievicz* Edited by Esther Roper pp 205 & 207.
6 *Ibid* p 90.
7 MSS letter, County Library, Sligo.

8 *In Jail with Madame Markiewicz* Nora Connolly, *Irish Citizen* September 1919.

9 Letter to the *Irish Times* from Maire Comerford 30 March 1966.

10 MSS, National Museum, Dublin.

11 *Prison Letters of Countess Markievicz* p 12.

12 MSS, National Library, Dublin.

13 MSS Letter, Sligo County Library.

14 Dorothy Macardle *op cit* pp 361–2 and Interim Report of the American Commission on Conditions in Ireland.

15 *Constance Markievicz* Sean O'Faolain p 275.

16 *Administration of Ireland* Major C. J. C. Street.

17 Private letter in the papers of Count Stanislas Dunin-Markiewicz.

CHAPTER 15

1 *Prison Letters of Countess Markievicz* Edited by Esther Roper pp 258–9.

2 *Ibid* p 262.

3 *The Irish Republic* Dorothy Macardle p 392.

4 *Ibid* p 416.

5 *Guerilla Days in Ireland* Tom Barry p 36.

6 *Seventy Years Young* Elizabeth Countess of Fingall p 400.

7 Dorothy Macardle *op cit* p 453.

8 *Craigavon: Ulsterman* St John Ervine p 417.

9 *Ibid* p 424.

10 *Ibid* p 422.

11 Dorothy Macardle *op cit* p 477.

12 MSS Letter, National Library, Dublin.

13 *Michael Collins* Piaris Beaslai p 311.

14 *Ibid* pp 311–12.

15 Official Report of Debate on the Treaty Between Great Britain and Ireland, Stationery Office, Dublin.

16 *Ibid* pp 34–5.

17 *Ibid* p 45.

18 *Ibid* pp 85, 88.

19 *Ibid* p 117.

20 *Ibid* pp 181–3, 186.

21 Dorothy Macardle *op cit* p 641.

22 *Treaty Debate op cit* pp 346–7.

23 *Prison Letters of Countess Markievicz op cit* p 102.

24 *Ibid* p 287.

25 MSS, National Library, Dublin.

26 *Prison Letters of Countess Markievicz op cit* p 287.

CHAPTER 16

1 Memorandum of Ex-Constable Jeremiah Mee for Count Stanislas Dunin-Markiewicz dated 27 October 1938.
2 *The Irish Republic* Dorothy Macardle p 718.
3 Dorothy Macardle *op cit* p 722.
4 *Arthur Griffith* Padraic Colum p 357.
5 *Protest in Arms* Edgar Holt p 295.
6 Information from Mrs Molony (Kathleen Barry) 1966.
7 *Kevin O'Higgins* Terence de Vere White p 83.
8 Padriac Colum *op cit* p 379.
9 Memorandum of Mr P. J. Hayes, Editor of the *Labour News*, Dublin.
10 MSS Letter from the late Mrs O'Carroll to Count Stanislas Dunin-Markiewicz.
11 Dorothy Macardle *op cit* p 802.
12 *Prison Letters of Countess Markievicz* Edited by Esther Roper p 238.
13 Dorothy Macardle *op cit* p 814.
14 *A Servant of the Queen* Maud Gonne MacBride pp 15–16.
15 MSS Letter, National Museum, Dublin.
16 Letter from Dorothy Macardle of 1 May 1923 in *Eire*.
17 Dorothy Macardle *op cit* p 862.
18 *Prison Letters of Countess Markievicz op cit* p 304.
19 Personal Recollections of Miss Baby and Miss Doty Bohan.
20 *Eire* 31 May 1924.
21 Letter of Summer 1924, National Museum, Dublin.
22 Letter of Autumn 1925, National Museum, Dublin.
23 Letter of 14 January 1926, National Museum, Dublin.
24 *Life and the Dream* Mary Colum pp 279–80.
25 Family Information.
26 The accounts of the death of Constance Markievicz are derived from Esther Roper's Biographical Sketch in *Prison Letters of Countess Markievicz* and from a memorandum written by Kathleen Lynn for Count Stanislas Dunin-Markiewicz.

Index